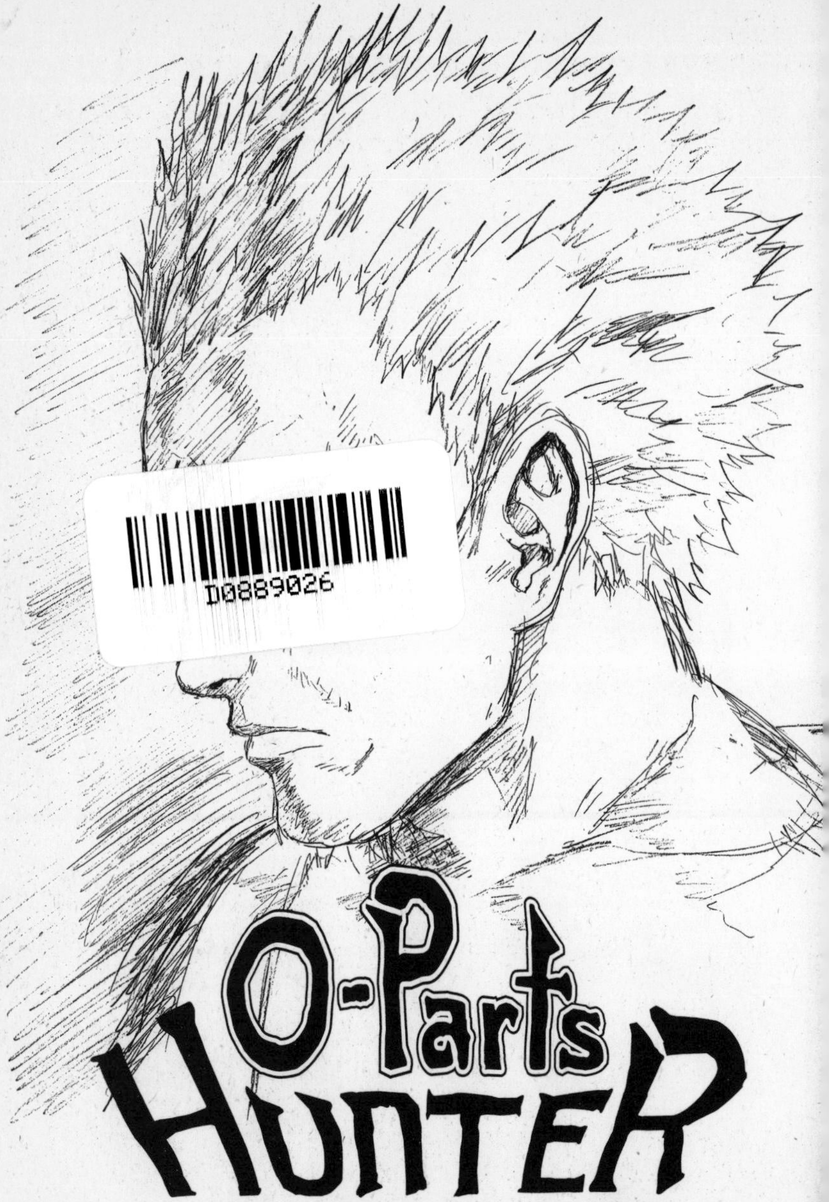

O-Parts HUNTER

SEIHI KISHIMOTO

12

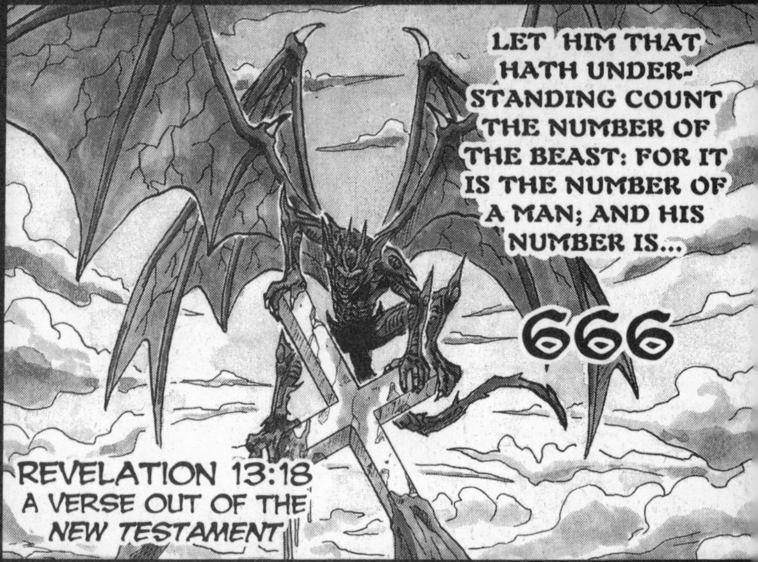
LET HIM THAT HATH UNDER-STANDING COUNT THE NUMBER OF THE BEAST: FOR IT IS THE NUMBER OF A MAN; AND HIS NUMBER IS...
666
REVELATION 13:18 A VERSE OUT OF THE *NEW TESTAMENT*

O-Parts Hunter

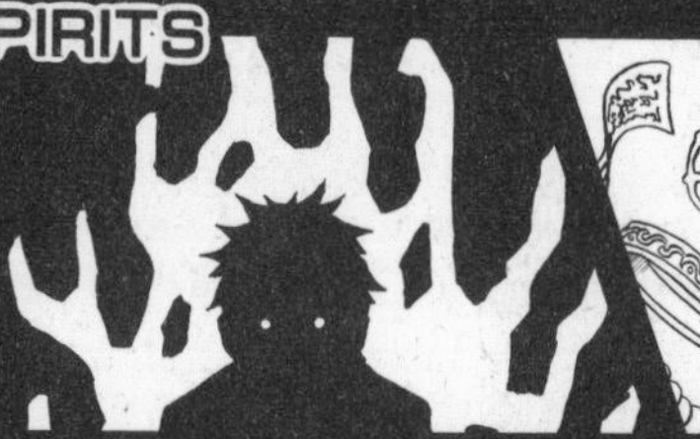
SPIRITS

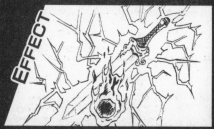

Spirit: A special energy force which only the O.P.T.s have. The amount of Spirit they have within them determines how strong of an O.P.T. they are.

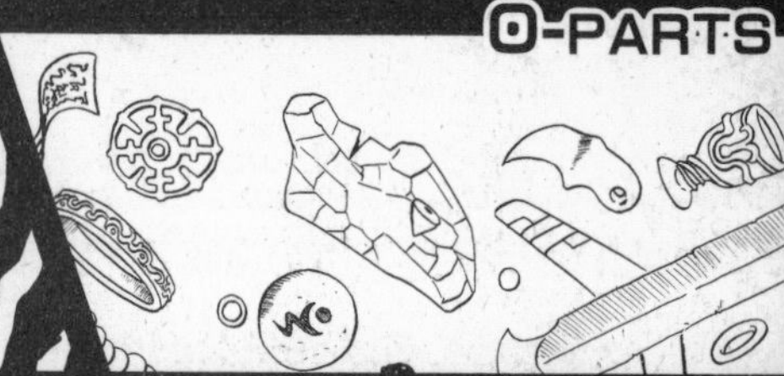
O-PARTS

O-Parts: Amazing artifacts with mystical powers left from an ancient civilization. They have been excavated from various ruins around the world. Depending on their Effects, O-Parts are given a rank from E to SS within a seven-tiered system.

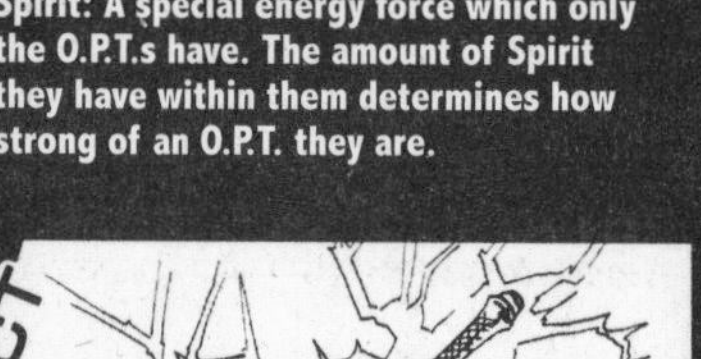
EFFECT

Effect: The special energy (power) the O-Parts possess. It can only be used when an O.P.T. sends his Spirit into an O-Part.

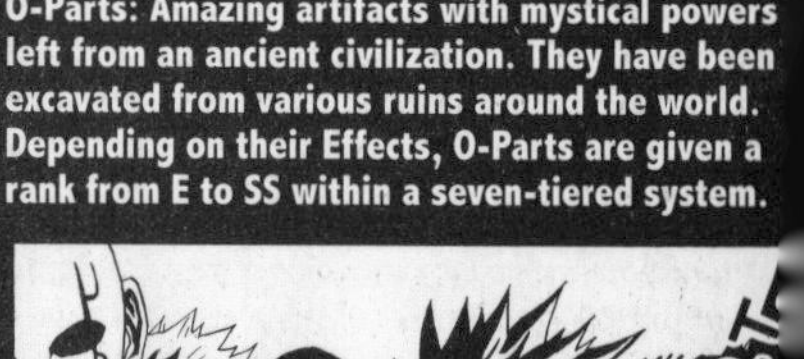
O.P.T.

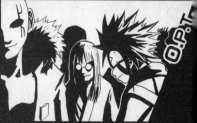

O.P.T.: One who has the ability to release and use the powers of the O-Parts. The name O.P.T. is an abbreviated form of O-Part Tactician.

CHARACTERS

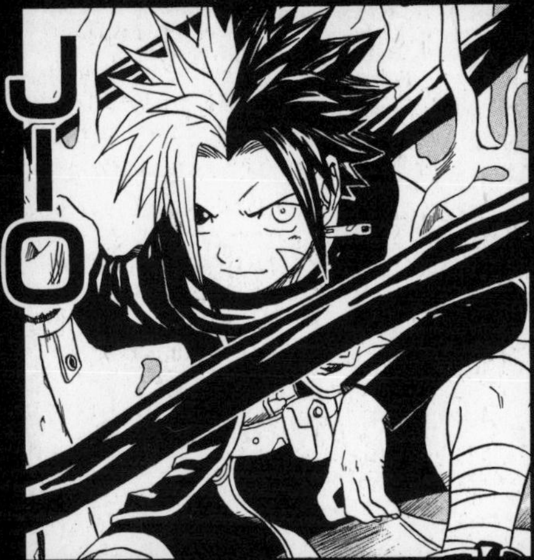
JIO

Jio Freed
A wild O.P.T. boy whose dream is world domination! He has been emotionally damaged by his experiences in the past, but is still gung-ho about his new adventures! O-Part: New Zero-shiki (Rank B)
Effect: Triple (Increasing power by a factor of three)

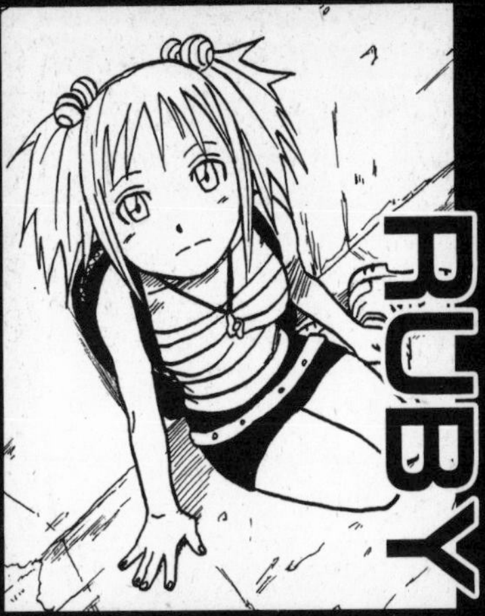
RUBY

Ruby
A treasure hunter who can decipher ancient texts. She meets Jio during her search for a legendary O-Part.

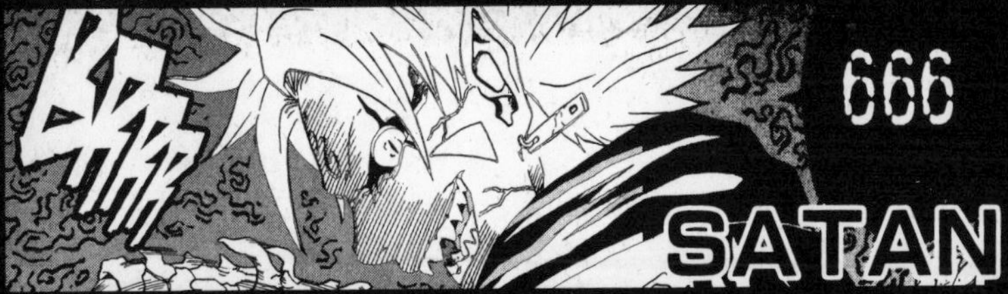
666
SATAN

Satan
This demon is thought to be a mutated form of Jio. It is a creature shrouded in mystery with earth-shattering powers.

STORY

Ascald: a world where people fight amongst themselves in order to get their hands on mystical objects left behind by an ancient civilization...the O-Parts.

In that world, a monster that strikes fear into the hearts of the strongest of men is rumored to exist. Those who have seen the monster all tell of the same thing–that the number of the beast, 666, is engraved on its forehead.

***

Jio, an O.P.T. boy who wants to rule the world, travels the globe with Ball, a novice O.P.T., and Ruby, a girl searching for a legendary O-Part and her missing father. On a quest to find the Kabbalah before the Stea Government or the Zenom Syndicate can use it to take over the world, Jio's team stumbles onto the city of Rock Bird, where Olympia, a deadly world tournament for O.P.T.s, is taking place. Little do they know that Olympia is merely a ruse to ensnare angels, demons, and the world's most powerful O.P.T.s for the city's own nefarious purposes. When the leader of Rock Bird abducts Ruby to get at Jio—aka Satan, the best prize of all—will Jio walk right into his trap?

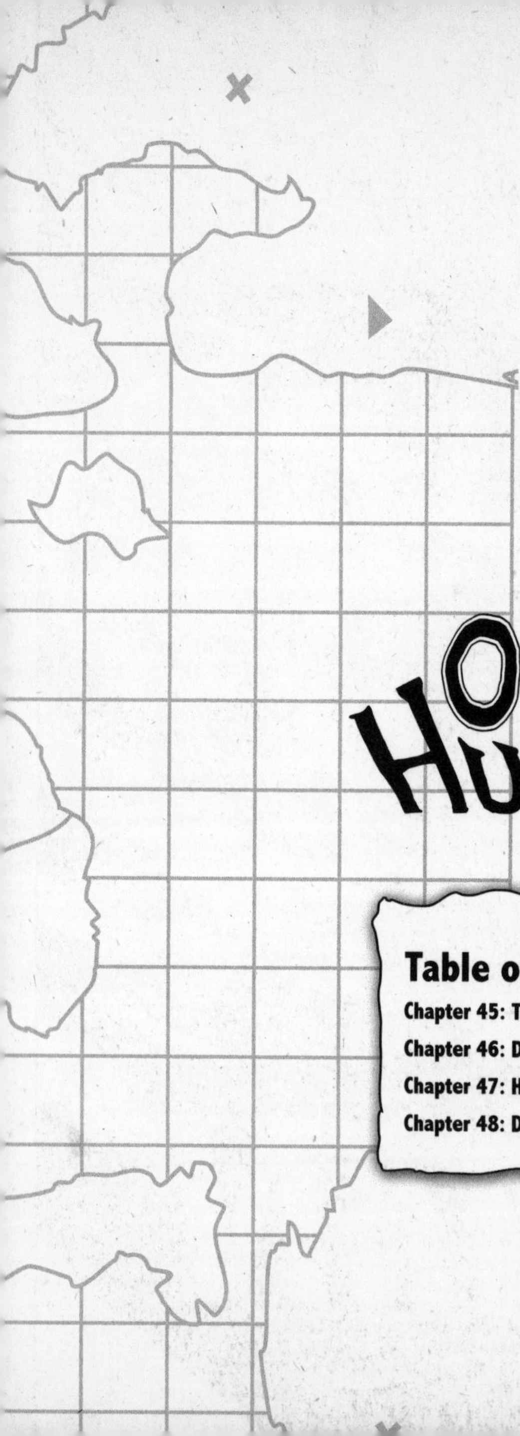

O-Parts Hunter

12

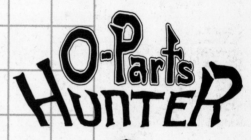

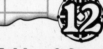

Table of Contents

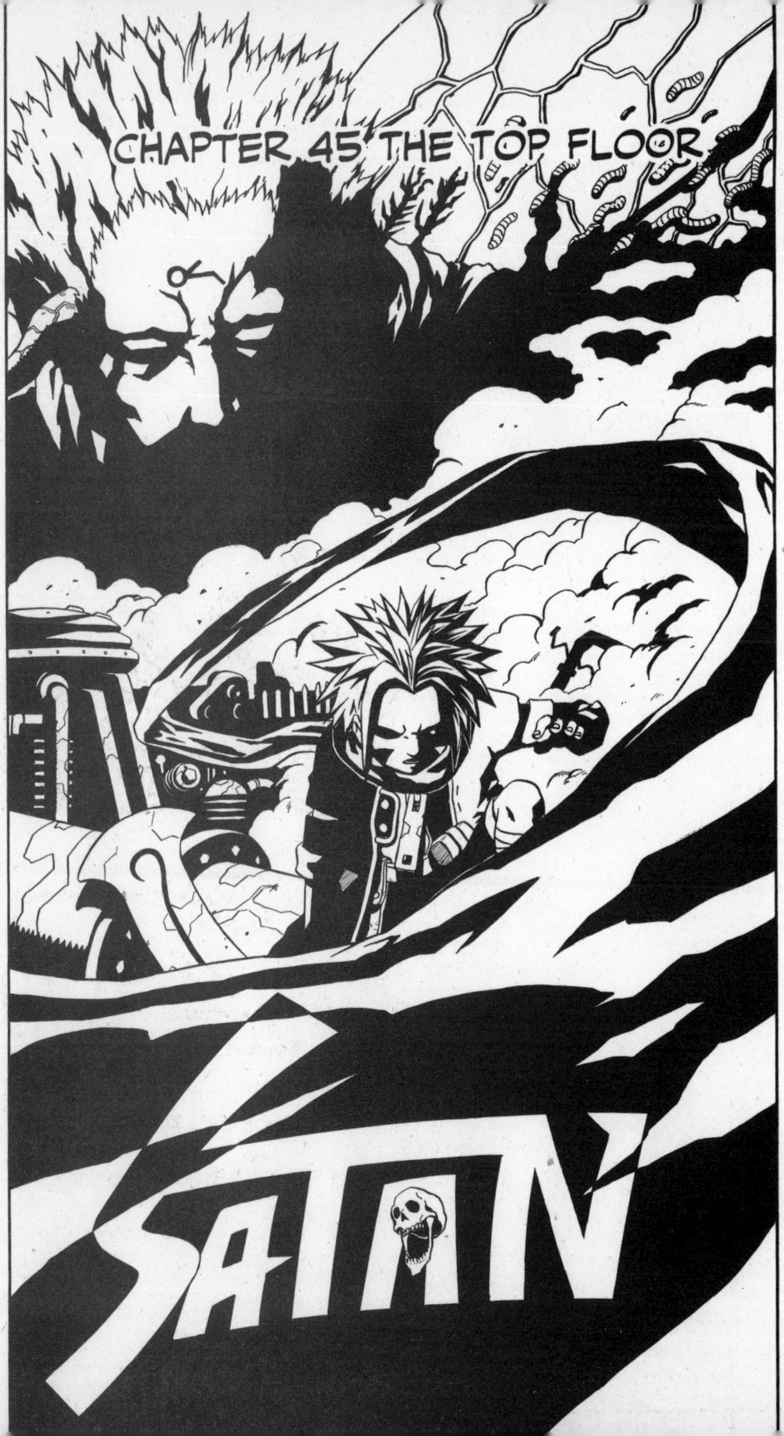
CHAPTER 45 THE TOP FLOOR
SATAN

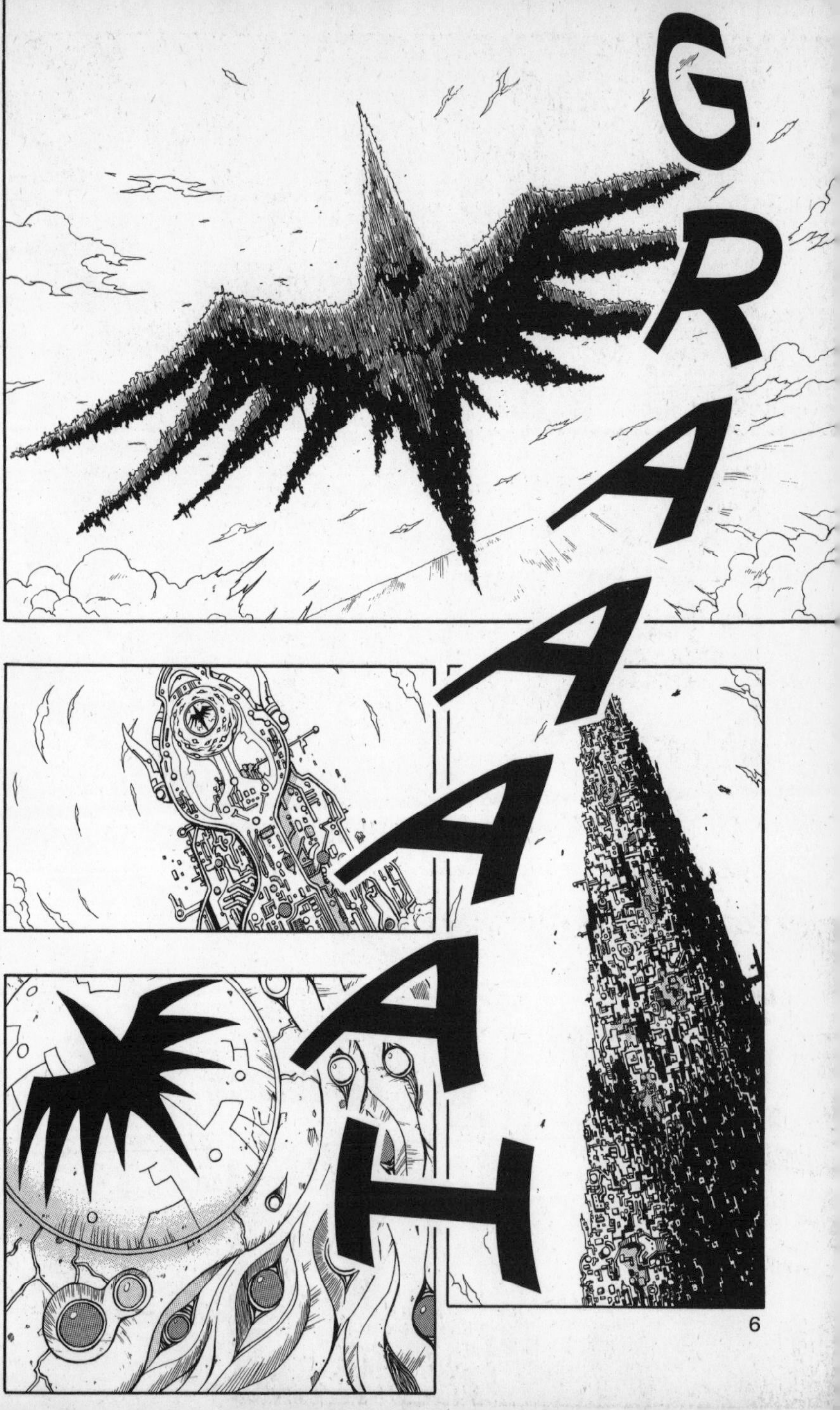
GRAAAAH

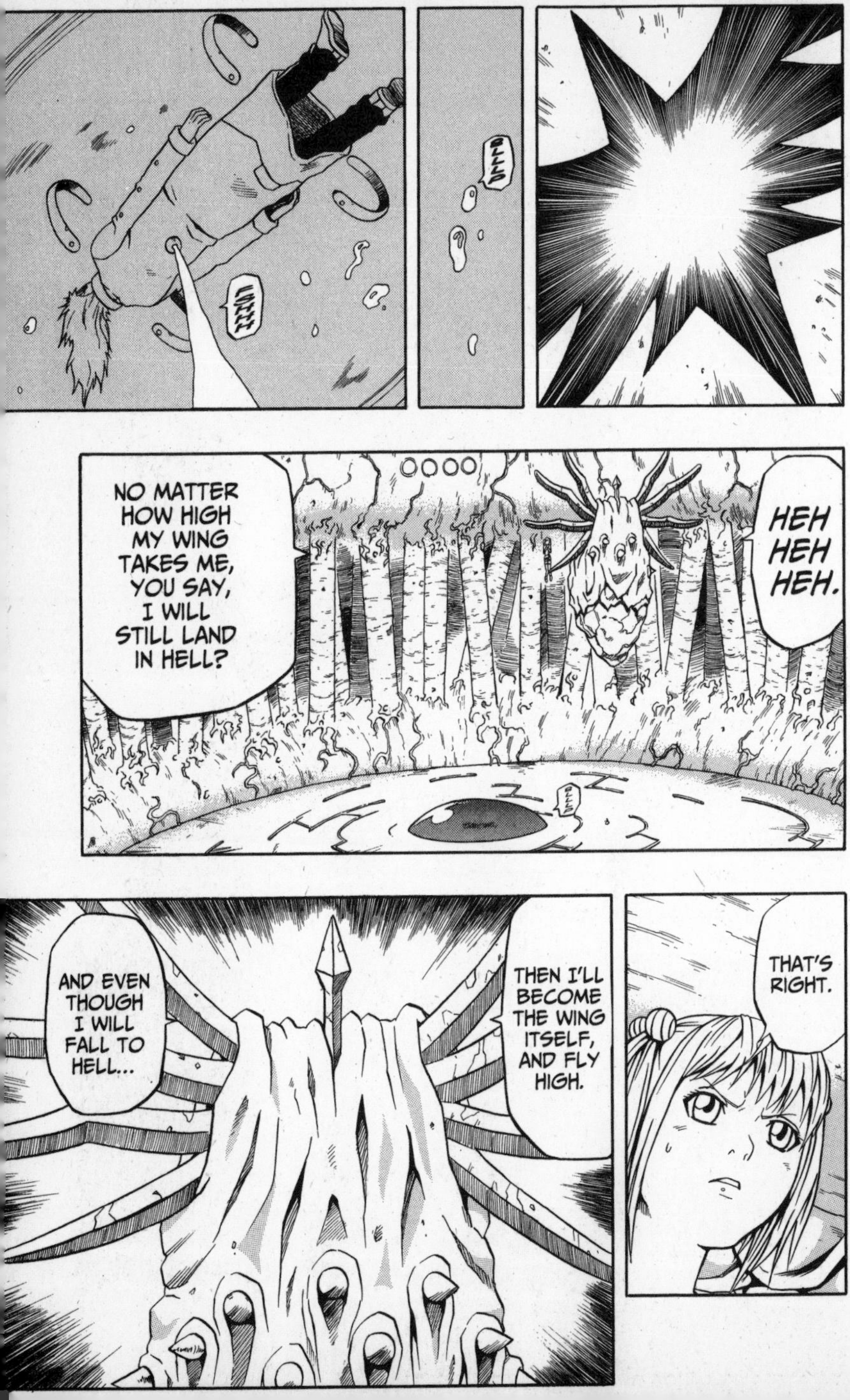
BLLLP
FSHHH
HEH HEH HEH.
NO MATTER HOW HIGH MY WING TAKES ME, YOU SAY, I WILL STILL LAND IN HELL?
BLLLP
THAT'S RIGHT.
THEN I'LL BECOME THE WING ITSELF, AND FLY HIGH.
AND EVEN THOUGH I WILL FALL TO HELL...

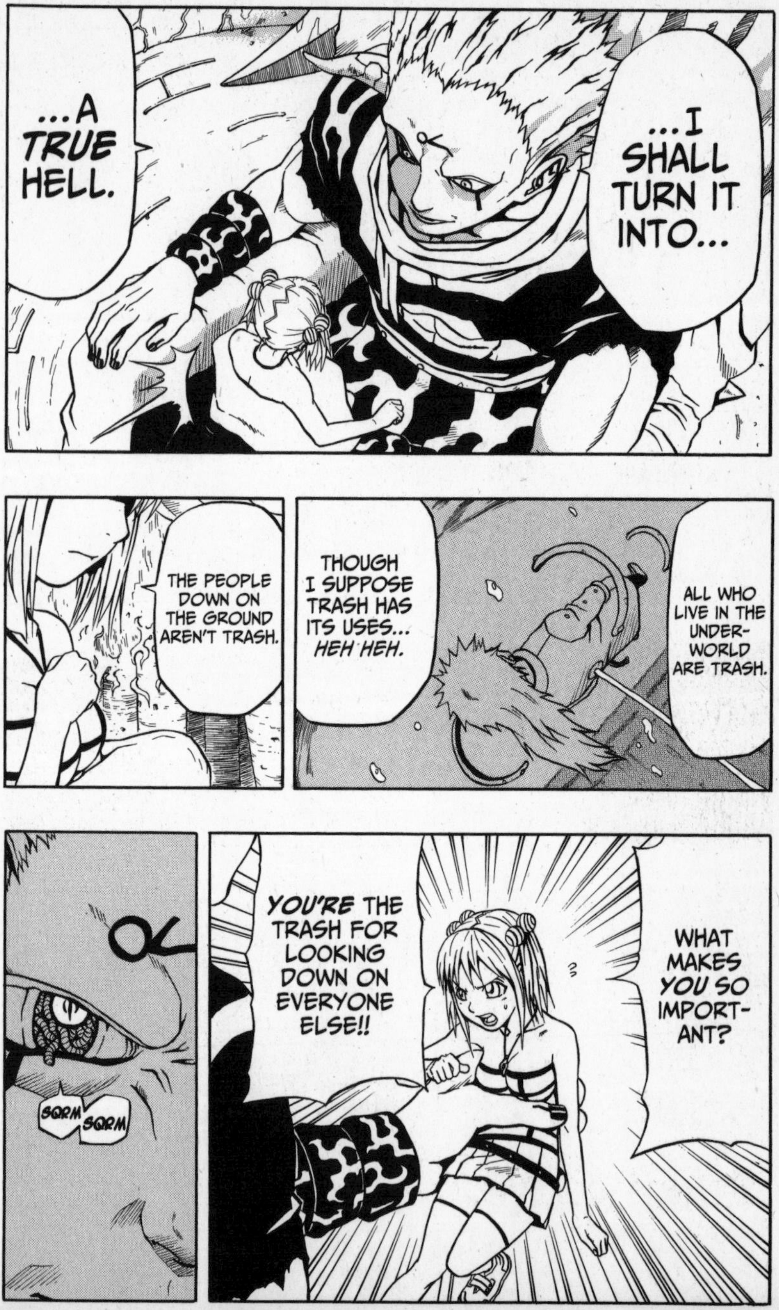
...I SHALL TURN IT INTO...
...A *TRUE* HELL.
ALL WHO LIVE IN THE UNDER-WORLD ARE TRASH.
THOUGH I SUPPOSE TRASH HAS ITS USES... *HEH HEH.*
THE PEOPLE DOWN ON THE GROUND AREN'T TRASH.
WHAT MAKES *YOU* SO IMPORT-ANT?
YOU'RE THE TRASH FOR LOOKING DOWN ON EVERYONE ELSE!!
SQRM SQRM

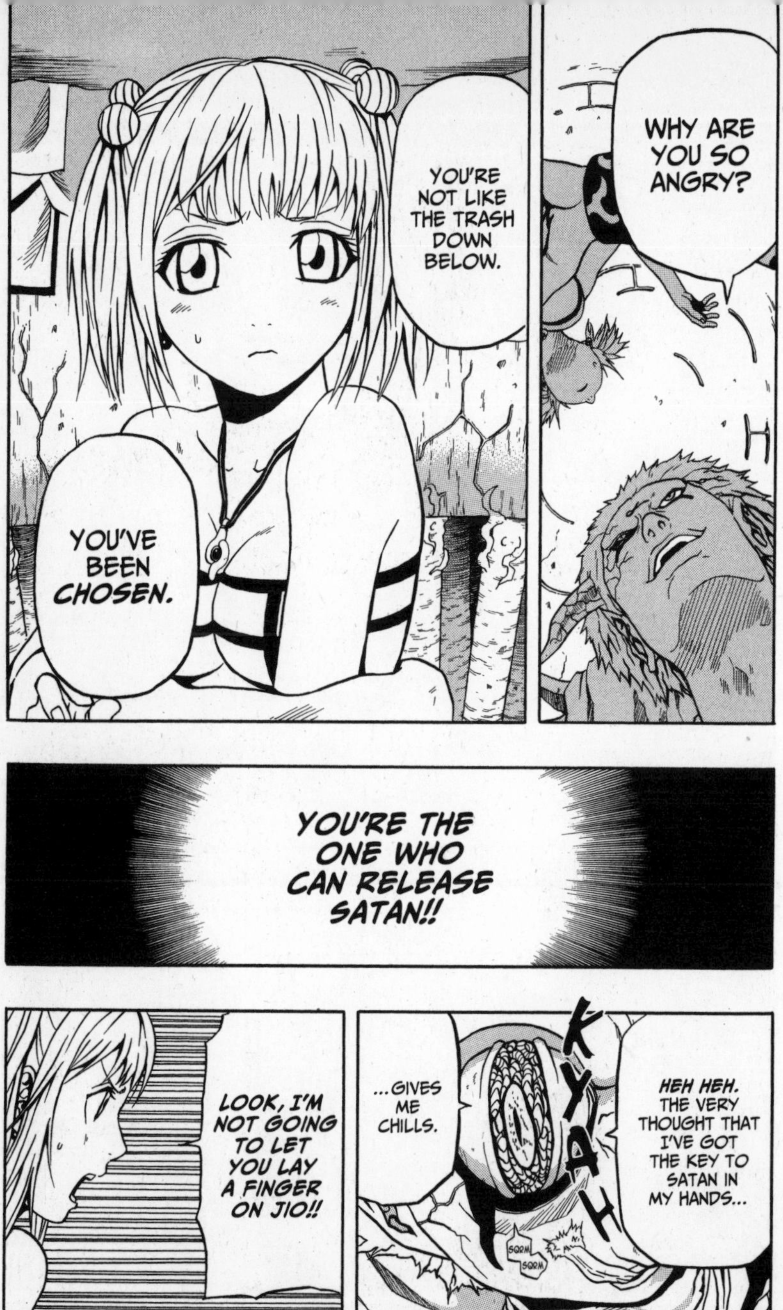
WHY ARE YOU SO ANGRY?
YOU'RE NOT LIKE THE TRASH DOWN BELOW.
YOU'VE BEEN CHOSEN.
YOU'RE THE ONE WHO CAN RELEASE SATAN!!
HEH HEH. THE VERY THOUGHT THAT I'VE GOT THE KEY TO SATAN IN MY HANDS...
KYAH
...GIVES ME CHILLS.
SQRM SQRM
LOOK, I'M NOT GOING TO LET YOU LAY A FINGER ON JIO!!

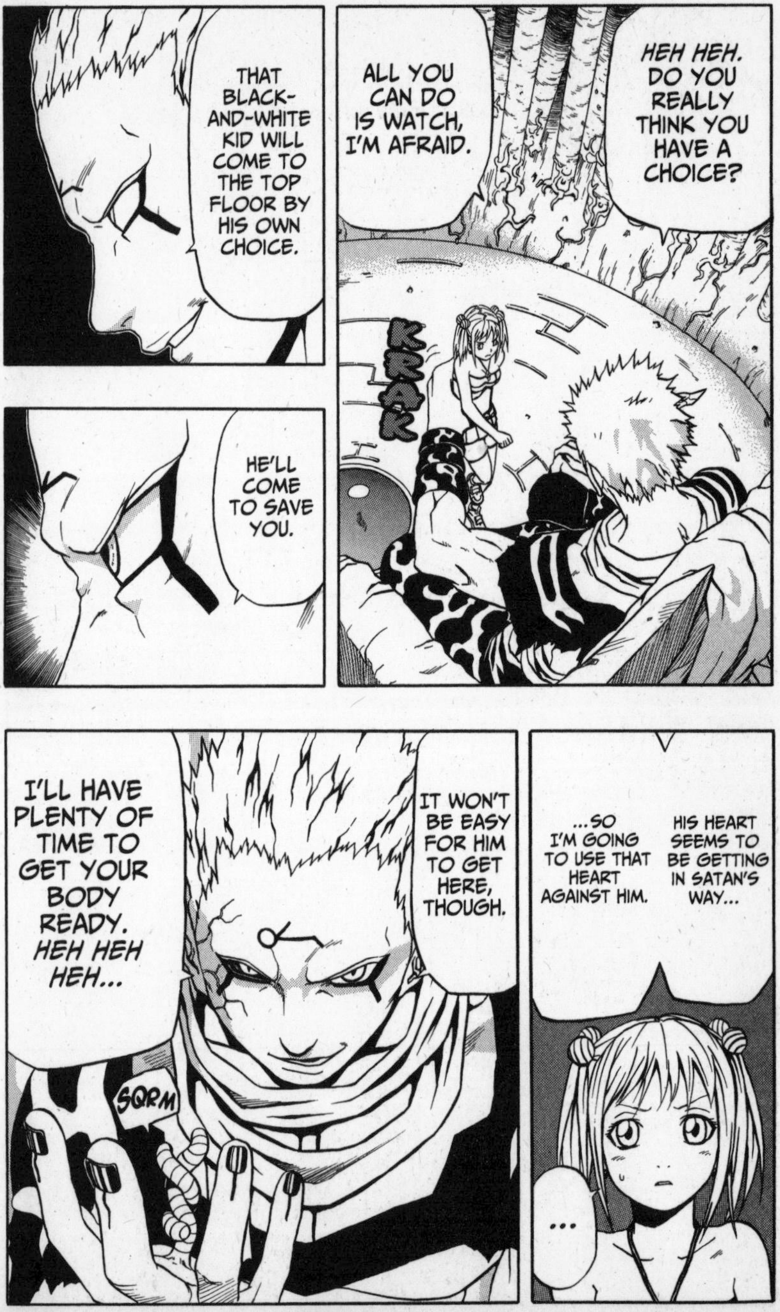
HEH HEH. DO YOU REALLY THINK YOU HAVE A CHOICE?
ALL YOU CAN DO IS WATCH, I'M AFRAID.
KRAK
THAT BLACK-AND-WHITE KID WILL COME TO THE TOP FLOOR BY HIS OWN CHOICE.
HE'LL COME TO SAVE YOU.
HIS HEART SEEMS TO BE GETTING IN SATAN'S WAY...
...SO I'M GOING TO USE THAT HEART AGAINST HIM.
...
IT WON'T BE EASY FOR HIM TO GET HERE, THOUGH.
I'LL HAVE PLENTY OF TIME TO GET YOUR BODY READY. HEH HEH HEH HEH...
SQRM

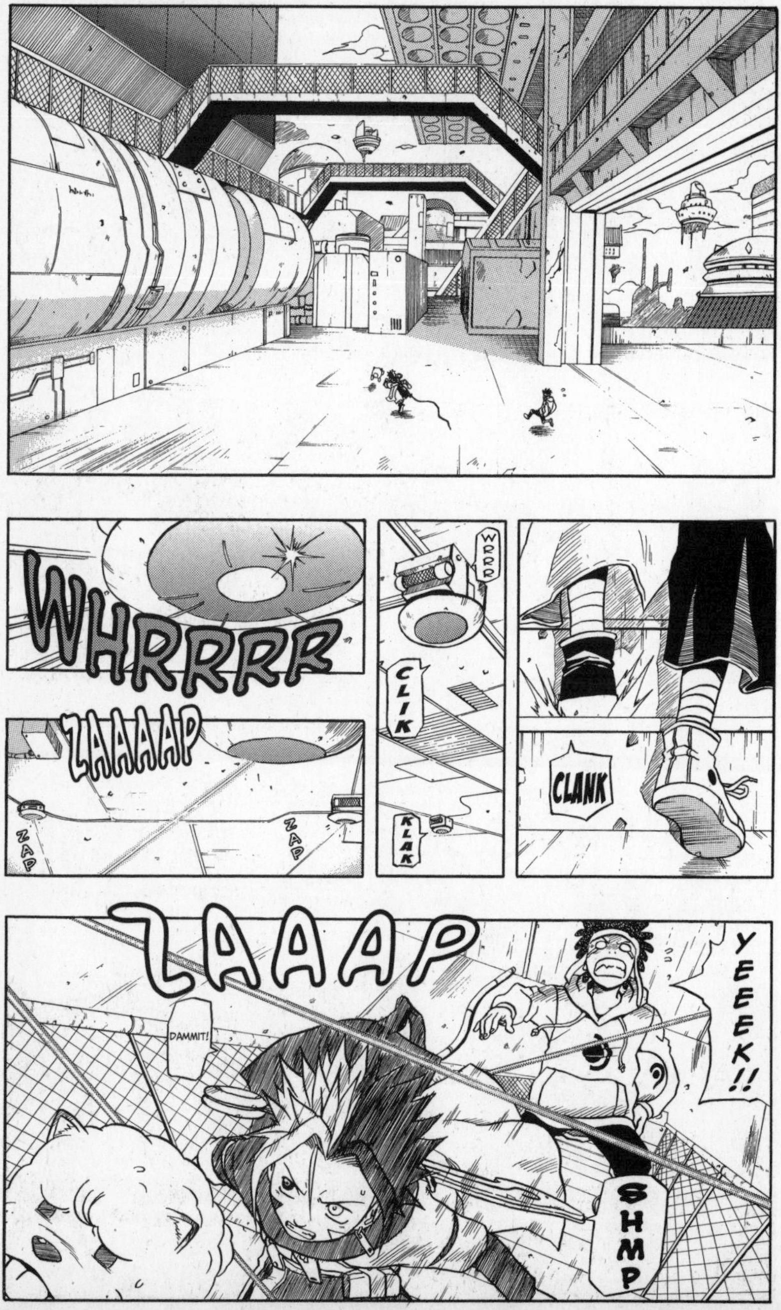
CLANK
WRRR
CLIK
KLAK
WHRRRR
ZAAAAP
ZAP
ZAP
YEEEEK!!
ZAAAP
SHMP
DAMMIT!

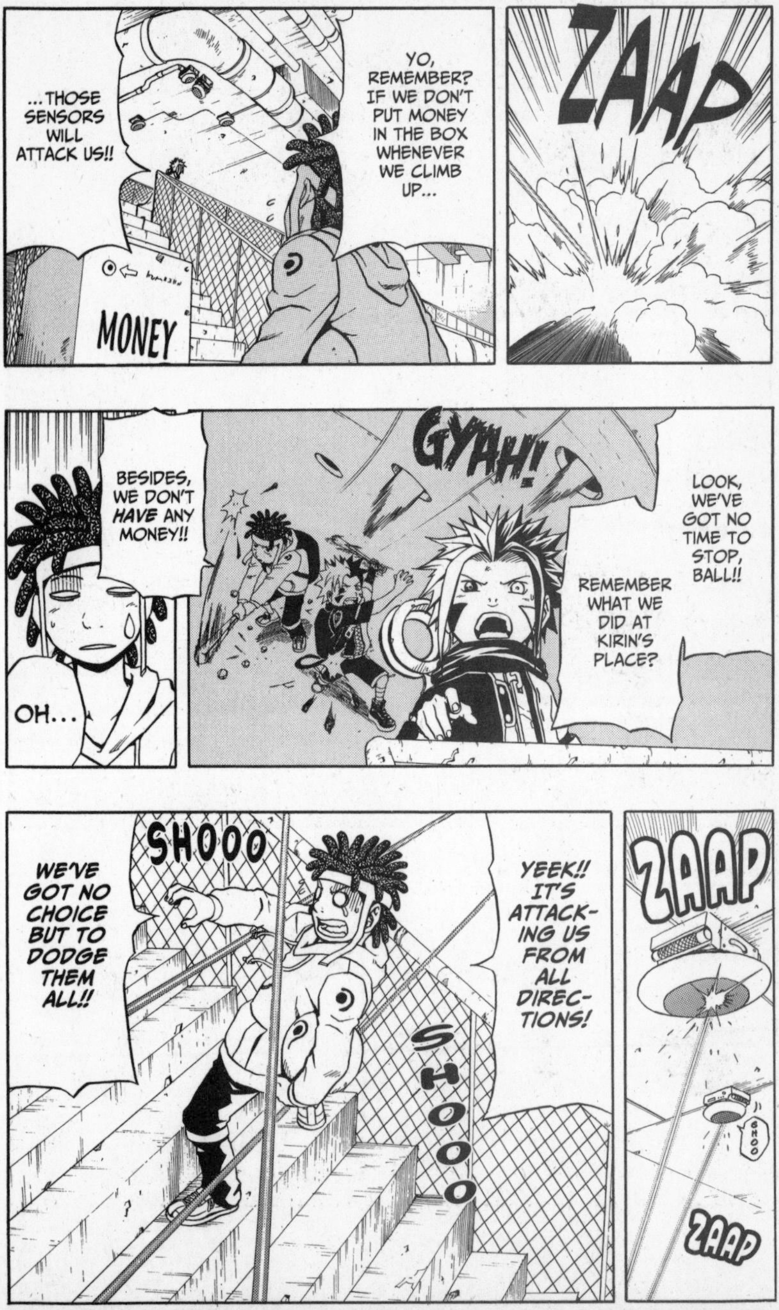
ZAAP
YO, REMEMBER? IF WE DON'T PUT MONEY IN THE BOX WHENEVER WE CLIMB UP...
...THOSE SENSORS WILL ATTACK US!!
MONEY
GYAH!
LOOK, WE'VE GOT NO TIME TO STOP, BALL!!
REMEMBER WHAT WE DID AT KIRIN'S PLACE?
BESIDES, WE DON'T *HAVE* ANY MONEY!!
OH...
ZAAP
SHOO
ZAAP
SHOOO
YEEK!! IT'S ATTACKING US FROM ALL DIRECTIONS!
WE'VE GOT NO CHOICE BUT TO DODGE THEM ALL!!
SHOOOO

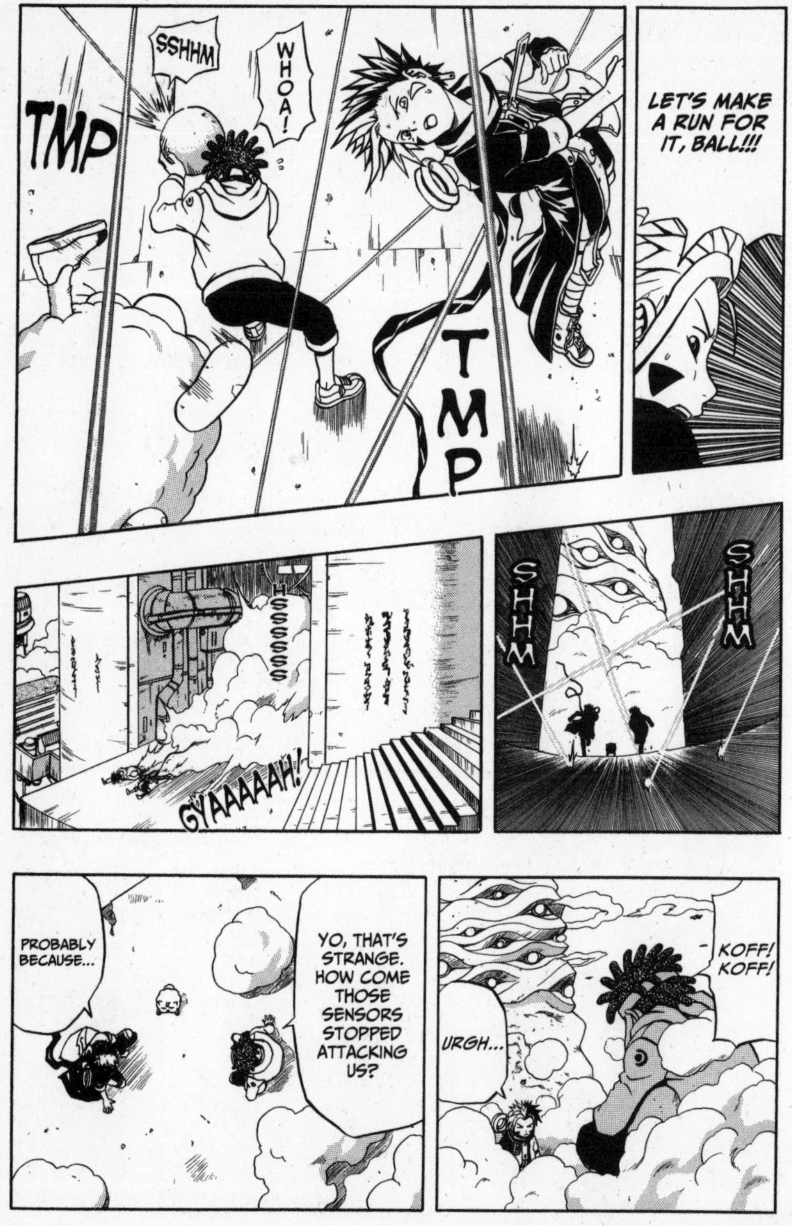
LET'S MAKE A RUN FOR IT, BALL!!!
TMP
WHOA!
SSHHM
TMP
SHHM
SHHM
HSSSSSS
GYAAAAAH!
KOFF! KOFF!
URGH...
YO, THAT'S STRANGE. HOW COME THOSE SENSORS STOPPED ATTACKING US?
PROBABLY BECAUSE...

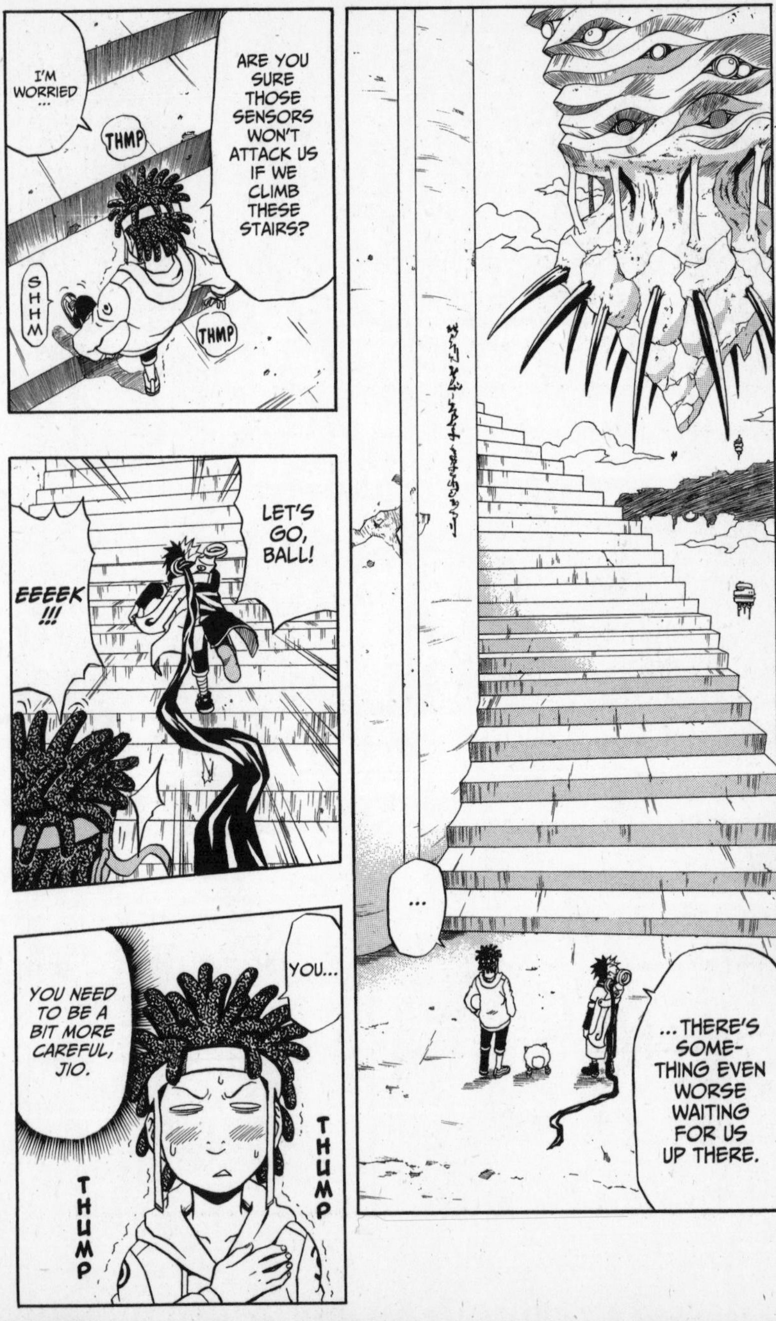
...
...THERE'S SOME-THING EVEN WORSE WAITING FOR US UP THERE.
ARE YOU SURE THOSE SENSORS WON'T ATTACK US IF WE CLIMB THESE STAIRS?
I'M WORRIED...
THMP
SHHM
THMP
LET'S GO, BALL!
EEEEK!!!
YOU...
YOU NEED TO BE A BIT MORE CAREFUL, JIO.
THUMP
THUMP

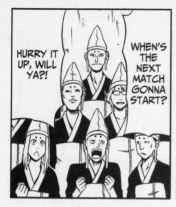

RAAH
RAAH
地
RAAH
WHEN'S THE NEXT MATCH GONNA START?
HURRY IT UP, WILL YA?!
RAAAH
RAAAAH
RAAAAH
ER...IT LOOKS LIKE OLYMPIA'S OVER FOR THIS YEAR.
HOW SHALL I EXPLAIN THIS TO THEM...?
HYAAA!
HFF
HFF
!

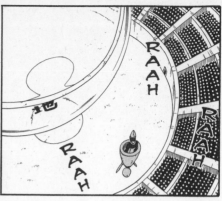

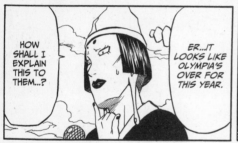

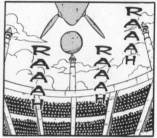

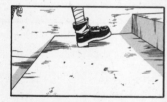

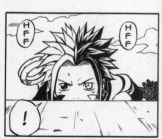

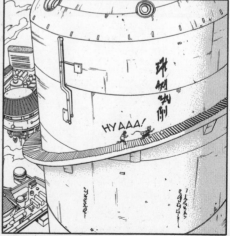

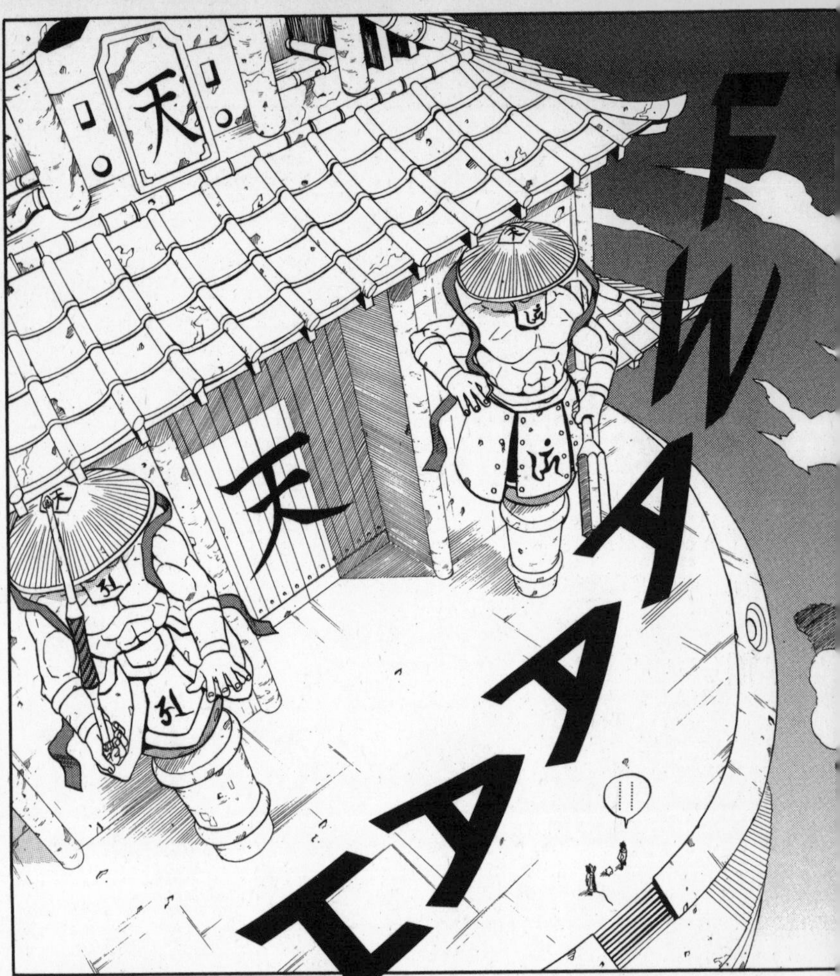
FWAAAAI
!!

SIGN ON GATE: HEAVEN

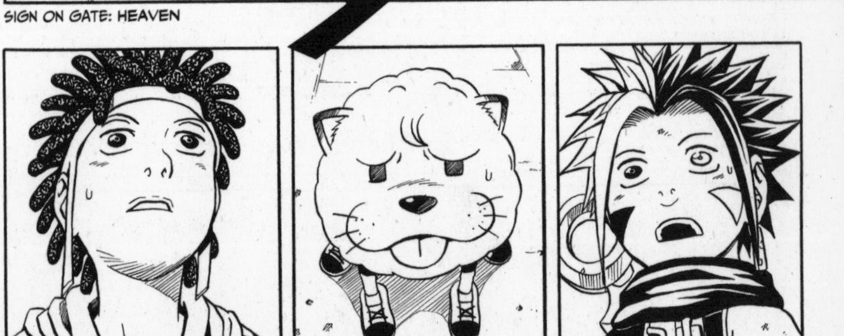

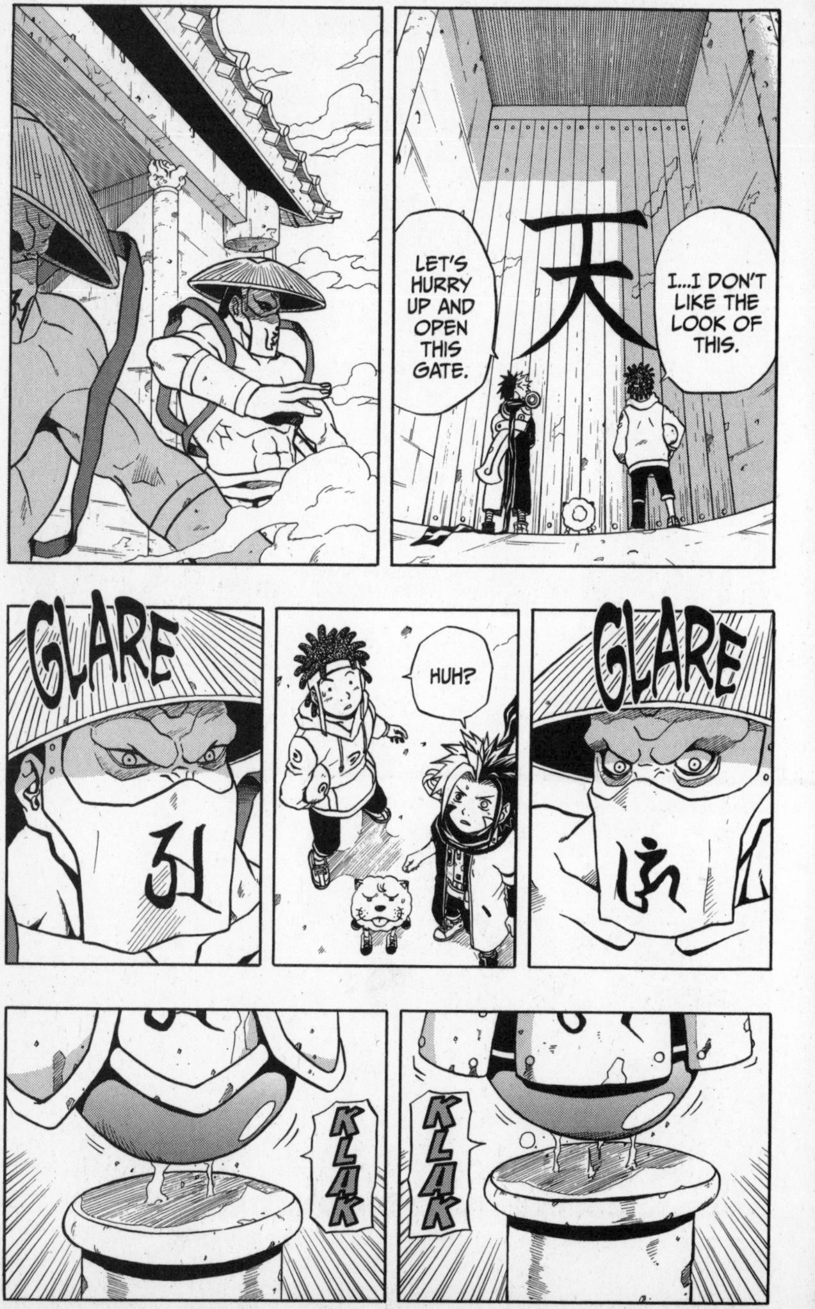
I...I DON'T LIKE THE LOOK OF THIS.
LET'S HURRY UP AND OPEN THIS GATE.
天
GLARE
HUH?
GLARE
KLAK
KLAK

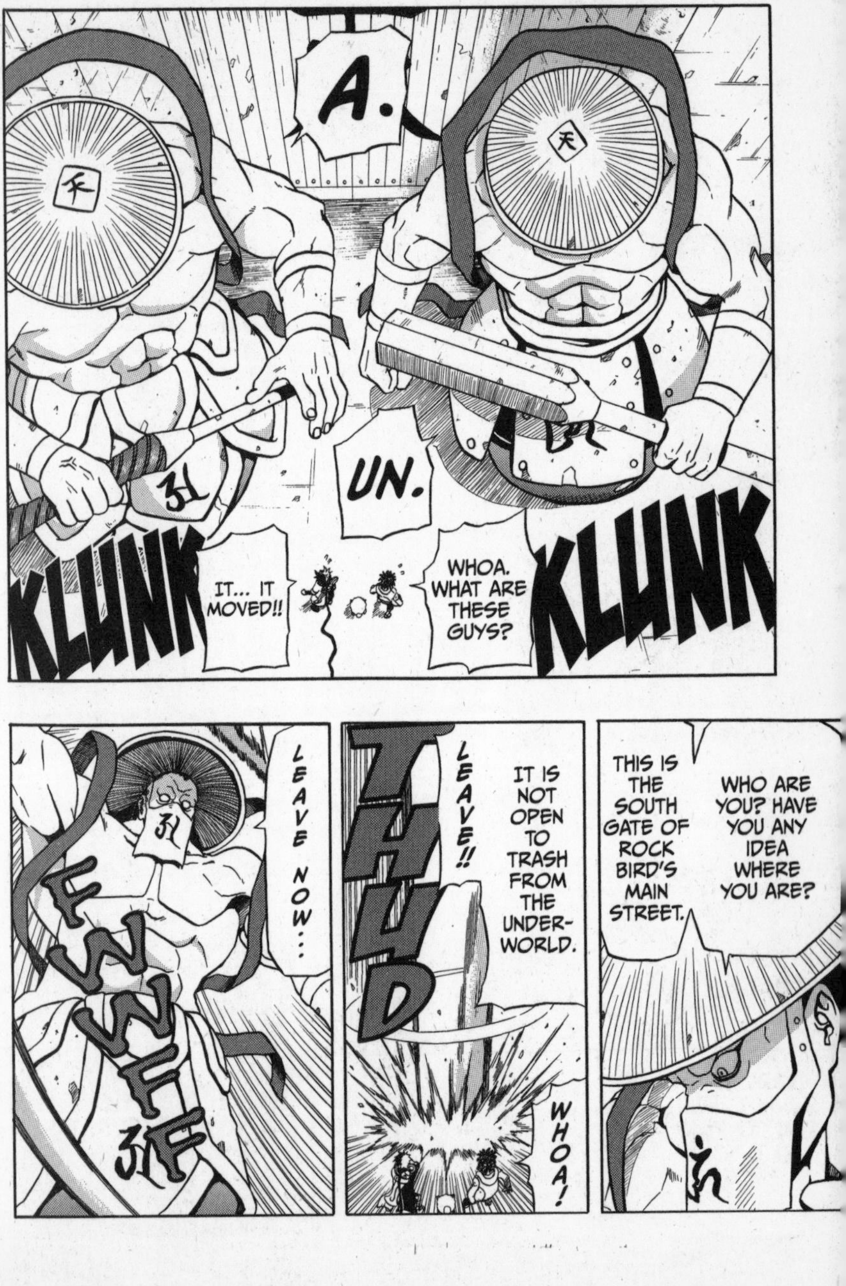
A.
UN.
WHOA. WHAT ARE THESE GUYS?
KLUNK
IT... IT MOVED!!
KLUNK
WHO ARE YOU? HAVE YOU ANY IDEA WHERE YOU ARE?
THIS IS THE SOUTH GATE OF ROCK BIRD'S MAIN STREET.
IT IS NOT OPEN TO TRASH FROM THE UNDER-WORLD.
LEAVE!!
THUD
WHOA!
LEAVE NOW...
FWWF

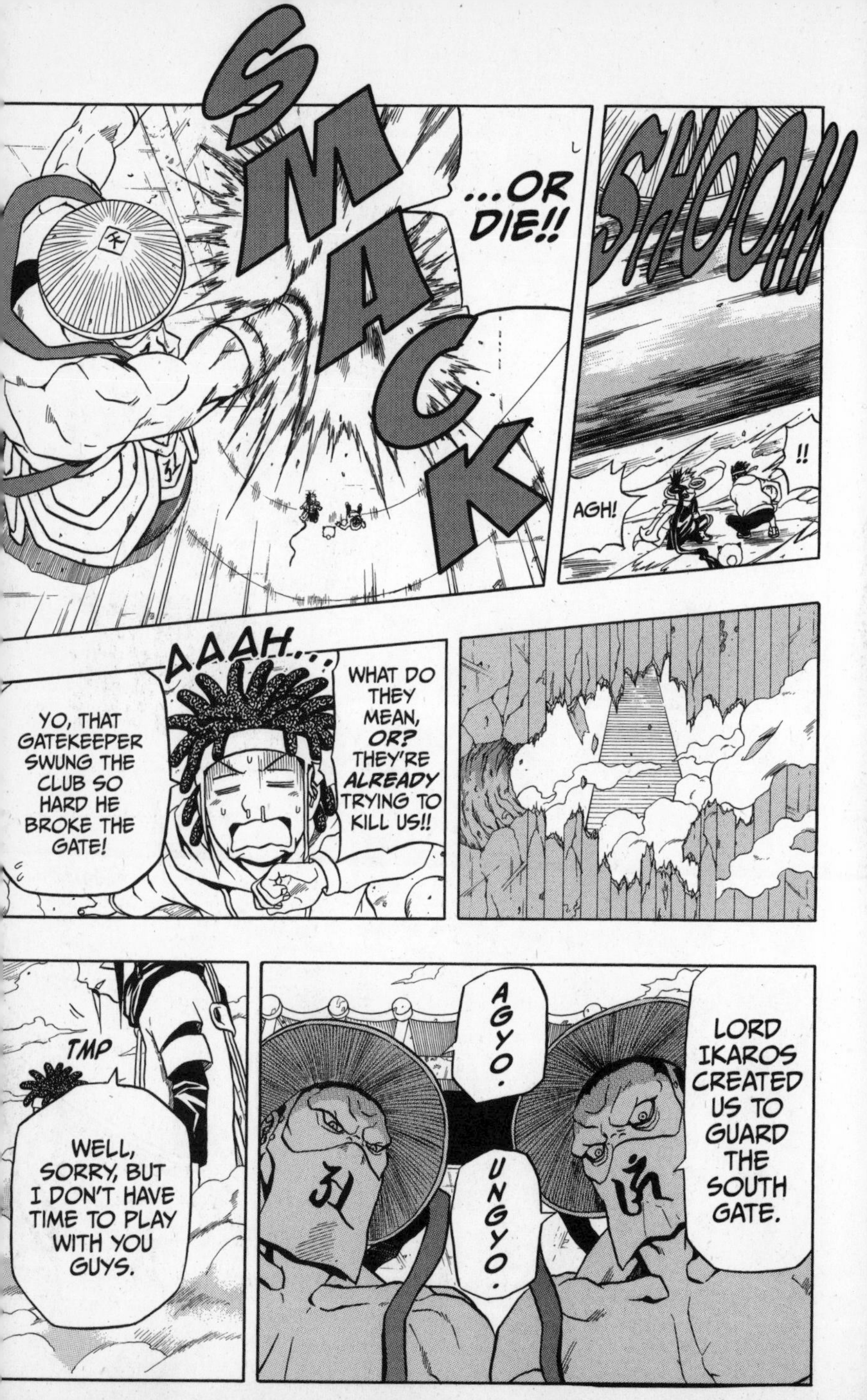
SHOOM
!!
AGH!
SMACK
...OR DIE!!
AAAH...
WHAT DO THEY MEAN, OR? THEY'RE ALREADY TRYING TO KILL US!!
YO, THAT GATEKEEPER SWUNG THE CLUB SO HARD HE BROKE THE GATE!
LORD IKAROS CREATED US TO GUARD THE SOUTH GATE.
AGYO.
UNGYO.
TMP
WELL, SORRY, BUT I DON'T HAVE TIME TO PLAY WITH YOU GUYS.

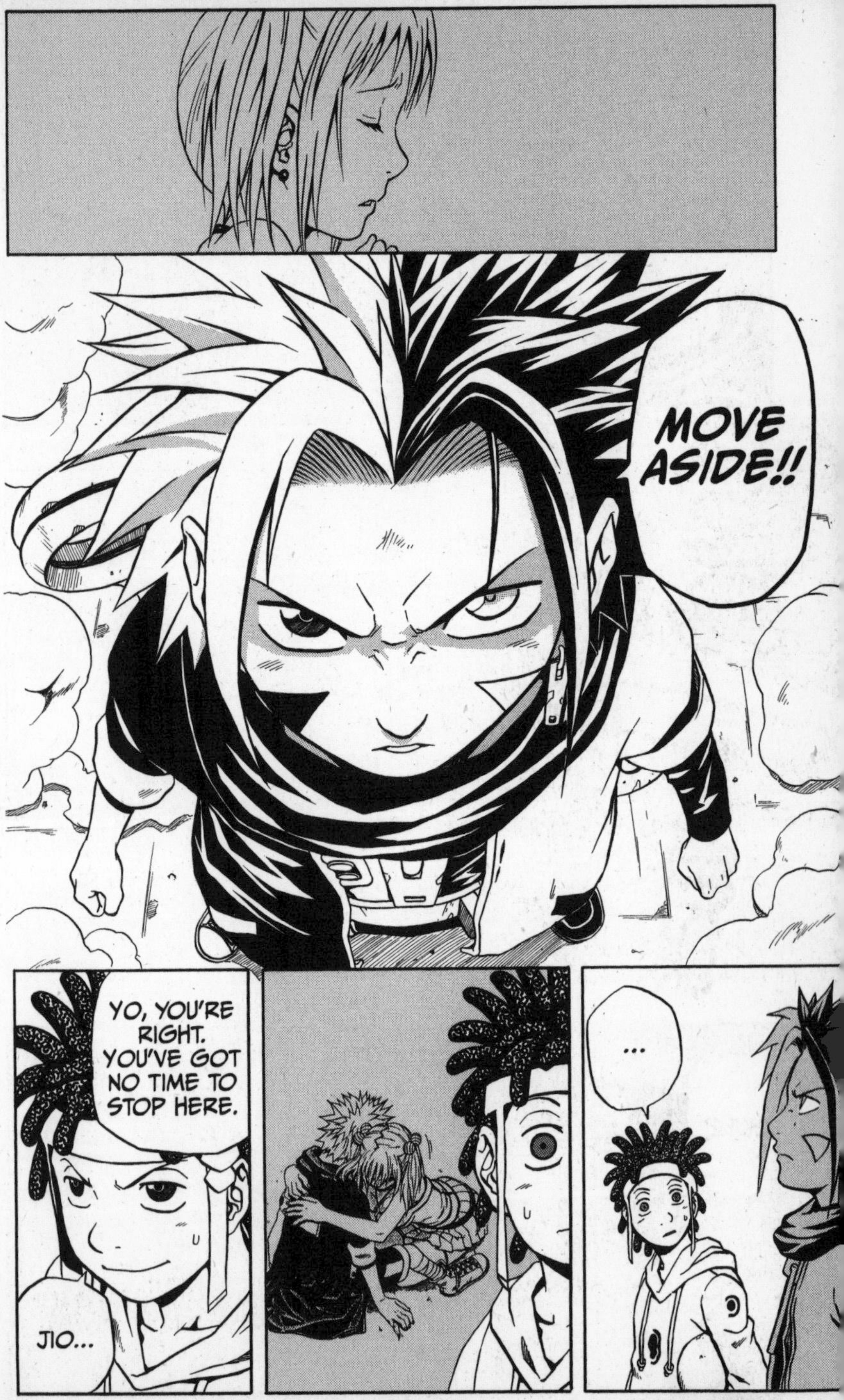
MOVE ASIDE!!
...
YO, YOU'RE RIGHT. YOU'VE GOT NO TIME TO STOP HERE.
JIO...

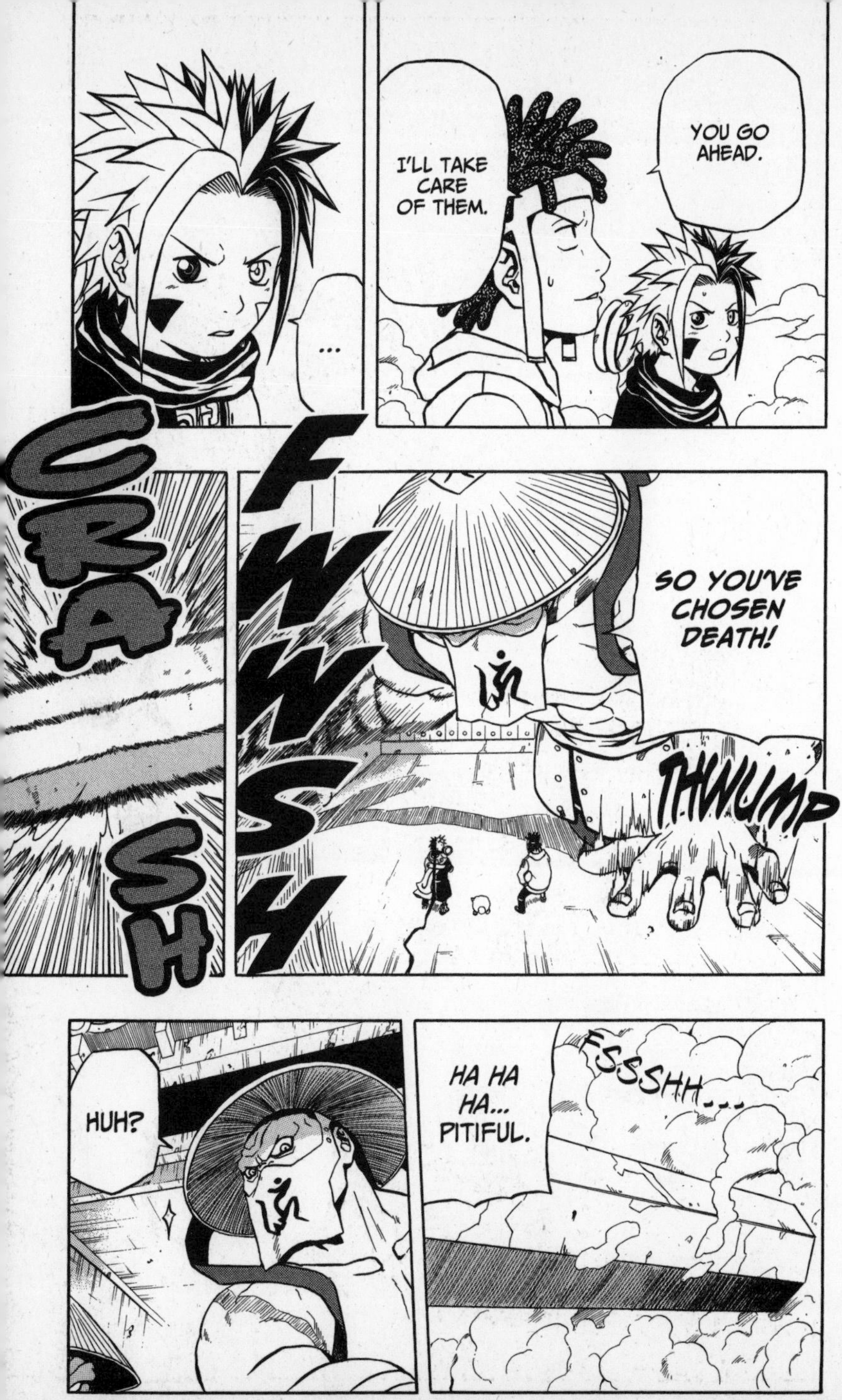
YOU GO AHEAD.
I'LL TAKE CARE OF THEM.
...
SO YOU'VE CHOSEN DEATH!
THWUMP
FWWWSSH
CRASH
FSSSHH...
HA HA HA... PITIFUL.
HUH?

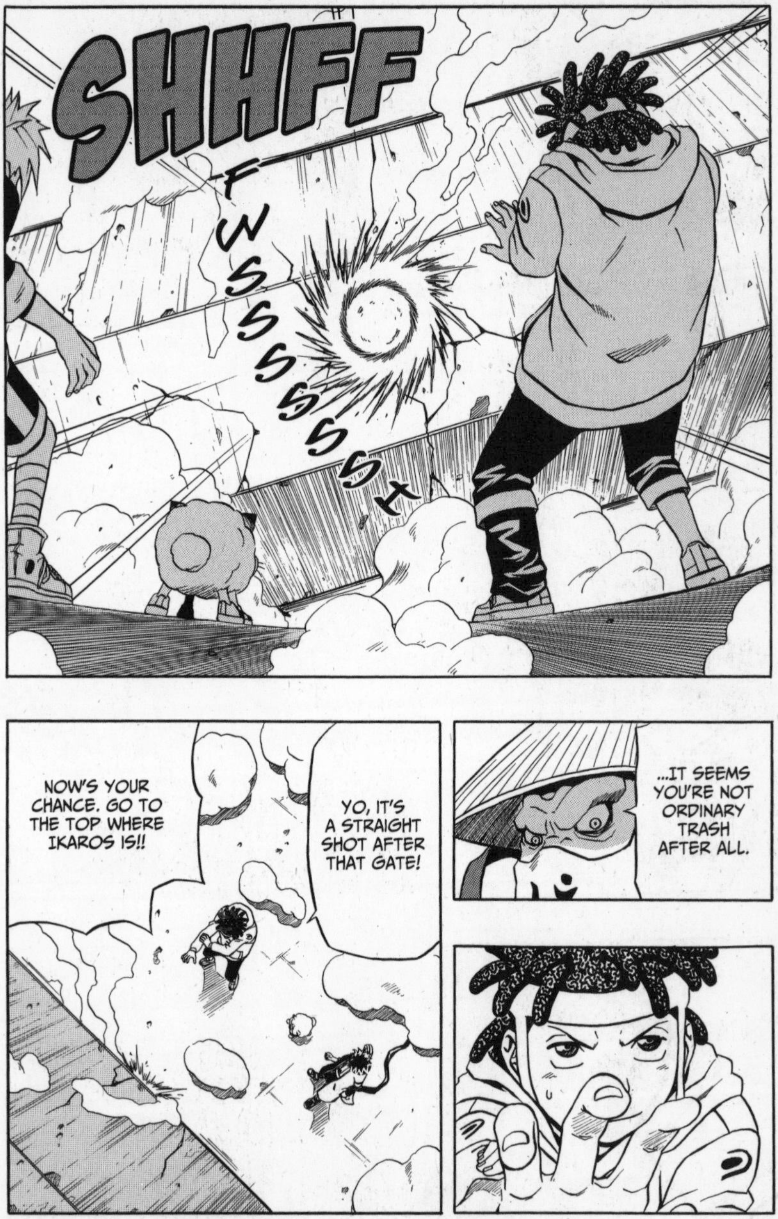
SHHFF
FWSSSSSSH
...IT SEEMS YOU'RE NOT ORDINARY TRASH AFTER ALL.
YO, IT'S A STRAIGHT SHOT AFTER THAT GATE!
NOW'S YOUR CHANCE. GO TO THE TOP WHERE IKAROS IS!!

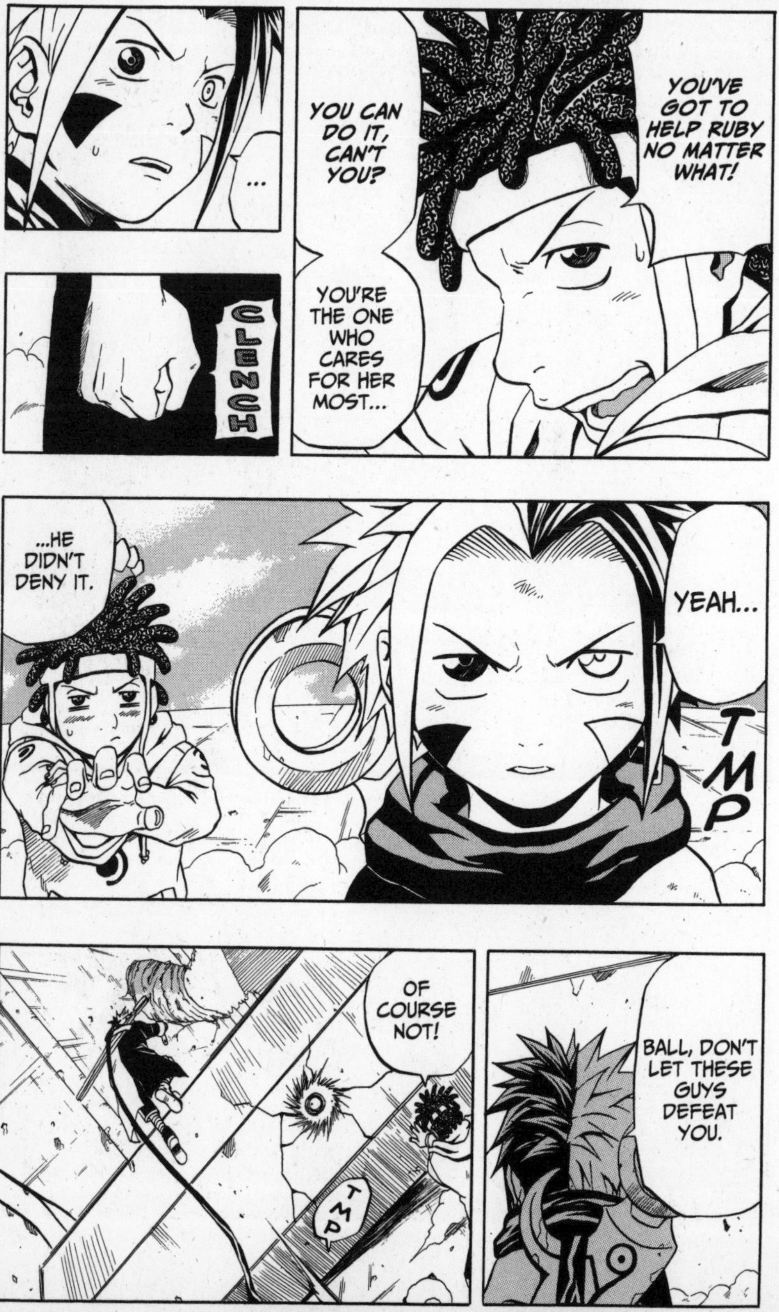
YOU'VE GOT TO HELP RUBY NO MATTER WHAT!
YOU CAN DO IT, CAN'T YOU?
YOU'RE THE ONE WHO CARES FOR HER MOST...
...
CLENCH
YEAH...
TMP
...HE DIDN'T DENY IT.
BALL, DON'T LET THESE GUYS DEFEAT YOU.
OF COURSE NOT!
TMP

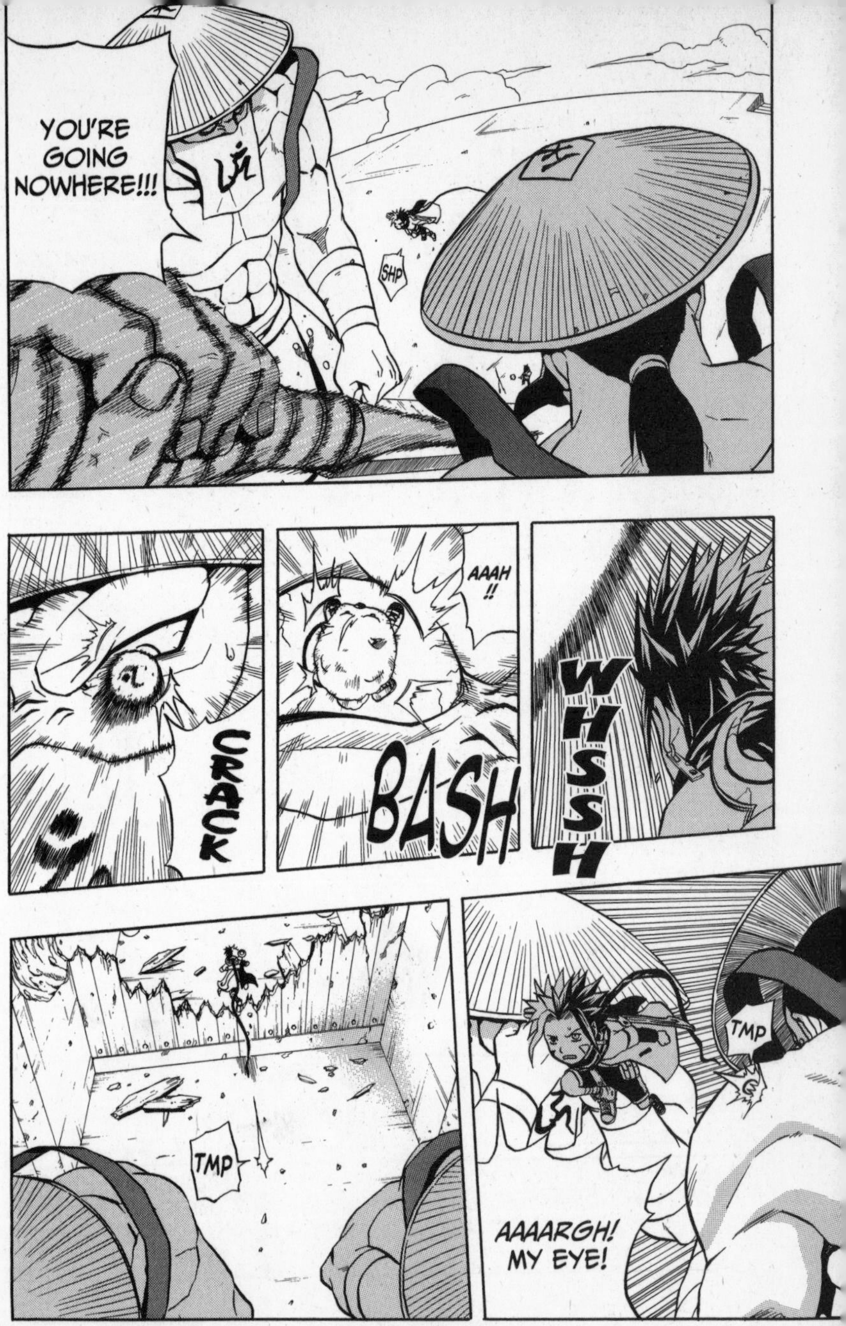
YOU'RE GOING NOWHERE!!!
SHP
WHISSH
AAAH !!
BASH
CRACK
TMP
AAAARGH! MY EYE!
TMP

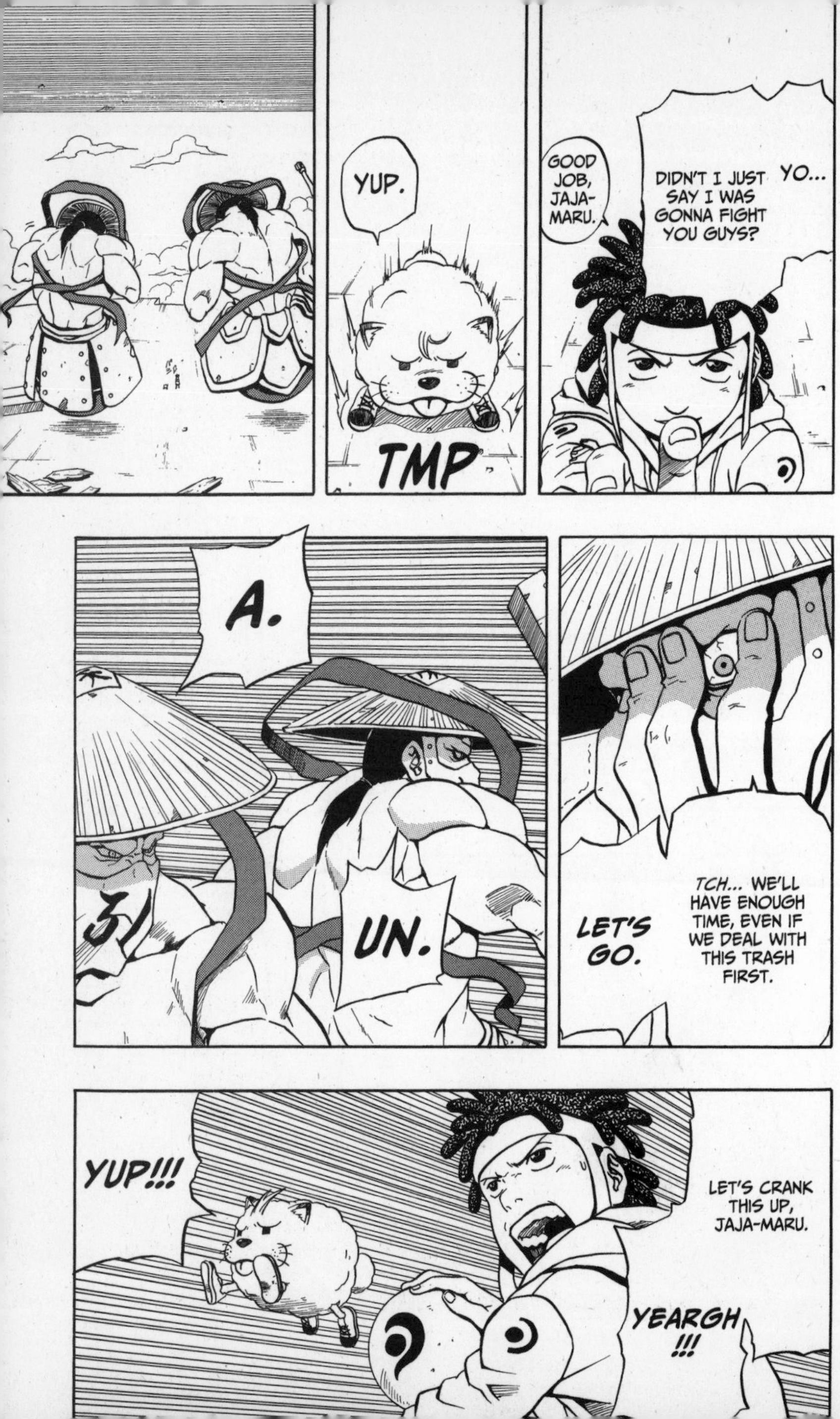
YO...
DIDN'T I JUST SAY I WAS GONNA FIGHT YOU GUYS?
GOOD JOB, JAJA-MARU.
YUP.
TMP
TCH... WE'LL HAVE ENOUGH TIME, EVEN IF WE DEAL WITH THIS TRASH FIRST.
LET'S GO.
A.
UN.
LET'S CRANK THIS UP, JAJA-MARU.
YEARGH!!!
YUP!!!

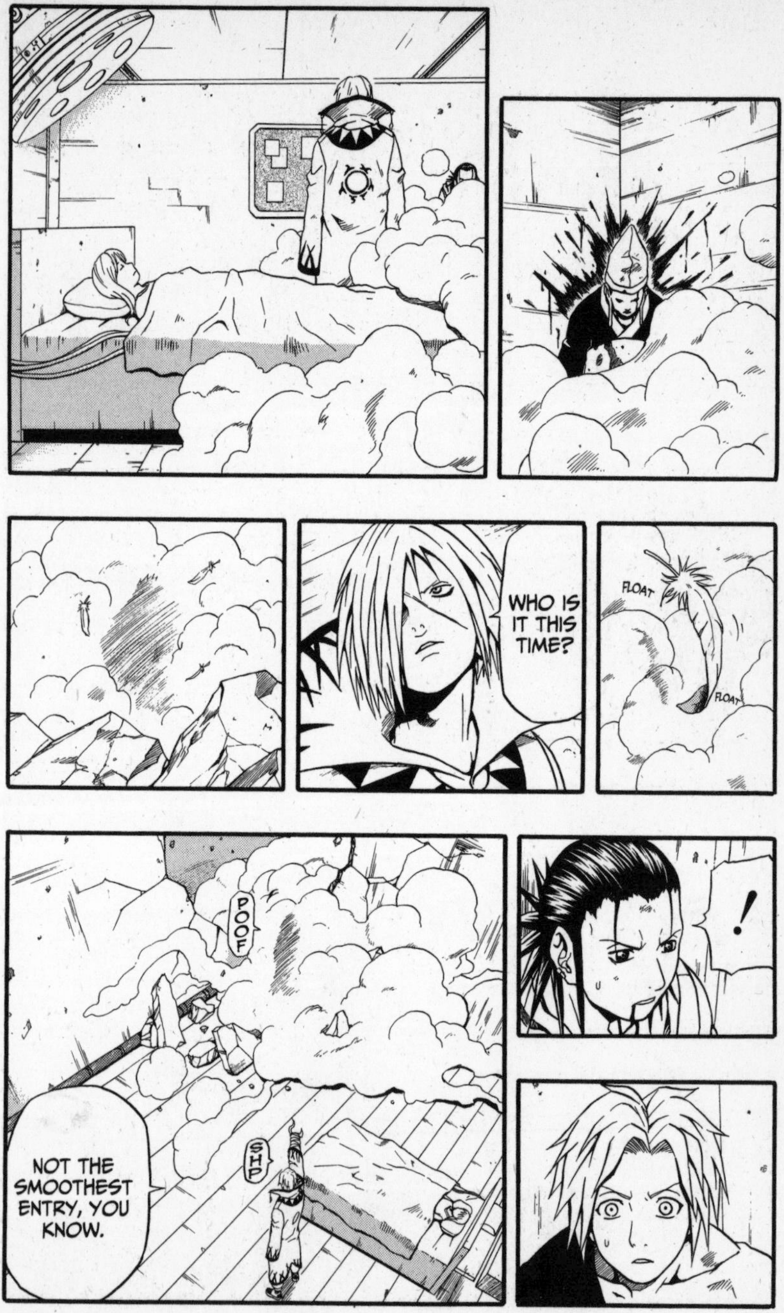
FLOAT
FLOAT
WHO IS IT THIS TIME?
!
POOF
SHP
NOT THE SMOOTHEST ENTRY, YOU KNOW.

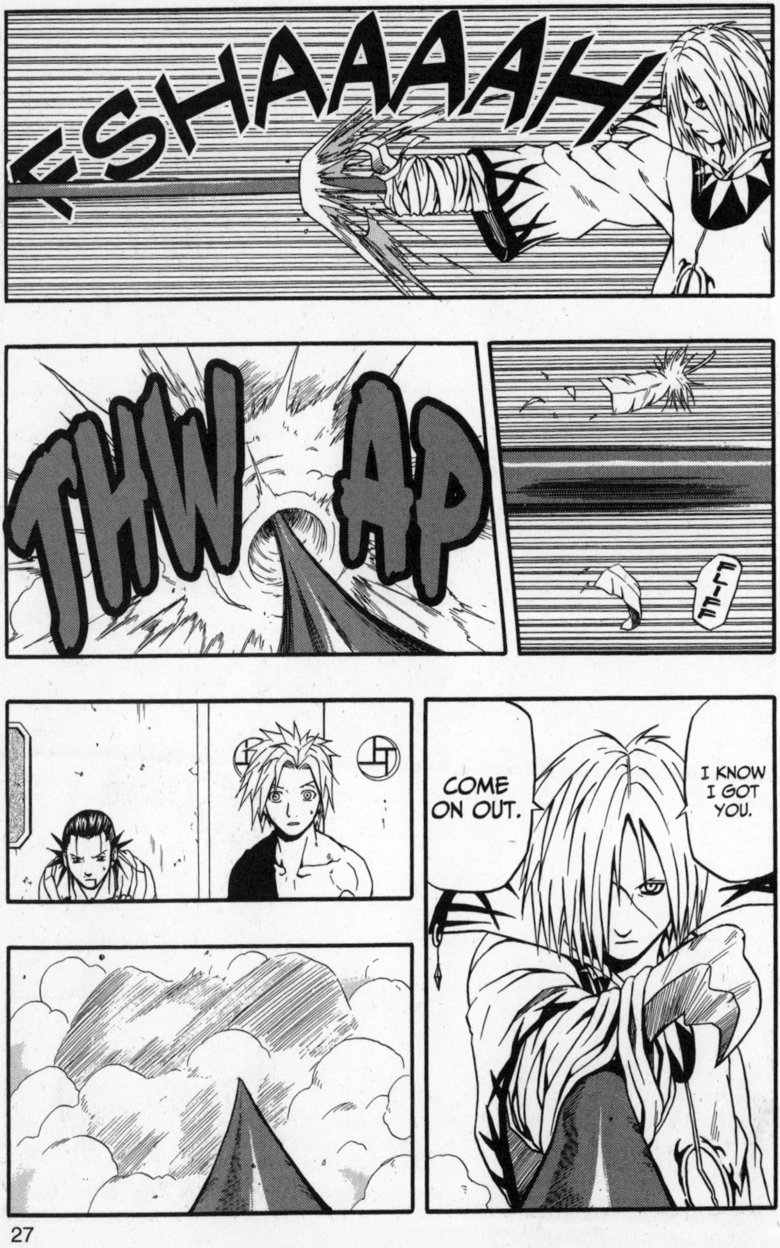
FSHAAAAH
FLIFF
THWAP
I KNOW I GOT YOU.
COME ON OUT.

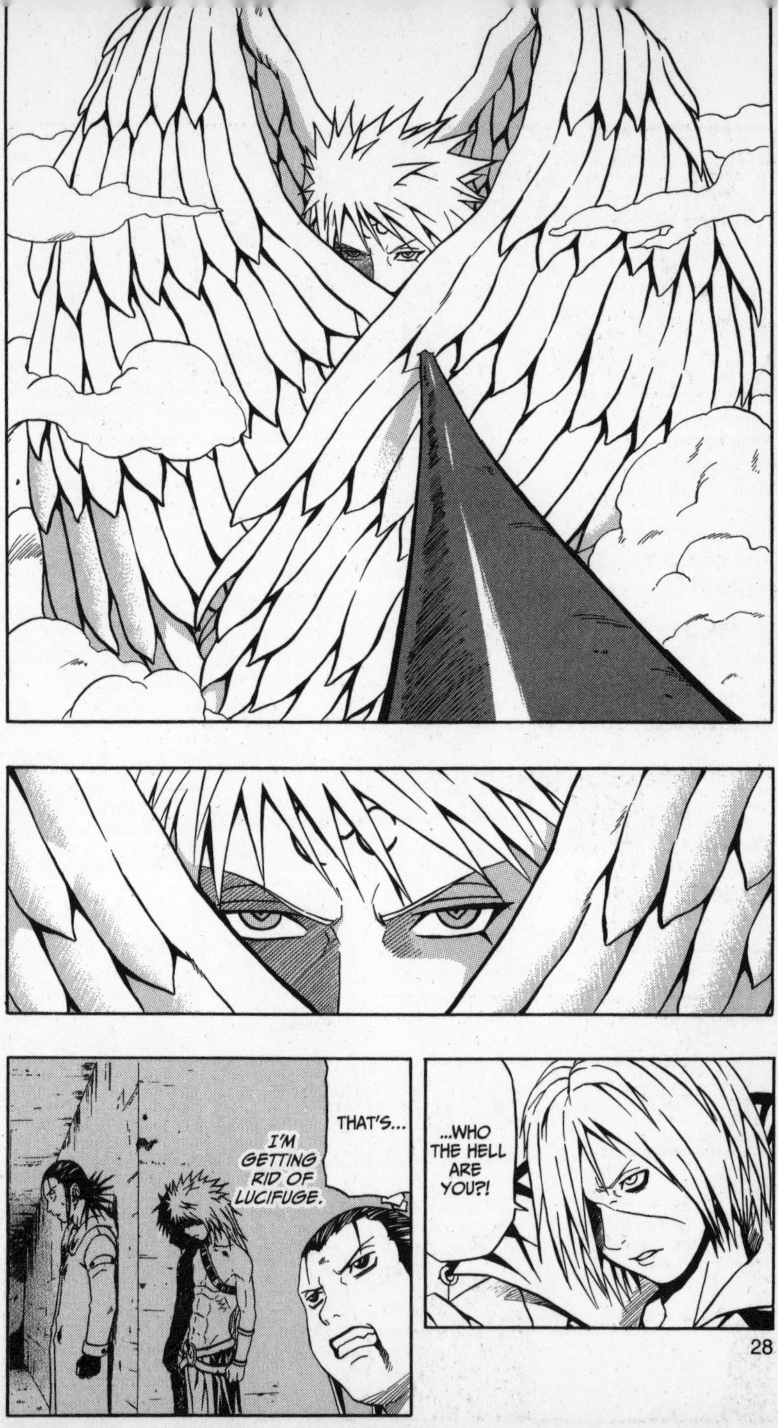
...WHO THE HELL ARE YOU?!
THAT'S...
I'M GETTING RID OF LUCIFUGE.

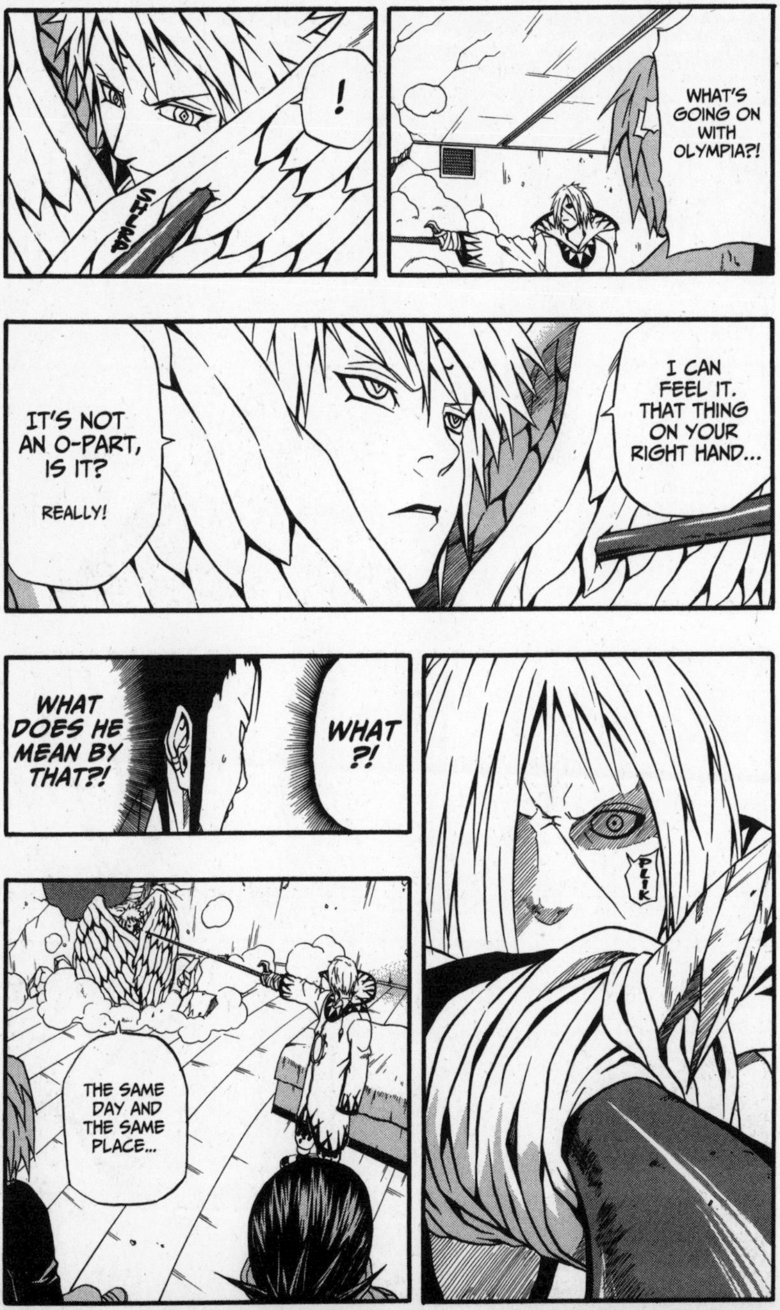

WHAT'S GOING ON WITH OLYMPIA?!
!
SHLRP
I CAN FEEL IT. THAT THING ON YOUR RIGHT HAND...
IT'S NOT AN O-PART, IS IT?
REALLY!
PLIK
WHAT?!
WHAT DOES HE MEAN BY THAT?!
THE SAME DAY AND THE SAME PLACE...

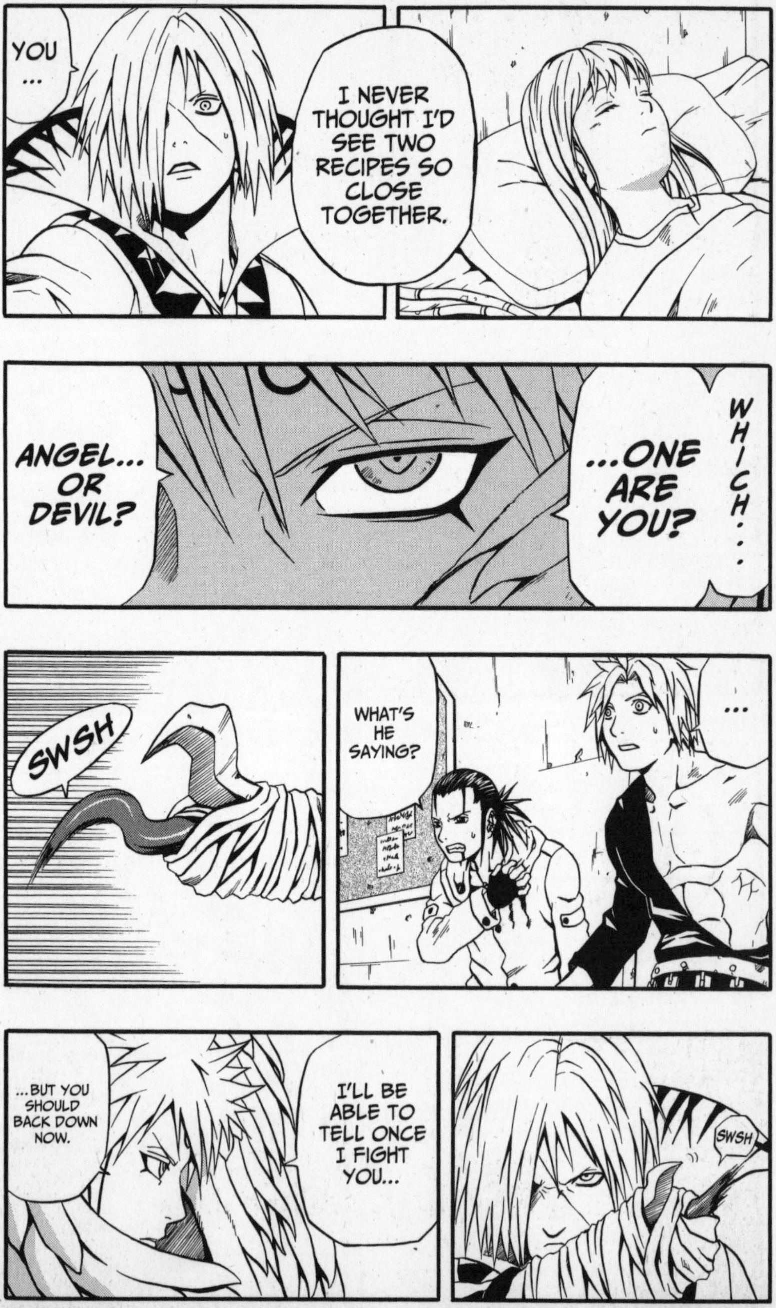
I NEVER THOUGHT I'D SEE TWO RECIPES SO CLOSE TOGETHER.
YOU ...
WHICH...
...ONE ARE YOU?
ANGEL... OR DEVIL?
...
WHAT'S HE SAYING?
SWSH
SWSH
I'LL BE ABLE TO TELL ONCE I FIGHT YOU...
...BUT YOU SHOULD BACK DOWN NOW.

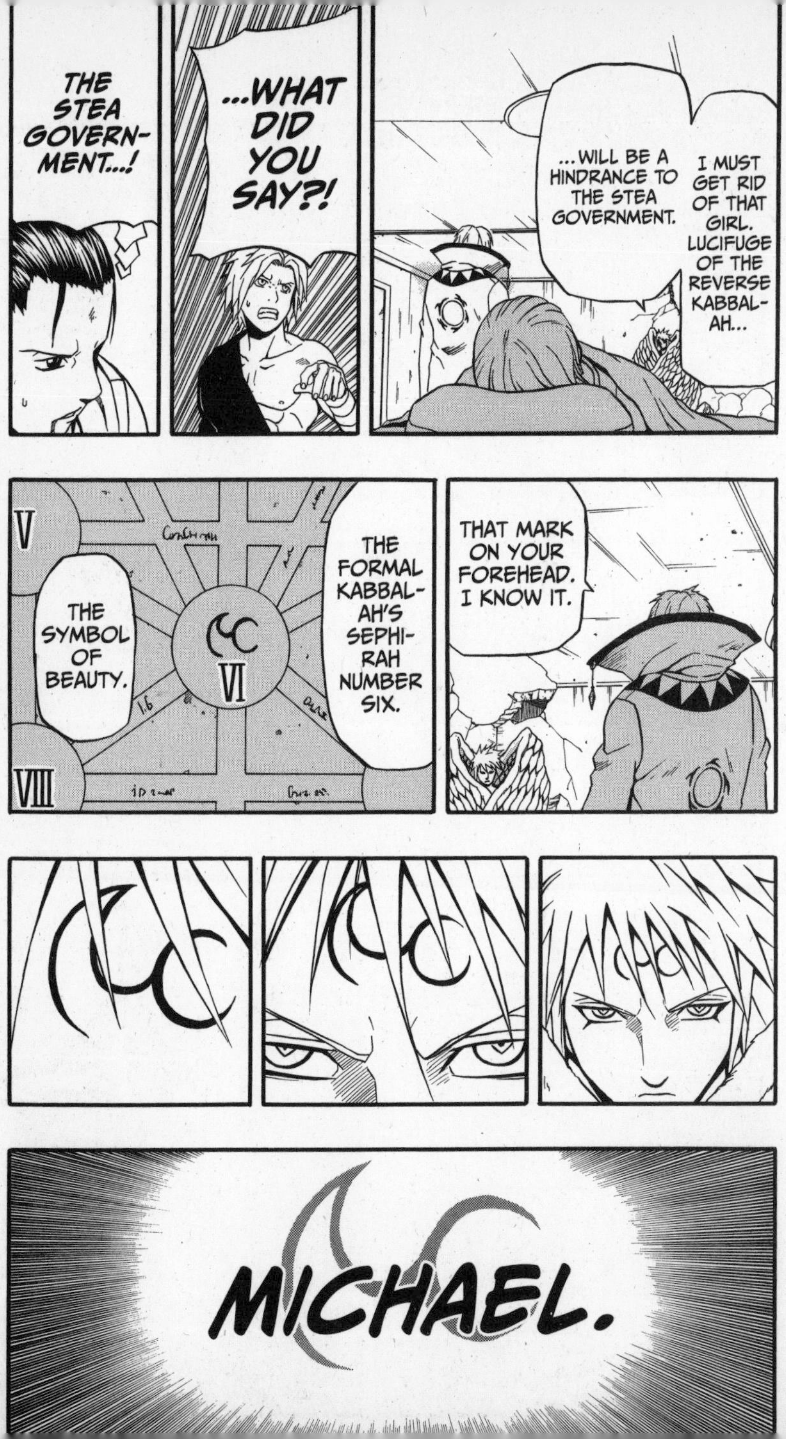
I MUST GET RID OF THAT GIRL. LUCIFUGE OF THE REVERSE KABBAL-AH...
...WILL BE A HINDRANCE TO THE STEA GOVERNMENT.
...WHAT DID YOU SAY?!
THE STEA GOVERN-MENT...!
THAT MARK ON YOUR FOREHEAD. I KNOW IT.
THE FORMAL KABBAL-AH'S SEPHI-RAH NUMBER SIX.
THE SYMBOL OF BEAUTY.
V
VI
VIII
MICHAEL.

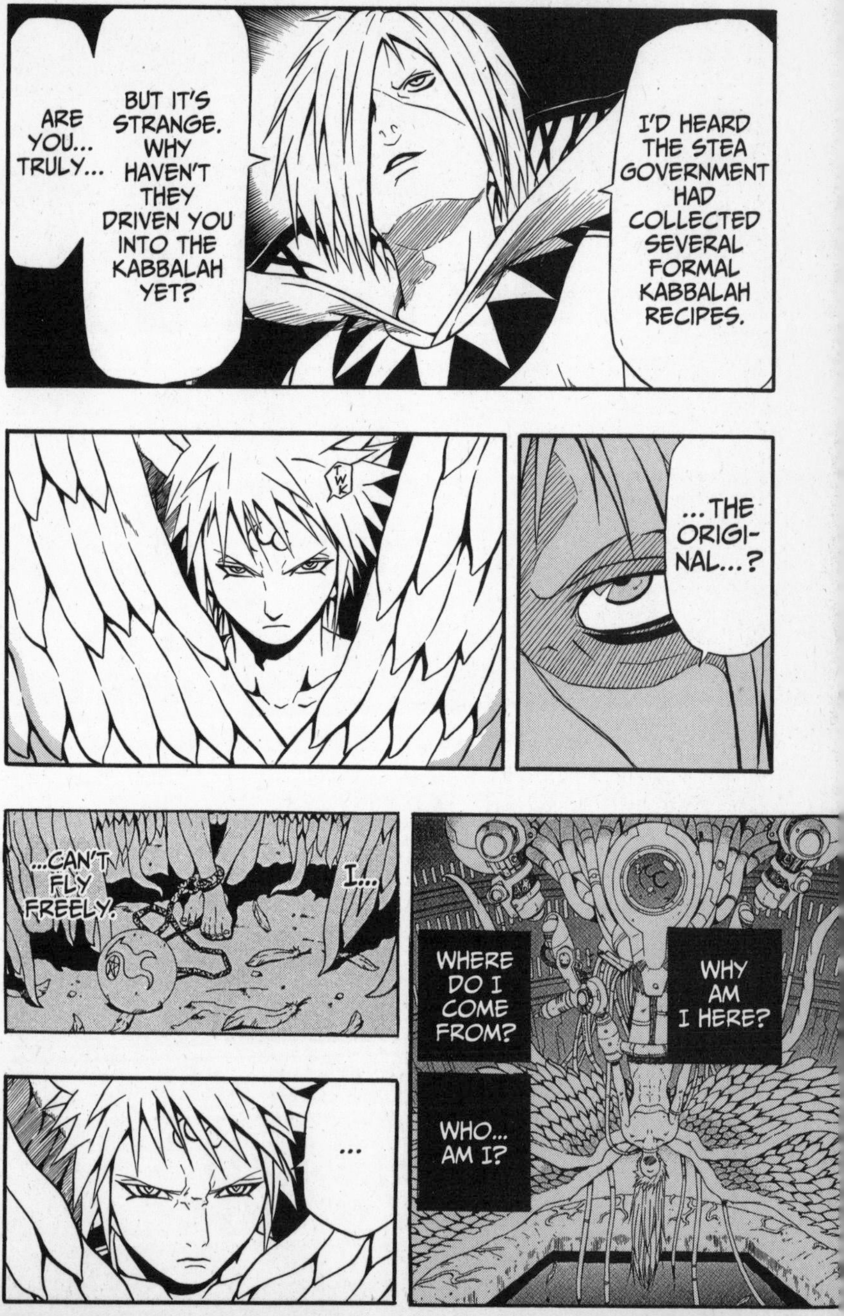
I'D HEARD THE STEA GOVERNMENT HAD COLLECTED SEVERAL FORMAL KABBALAH RECIPES.
BUT IT'S STRANGE. WHY HAVEN'T THEY DRIVEN YOU INTO THE KABBALAH YET?
ARE YOU... TRULY...
...THE ORIGI-NAL...?
TWK
WHY AM I HERE?
WHERE DO I COME FROM?
WHO... AM I?
I...
...CAN'T FLY FREELY.
...

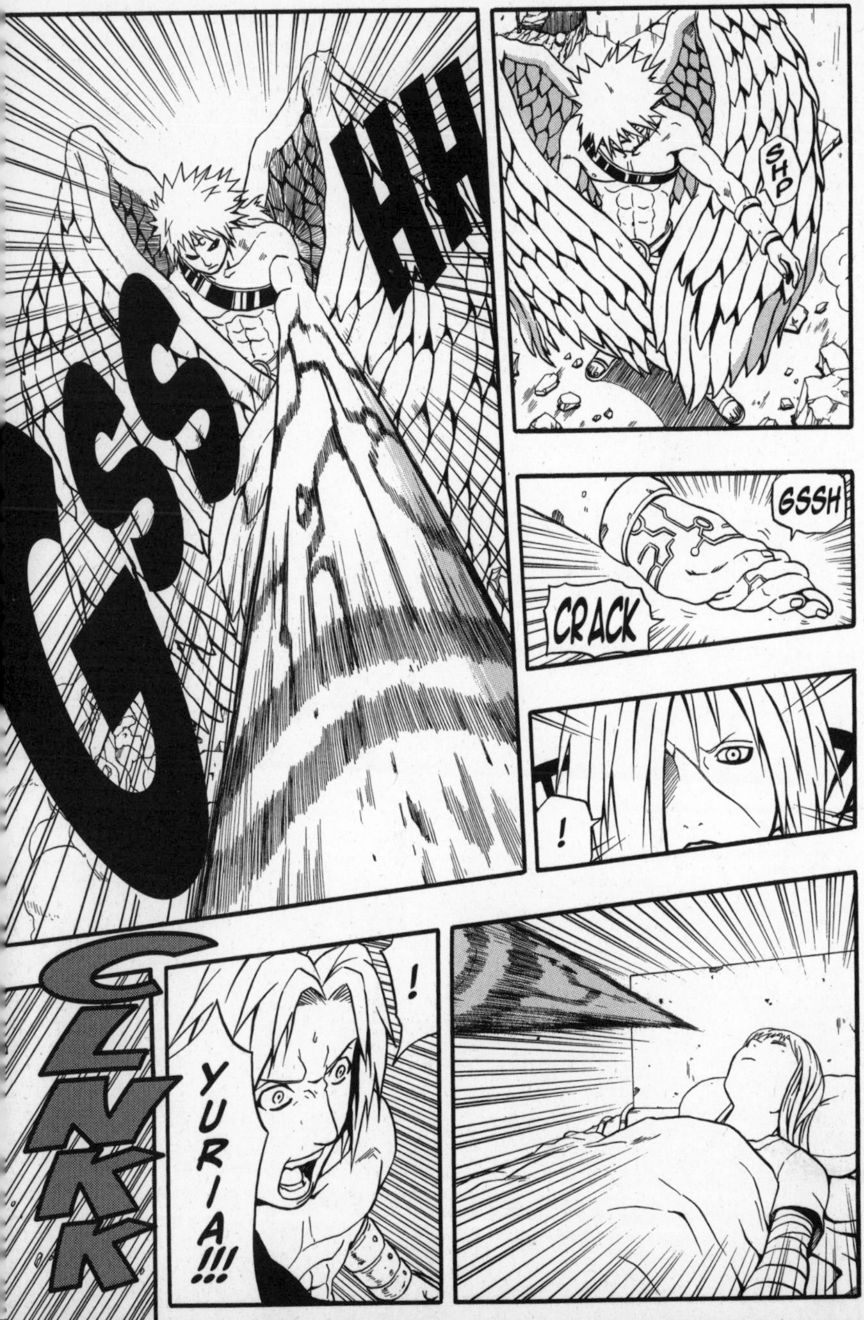
SHP
GSSH
CRACK
!
GSSHH
!
YURIA!!!
CLNKK

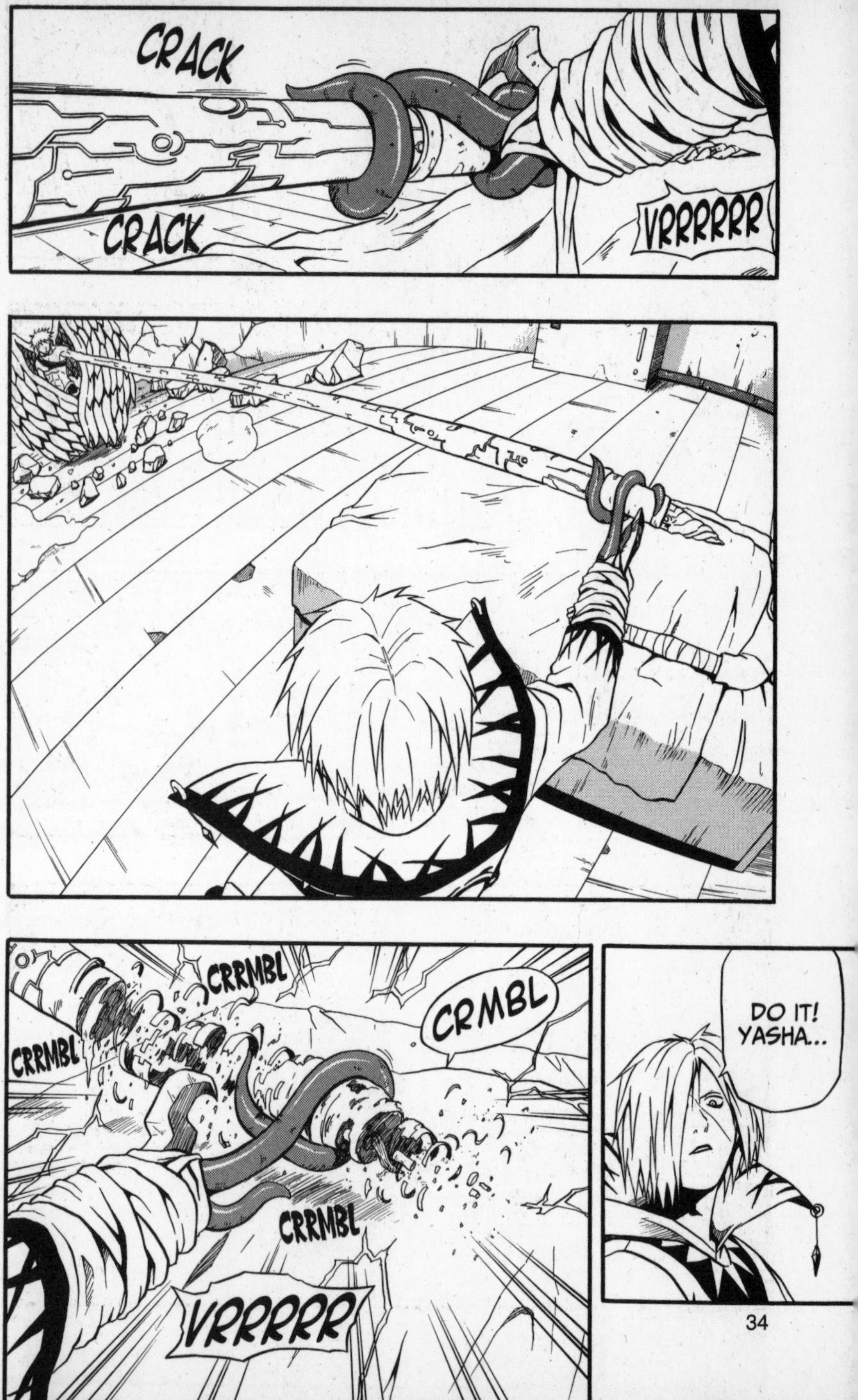
CRACK
VRRRRRR
CRACK
DO IT! YASHA...
CRMBL
CRRMBL
CRRMBL
CRRMBL
VRRRRR

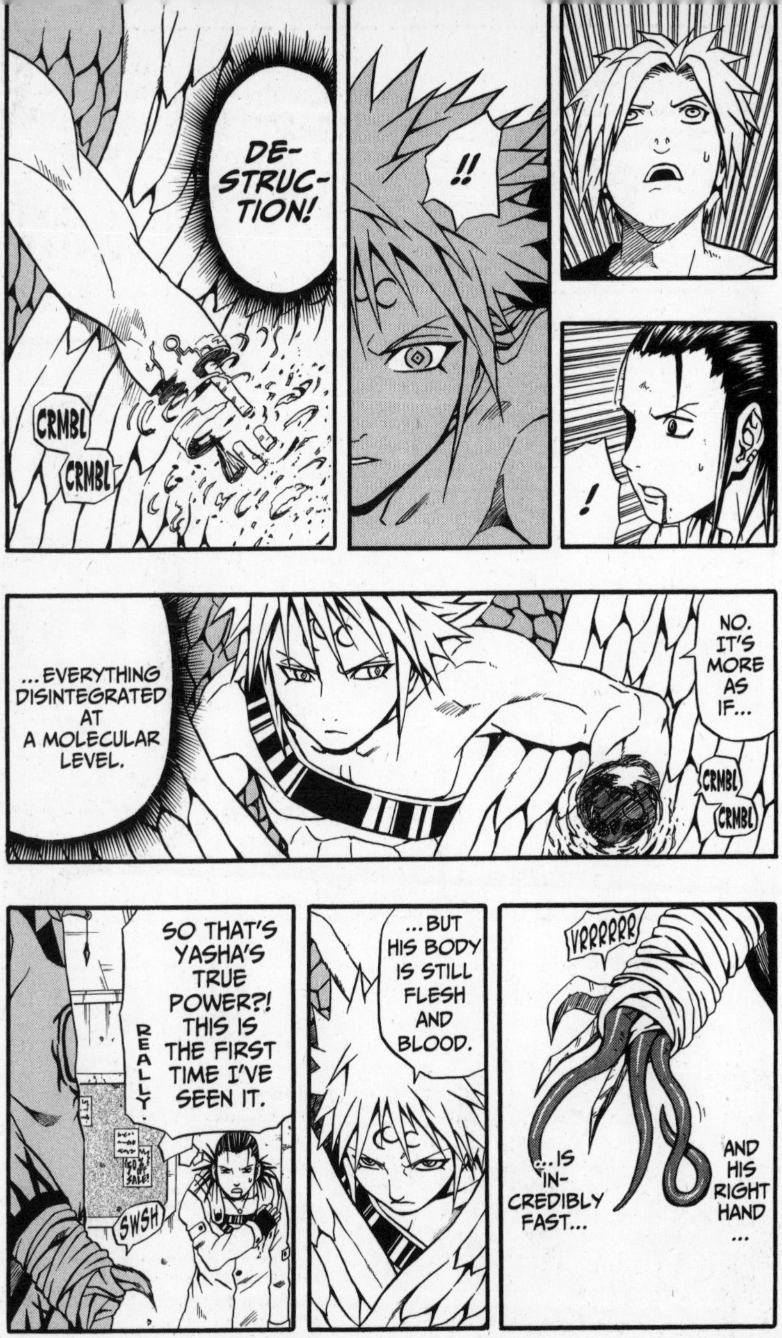
!
!!
DE-STRUCTION!
CRMBL
CRMBL
NO. IT'S MORE AS IF...
CRMBL
CRMBL
...EVERYTHING DISINTEGRATED AT A MOLECULAR LEVEL.
VRRRRRR
AND HIS RIGHT HAND ...
...IS INCREDIBLY FAST...
...BUT HIS BODY IS STILL FLESH AND BLOOD.
SO THAT'S YASHA'S TRUE POWER?! THIS IS THE FIRST TIME I'VE SEEN IT.
REALLY.
SWSH

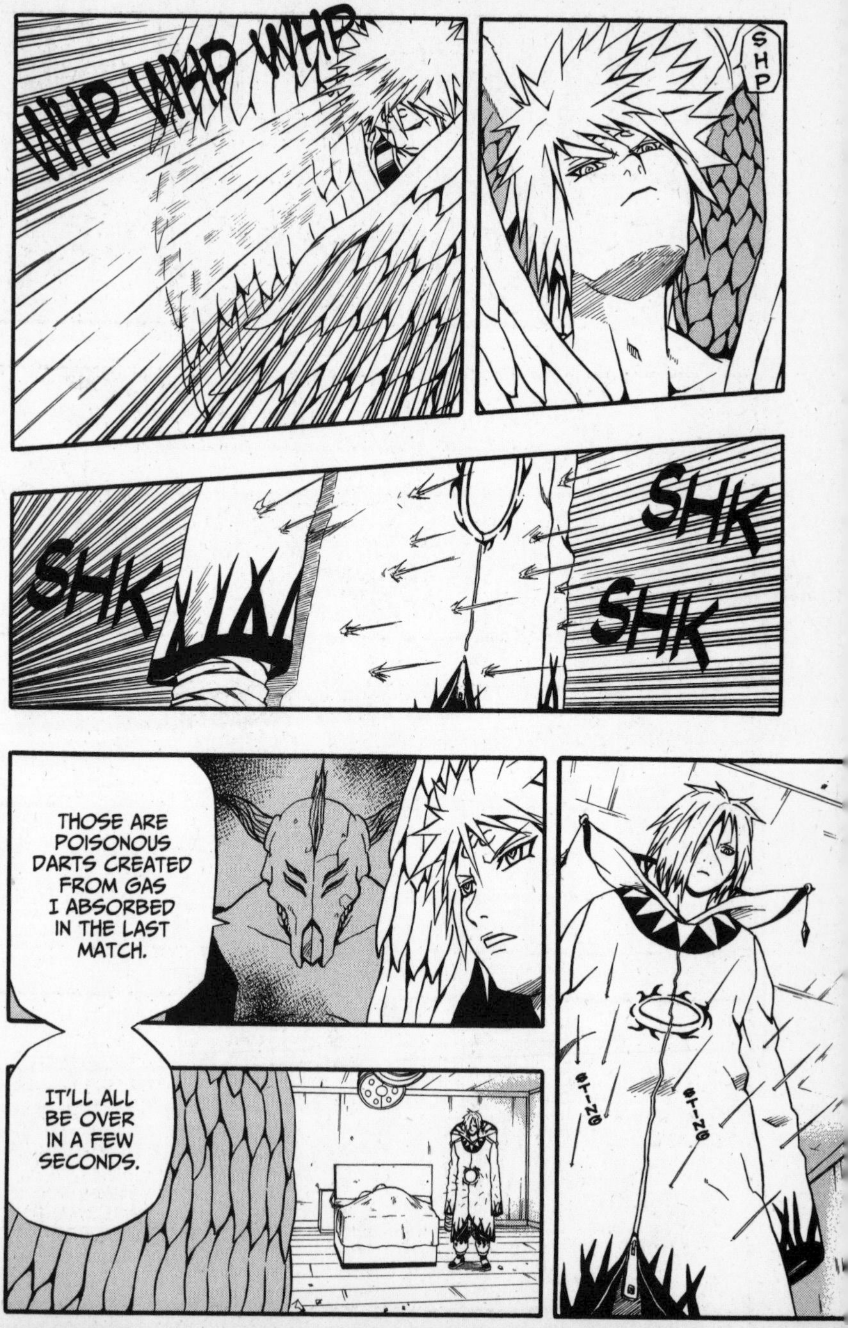
SHP
WHP WHP WHP
SHK
SHK
SHK
STING
STING
THOSE ARE POISONOUS DARTS CREATED FROM GAS I ABSORBED IN THE LAST MATCH.
IT'LL ALL BE OVER IN A FEW SECONDS.

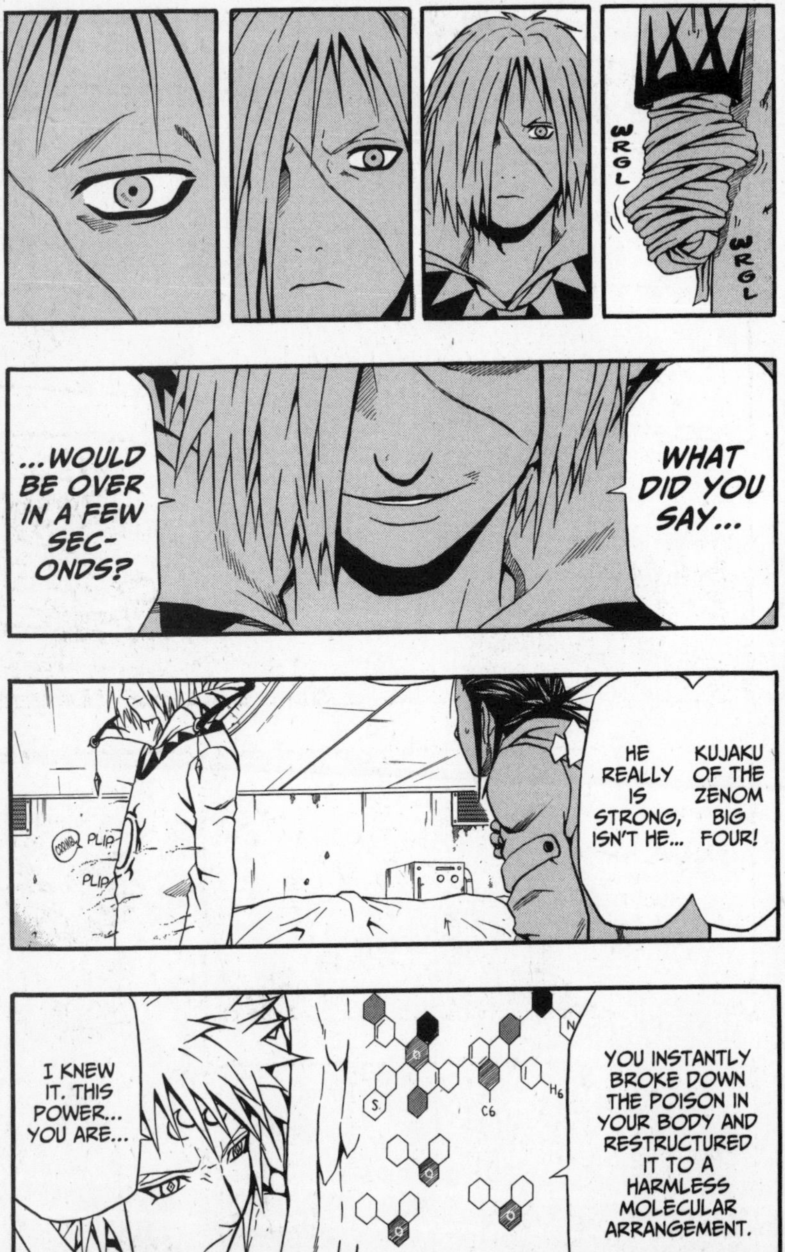
WRGL
WRGL
WHAT DID YOU SAY...
...WOULD BE OVER IN A FEW SEC-ONDS?
KUJAKU OF THE ZENOM BIG FOUR!
HE REALLY IS STRONG, ISN'T HE...
PLIP
PLIP
YOU INSTANTLY BROKE DOWN THE POISON IN YOUR BODY AND RESTRUCTURED IT TO A HARMLESS MOLECULAR ARRANGEMENT.
I KNEW IT. THIS POWER... YOU ARE...

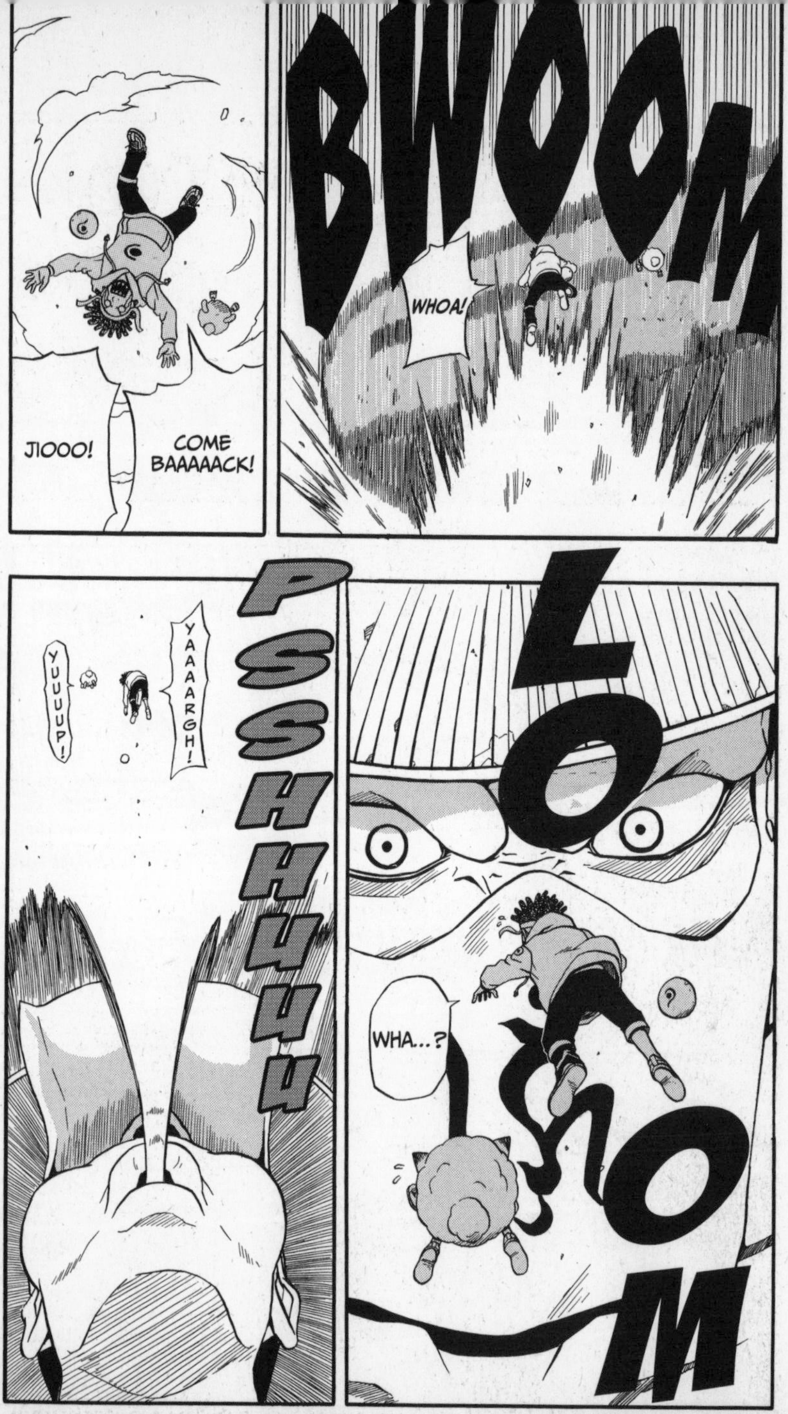
BWOOM
WHOA!
COME BAAAAACK!
JIOOO!
LOOM
WHA...?
PSSHHUUU
YAAAARGH!
YUUUUP!

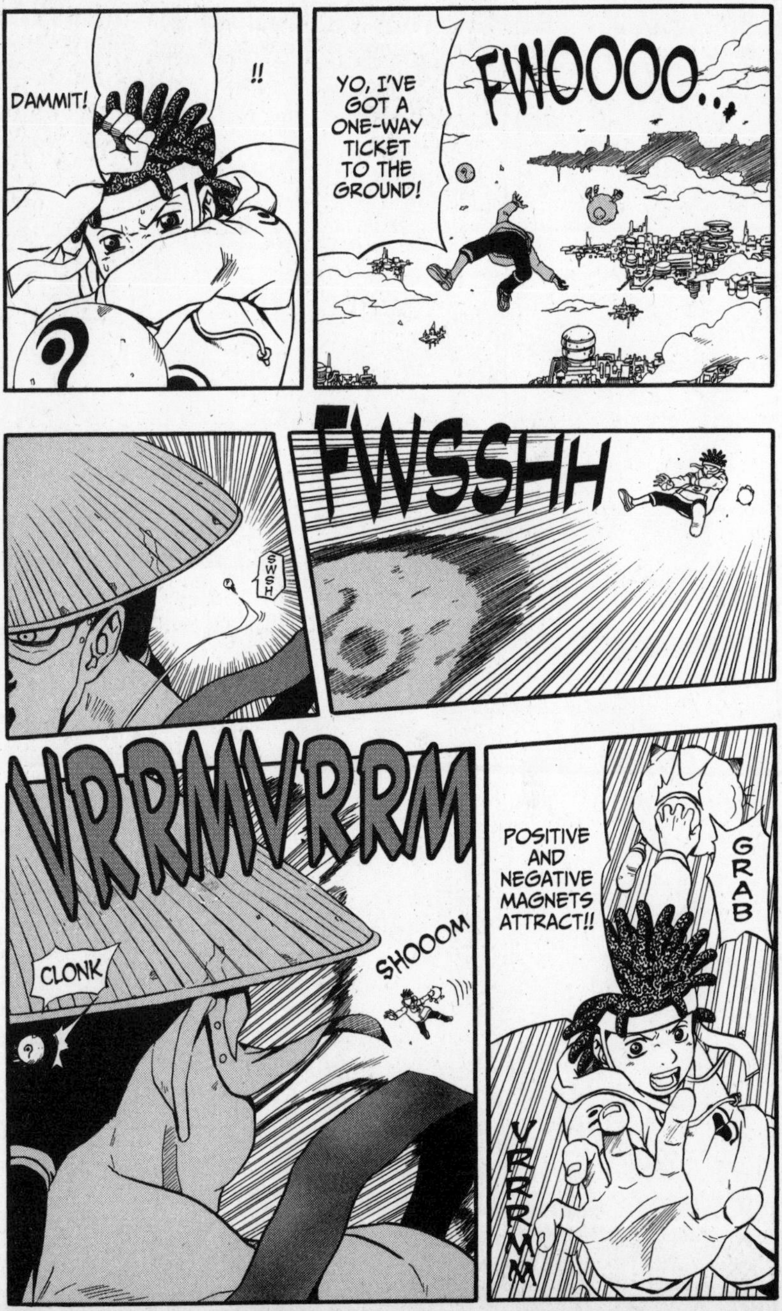
YO, I'VE GOT A ONE-WAY TICKET TO THE GROUND!
FWOOOO...
!!
DAMMIT!
FWSSHH
SWSH
POSITIVE AND NEGATIVE MAGNETS ATTRACT!!
GRAB
VRRRMM
VRRMVRRM
SHOOOM
CLONK

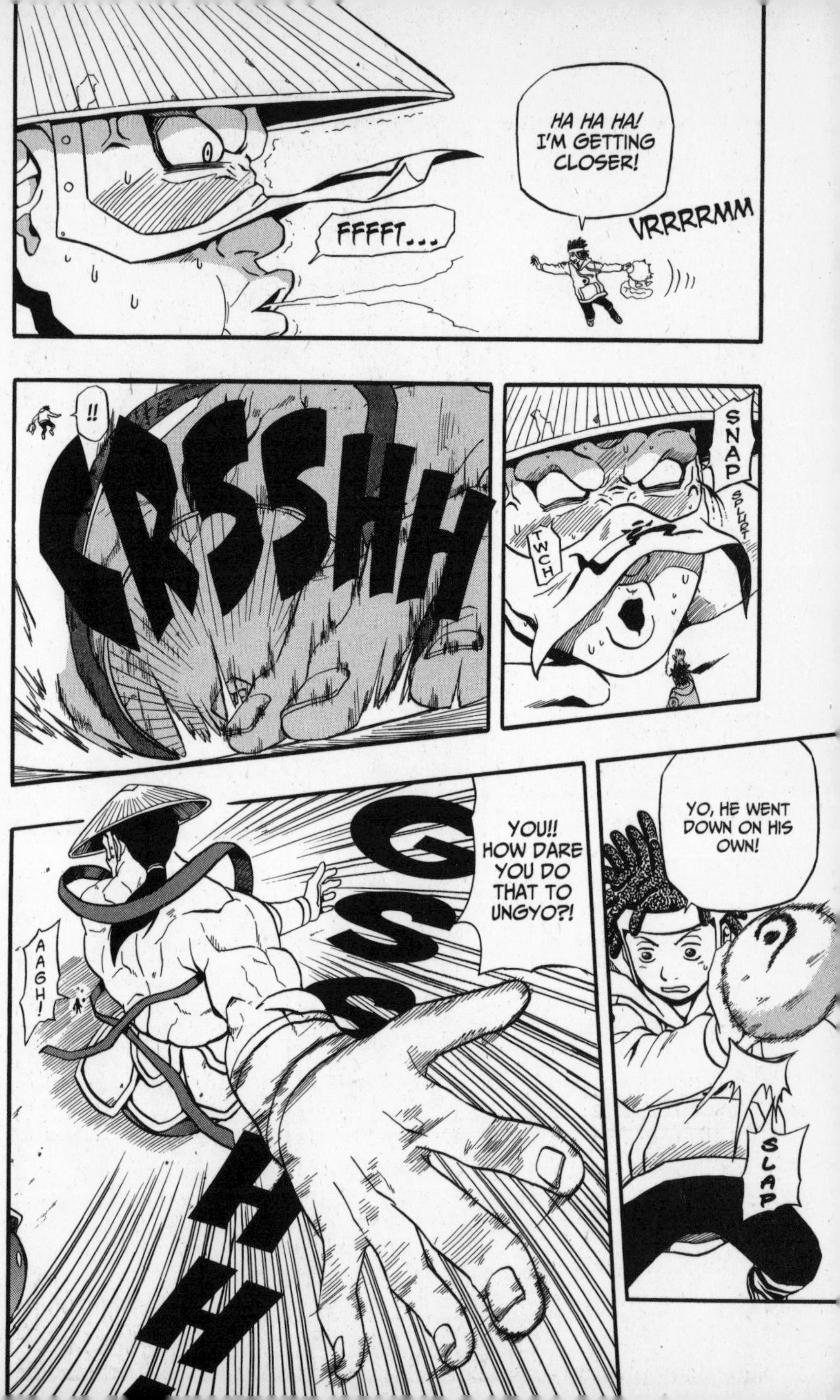

HA HA HA! I'M GETTING CLOSER!
VRRRRMM
FFFFT...
SNAP
SPLURT
TWCH
!!
CRSSHH
YO, HE WENT DOWN ON HIS OWN!
SLAP
YOU!! HOW DARE YOU DO THAT TO UNGYO?!
GSSHHH
AAGH!

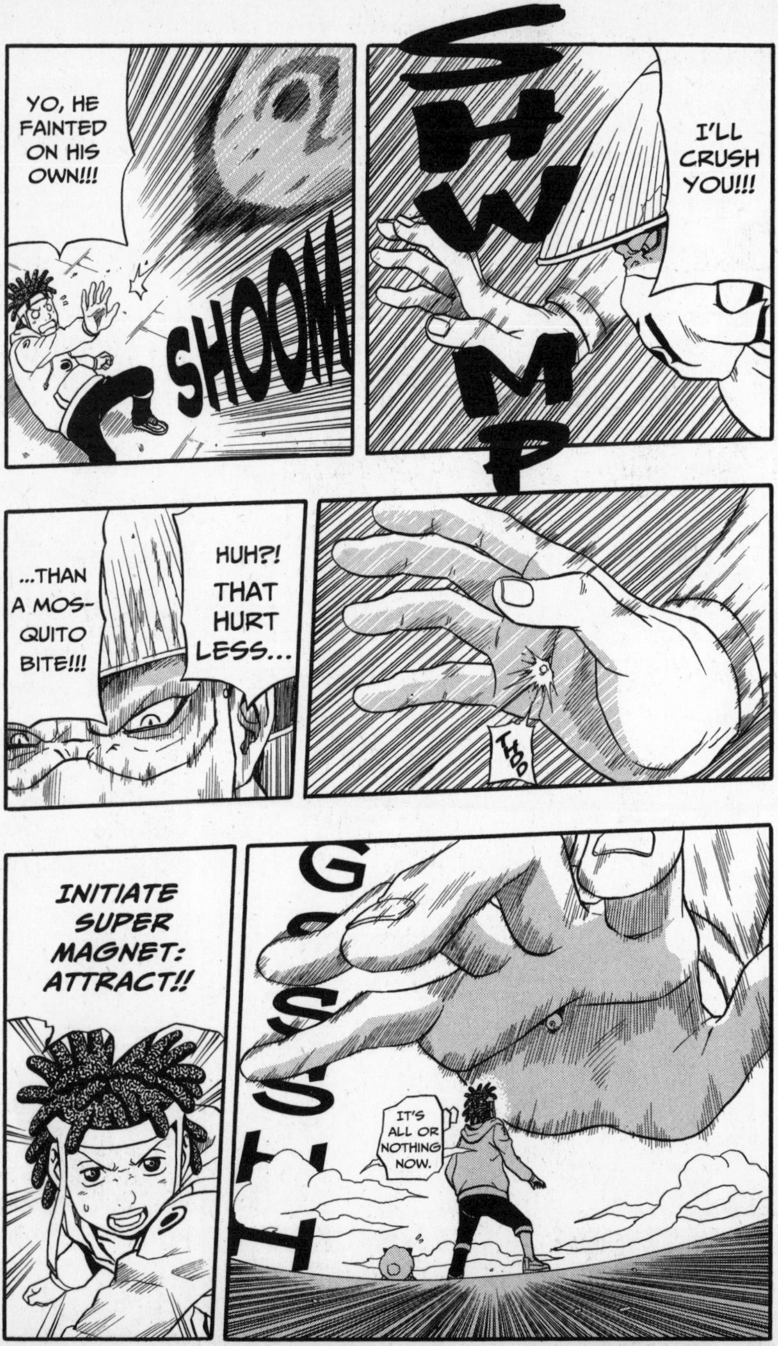
SHWMP
I'LL CRUSH YOU!!!
SHOOM
YO, HE FAINTED ON HIS OWN!!!
THOO
HUH?! THAT HURT LESS...
...THAN A MOS-QUITO BITE!!!
IT'S ALL OR NOTHING NOW.
INITIATE SUPER MAGNET: ATTRACT!!

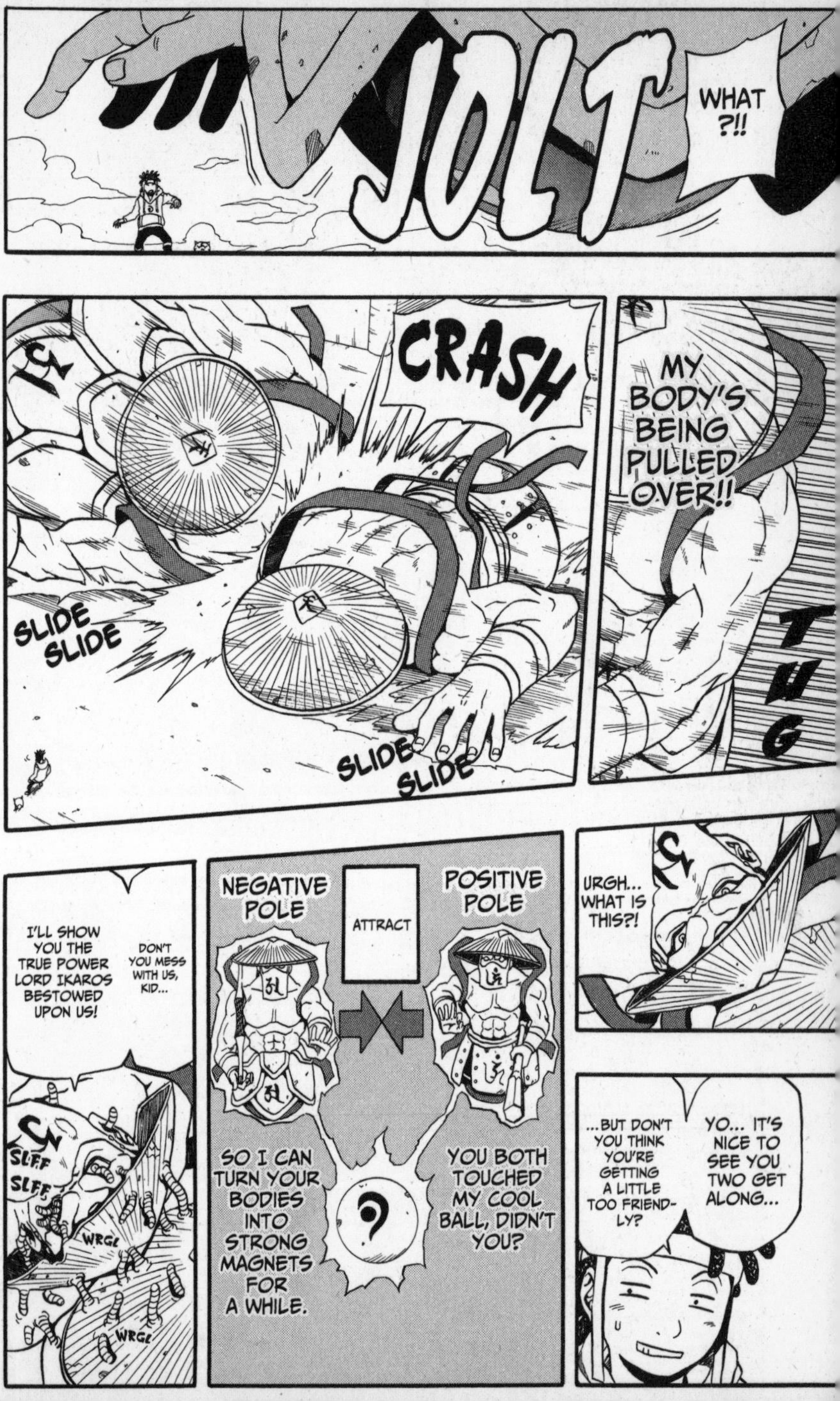
JOLT
WHAT ?!!
MY BODY'S BEING PULLED OVER!!
TUG
CRASH
SLIDE SLIDE
SLIDE SLIDE
URGH... WHAT IS THIS?!
YO... IT'S NICE TO SEE YOU TWO GET ALONG...
...BUT DON'T YOU THINK YOU'RE GETTING A LITTLE TOO FRIEND-LY?
POSITIVE POLE
ATTRACT
NEGATIVE POLE
YOU BOTH TOUCHED MY COOL BALL, DIDN'T YOU?
SO I CAN TURN YOUR BODIES INTO STRONG MAGNETS FOR A WHILE.
DON'T YOU MESS WITH US, KID...
I'LL SHOW YOU THE TRUE POWER LORD IKAROS BESTOWED UPON US!
SLFF SLFF
WRGL
WRGL

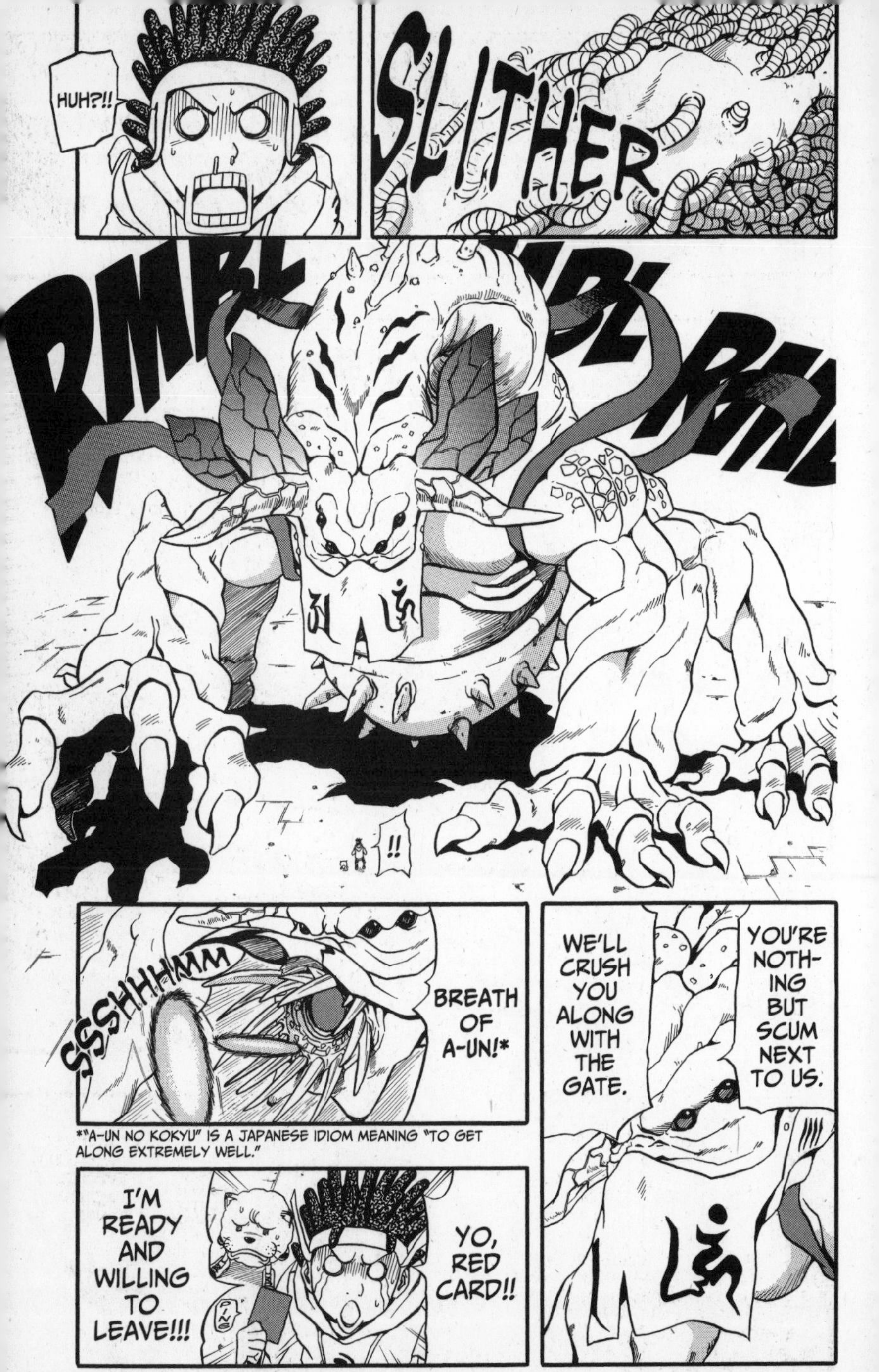
SLITHER
HUH?!!
RMBL
!!
YOU'RE NOTHING BUT SCUM NEXT TO US.
WE'LL CRUSH YOU ALONG WITH THE GATE.
BREATH OF A-UN!*
SSSHHMMM
YO, RED CARD!!
I'M READY AND WILLING TO LEAVE!!!

*"A-UN NO KOKYU" IS A JAPANESE IDIOM MEANING "TO GET ALONG EXTREMELY WELL."

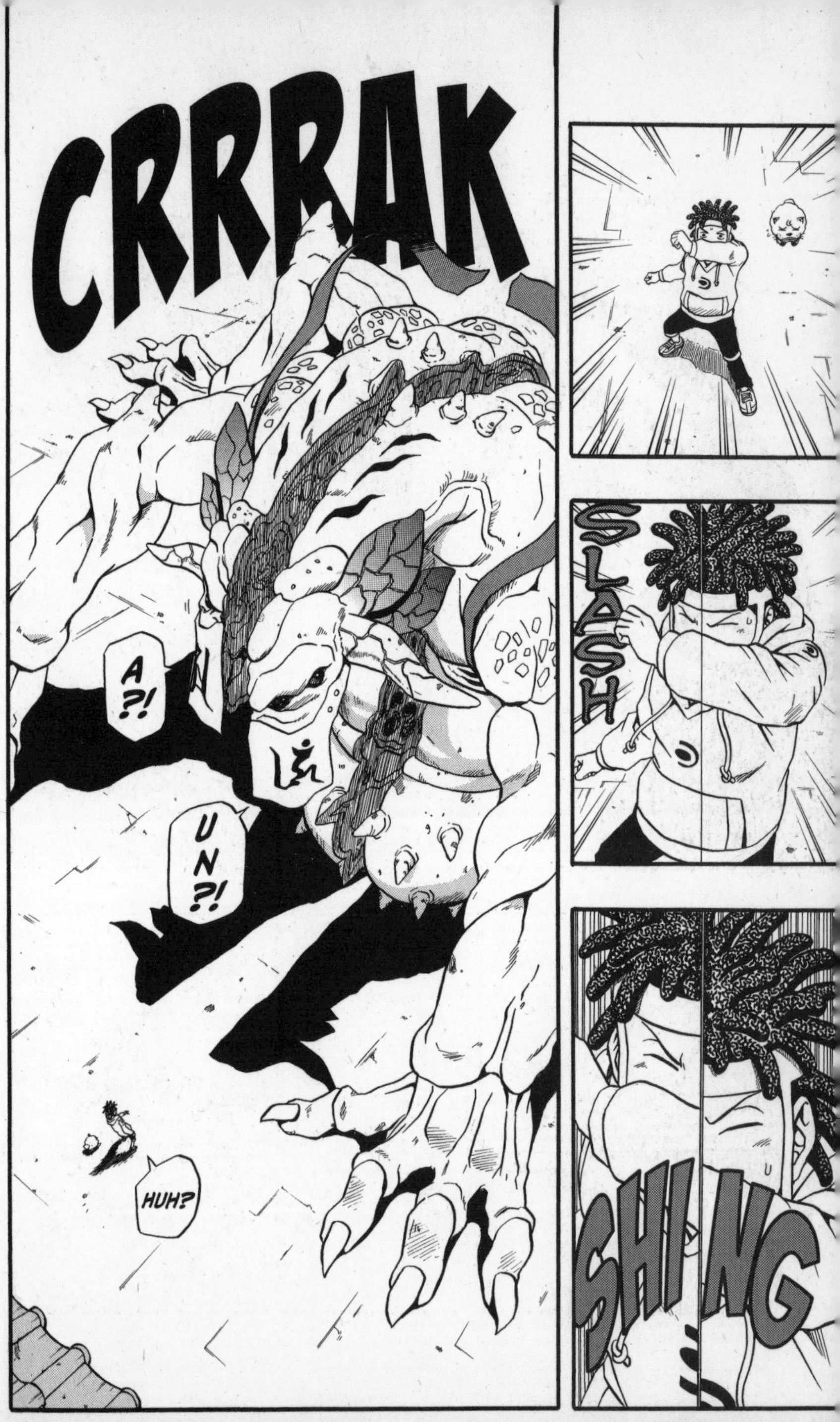
SLASH
SHING
CRRRAK
A?!
UN?!
HUH?

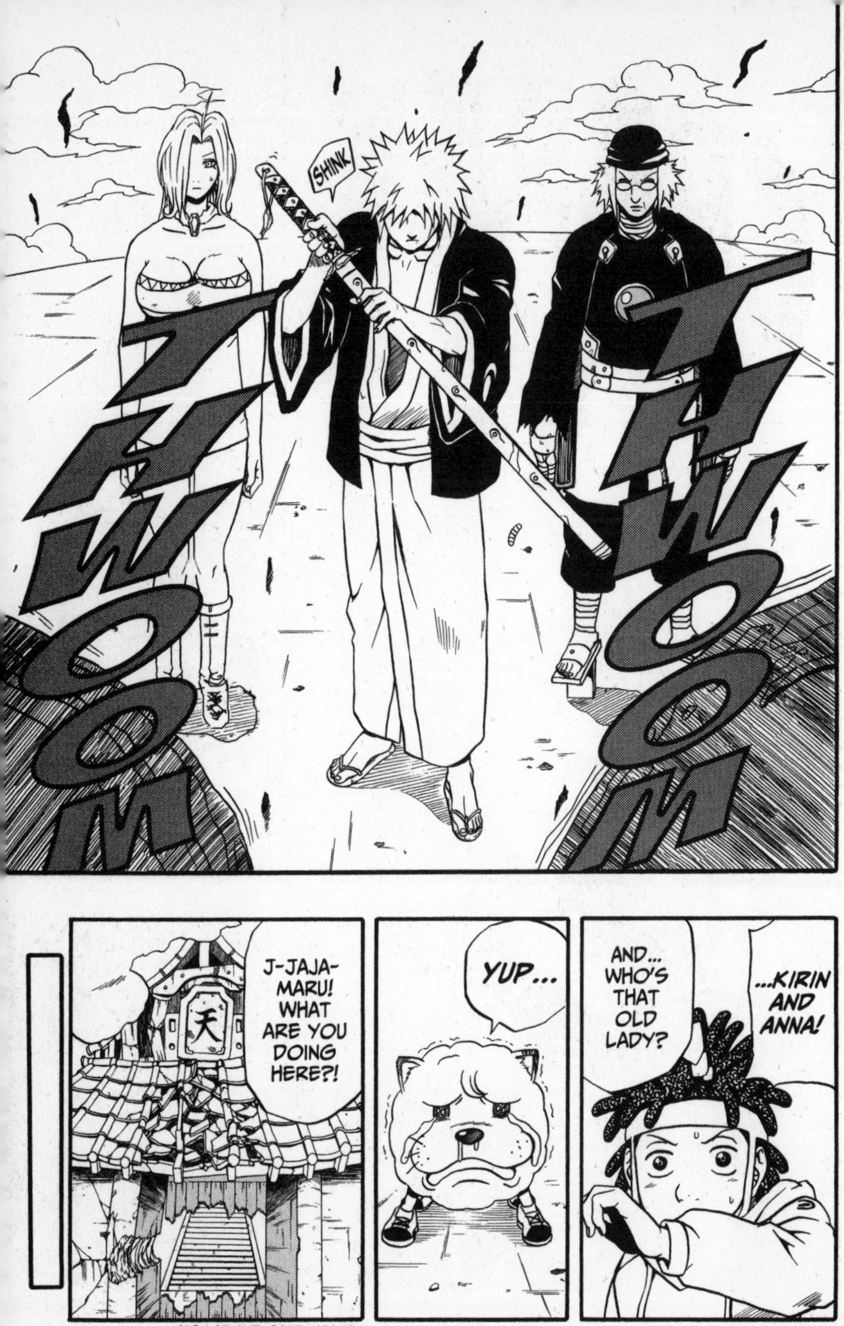
SHINK
THWOOM
THWOOM
...KIRIN AND ANNA!
AND... WHO'S THAT OLD LADY?
YUP...
J-JAJA-MARU! WHAT ARE YOU DOING HERE?!

SIGN ABOVE GATE: HEAVEN

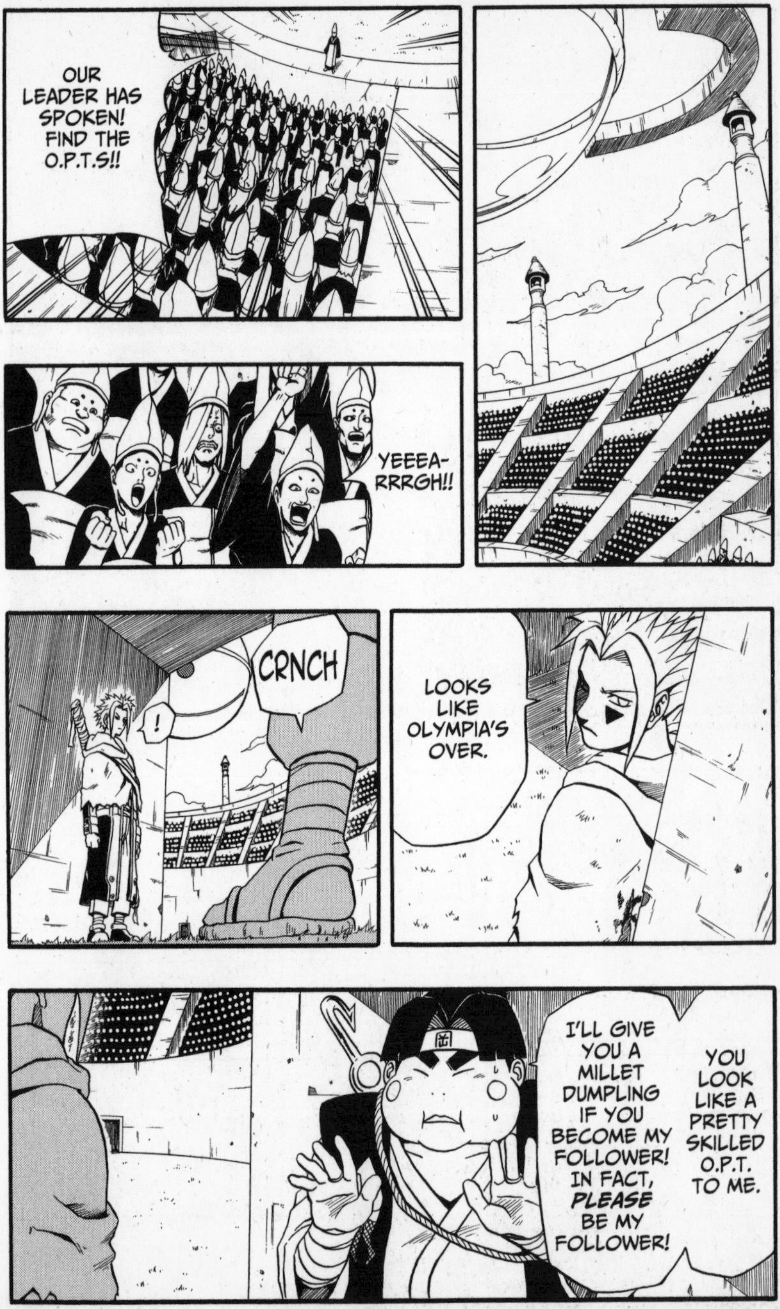
OUR LEADER HAS SPOKEN! FIND THE O.P.T.S!!
YEEEA-RRRGH!!
LOOKS LIKE OLYMPIA'S OVER.
CRNCH
!
YOU LOOK LIKE A PRETTY SKILLED O.P.T. TO ME.
I'LL GIVE YOU A MILLET DUMPLING IF YOU BECOME MY FOLLOWER! IN FACT, *PLEASE* BE MY FOLLOWER!

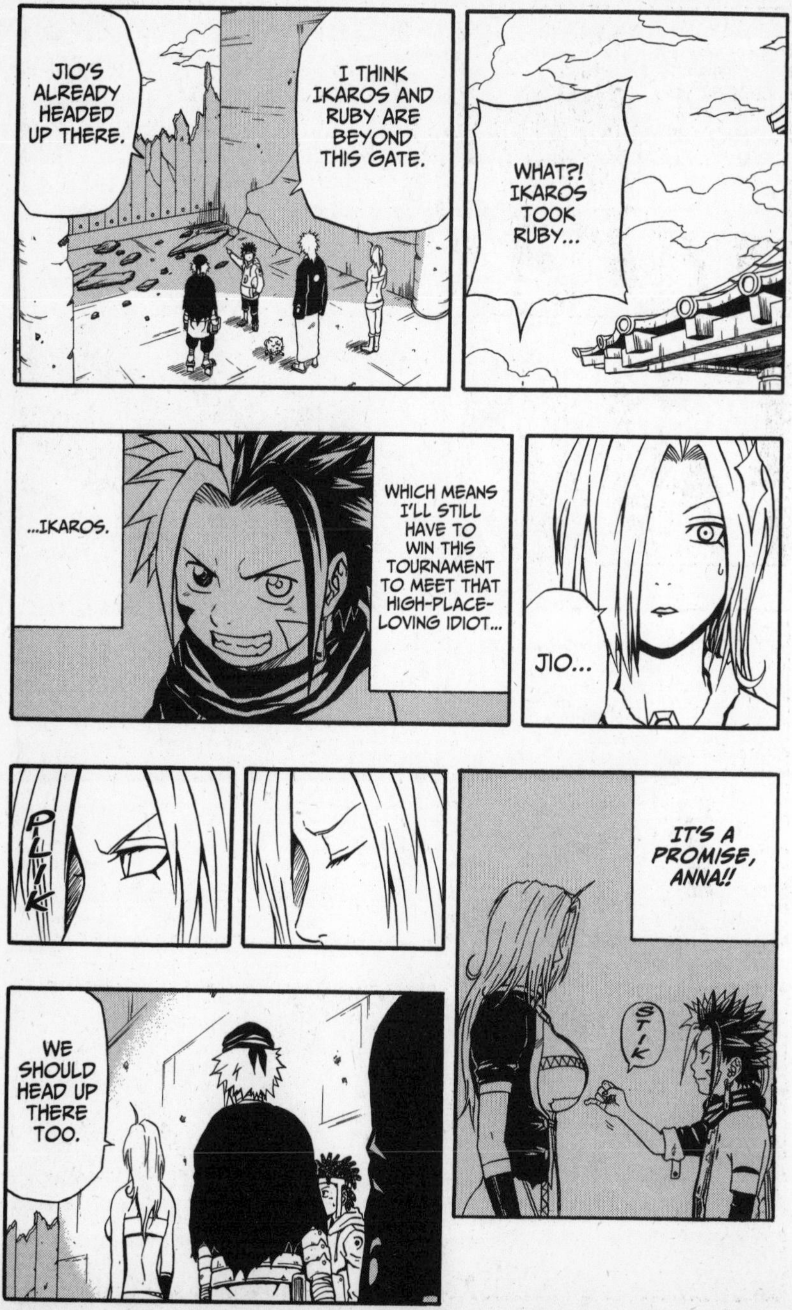
WHAT?! IKAROS TOOK RUBY...
I THINK IKAROS AND RUBY ARE BEYOND THIS GATE.
JIO'S ALREADY HEADED UP THERE.
JIO...
WHICH MEANS I'LL STILL HAVE TO WIN THIS TOURNAMENT TO MEET THAT HIGH-PLACE-LOVING IDIOT...
...IKAROS.
IT'S A PROMISE, ANNA!!
STIK
PLIK
WE SHOULD HEAD UP THERE TOO.

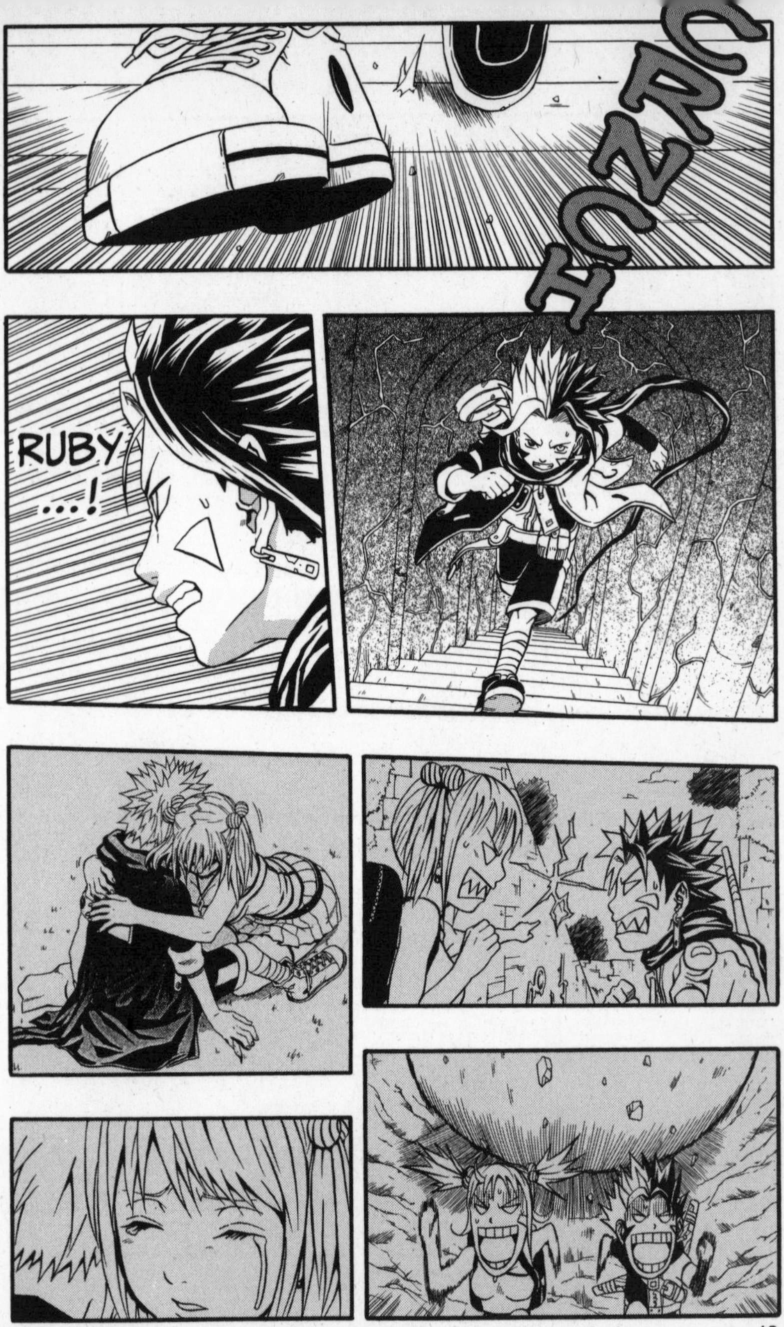
CRUNCH
RUBY ...!

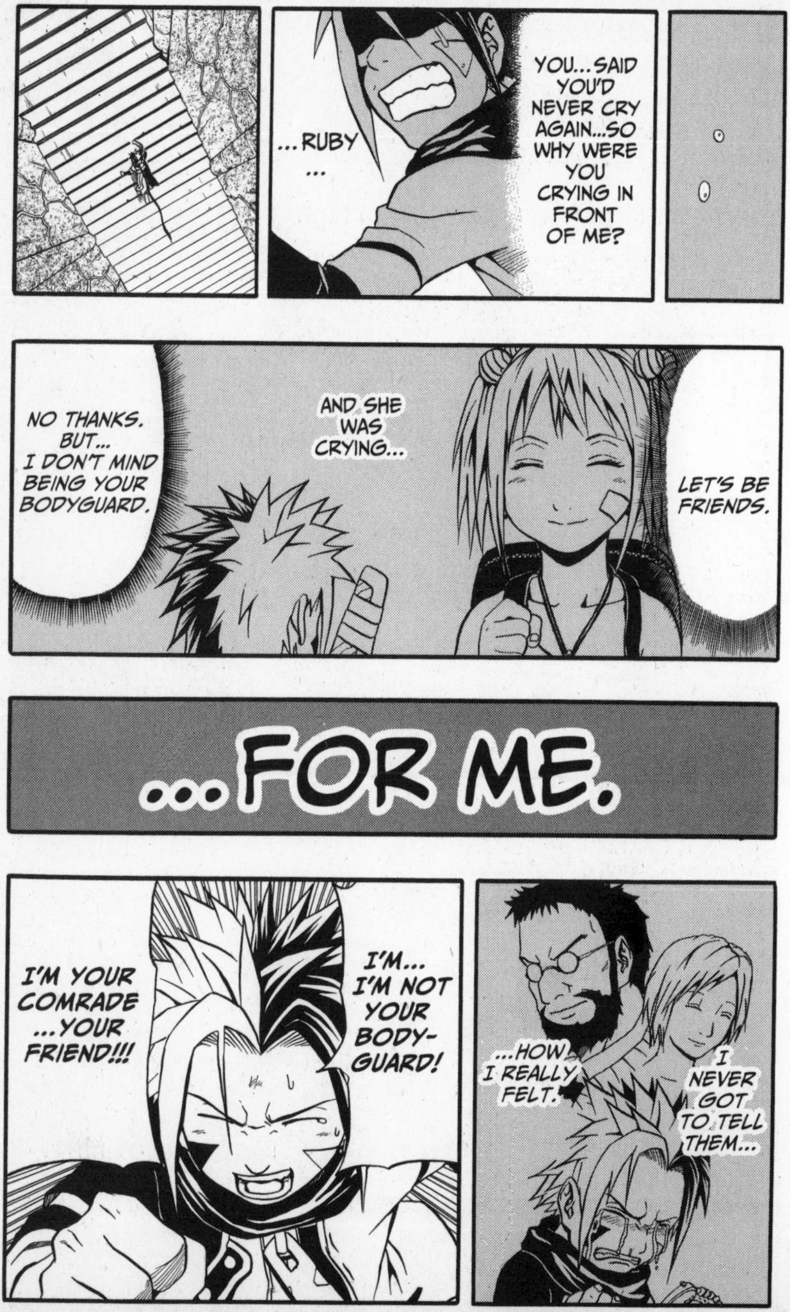
YOU...SAID YOU'D NEVER CRY AGAIN...SO WHY WERE YOU CRYING IN FRONT OF ME?
...RUBY ...
LET'S BE FRIENDS.
AND SHE WAS CRYING...
NO THANKS. BUT... I DON'T MIND BEING YOUR BODYGUARD.
...FOR ME.
I NEVER GOT TO TELL THEM...
...HOW I REALLY FELT.
I'M... I'M NOT YOUR BODY-GUARD!
I'M YOUR COMRADE ...YOUR FRIEND!!!

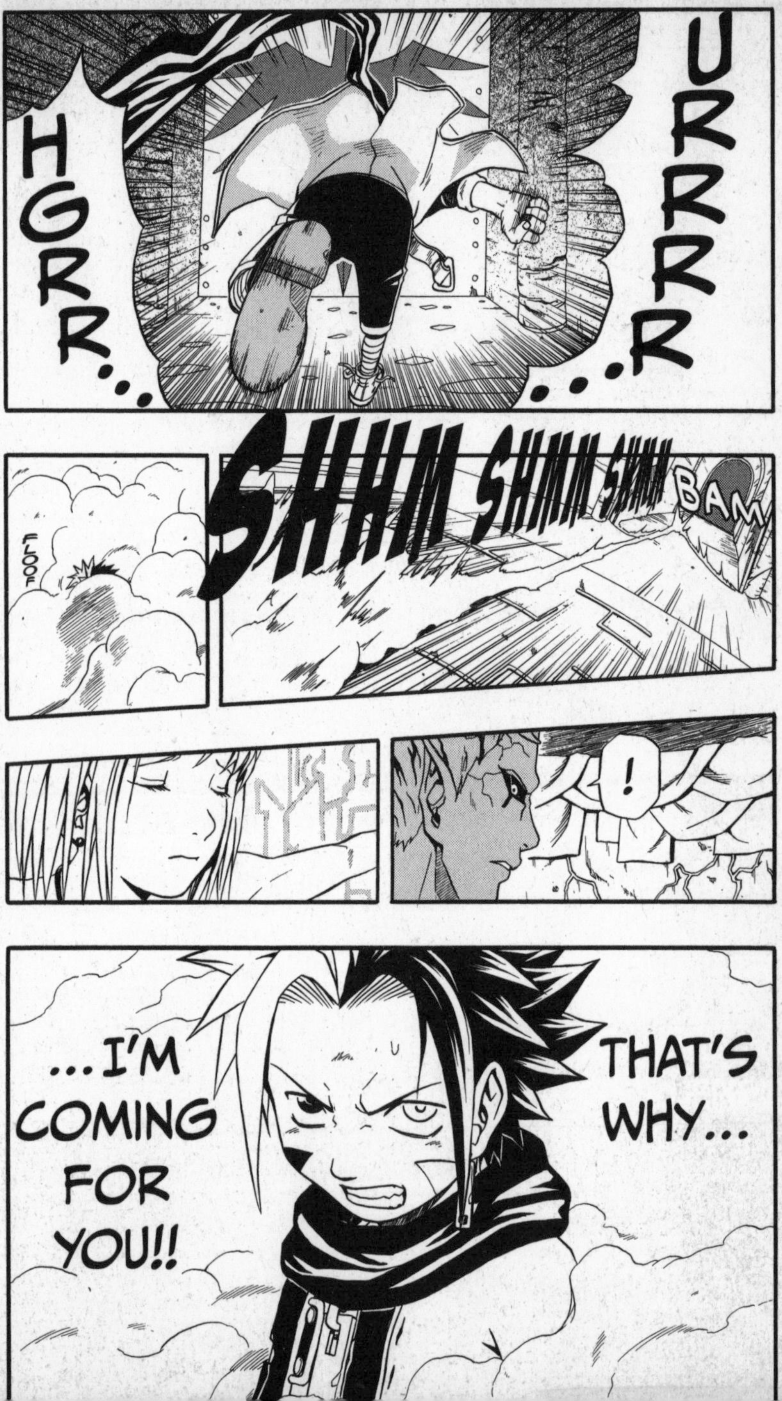

HGRR... ...URRRR...R
SHHM SHHM SHHM
BAM
FLOOF
!
THAT'S WHY...
...I'M COMING FOR YOU!!

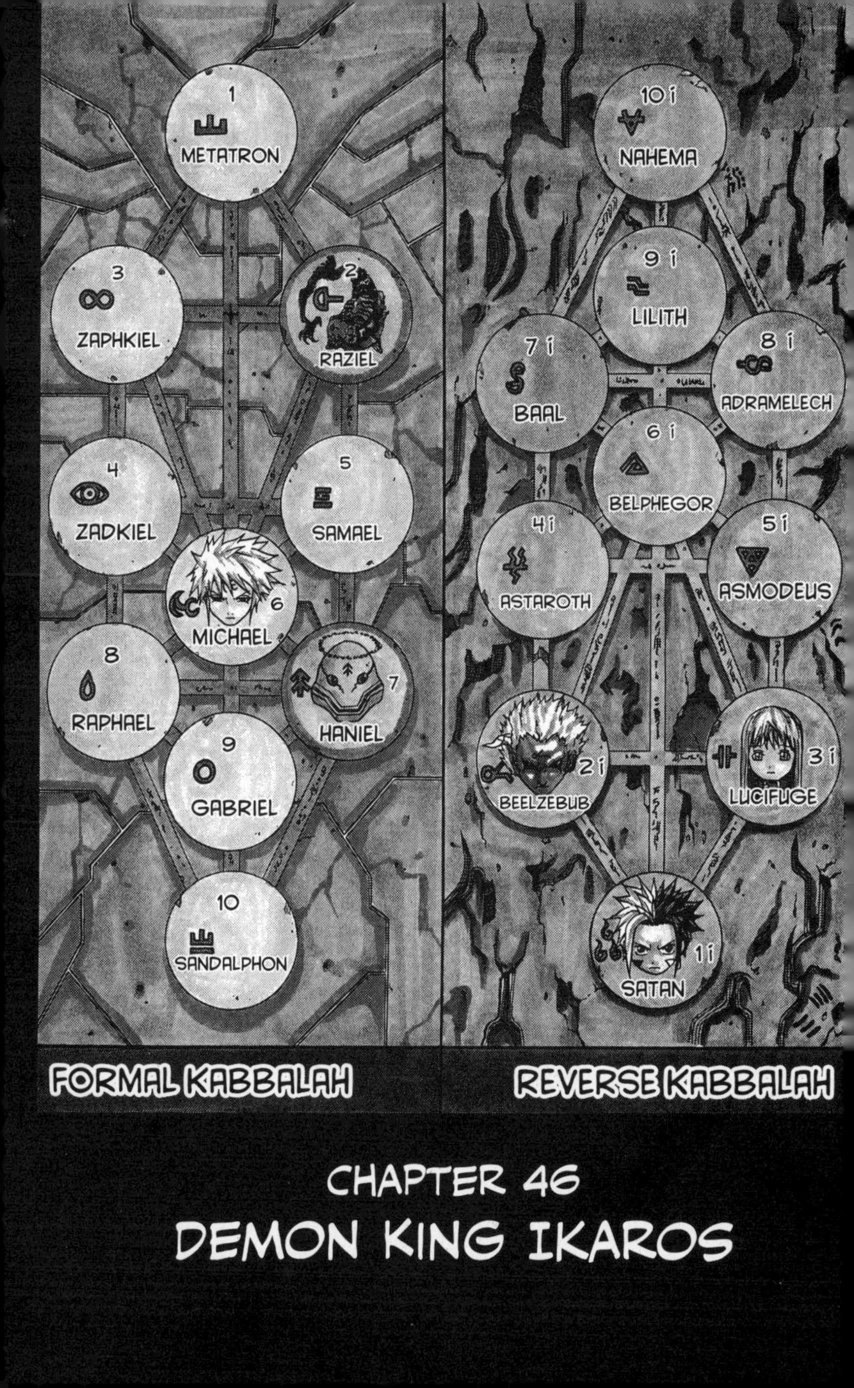
10 i
NAHEMA
9 i
LILITH
7 i
BAAL
8 i
ADRAMELECH
6 i
BELPHEGOR
4 i
ASTAROTH
5 i
ASMODEUS
2 i
BEELZEBUB
3 i
LUCIFUGE
1 i
SATAN
REVERSE KABBALAH
1
METATRON
3
ZAPHKIEL
2
RAZIEL
4
ZADKIEL
5
SAMAEL
6
MICHAEL
8
RAPHAEL
7
HANIEL
9
GABRIEL
10
SANDALPHON
FORMAL KABBALAH

CHAPTER 46
DEMON KING IKAROS

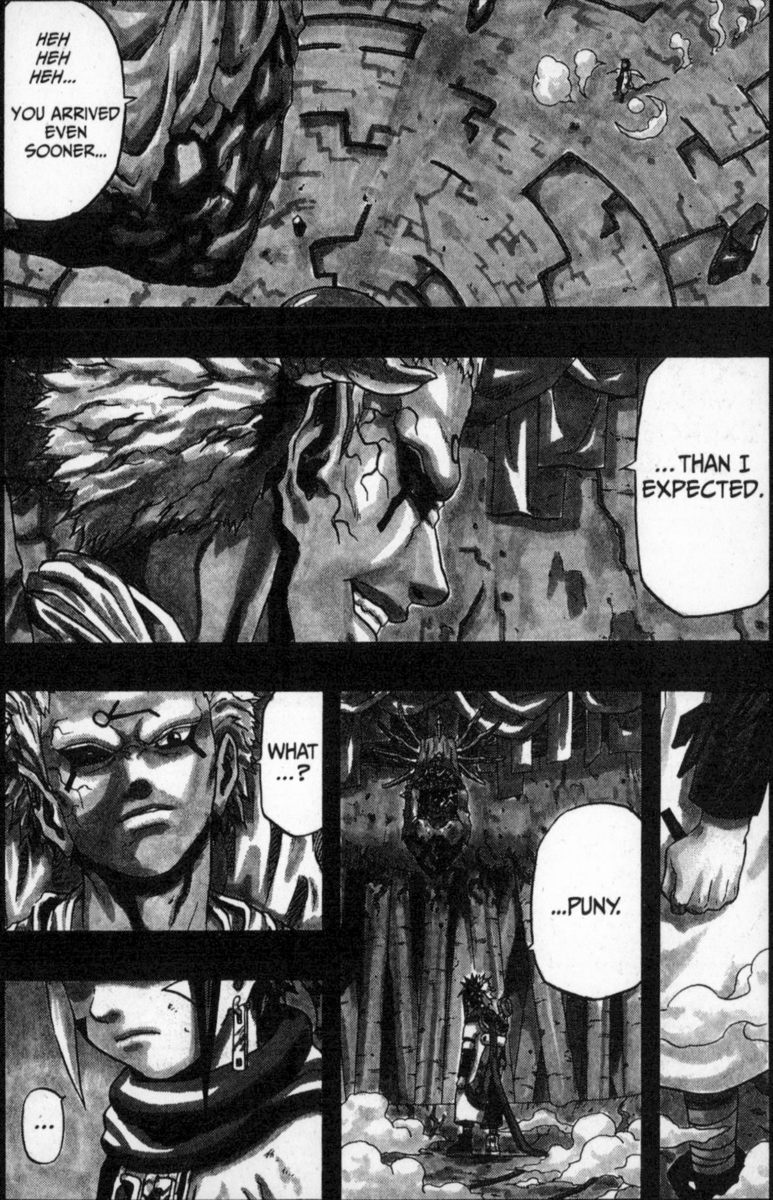
HEH HEH HEH...
YOU ARRIVED EVEN SOONER...
...THAN I EXPECTED.
...PUNY.
WHAT ...?
...

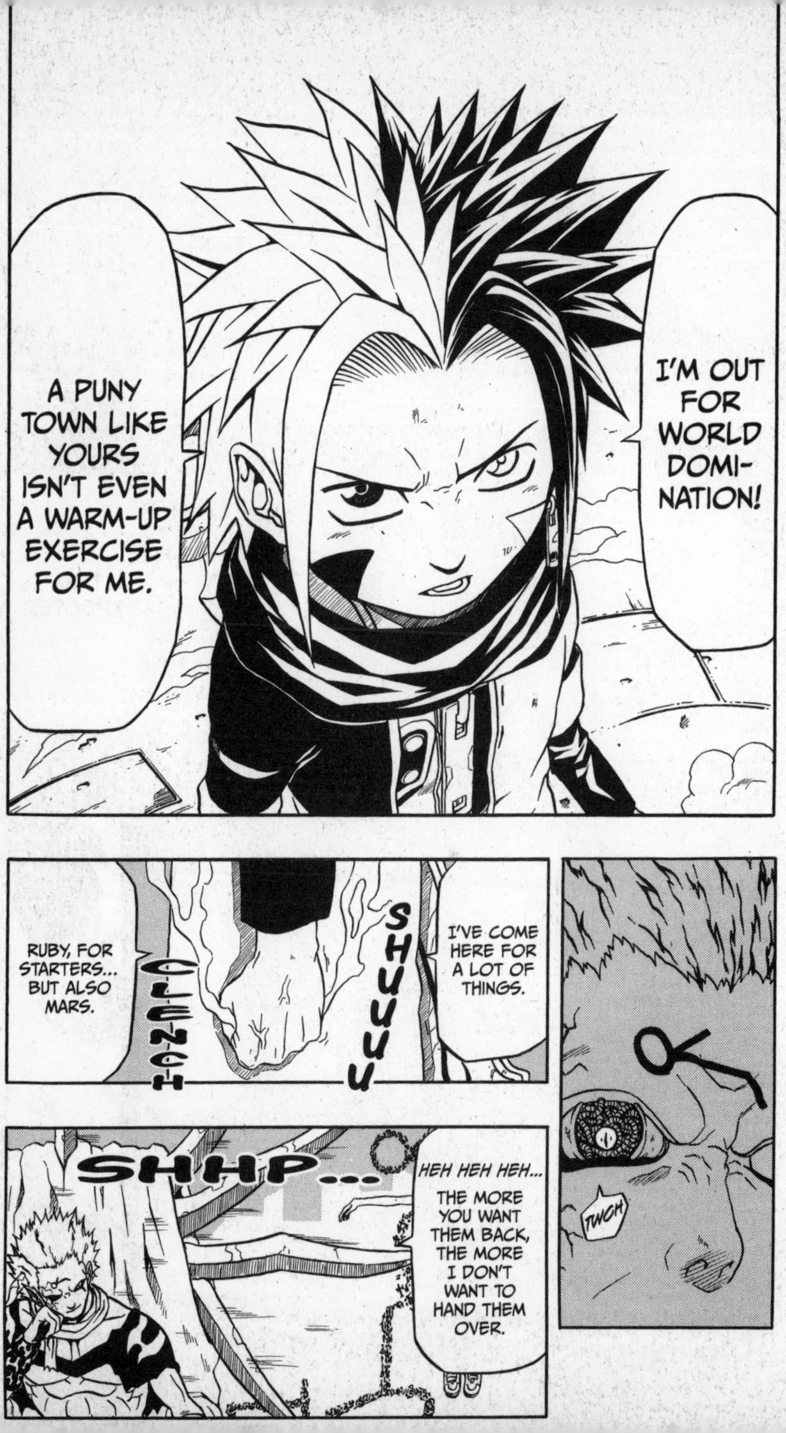

I'M OUT FOR WORLD DOMINATION!
A PUNY TOWN LIKE YOURS ISN'T EVEN A WARM-UP EXERCISE FOR ME.
TWCH
I'VE COME HERE FOR A LOT OF THINGS.
SHUUUUU
CLENCH
RUBY, FOR STARTERS... BUT ALSO MARS.
HEH HEH HEH... THE MORE YOU WANT THEM BACK, THE MORE I DON'T WANT TO HAND THEM OVER.
SHHP...

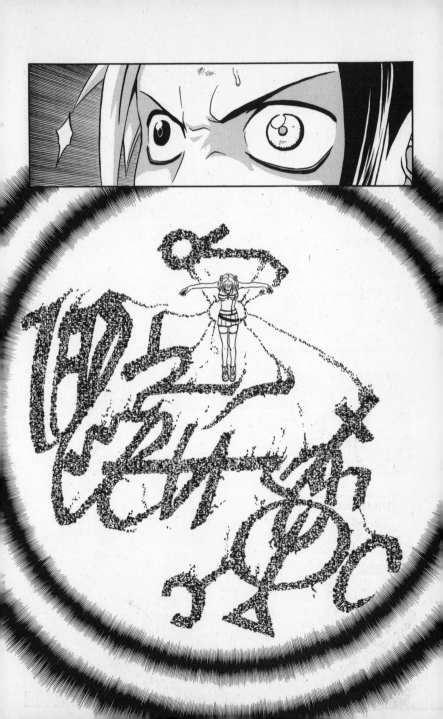

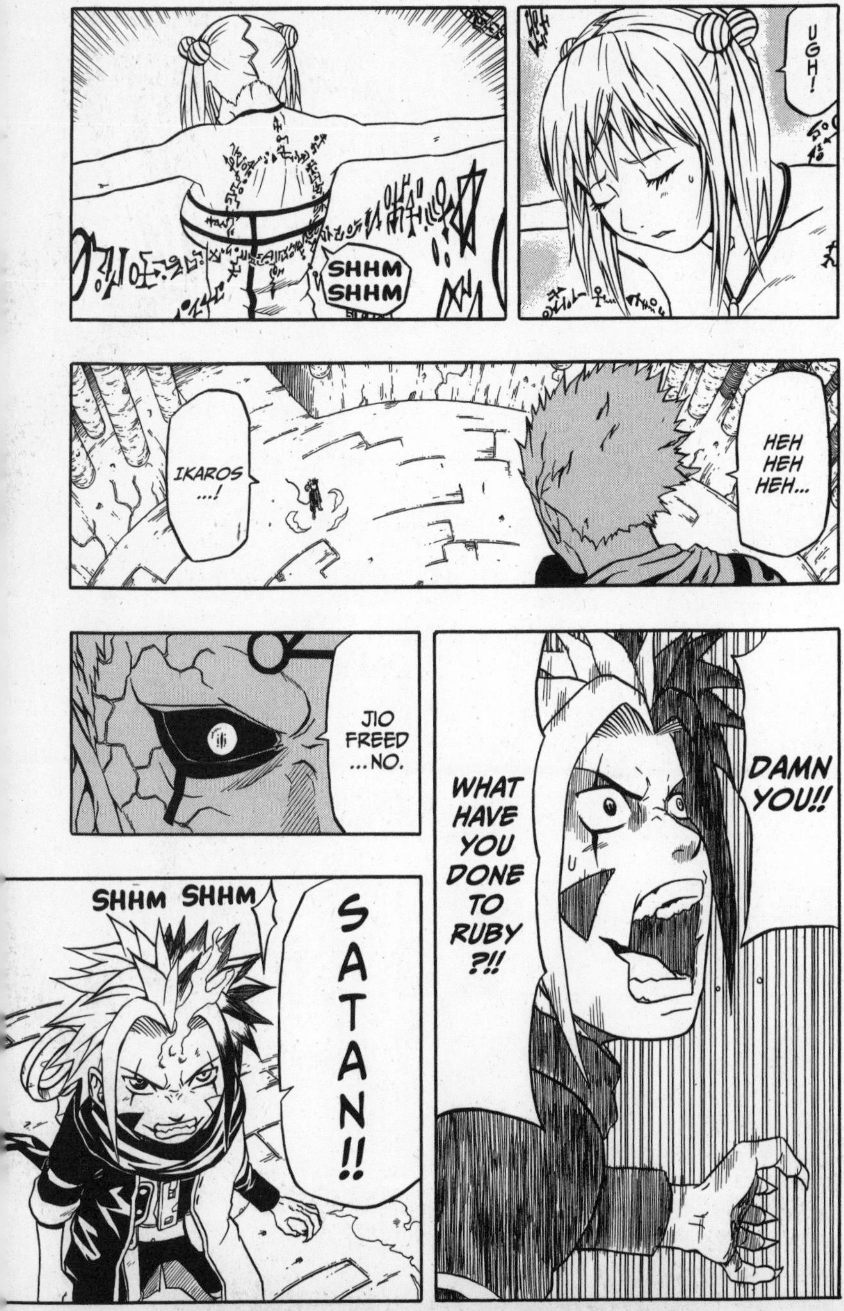
UGH!
SHHM SHHM
HEH HEH HEH...
IKAROS ...!
DAMN YOU!!
WHAT HAVE YOU DONE TO RUBY?!!
JIO FREED ...NO.
SHHM SHHM
SATAN!!

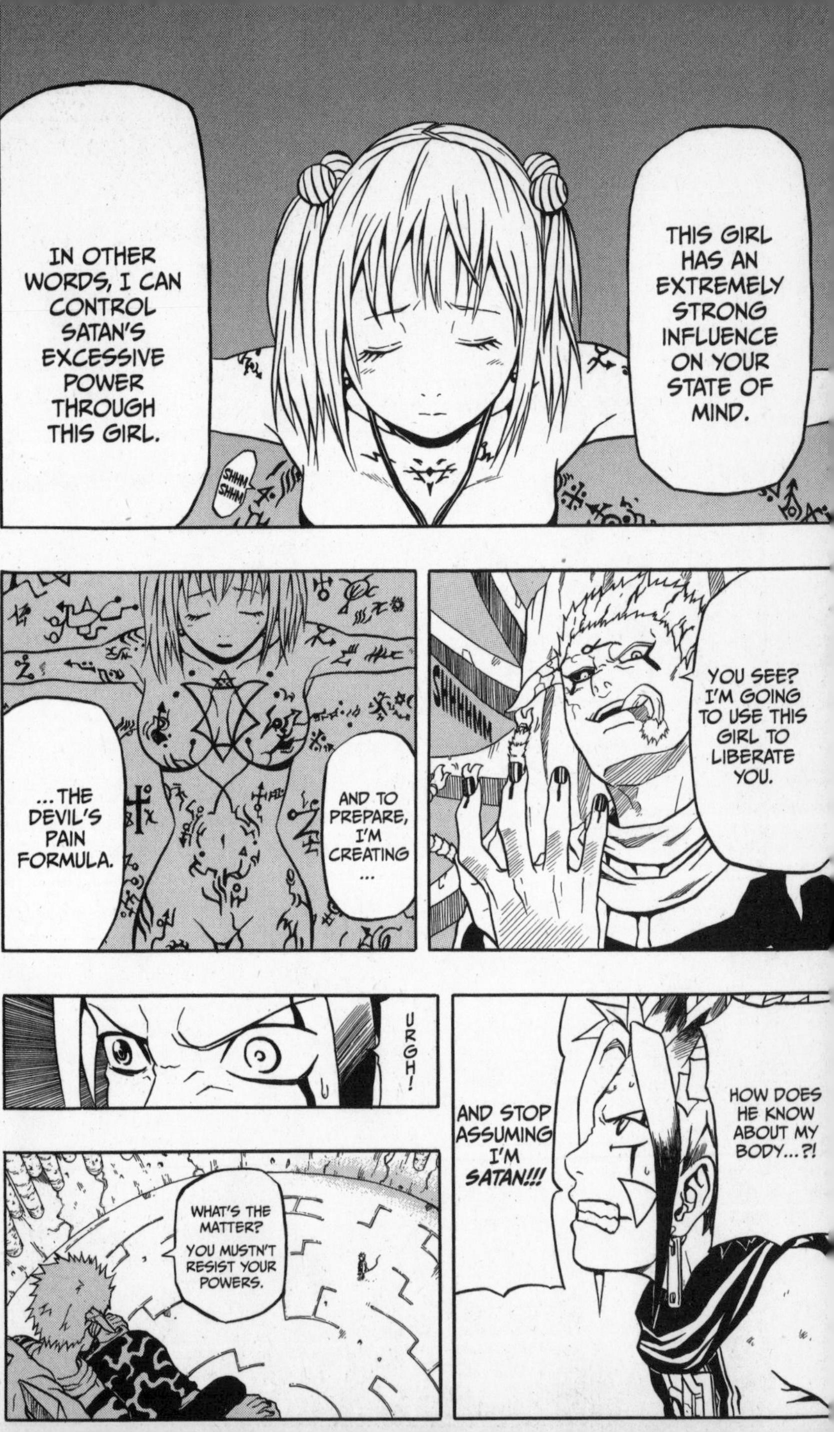
THIS GIRL HAS AN EXTREMELY STRONG INFLUENCE ON YOUR STATE OF MIND.
IN OTHER WORDS, I CAN CONTROL SATAN'S EXCESSIVE POWER THROUGH THIS GIRL.
SHHM SHHM
SHHHHMM
YOU SEE? I'M GOING TO USE THIS GIRL TO LIBERATE YOU.
AND TO PREPARE, I'M CREATING ...
...THE DEVIL'S PAIN FORMULA.
HOW DOES HE KNOW ABOUT MY BODY...?!
AND STOP ASSUMING I'M SATAN!!!
URGH!
WHAT'S THE MATTER?
YOU MUSTN'T RESIST YOUR POWERS.

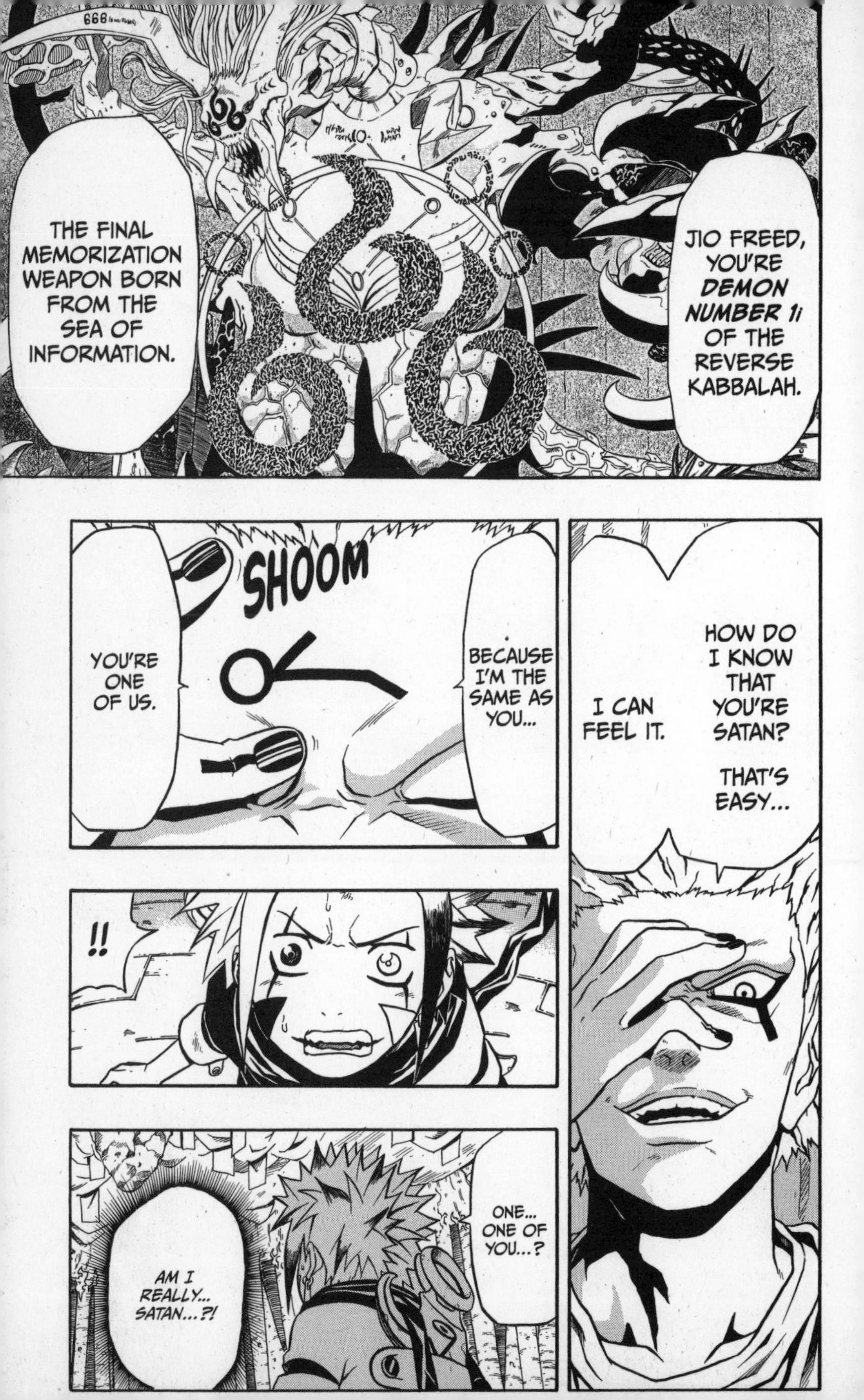
JIO FREED, YOU'RE *DEMON NUMBER 1!* OF THE REVERSE KABBALAH.
THE FINAL MEMORIZATION WEAPON BORN FROM THE SEA OF INFORMATION.
HOW DO I KNOW THAT YOU'RE SATAN?
THAT'S EASY...
I CAN FEEL IT.
BECAUSE I'M THE SAME AS YOU...
SHOOM
YOU'RE ONE OF US.
!!
ONE... ONE OF YOU...?
AM I REALLY... SATAN...?!

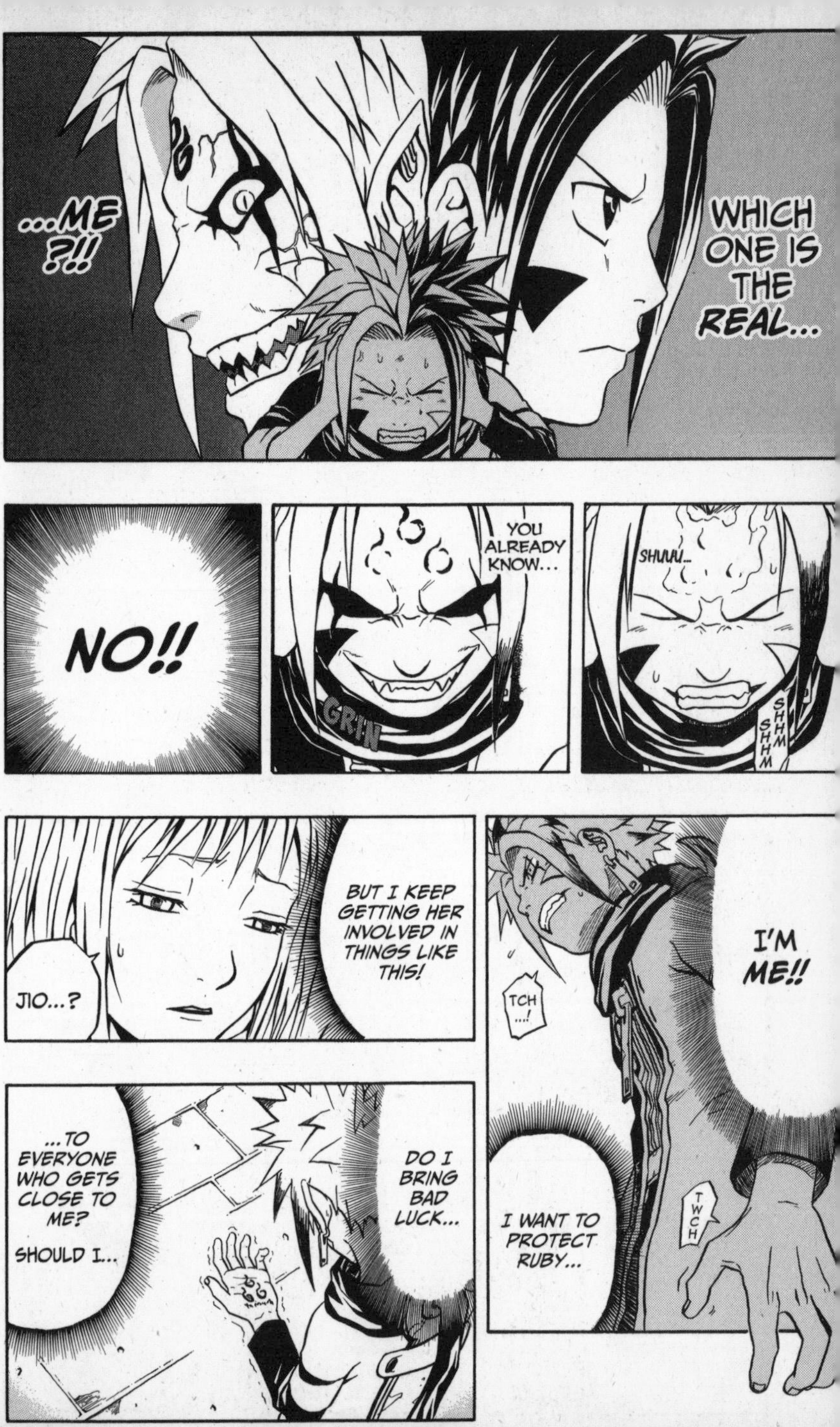
WHICH ONE IS THE REAL...
...ME ?!!
SHUUU...
SHHM SHHM
YOU ALREADY KNOW...
GRIN
NO!!
I'M ME!!
TCH ...!
I WANT TO PROTECT RUBY...
TWCH
BUT I KEEP GETTING HER INVOLVED IN THINGS LIKE THIS!
JIO...?
DO I BRING BAD LUCK...
...TO EVERYONE WHO GETS CLOSE TO ME?
SHOULD I...

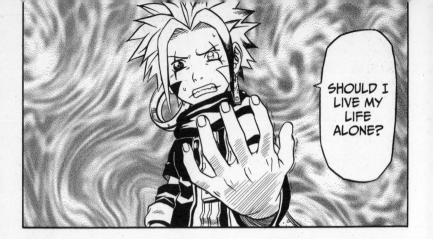

SHOULD I LIVE MY LIFE ALONE?
RUN...
RUN, JIO...!
SHHM SHHM
SHHM
WHEN THE TIME COMES, THIS GIRL WILL BE ACTIVATED AS THE SOFTWARE THAT WILL ERASE THE FIREWALL TO YOUR MEMORY, JIO FREED.
SHE WILL DRAG SATAN OUT OF YOU...AND HER OWN MIND WILL BE DESTROYED.

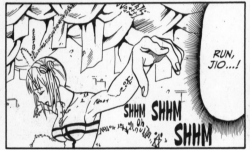

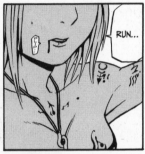

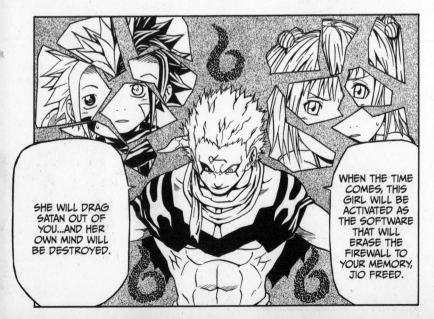

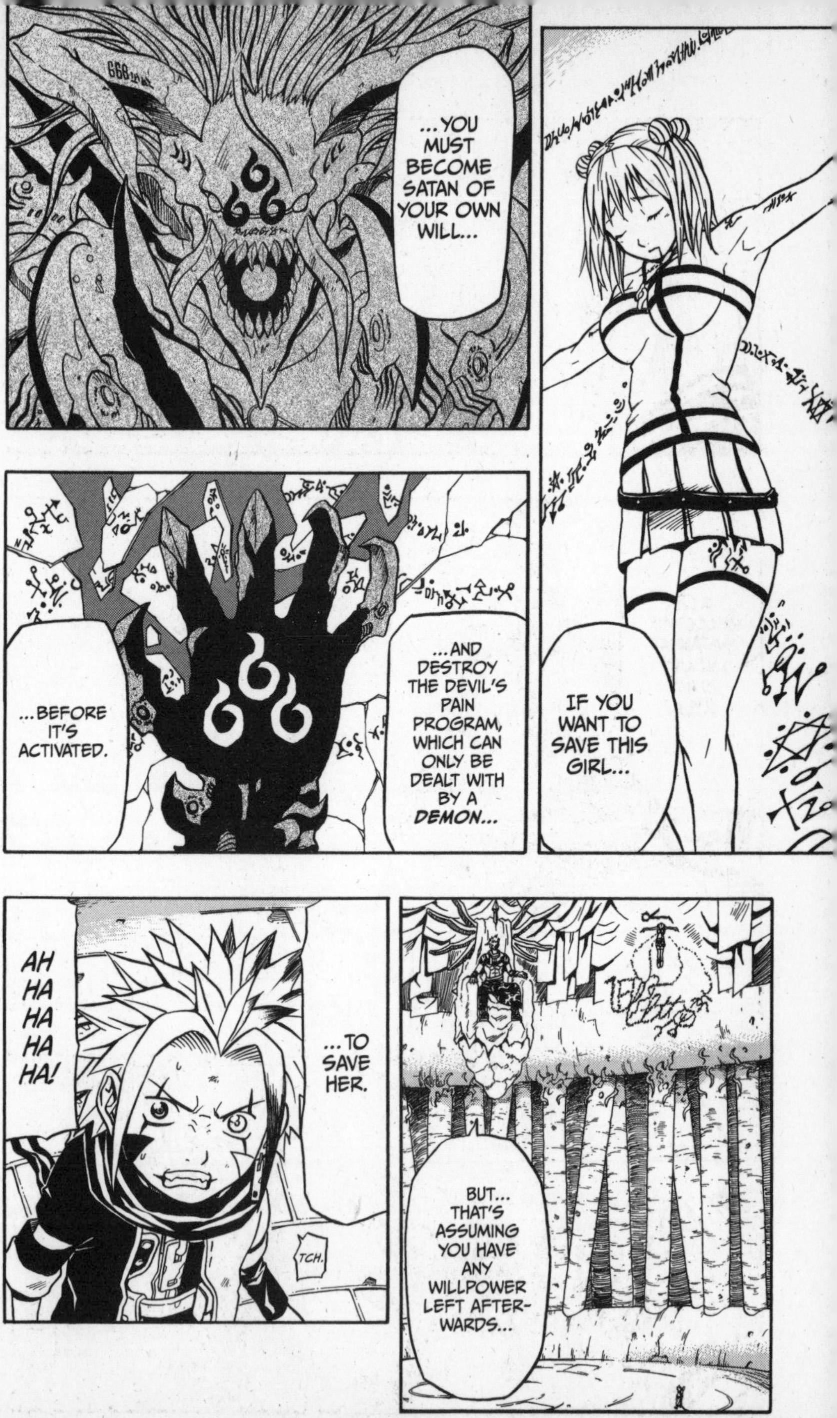
IF YOU WANT TO SAVE THIS GIRL...
...YOU MUST BECOME SATAN OF YOUR OWN WILL...
...AND DESTROY THE DEVIL'S PAIN PROGRAM, WHICH CAN ONLY BE DEALT WITH BY A DEMON...
...BEFORE IT'S ACTIVATED.
BUT... THAT'S ASSUMING YOU HAVE ANY WILLPOWER LEFT AFTER-WARDS...
...TO SAVE HER.
AH HA HA HA HA!
TCH.

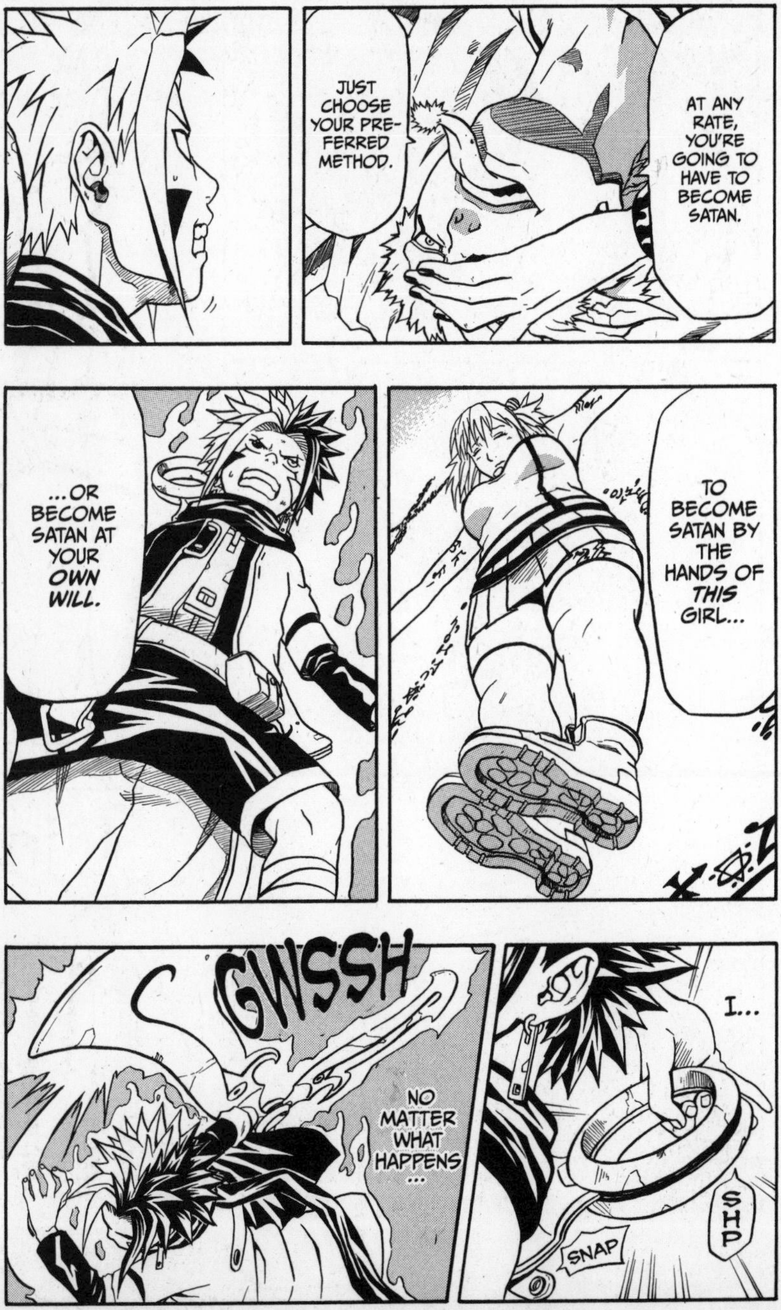
AT ANY RATE, YOU'RE GOING TO HAVE TO BECOME SATAN.
JUST CHOOSE YOUR PRE-FERRED METHOD.
TO BECOME SATAN BY THE HANDS OF *THIS* GIRL...
...OR BECOME SATAN AT YOUR *OWN WILL.*
I...
SHP
SNAP
GWSSH
NO MATTER WHAT HAPPENS...

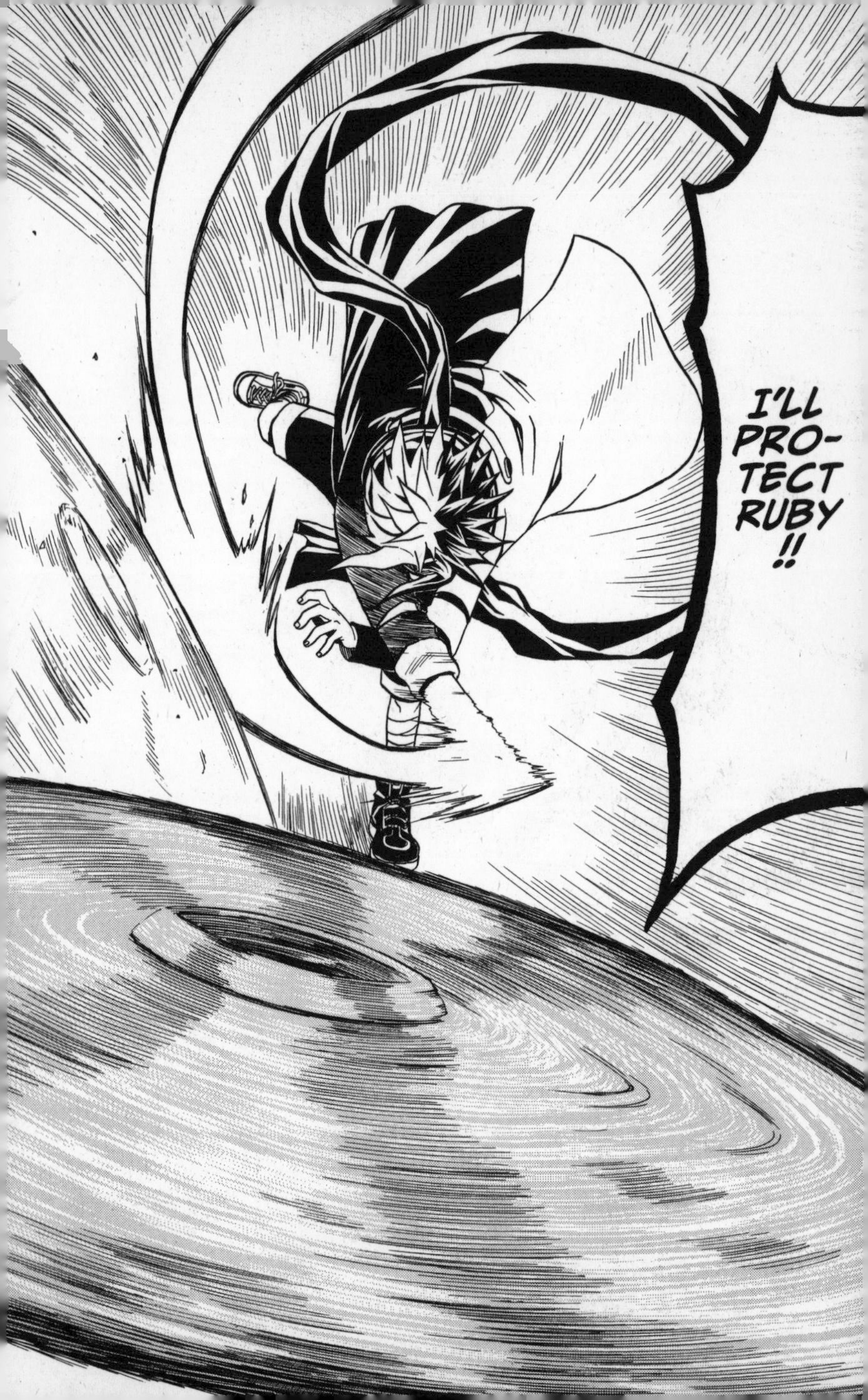
I'LL PRO-TECT RUBY!!

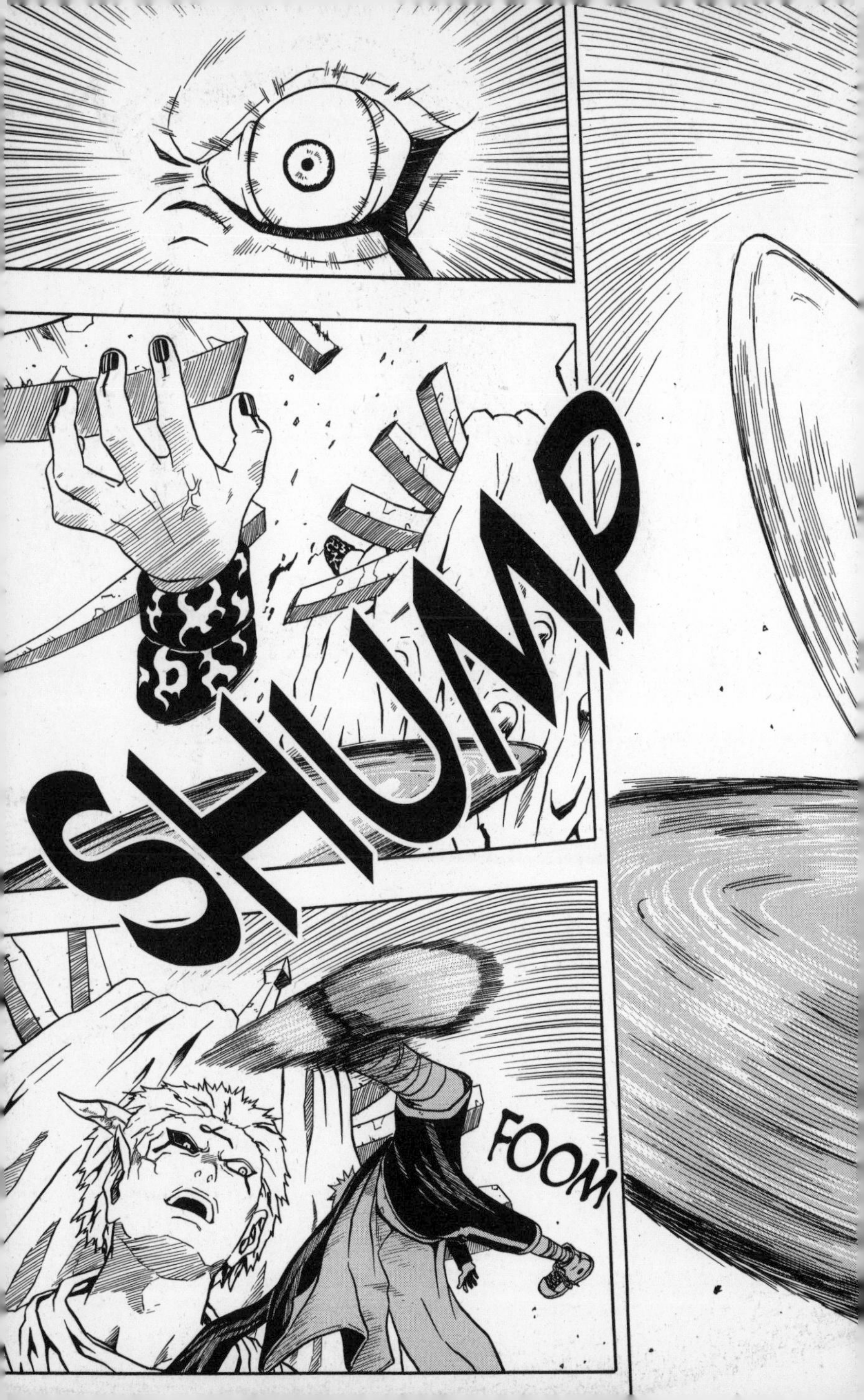
SHUMP
FOOM

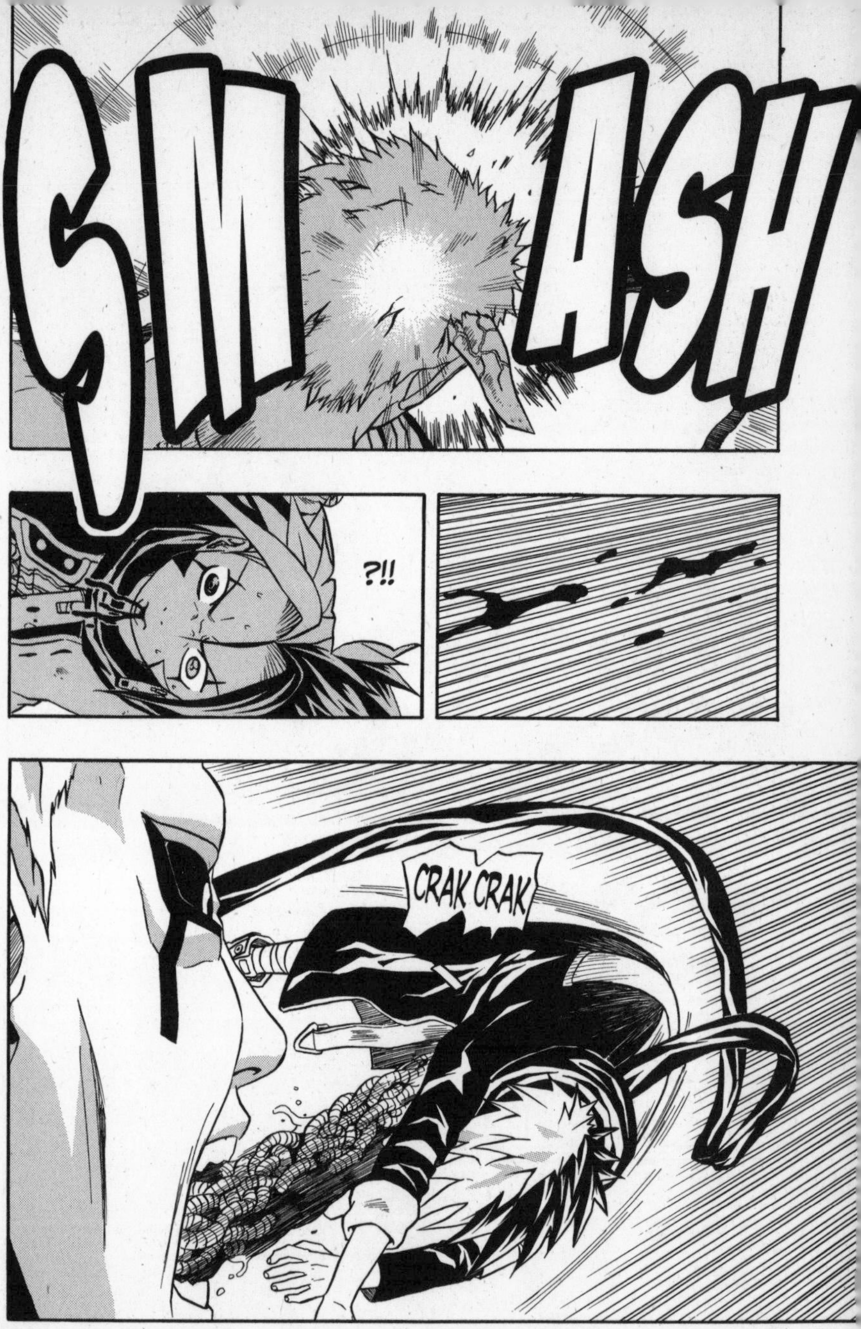
SMASH
?!!
CRAK CRAK

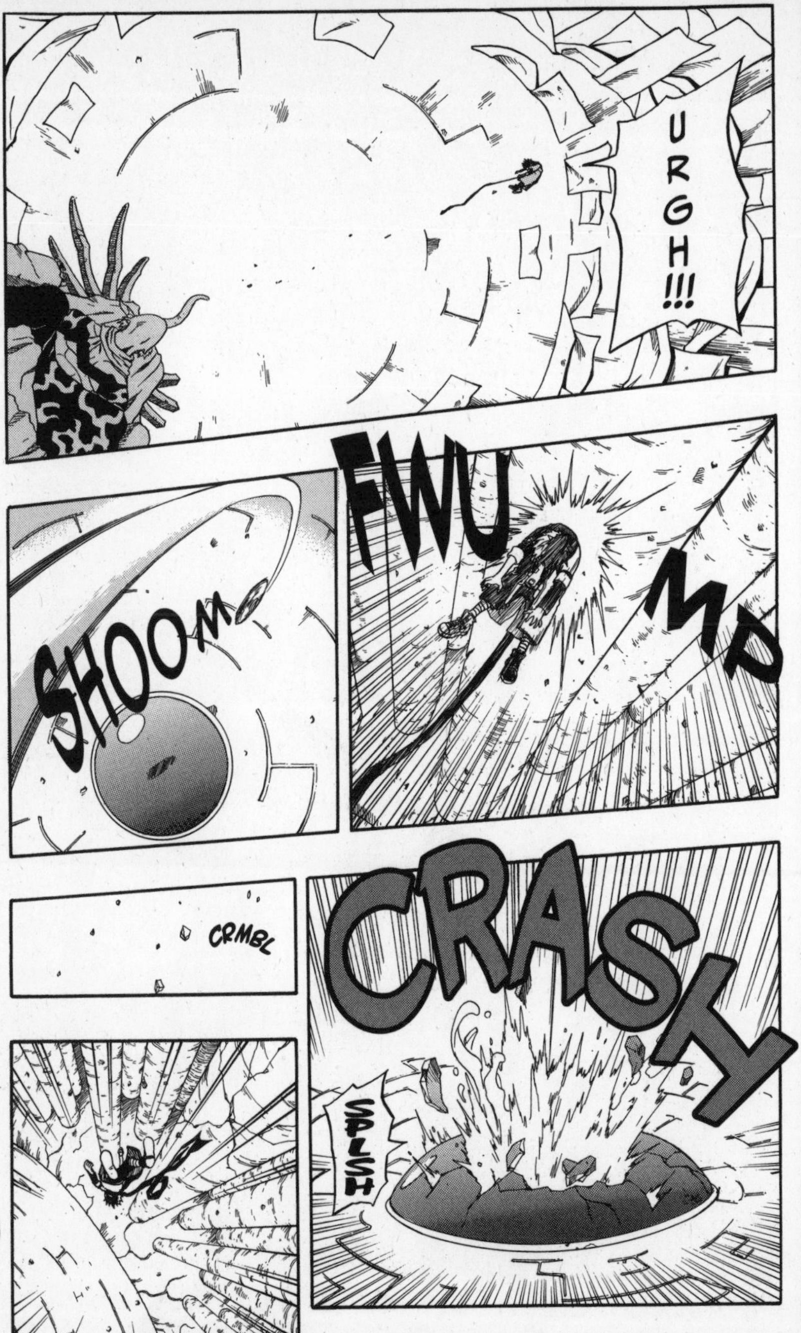
URGH!!!
FWUMP
SHOOM
CRASH
SPLSH
CRMBL

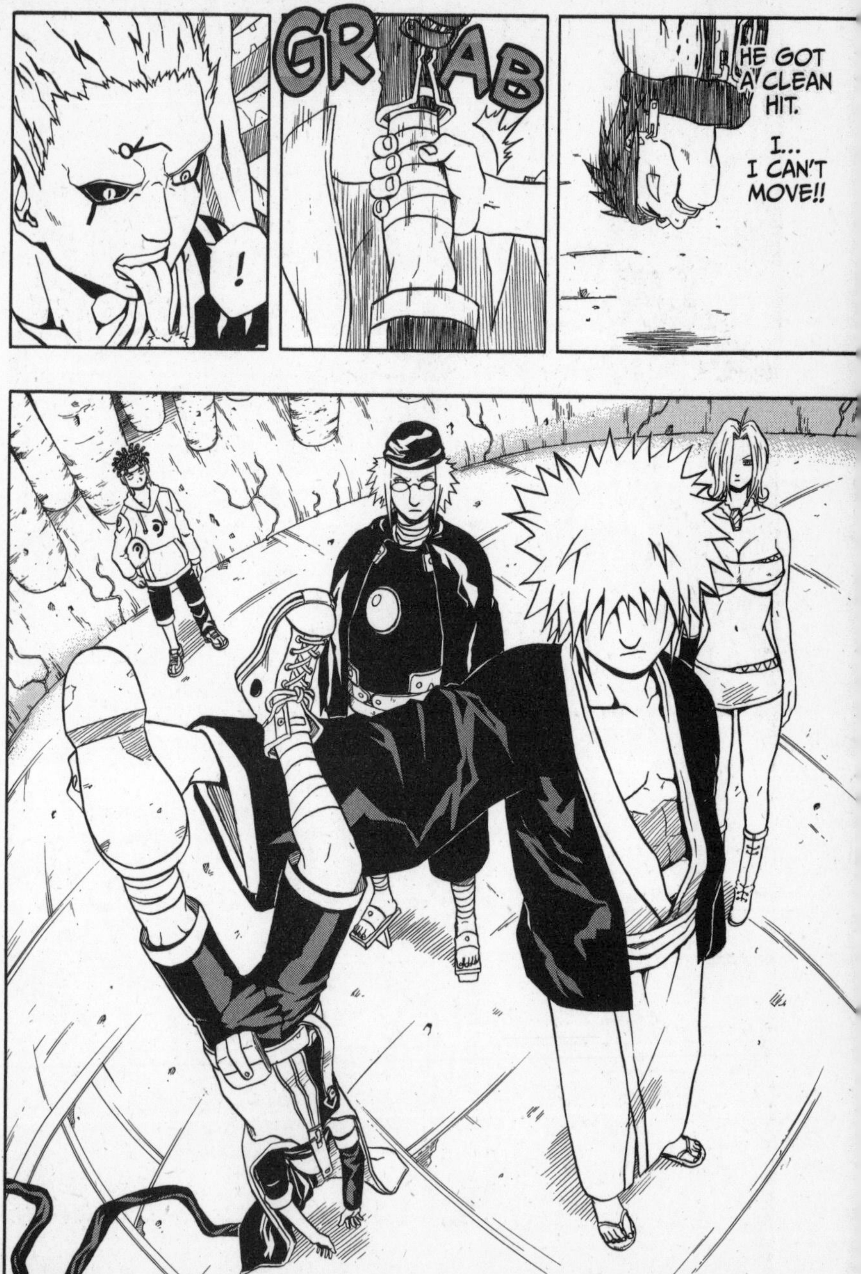
HE GOT A CLEAN HIT.
I... I CAN'T MOVE!!
GRAB
!

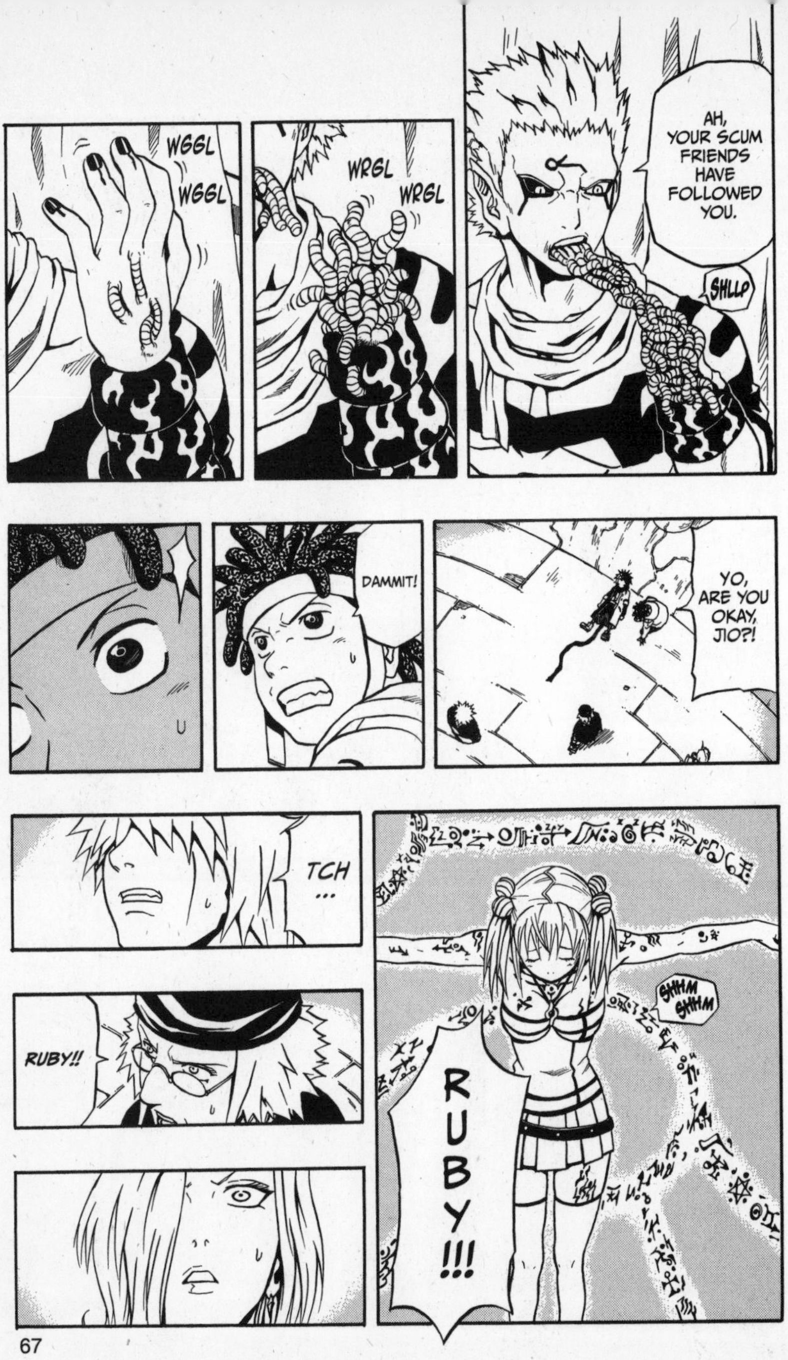
AH, YOUR SCUM FRIENDS HAVE FOLLOWED YOU.
SHLLP
WRGL WRGL
WGGL WGGL
YO, ARE YOU OKAY, JIO?!
DAMMIT!
SHHM SHHM
RUBY!!!
TCH ...
RUBY!!

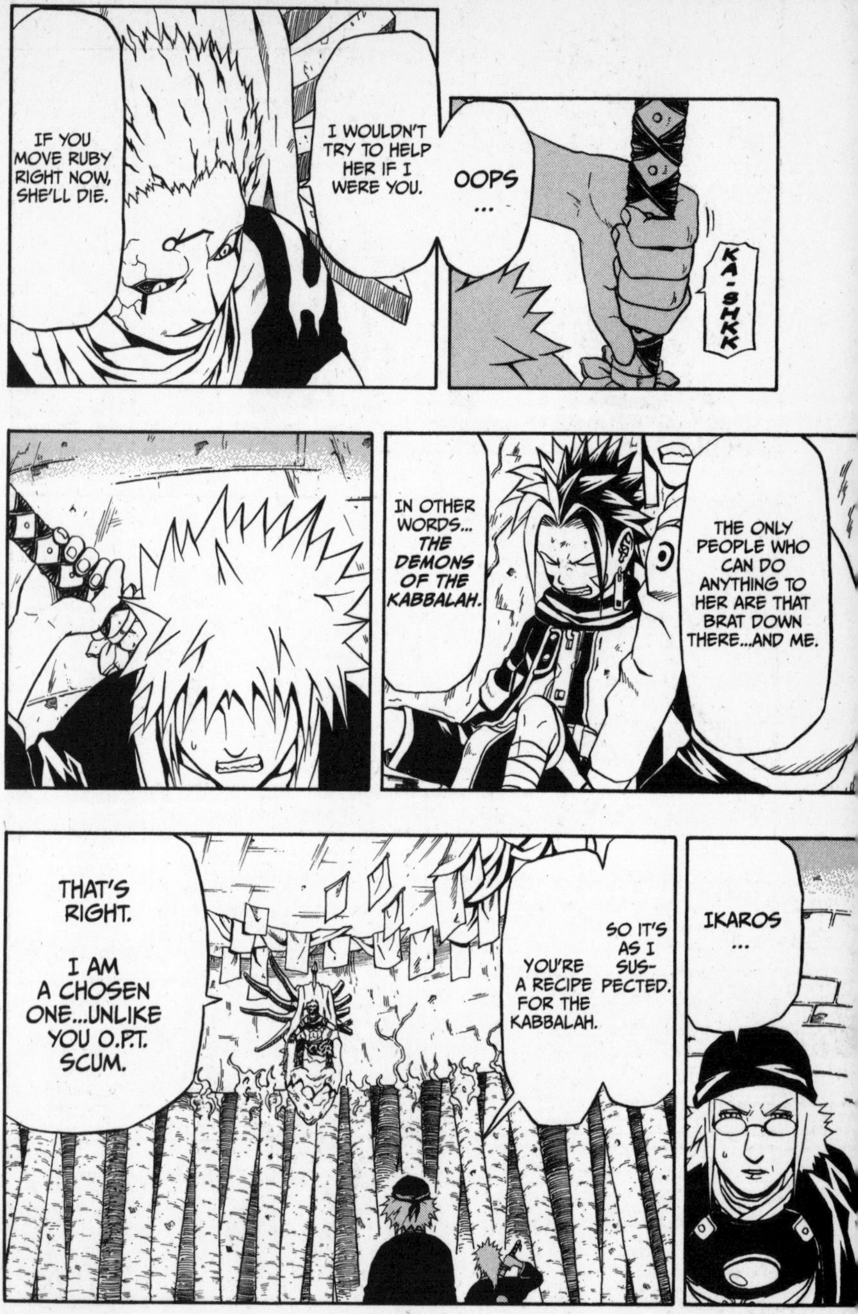
OOPS ...
KA-SHKK
I WOULDN'T TRY TO HELP HER IF I WERE YOU.
IF YOU MOVE RUBY RIGHT NOW, SHE'LL DIE.
THE ONLY PEOPLE WHO CAN DO ANYTHING TO HER ARE THAT BRAT DOWN THERE...AND ME.
IN OTHER WORDS... *THE DEMONS OF THE KABBALAH.*
IKAROS ...
SO IT'S AS I SUS-PECTED.
YOU'RE A RECIPE FOR THE KABBALAH.
THAT'S RIGHT.
I AM A CHOSEN ONE...UNLIKE YOU O.P.T. SCUM.

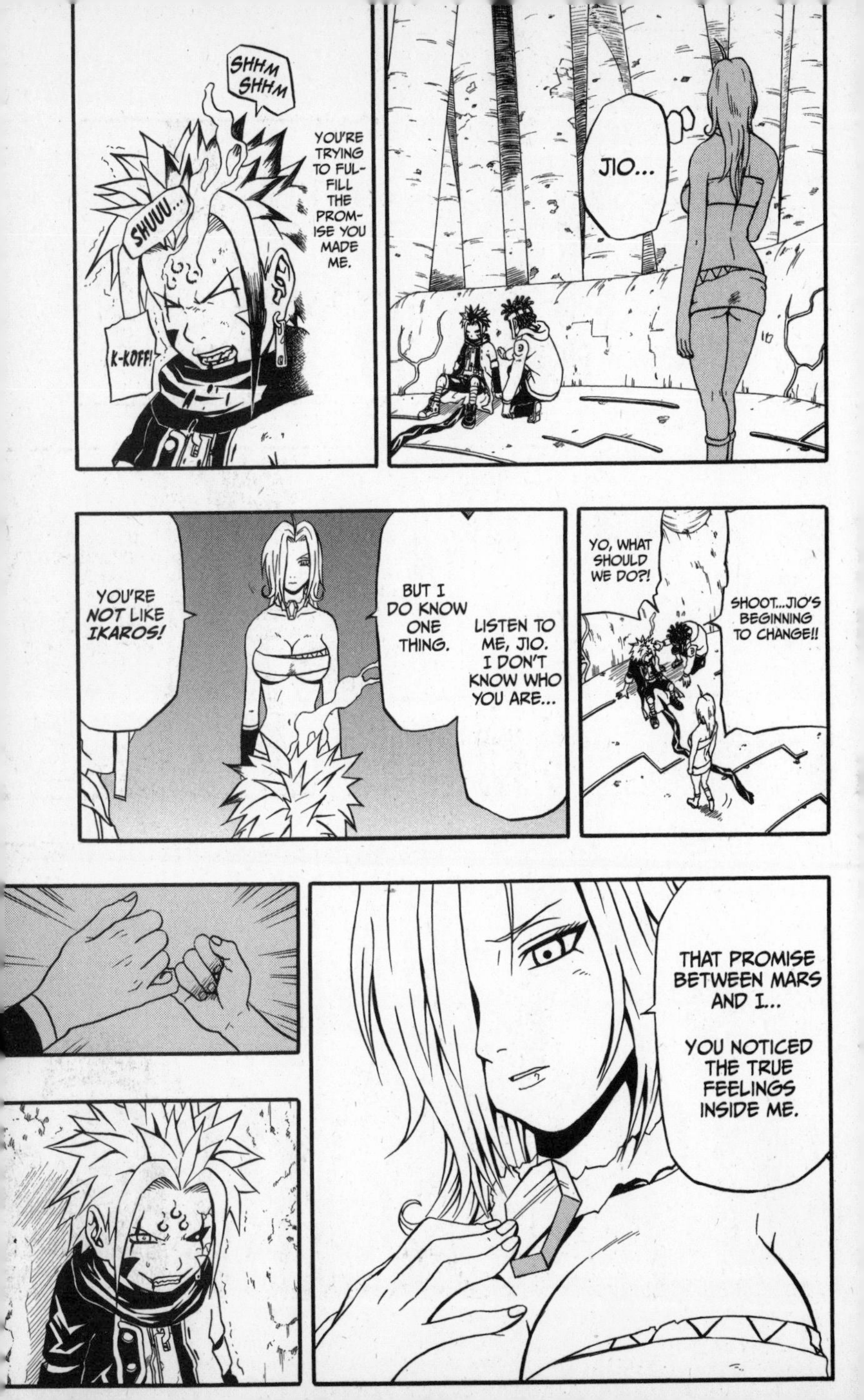
JIO...
SHHM SHHM
YOU'RE TRYING TO FUL-FILL THE PROM-ISE YOU MADE ME.
SHUUU...
K-KOFF!
YO, WHAT SHOULD WE DO?!
SHOOT...JIO'S BEGINNING TO CHANGE!!
LISTEN TO ME, JIO. I DON'T KNOW WHO YOU ARE...
BUT I DO KNOW ONE THING.
YOU'RE *NOT* LIKE *IKAROS!*
THAT PROMISE BETWEEN MARS AND I...
YOU NOTICED THE TRUE FEELINGS INSIDE ME.

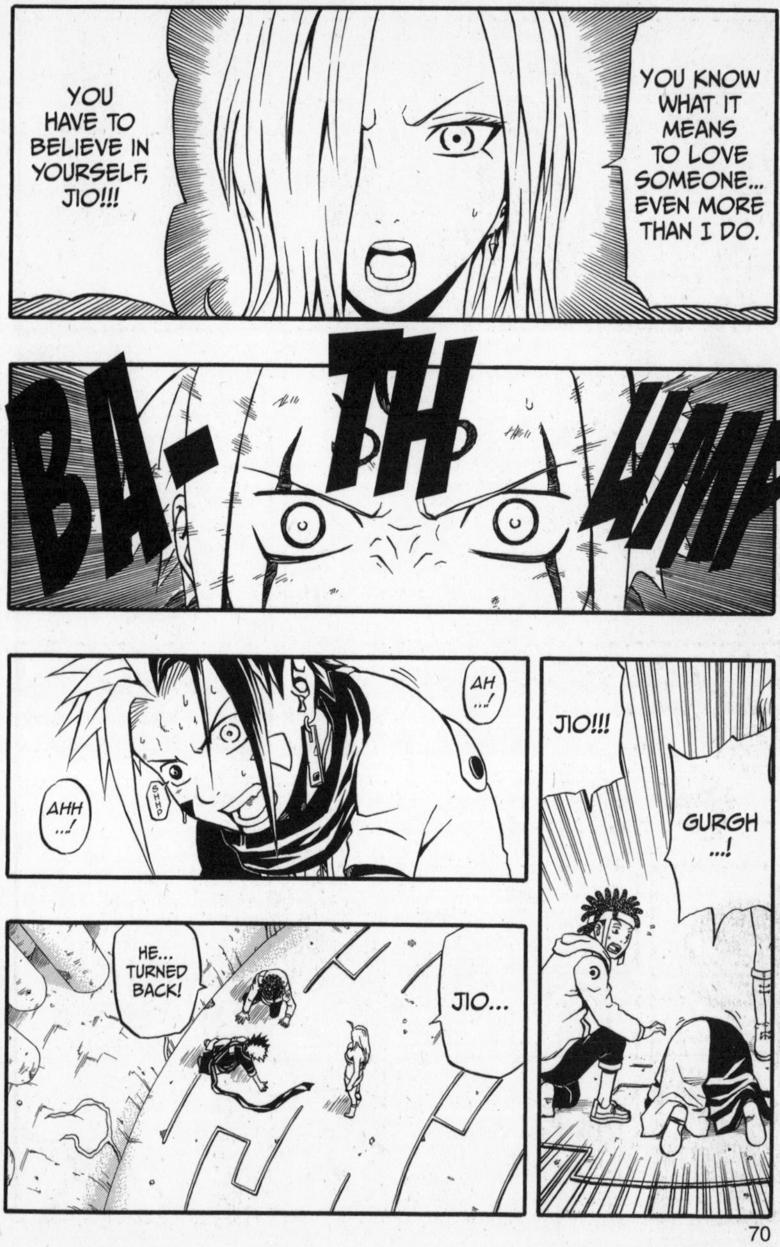
YOU KNOW WHAT IT MEANS TO LOVE SOMEONE... EVEN MORE THAN I DO.
YOU HAVE TO BELIEVE IN YOURSELF, JIO!!!
BA-THUMP
JIO!!!
GURGH ...!
AH ...!
SHHP
AHH ...!
JIO...
HE... TURNED BACK!

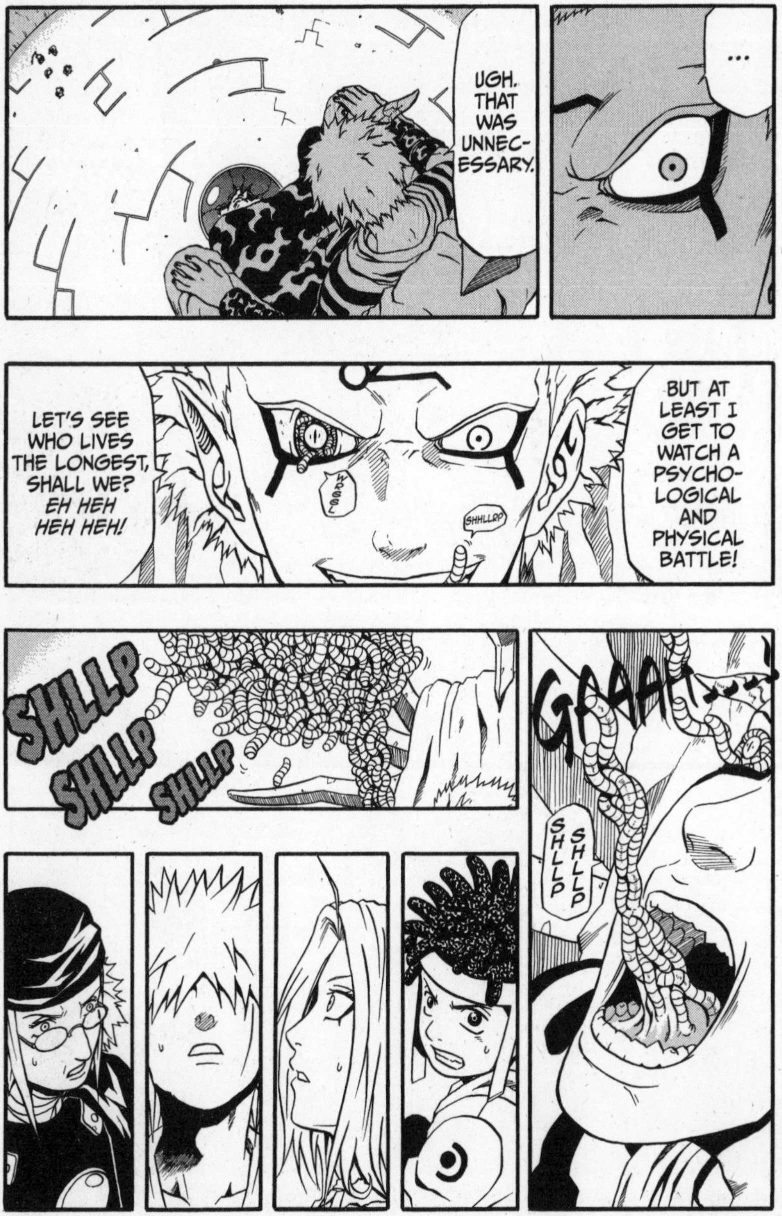
...
UGH. THAT WAS UNNECESSARY.
BUT AT LEAST I GET TO WATCH A PSYCHOLOGICAL AND PHYSICAL BATTLE!
WRSSL
SHHLLRP
LET'S SEE WHO LIVES THE LONGEST, SHALL WE? EH HEH HEH HEH!
GAAAH...!
SHLLP SHLLP
SHLLP SHLLP SHLLP

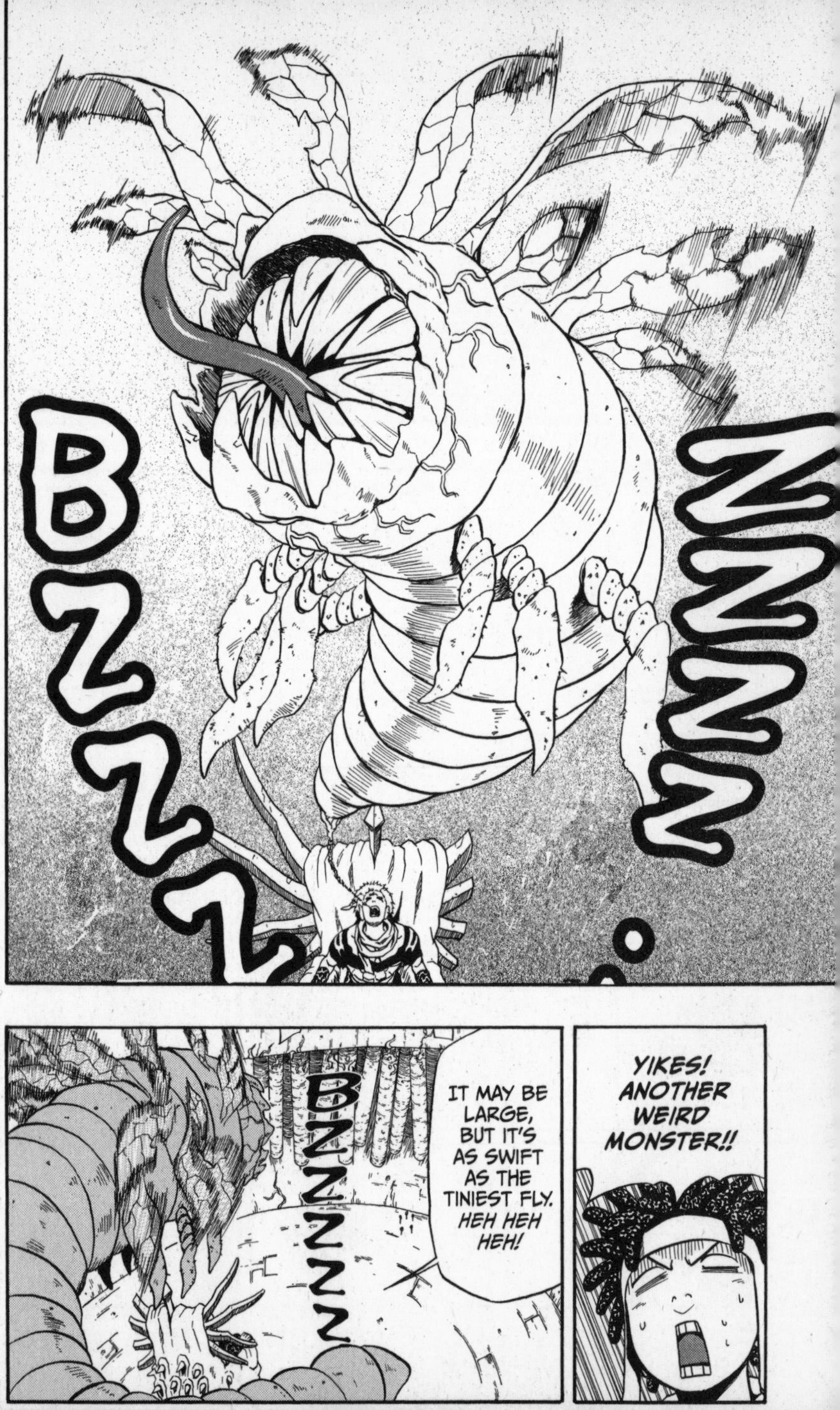
BZZZZ
ZZZZZ..
YIKES! ANOTHER WEIRD MONSTER!!
IT MAY BE LARGE, BUT IT'S AS SWIFT AS THE TINIEST FLY. HEH HEH HEH!
BZZZZZZ

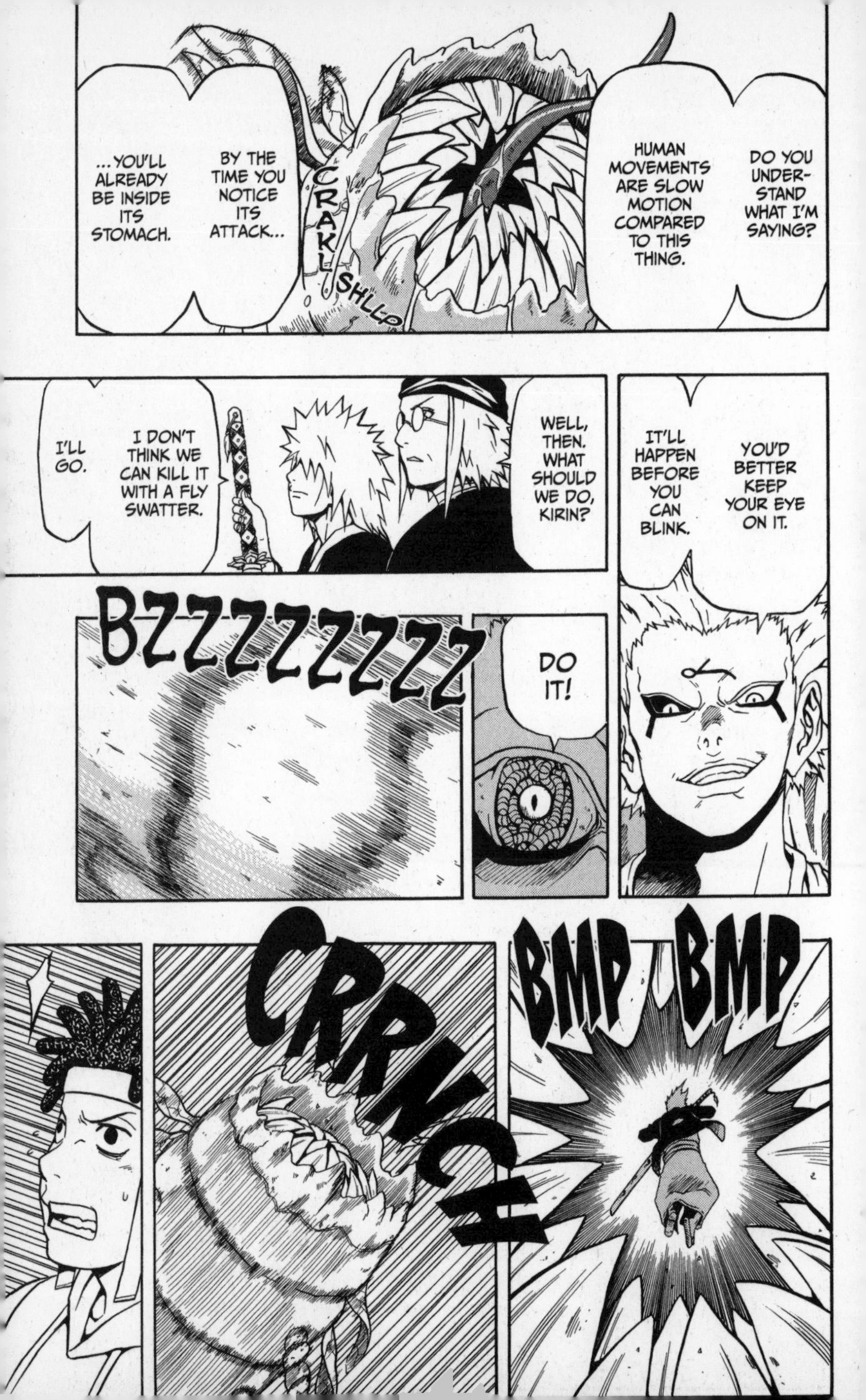
DO YOU UNDERSTAND WHAT I'M SAYING?
HUMAN MOVEMENTS ARE SLOW MOTION COMPARED TO THIS THING.
CRAKL
SHLLP
BY THE TIME YOU NOTICE ITS ATTACK...
...YOU'LL ALREADY BE INSIDE ITS STOMACH.
YOU'D BETTER KEEP YOUR EYE ON IT.
IT'LL HAPPEN BEFORE YOU CAN BLINK.
WELL, THEN. WHAT SHOULD WE DO, KIRIN?
I DON'T THINK WE CAN KILL IT WITH A FLY SWATTER.
I'LL GO.
DO IT!
BZZZZZZZZZ
BMP BMP
CRRNCH

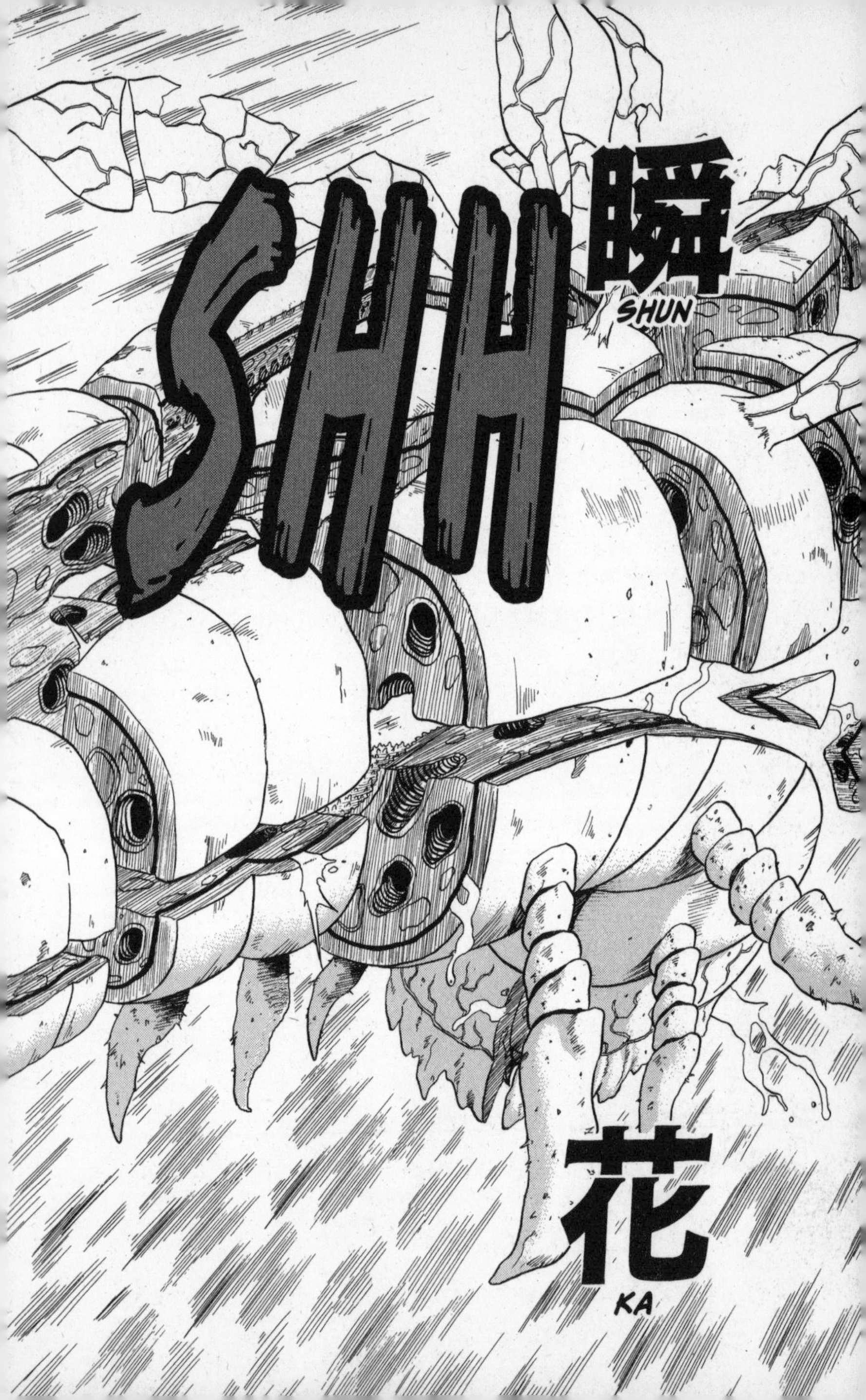

SHH
瞬
SHUN
花
KA

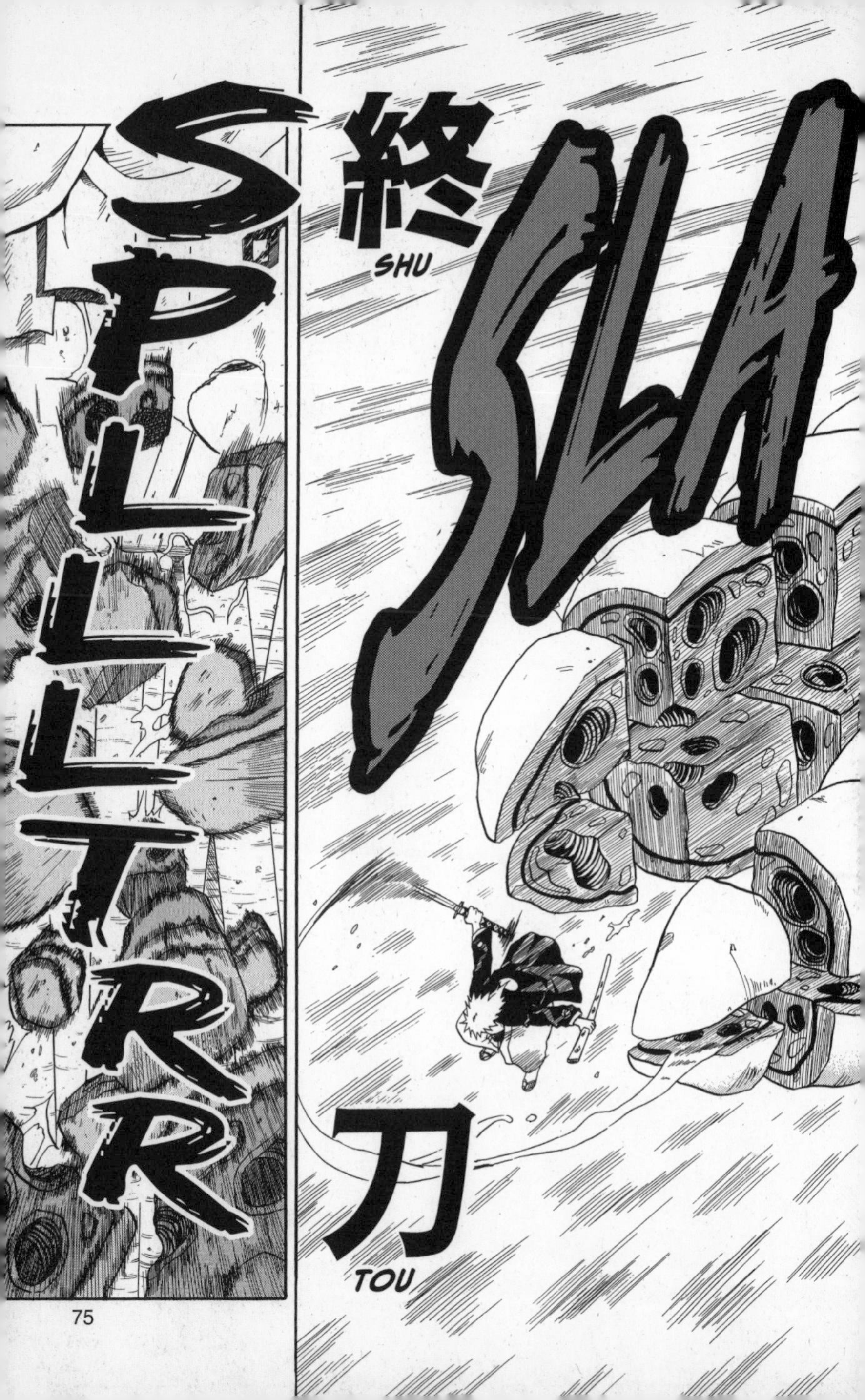
終
SHU
SLA
刀
TOU
SPLLTRR

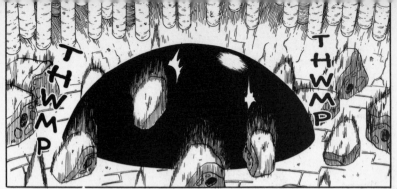

THWMP
THWMP
SLSH SLSH SLSH
SHHMPP
PLAP
TMP
NOW THAT'S WHAT I CALL...
...BEFORE YOU CAN BLINK!
KLINK

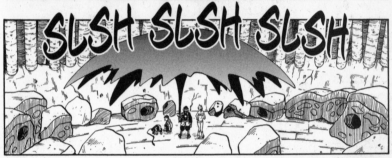

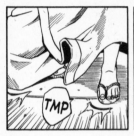

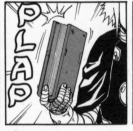

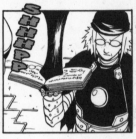

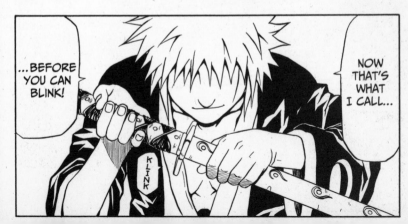

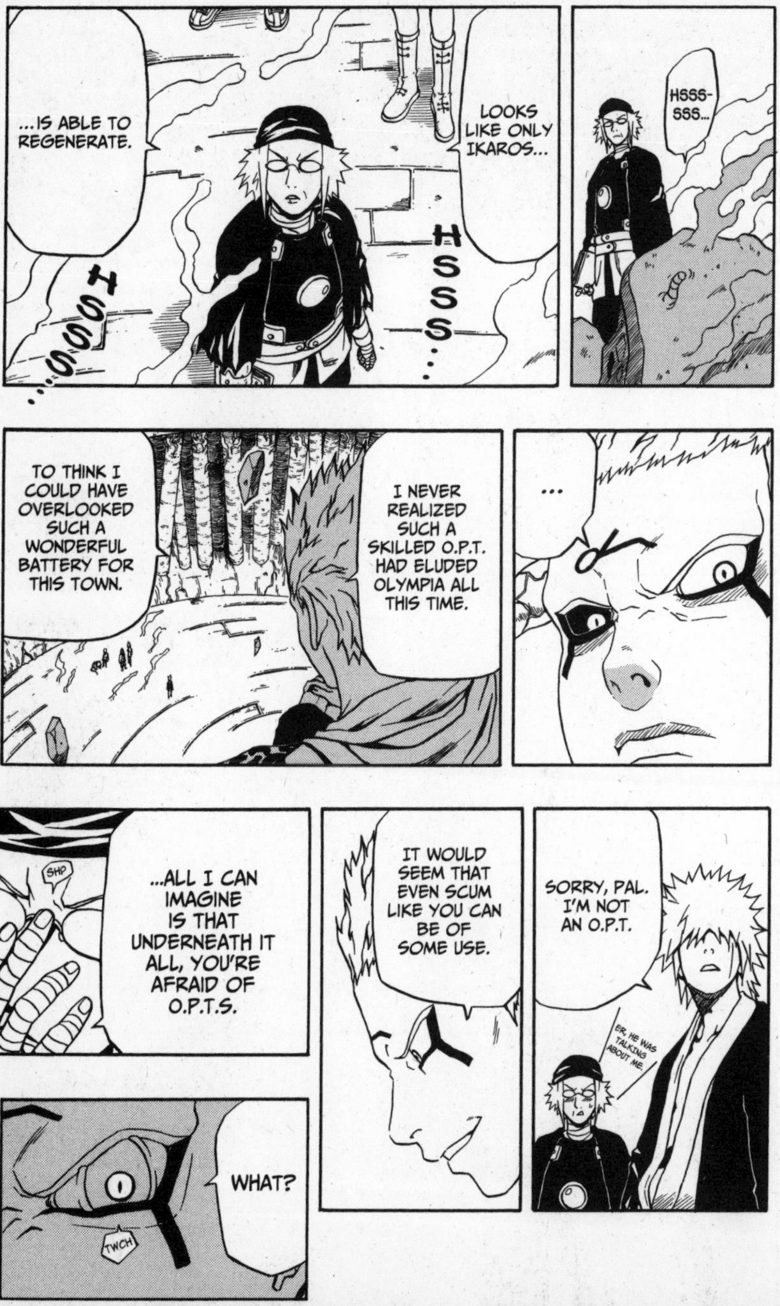
HSSS-SSS...
LOOKS LIKE ONLY IKAROS...
...IS ABLE TO REGENERATE.
HSSS...
HSSS...
...
I NEVER REALIZED SUCH A SKILLED O.P.T. HAD ELUDED OLYMPIA ALL THIS TIME.
TO THINK I COULD HAVE OVERLOOKED SUCH A WONDERFUL BATTERY FOR THIS TOWN.
SORRY, PAL. I'M NOT AN O.P.T.
ER, HE WAS TALKING ABOUT ME.
IT WOULD SEEM THAT EVEN SCUM LIKE YOU CAN BE OF SOME USE.
SHP
...ALL I CAN IMAGINE IS THAT UNDERNEATH IT ALL, YOU'RE AFRAID OF O.P.T.S.
WHAT?
TWCH

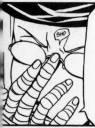

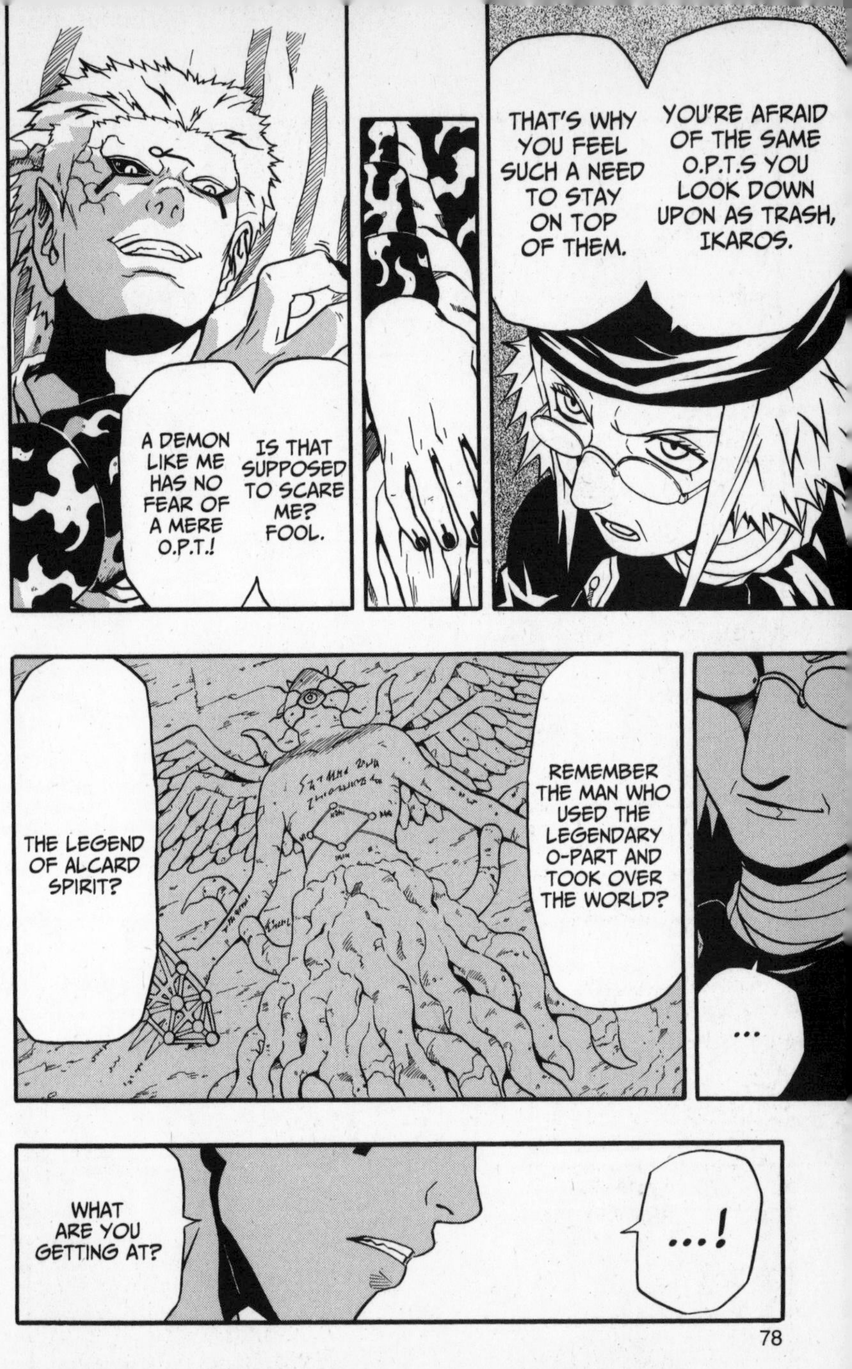
YOU'RE AFRAID OF THE SAME O.P.T.S YOU LOOK DOWN UPON AS TRASH, IKAROS.
THAT'S WHY YOU FEEL SUCH A NEED TO STAY ON TOP OF THEM.
IS THAT SUPPOSED TO SCARE ME? FOOL.
A DEMON LIKE ME HAS NO FEAR OF A MERE O.P.T.!
...
REMEMBER THE MAN WHO USED THE LEGENDARY O-PART AND TOOK OVER THE WORLD?
THE LEGEND OF ALCARD SPIRIT?
...!
WHAT ARE YOU GETTING AT?

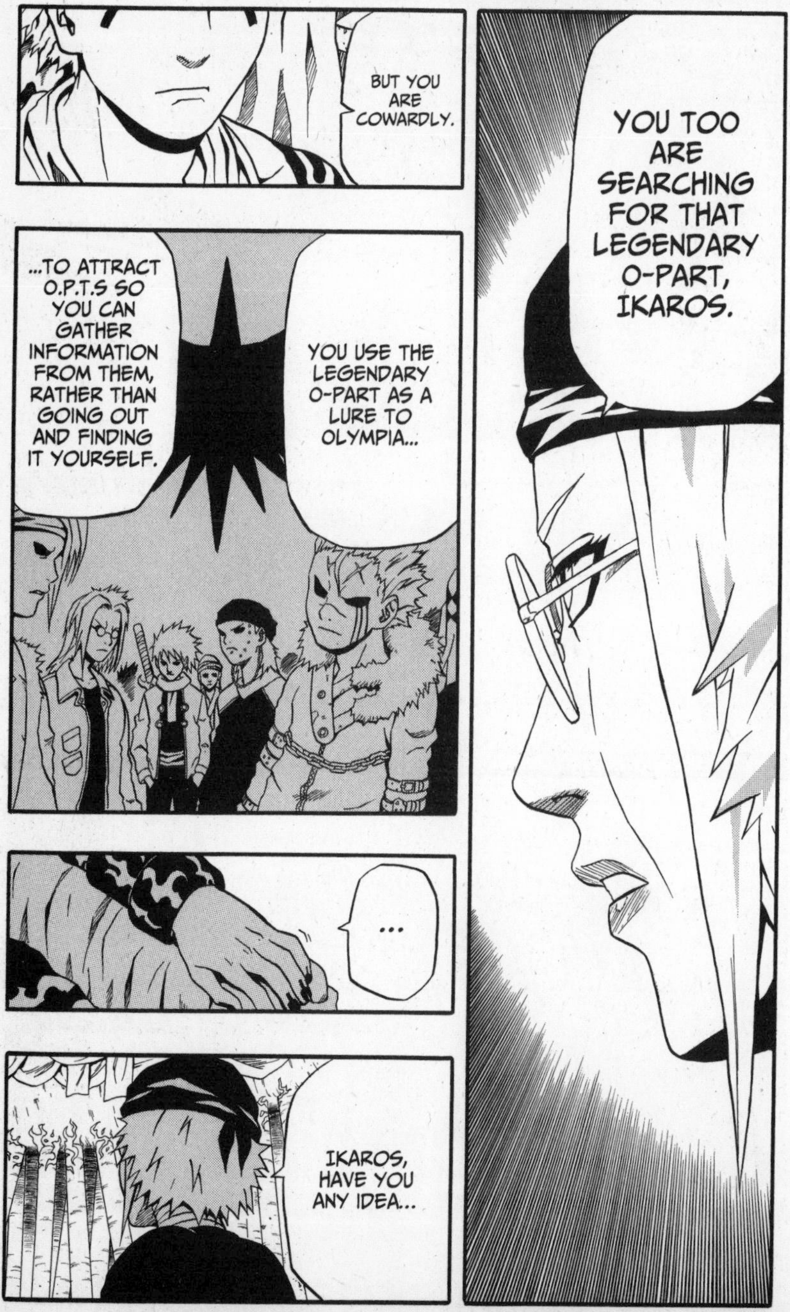
YOU TOO ARE SEARCHING FOR THAT LEGENDARY O-PART, IKAROS.
BUT YOU ARE COWARDLY.
YOU USE THE LEGENDARY O-PART AS A LURE TO OLYMPIA...
...TO ATTRACT O.P.T.S SO YOU CAN GATHER INFORMATION FROM THEM, RATHER THAN GOING OUT AND FINDING IT YOURSELF.
...
IKAROS, HAVE YOU ANY IDEA...

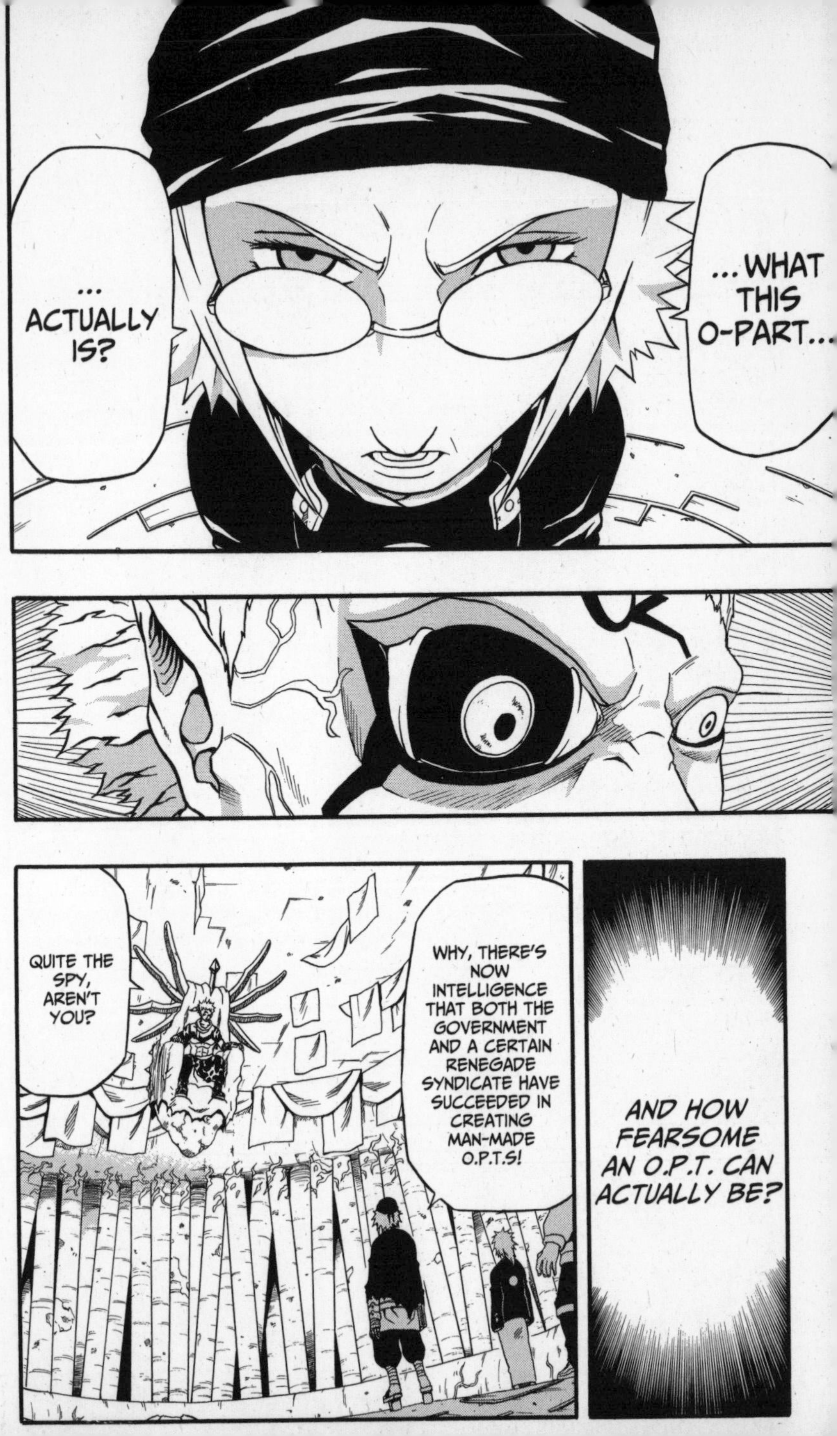
...WHAT THIS O-PART...
... ACTUALLY IS?
AND HOW FEARSOME AN O.P.T. CAN ACTUALLY BE?
WHY, THERE'S NOW INTELLIGENCE THAT BOTH THE GOVERNMENT AND A CERTAIN RENEGADE SYNDICATE HAVE SUCCEEDED IN CREATING MAN-MADE O.P.T.S!
QUITE THE SPY, AREN'T YOU?

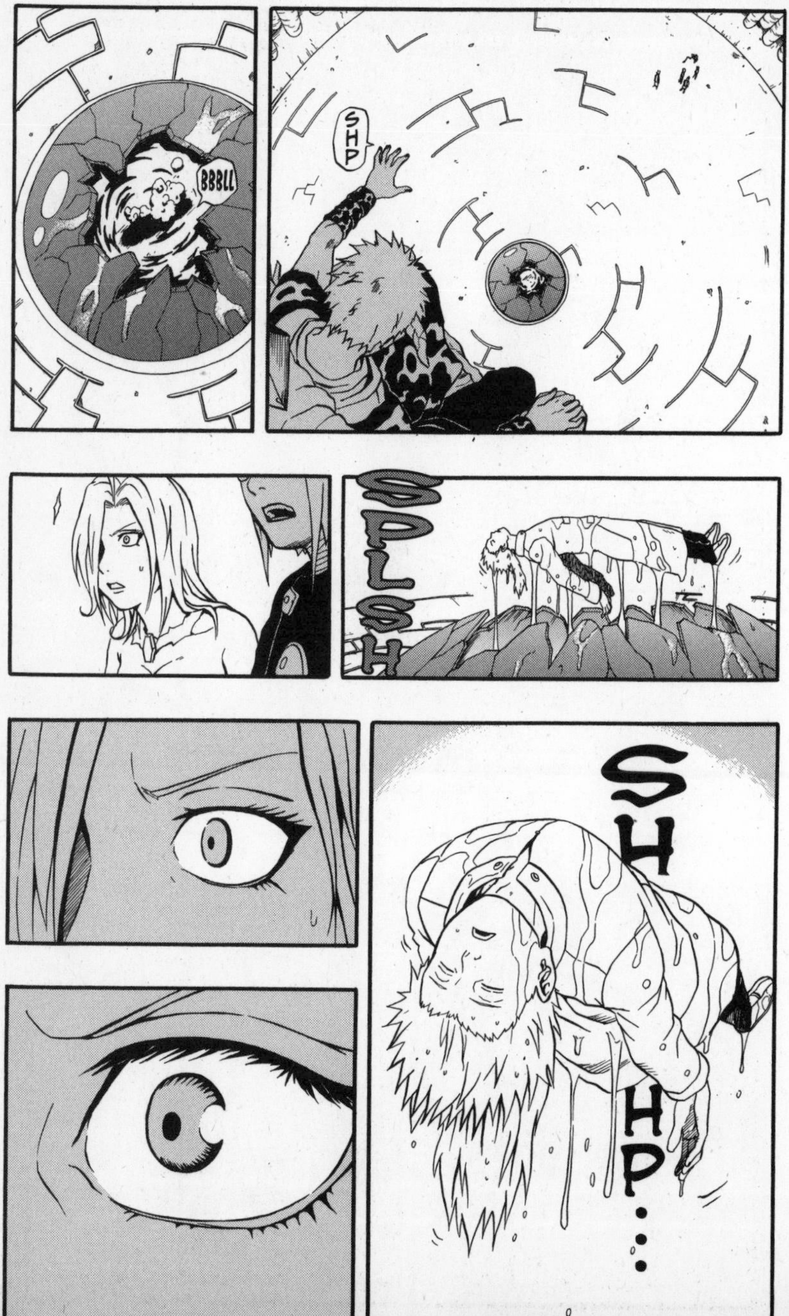
SHP
BBBLL
SPLSH
SHHP...

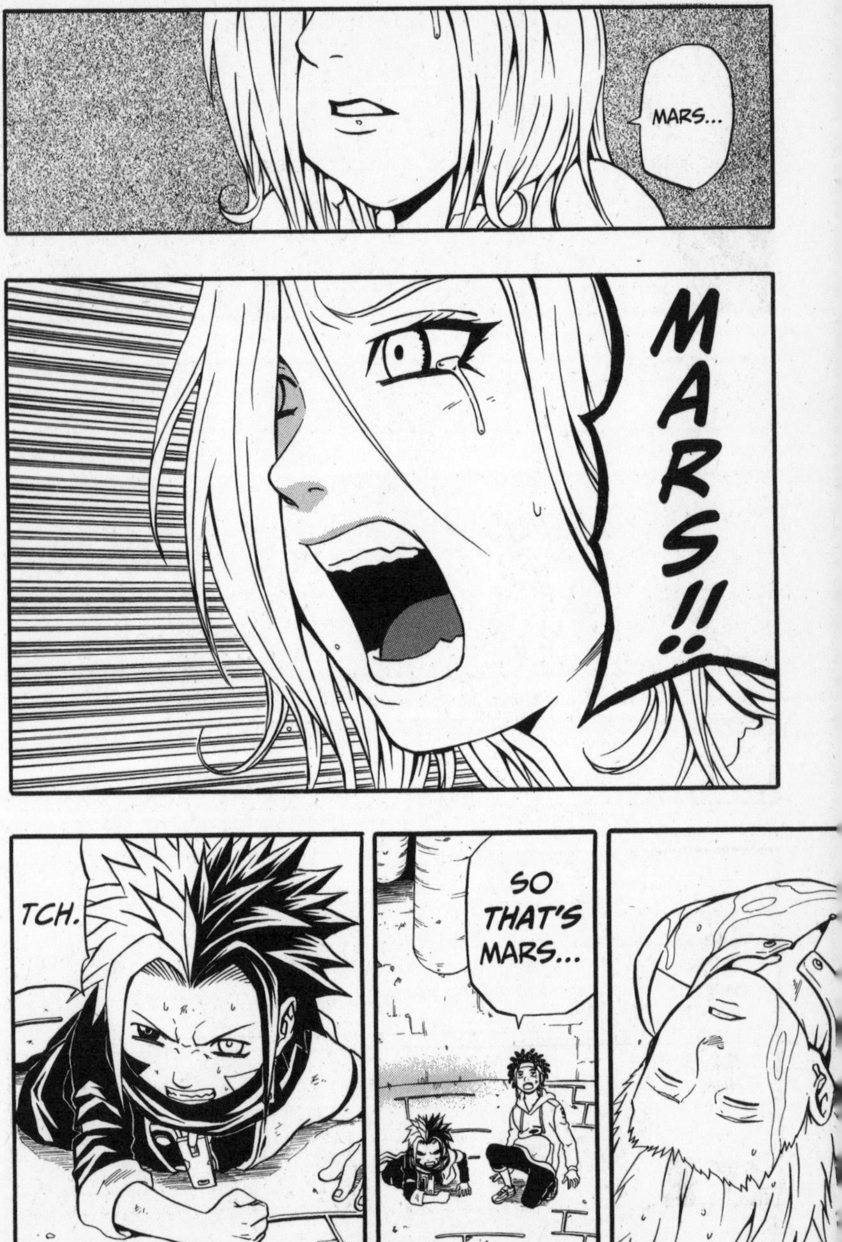
MARS...
MARS!!
SO THAT'S MARS...
TCH.

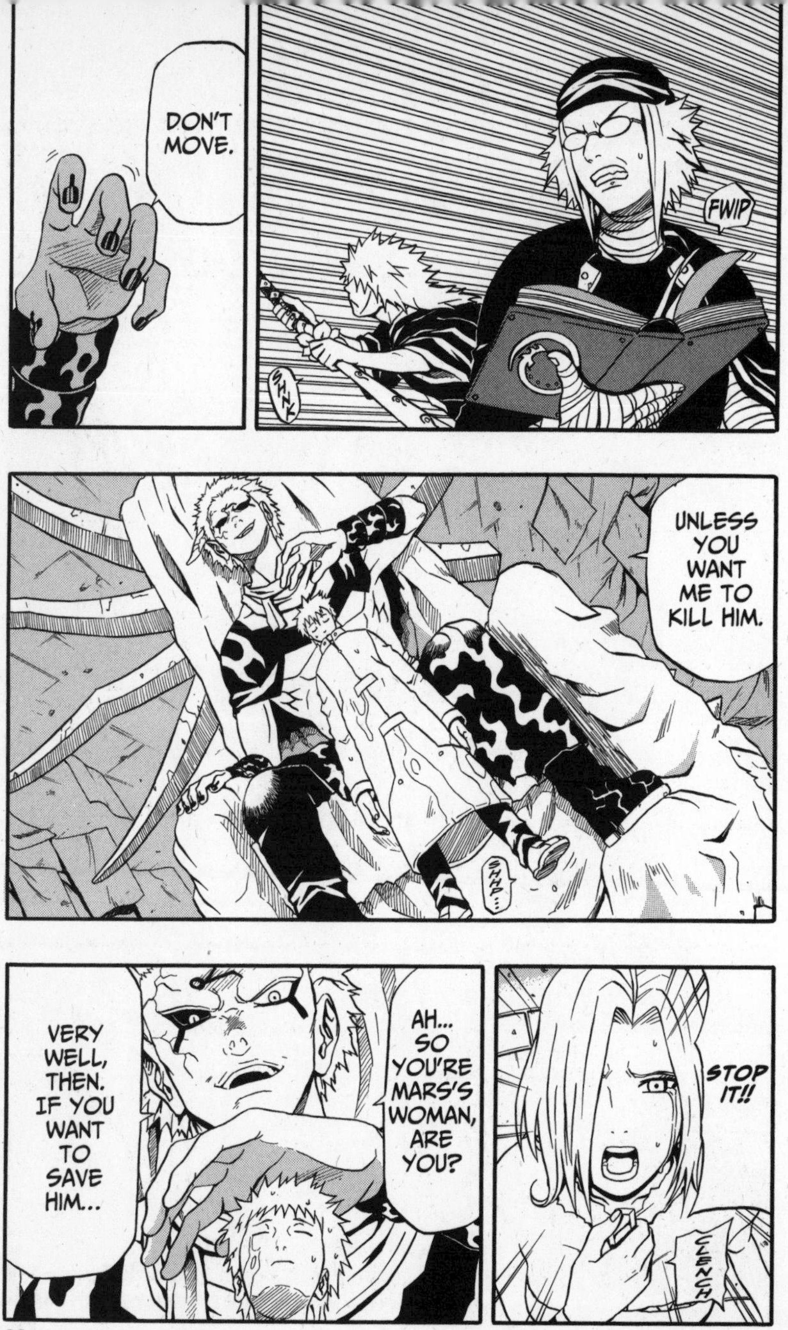
FWIP
SHNK
DON'T MOVE.
UNLESS YOU WANT ME TO KILL HIM.
SHHP...
STOP IT!!
CLENCH
AH... SO YOU'RE MARS'S WOMAN, ARE YOU?
VERY WELL, THEN. IF YOU WANT TO SAVE HIM...

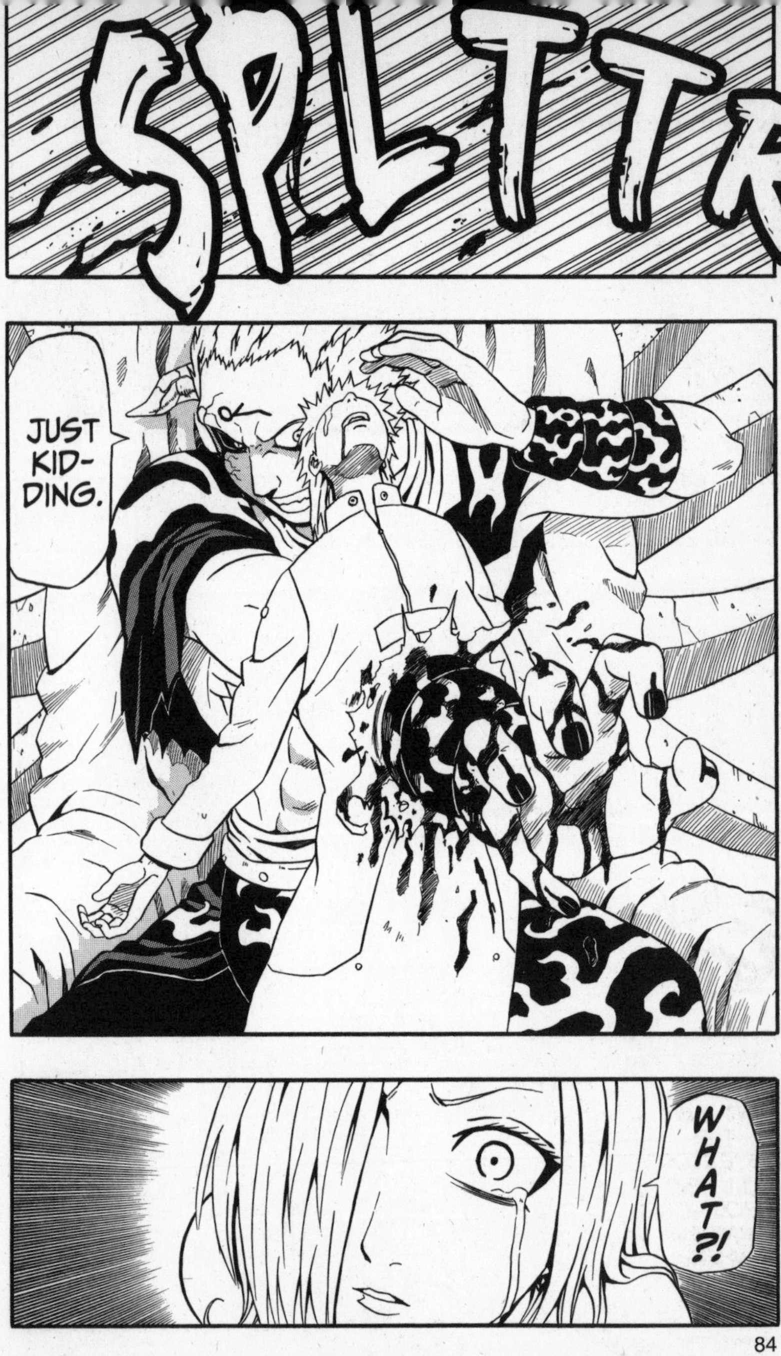
SPLTTR
JUST KID-DING.
WHAT?!

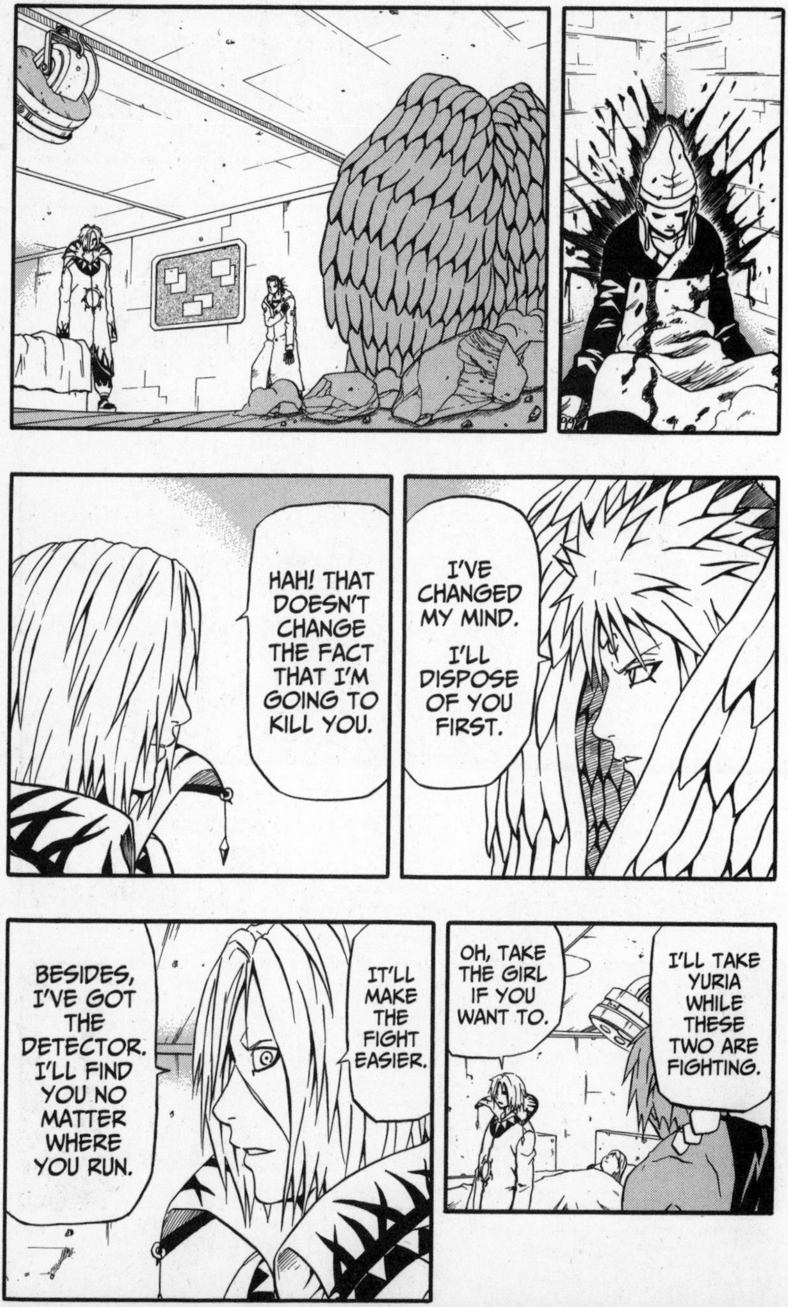
I'VE CHANGED MY MIND.
I'LL DISPOSE OF YOU FIRST.
HAH! THAT DOESN'T CHANGE THE FACT THAT I'M GOING TO KILL YOU.
I'LL TAKE YURIA WHILE THESE TWO ARE FIGHTING.
OH, TAKE THE GIRL IF YOU WANT TO.
IT'LL MAKE THE FIGHT EASIER.
BESIDES, I'VE GOT THE DETECTOR. I'LL FIND YOU NO MATTER WHERE YOU RUN.

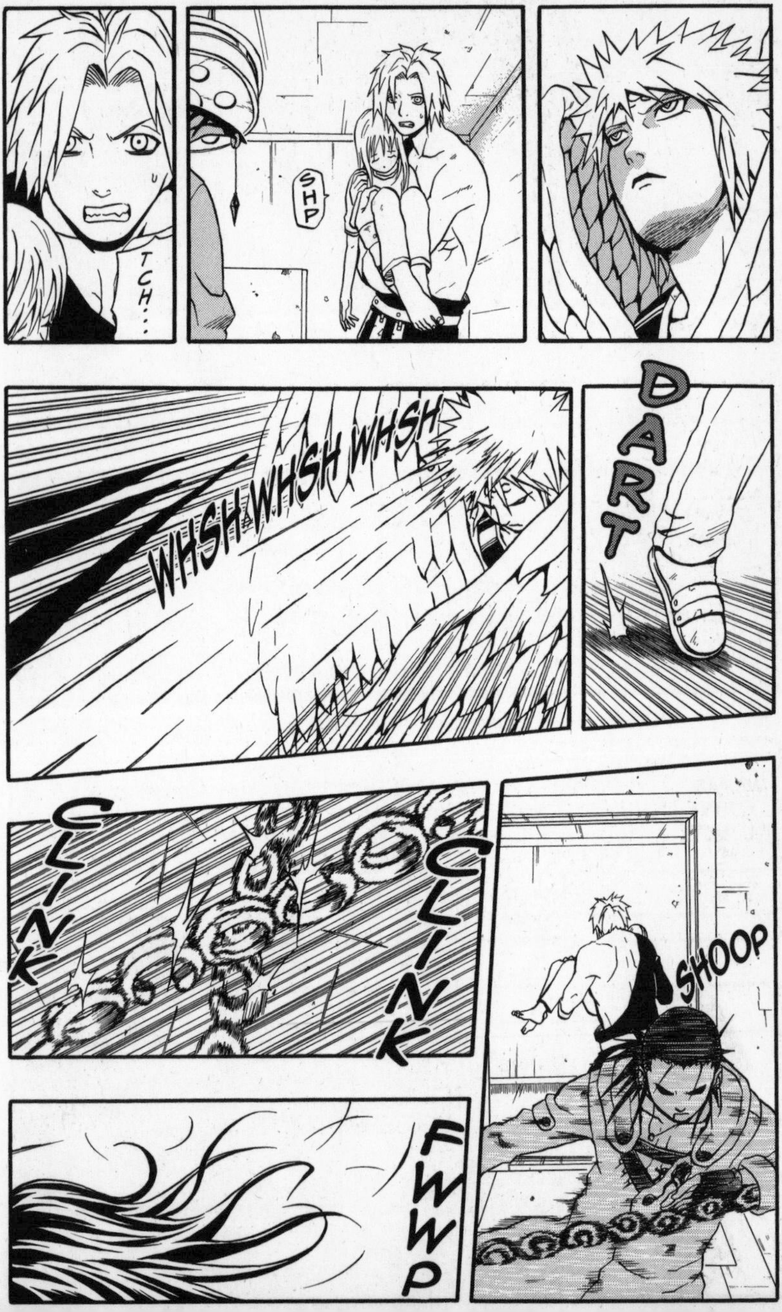
SHP
TCH...
DART
WHSH WHSH WHSH
SHOOP
CLINK
CLINK
FWWP

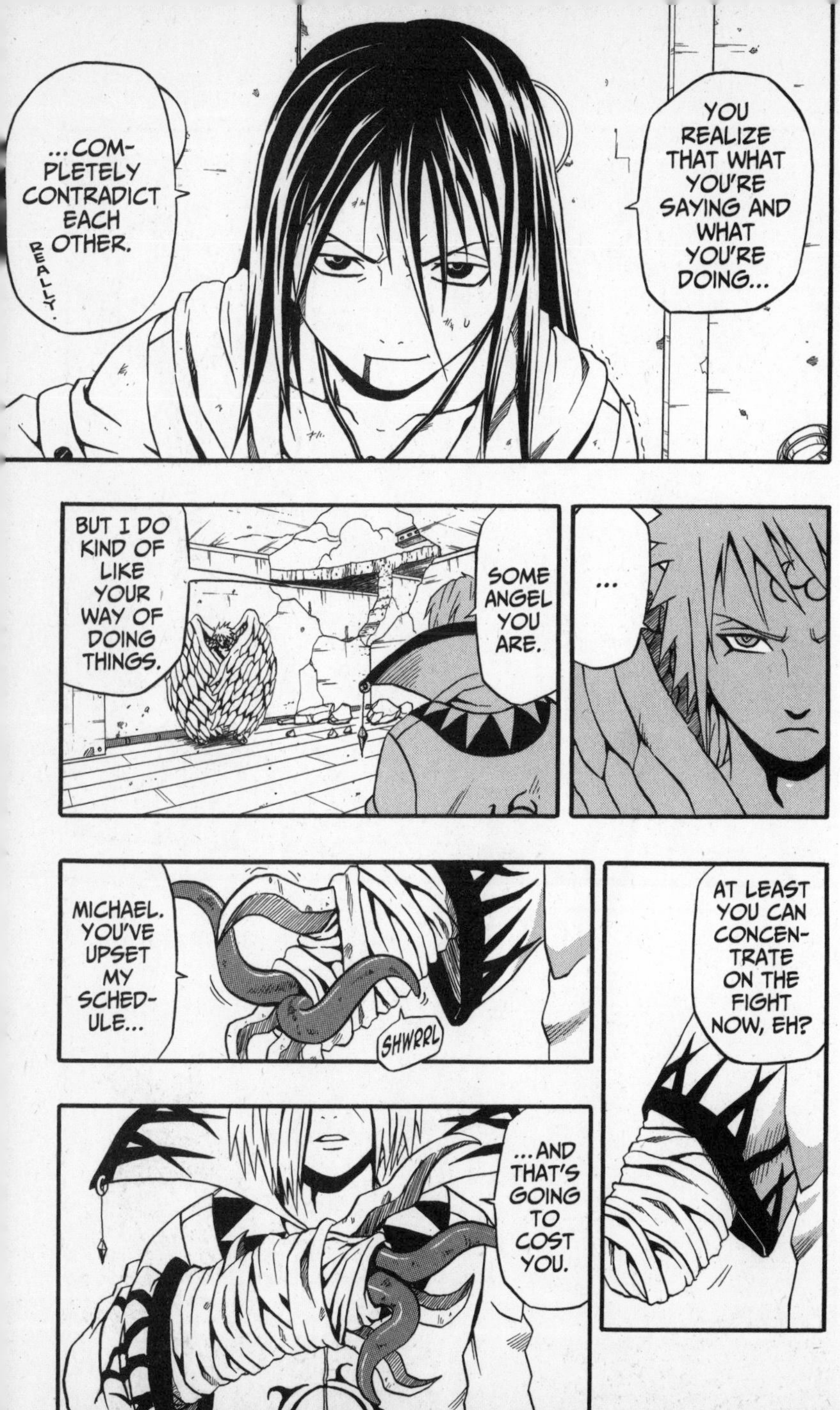
YOU REALIZE THAT WHAT YOU'RE SAYING AND WHAT YOU'RE DOING...
...COMPLETELY CONTRADICT EACH OTHER.
REALLY.
...
SOME ANGEL YOU ARE.
BUT I DO KIND OF LIKE YOUR WAY OF DOING THINGS.
AT LEAST YOU CAN CONCENTRATE ON THE FIGHT NOW, EH?
MICHAEL. YOU'VE UPSET MY SCHEDULE...
SHWRRL
...AND THAT'S GOING TO COST YOU.

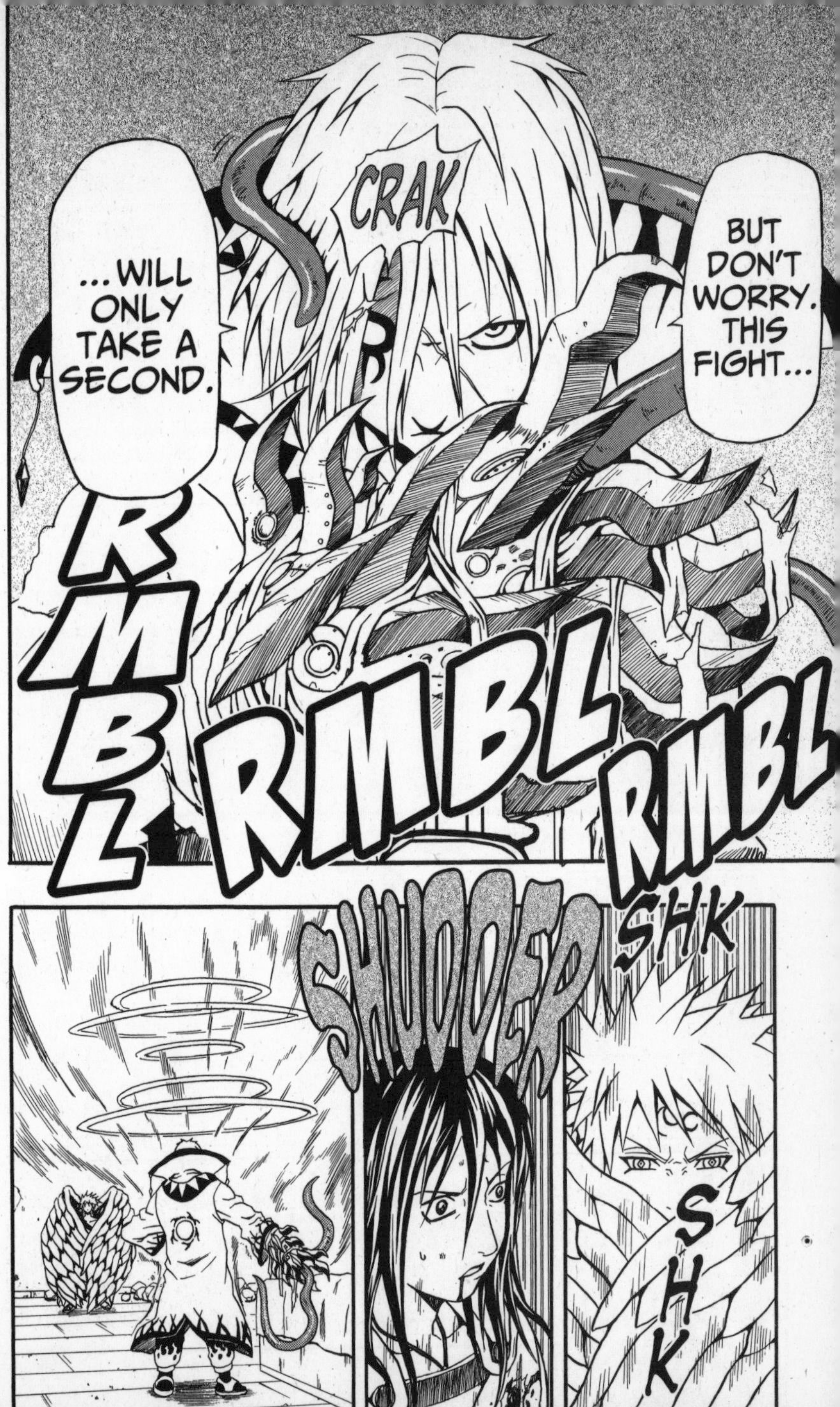
CRAK
BUT DON'T WORRY. THIS FIGHT...
...WILL ONLY TAKE A SECOND.
RMBL
RMBL
RMBL
SHK
SHK

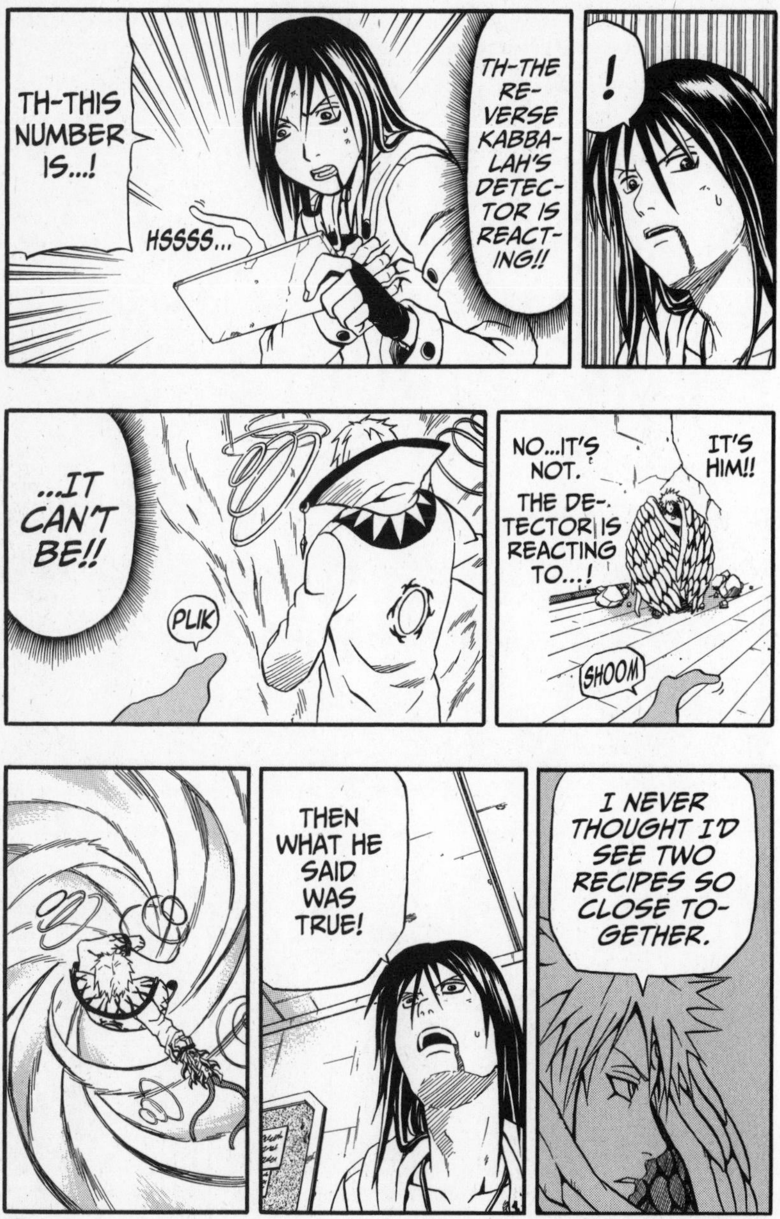
!
TH-THE REVERSE KABBALAH'S DETECTOR IS REACTING!!
TH-THIS NUMBER IS...!
HSSSS...
IT'S HIM!!
NO...IT'S NOT.
THE DETECTOR IS REACTING TO...!
SHOOM
...IT CAN'T BE!!
PLIK
I NEVER THOUGHT I'D SEE TWO RECIPES SO CLOSE TOGETHER.
THEN WHAT HE SAID WAS TRUE!

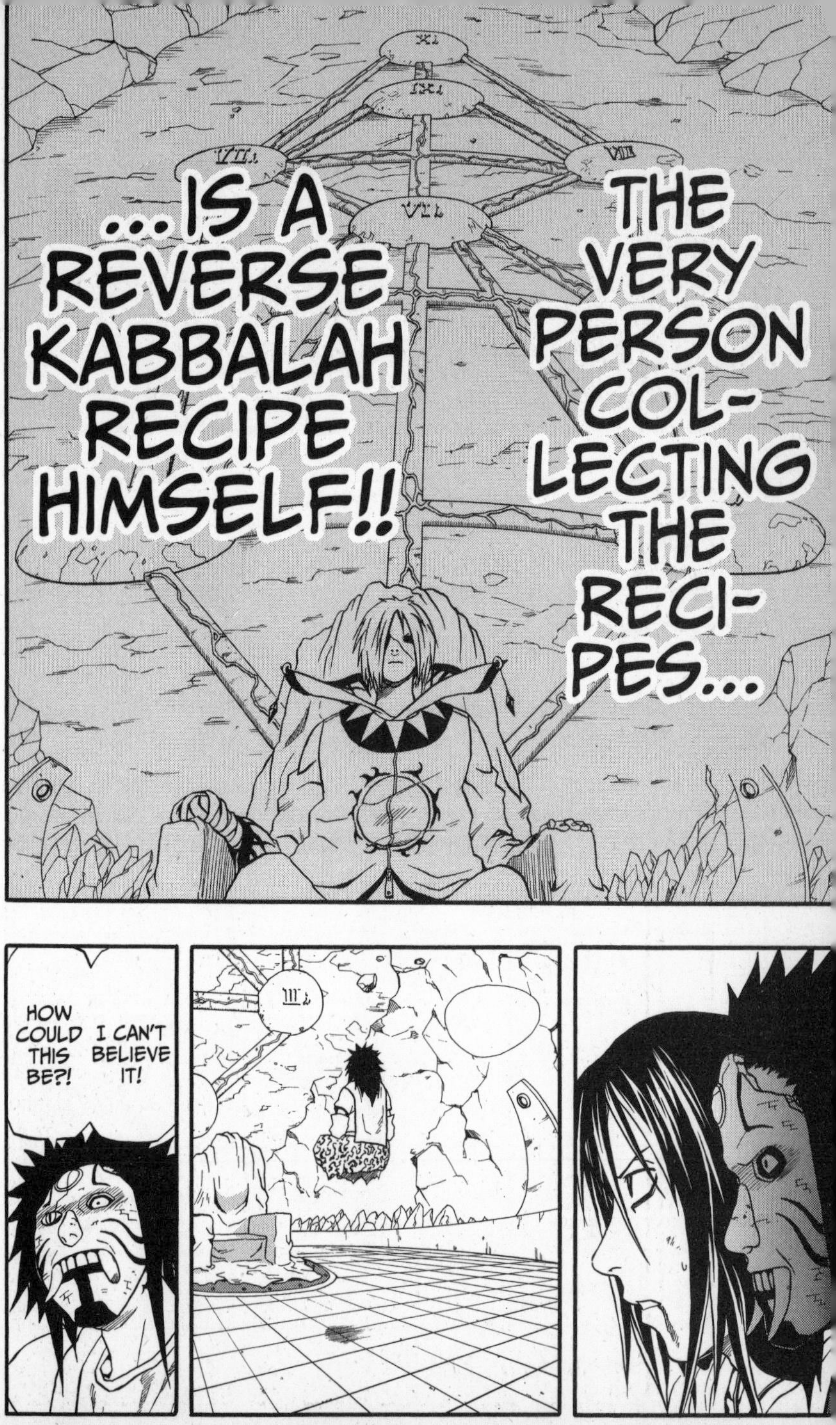
THE VERY PERSON COL-LECTING THE RECI-PES...
...IS A REVERSE KABBALAH RECIPE HIMSELF!!
I CAN'T BELIEVE IT!
HOW COULD THIS BE?!

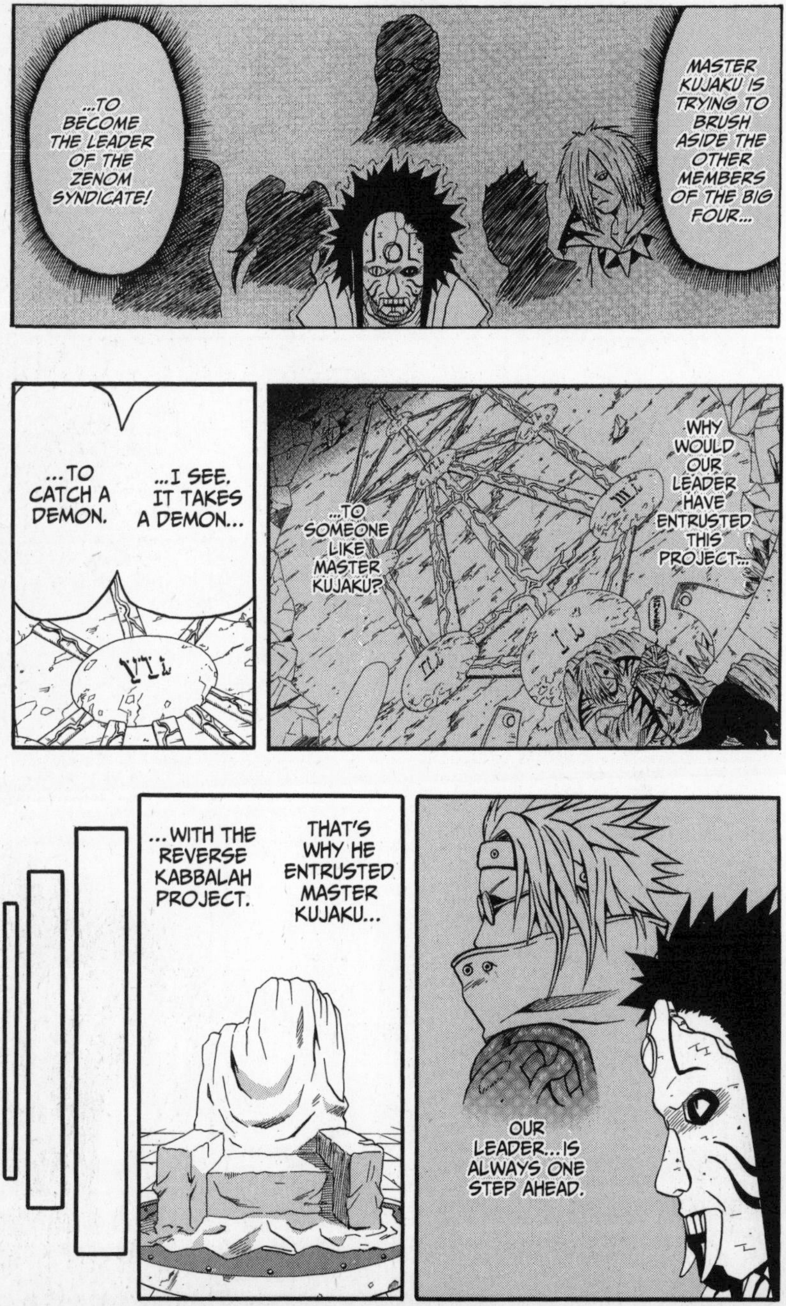
MASTER KUJAKU IS TRYING TO BRUSH ASIDE THE OTHER MEMBERS OF THE BIG FOUR...
...TO BECOME THE LEADER OF THE ZENOM SYNDICATE!
WHY WOULD OUR LEADER HAVE ENTRUSTED THIS PROJECT...
...TO SOMEONE LIKE MASTER KUJAKU?
...I SEE. IT TAKES A DEMON...
...TO CATCH A DEMON.
OUR LEADER...IS ALWAYS ONE STEP AHEAD.
THAT'S WHY HE ENTRUSTED MASTER KUJAKU...
...WITH THE REVERSE KABBALAH PROJECT.

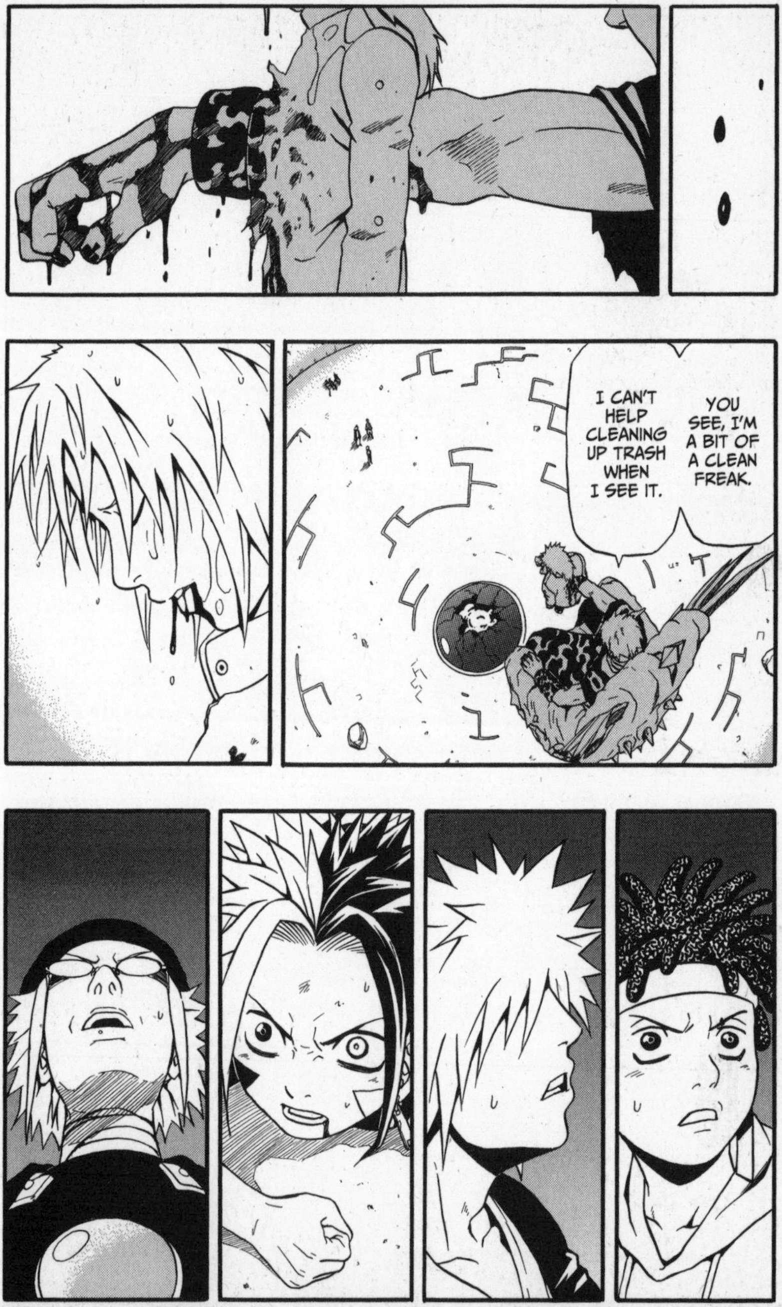
YOU SEE, I'M A BIT OF A CLEAN FREAK.
I CAN'T HELP CLEANING UP TRASH WHEN I SEE IT.

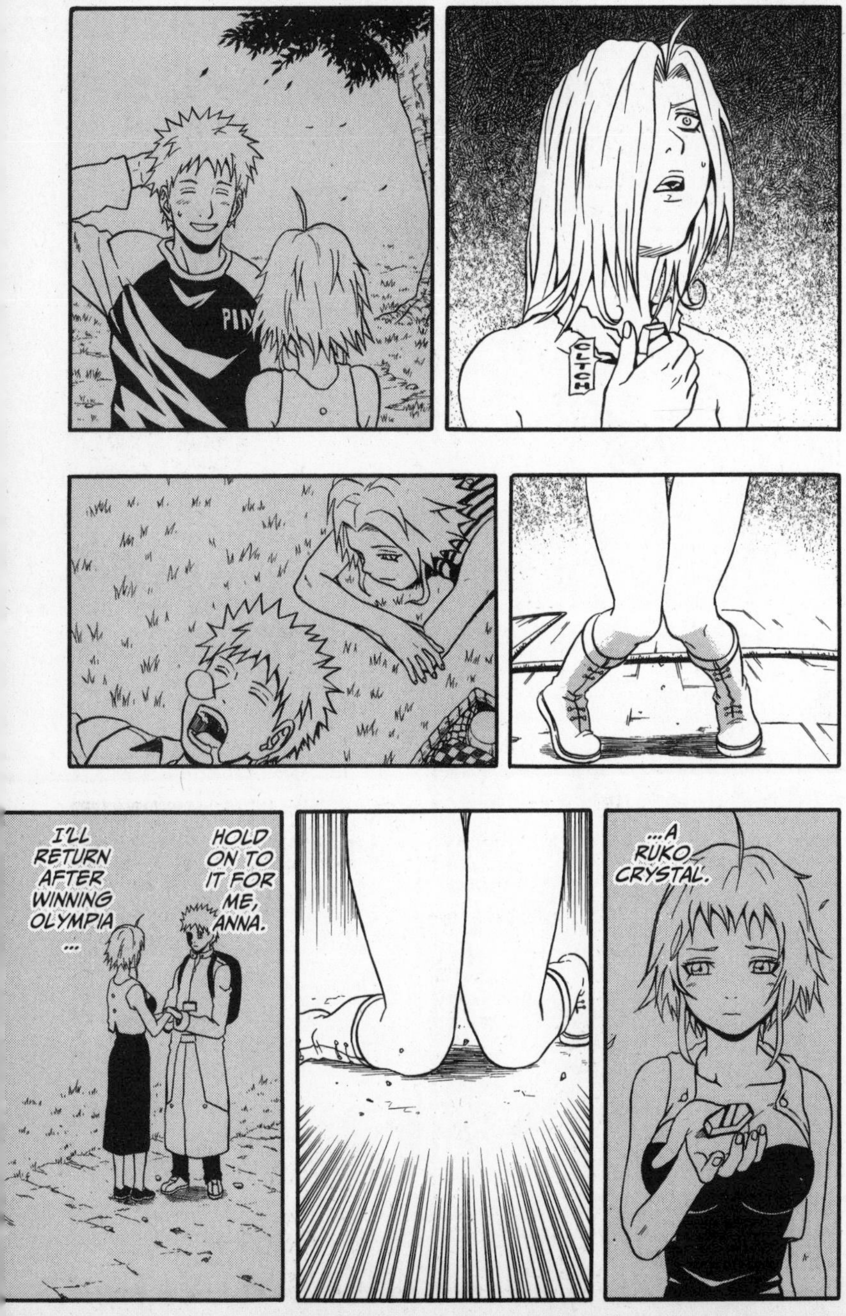
CLTCH
...A RUKO CRYSTAL.
HOLD ON TO IT FOR ME, ANNA.
I'LL RETURN AFTER WINNING OLYMPIA ...

I PROMISE.

...AND THEN WE CAN MAKE RINGS OUT OF IT...FOR BOTH OF US.

PLEASE UNDERSTAND. THIS GUY IS NOTHING MORE THAN AN EXHAUSTED BATTERY. HE HAS NO SPIRIT LEFT.

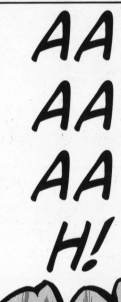

AA AA AA H!

CRAK

SHLKK

TRASH BELONGS IN A TRASHCAN, DOES IT NOT?

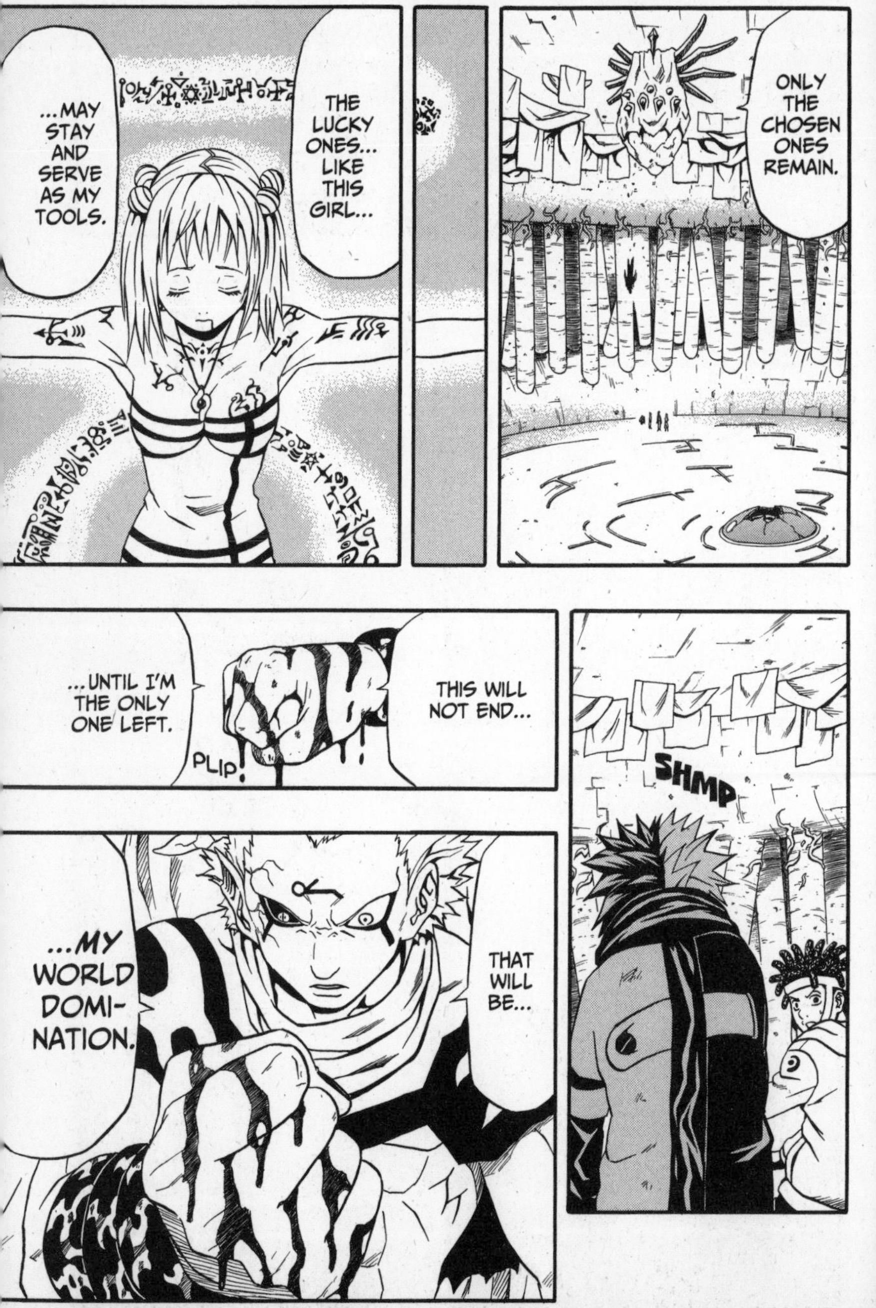
ONLY THE CHOSEN ONES REMAIN.
THE LUCKY ONES... LIKE THIS GIRL...
...MAY STAY AND SERVE AS MY TOOLS.
SHMP
THIS WILL NOT END...
...UNTIL I'M THE ONLY ONE LEFT.
PLIP!
THAT WILL BE...
...MY WORLD DOMINATION.

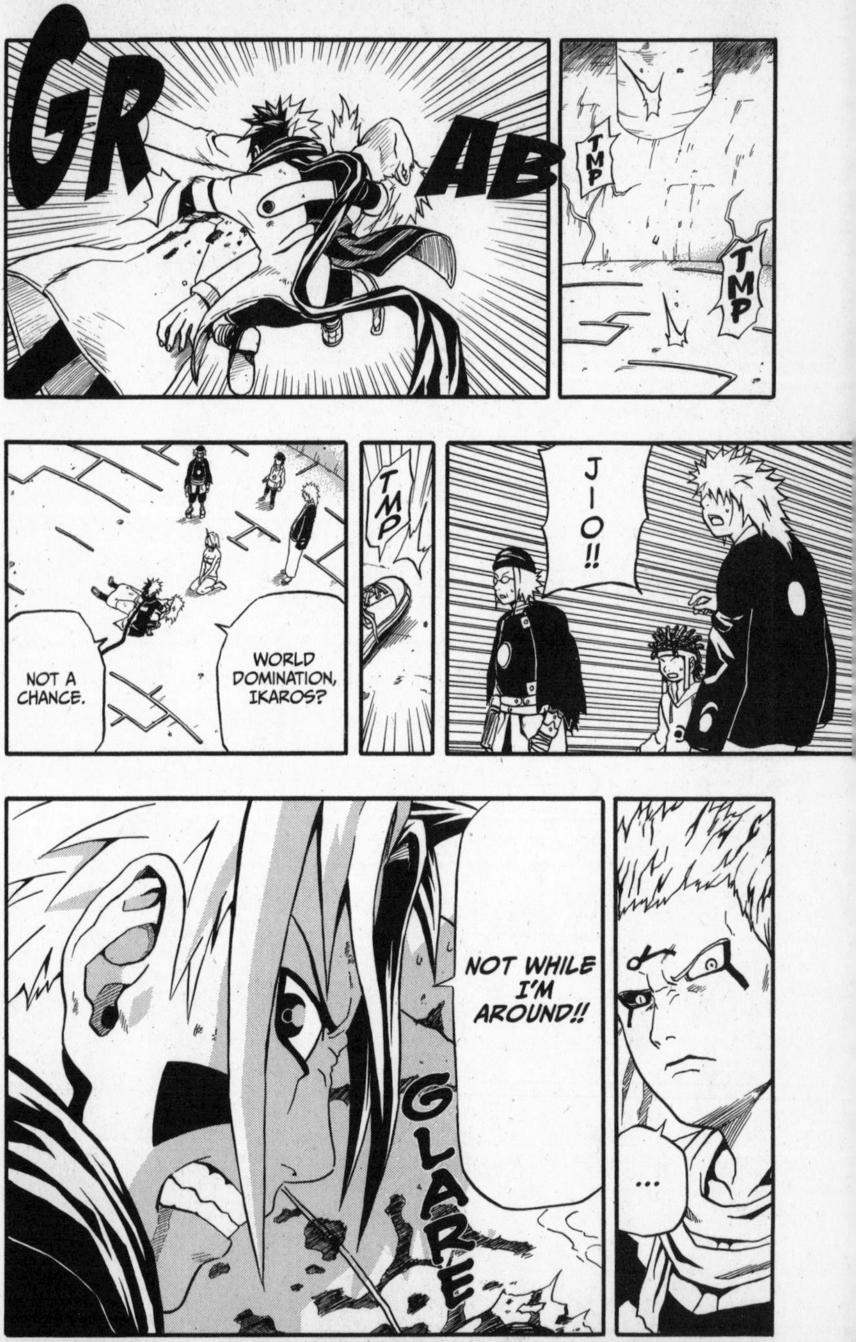
TMP
TMP
GRAB
JIO!!
TMP
WORLD DOMINATION, IKAROS?
NOT A CHANCE.
...
NOT WHILE I'M AROUND!!
GLARE

[redacted]

CHAPTER 47 HEART

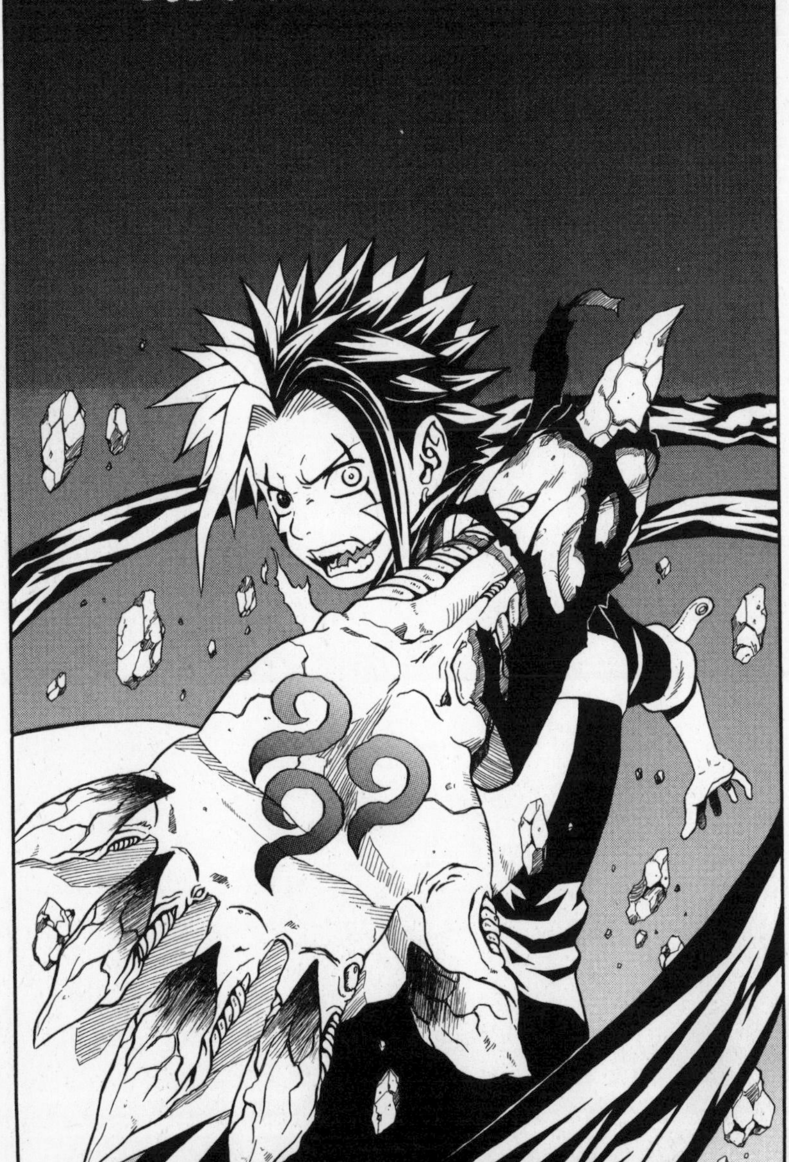

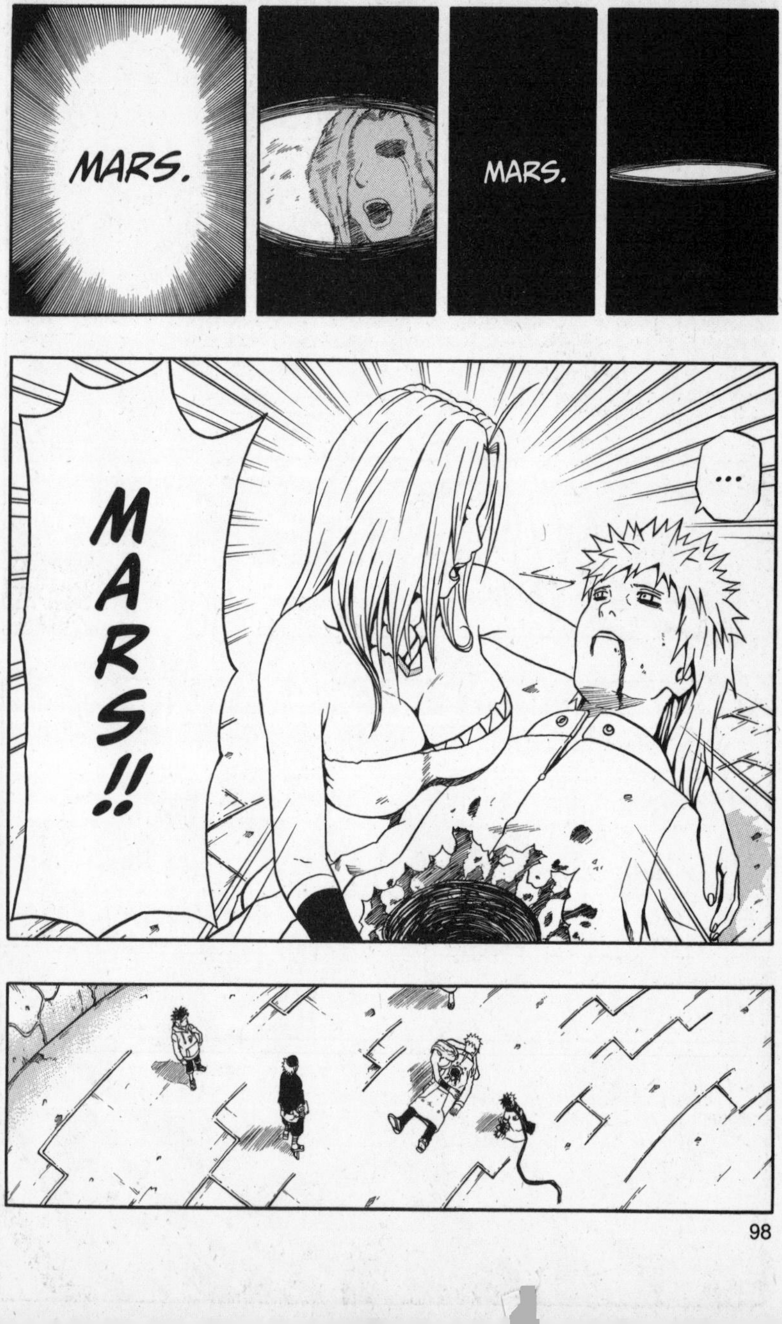
MARS.
MARS.
...
MARS!!

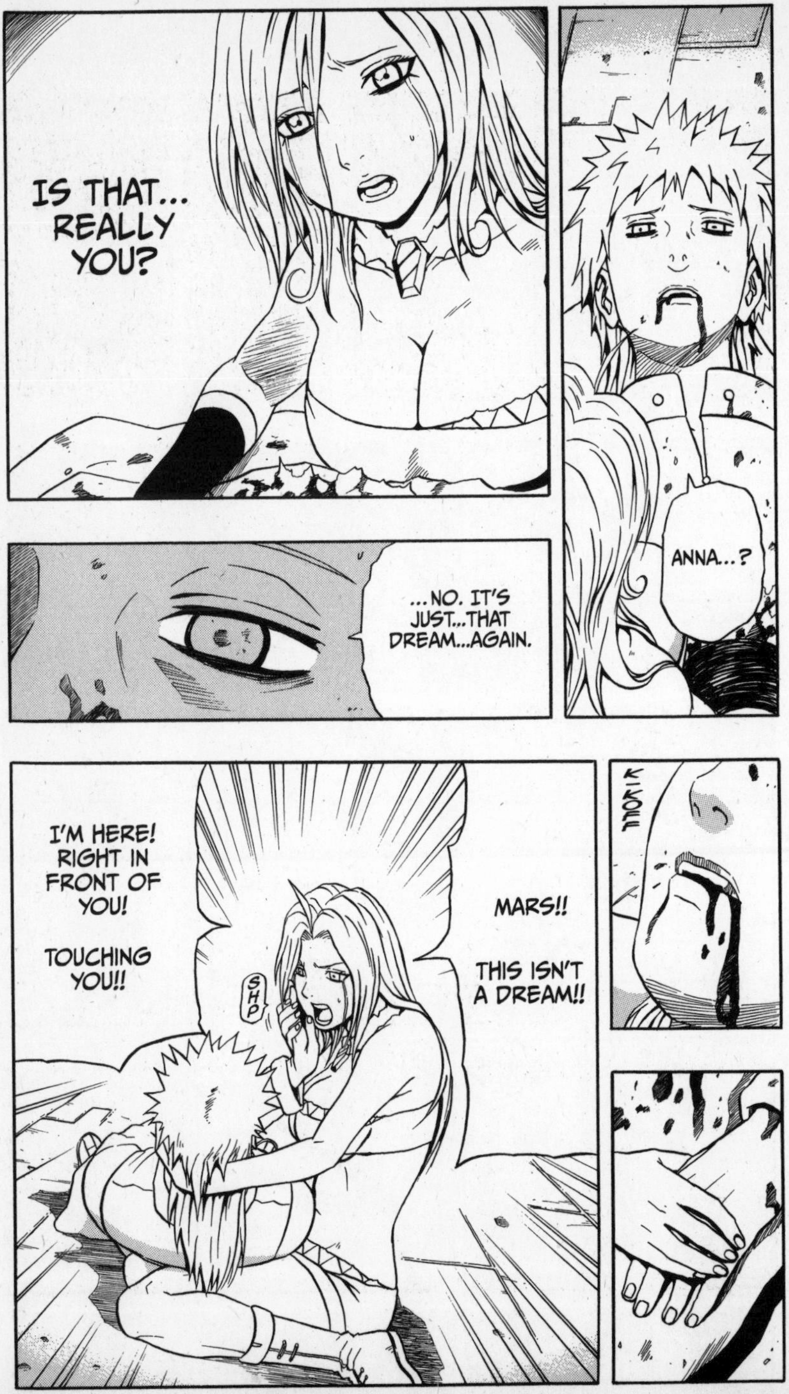
ANNA...?
IS THAT... REALLY YOU?
...NO. IT'S JUST...THAT DREAM...AGAIN.
K-KOFF
MARS!!
THIS ISN'T A DREAM!!
I'M HERE! RIGHT IN FRONT OF YOU!
TOUCHING YOU!!
SHP

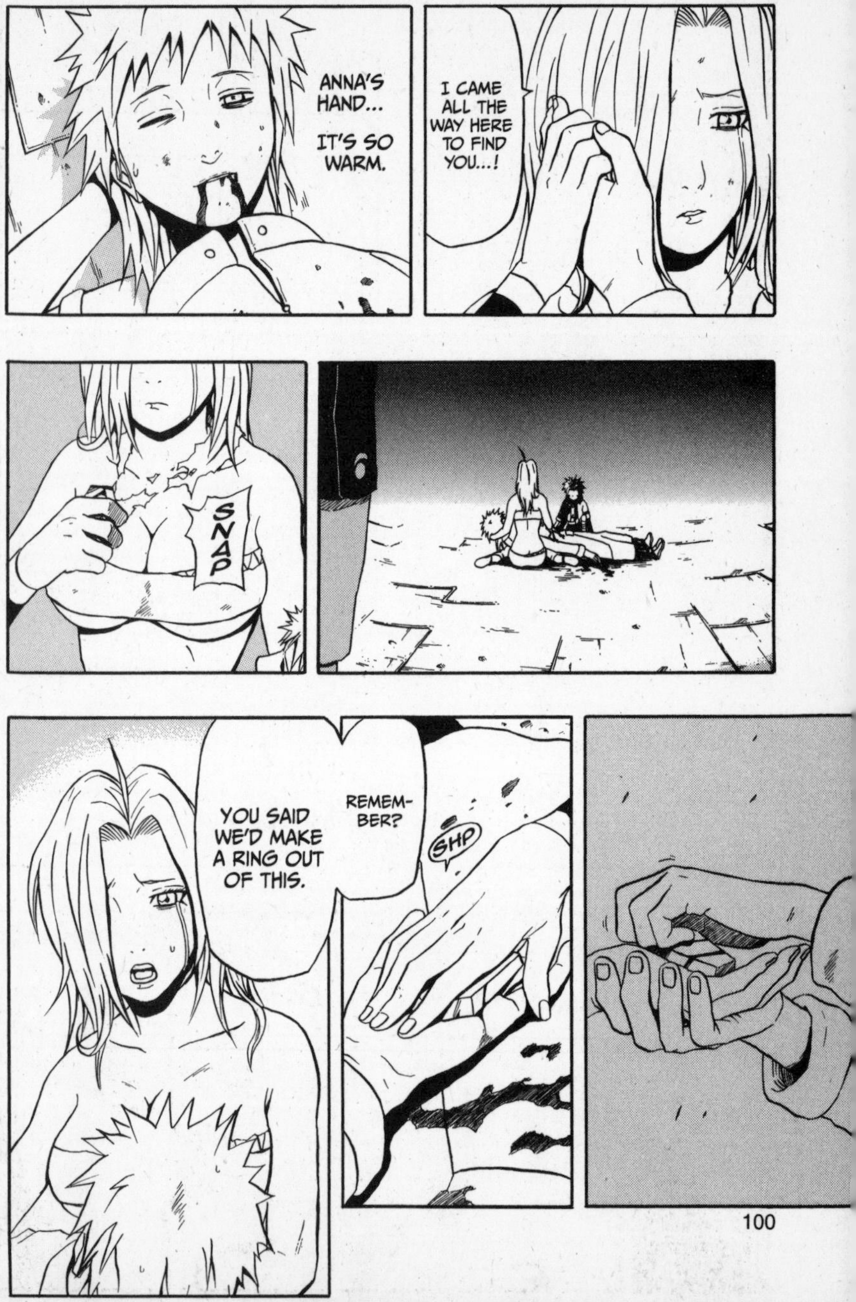
I CAME ALL THE WAY HERE TO FIND YOU...!
ANNA'S HAND...
IT'S SO WARM.
SNAP
REMEM- BER?
YOU SAID WE'D MAKE A RING OUT OF THIS.
SHP

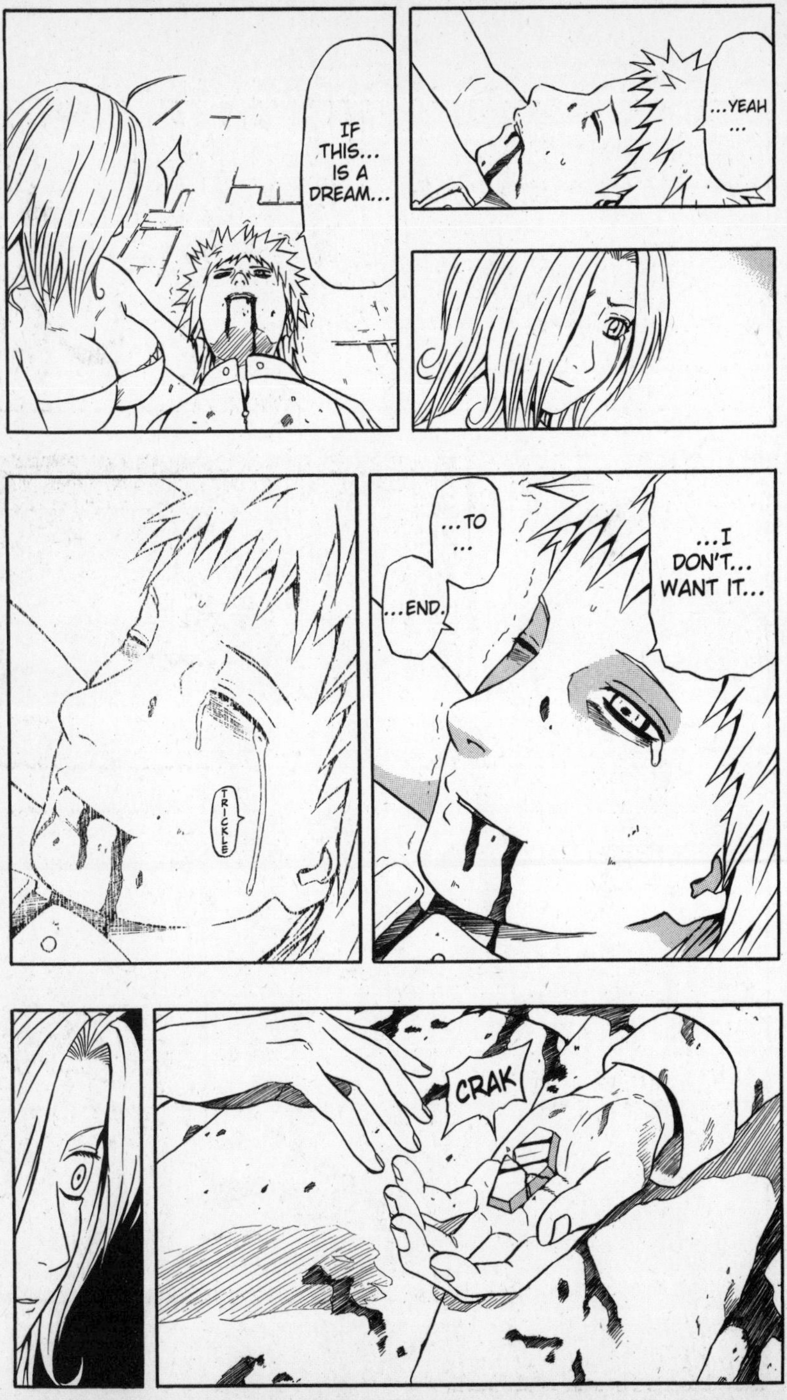
...YEAH ...
IF THIS... IS A DREAM...
...I DON'T... WANT IT...
...TO ...
...END.
TRICKLE
CRAK

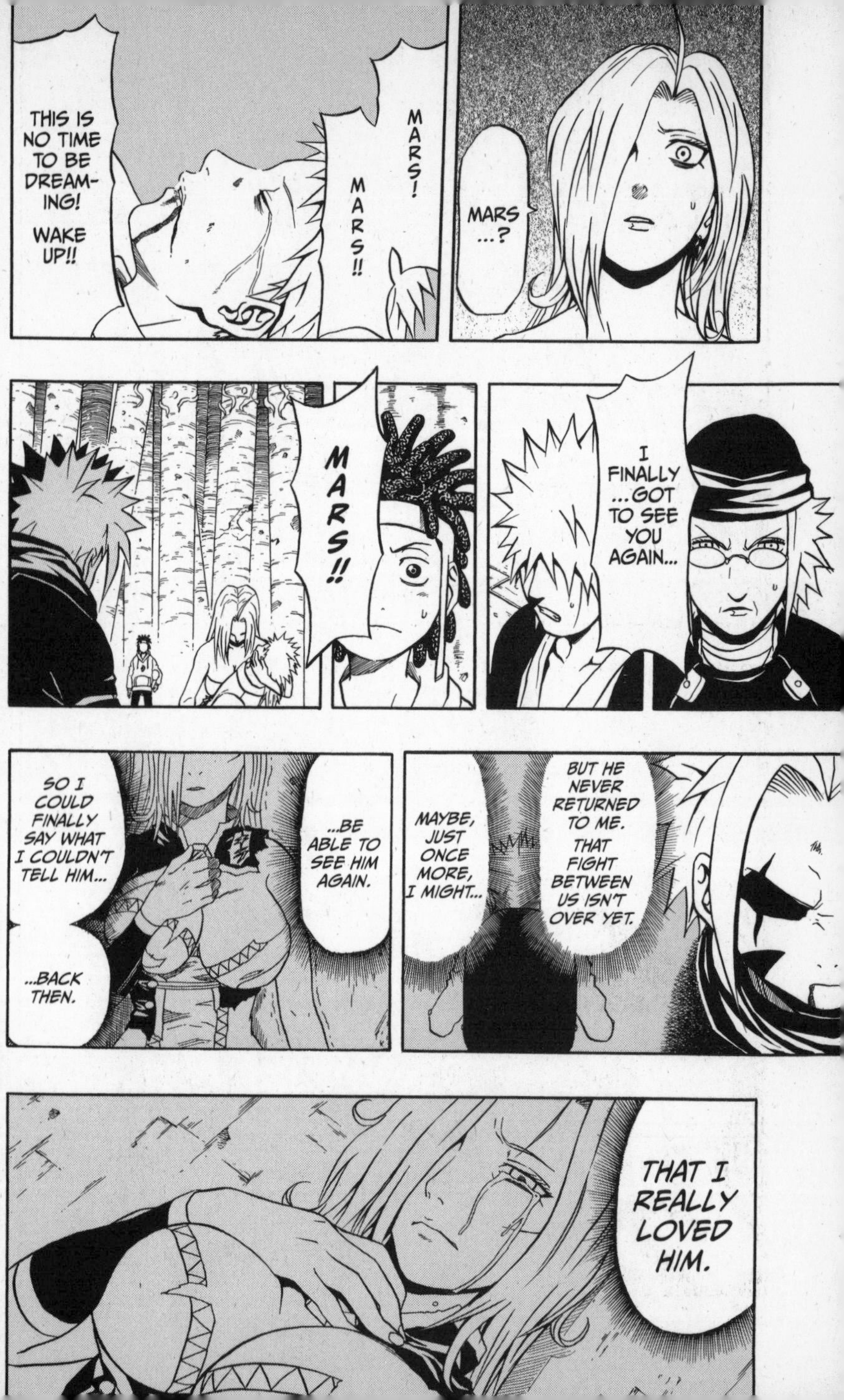
MARS ...?
MARS!
MARS!!
THIS IS NO TIME TO BE DREAMING!
WAKE UP!!
I FINALLY ...GOT TO SEE YOU AGAIN...
MARS!!
BUT HE NEVER RETURNED TO ME.
THAT FIGHT BETWEEN US ISN'T OVER YET.
MAYBE, JUST ONCE MORE, I MIGHT...
...BE ABLE TO SEE HIM AGAIN.
SO I COULD FINALLY SAY WHAT I COULDN'T TELL HIM...
...BACK THEN.
THAT I REALLY LOVED HIM.

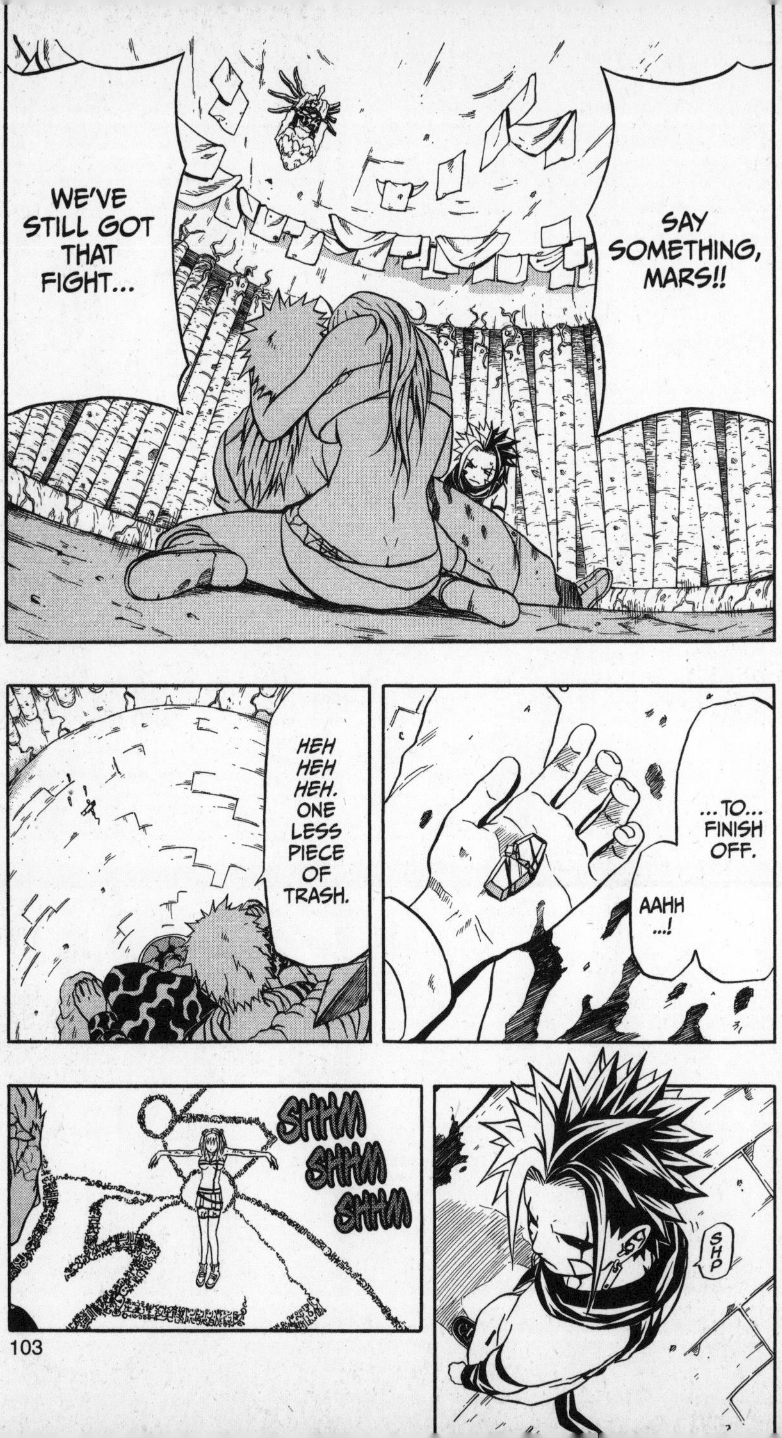
SAY SOMETHING, MARS!!
WE'VE STILL GOT THAT FIGHT...
...TO... FINISH OFF.
AAHH ...!
HEH HEH HEH. ONE LESS PIECE OF TRASH.
SHP
SHHM SHHM SHHM

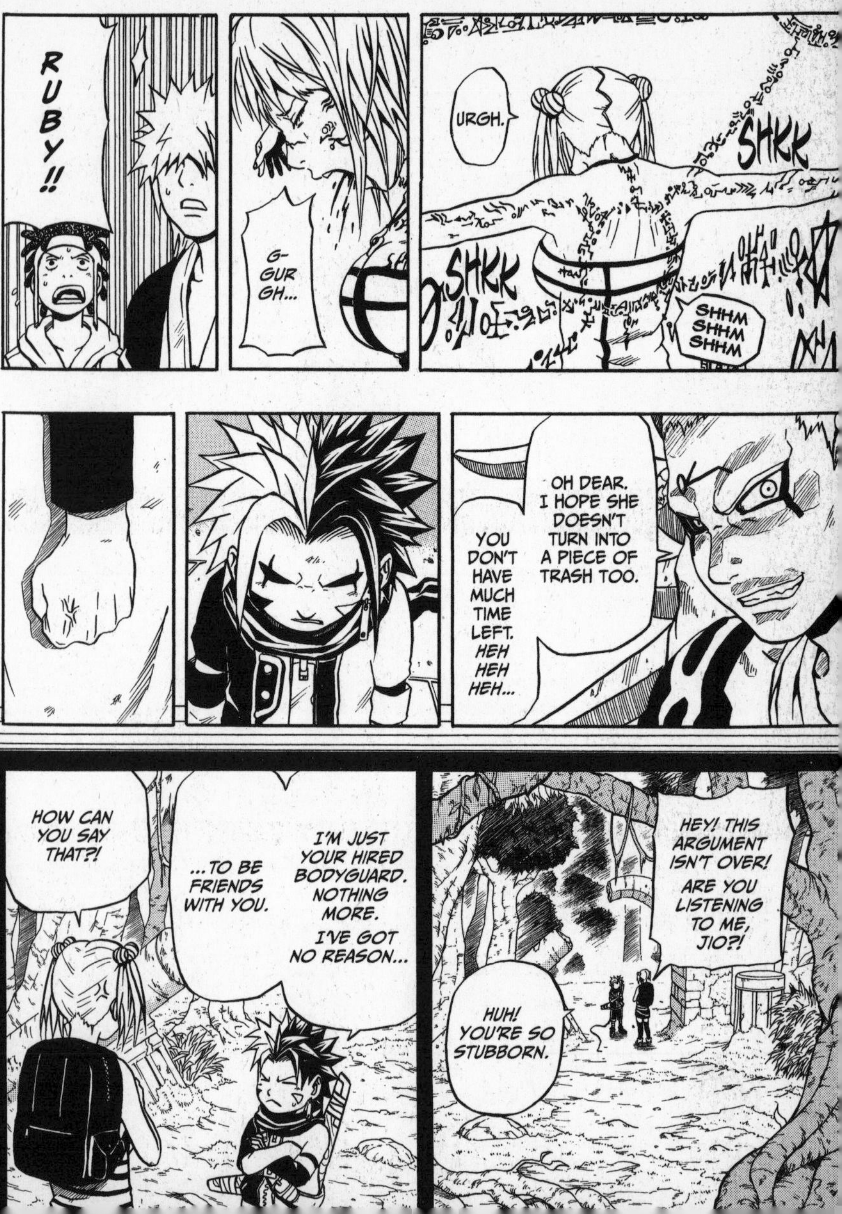
URGH.
SHKK
SHKK
SHHM SHHM SHHM
G-GURGH...
RUBY!!
OH DEAR. I HOPE SHE DOESN'T TURN INTO A PIECE OF TRASH TOO.
YOU DON'T HAVE MUCH TIME LEFT. HEH HEH HEH...
HEY! THIS ARGUMENT ISN'T OVER! ARE YOU LISTENING TO ME, JIO?!
HUH! YOU'RE SO STUBBORN.
I'M JUST YOUR HIRED BODYGUARD. NOTHING MORE. I'VE GOT NO REASON...
...TO BE FRIENDS WITH YOU.
HOW CAN YOU SAY THAT?!

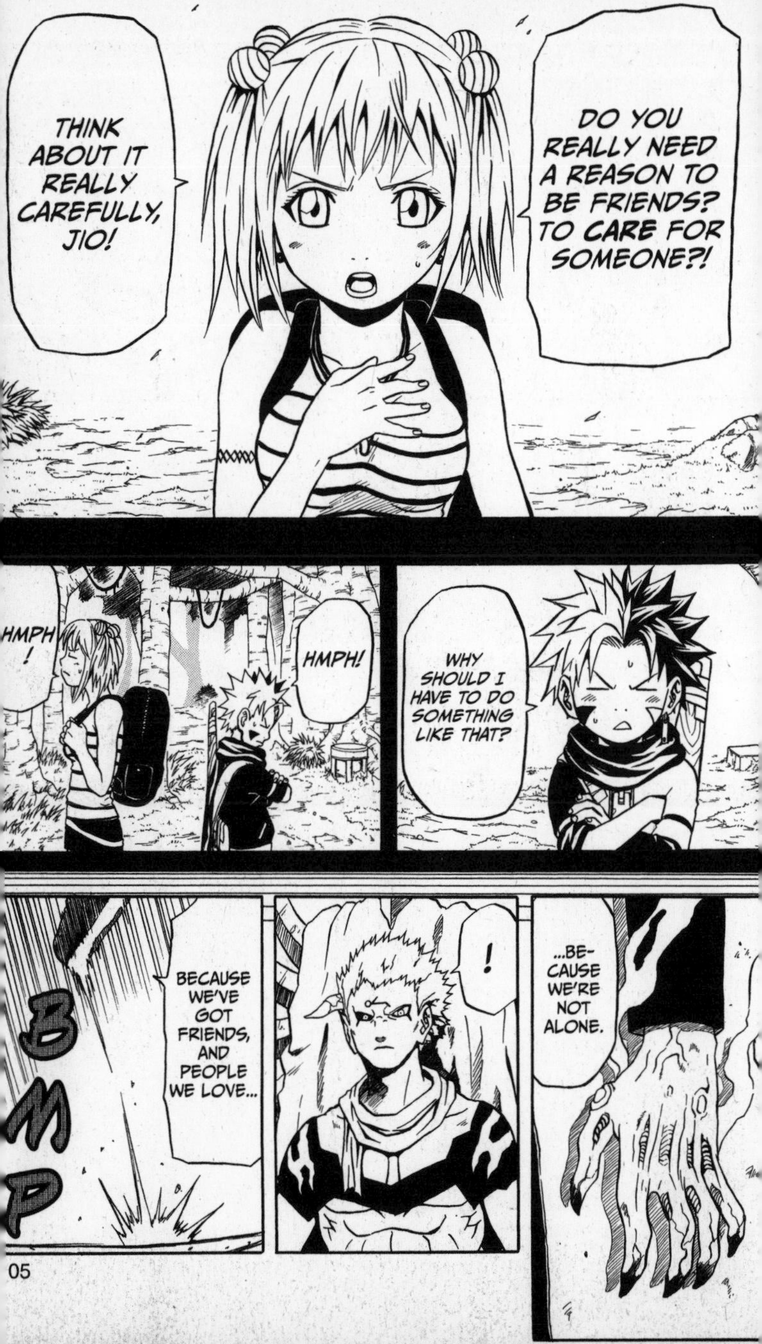
DO YOU REALLY NEED A REASON TO BE FRIENDS? TO **CARE** FOR SOMEONE?!
THINK ABOUT IT REALLY CAREFULLY, JIO!
WHY SHOULD I HAVE TO DO SOMETHING LIKE THAT?
HMPH!
HMPH!
...BE-CAUSE WE'RE NOT ALONE.
!
BECAUSE WE'VE GOT FRIENDS, AND PEOPLE WE LOVE...
BMP

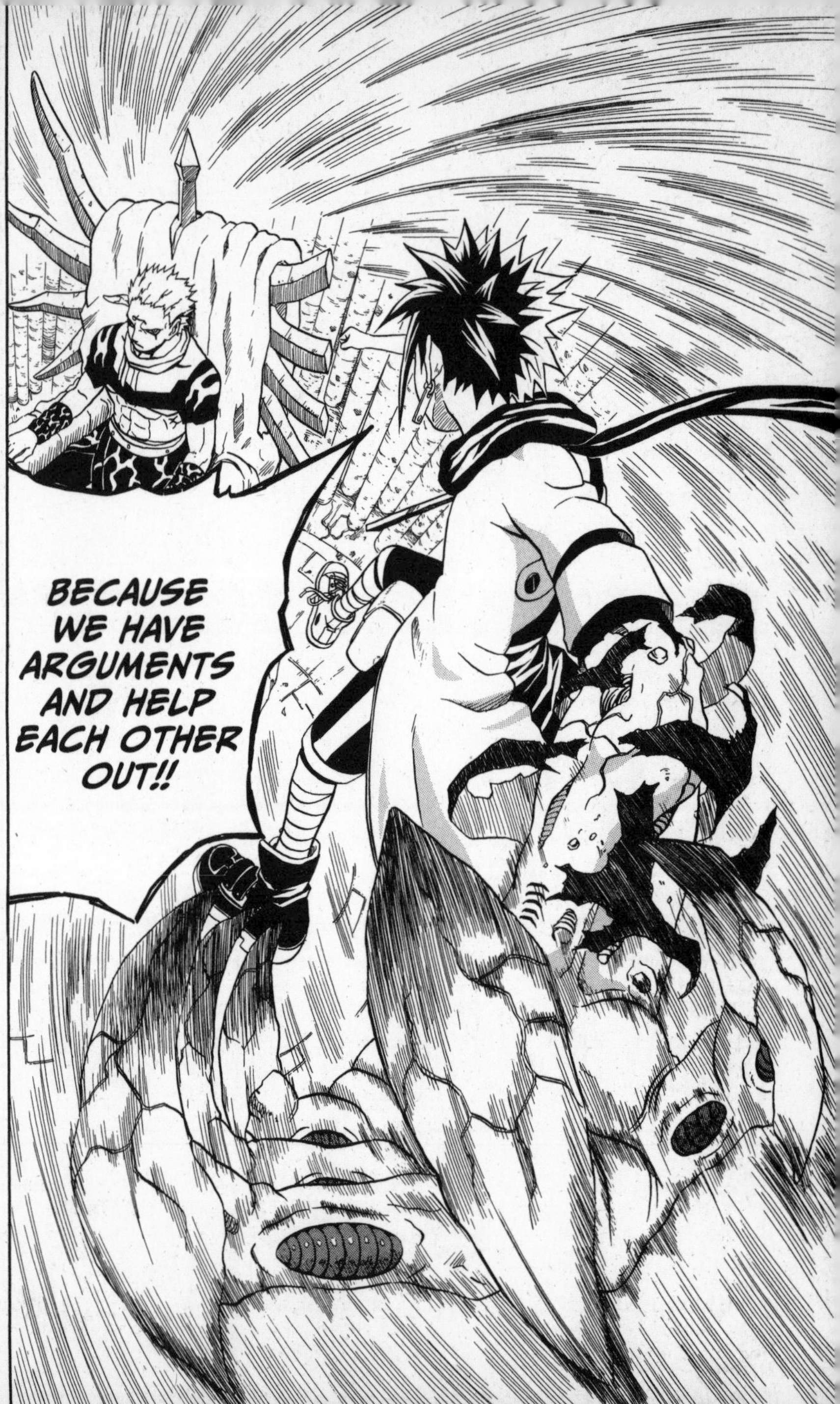
BECAUSE WE HAVE ARGUMENTS AND HELP EACH OTHER OUT!!

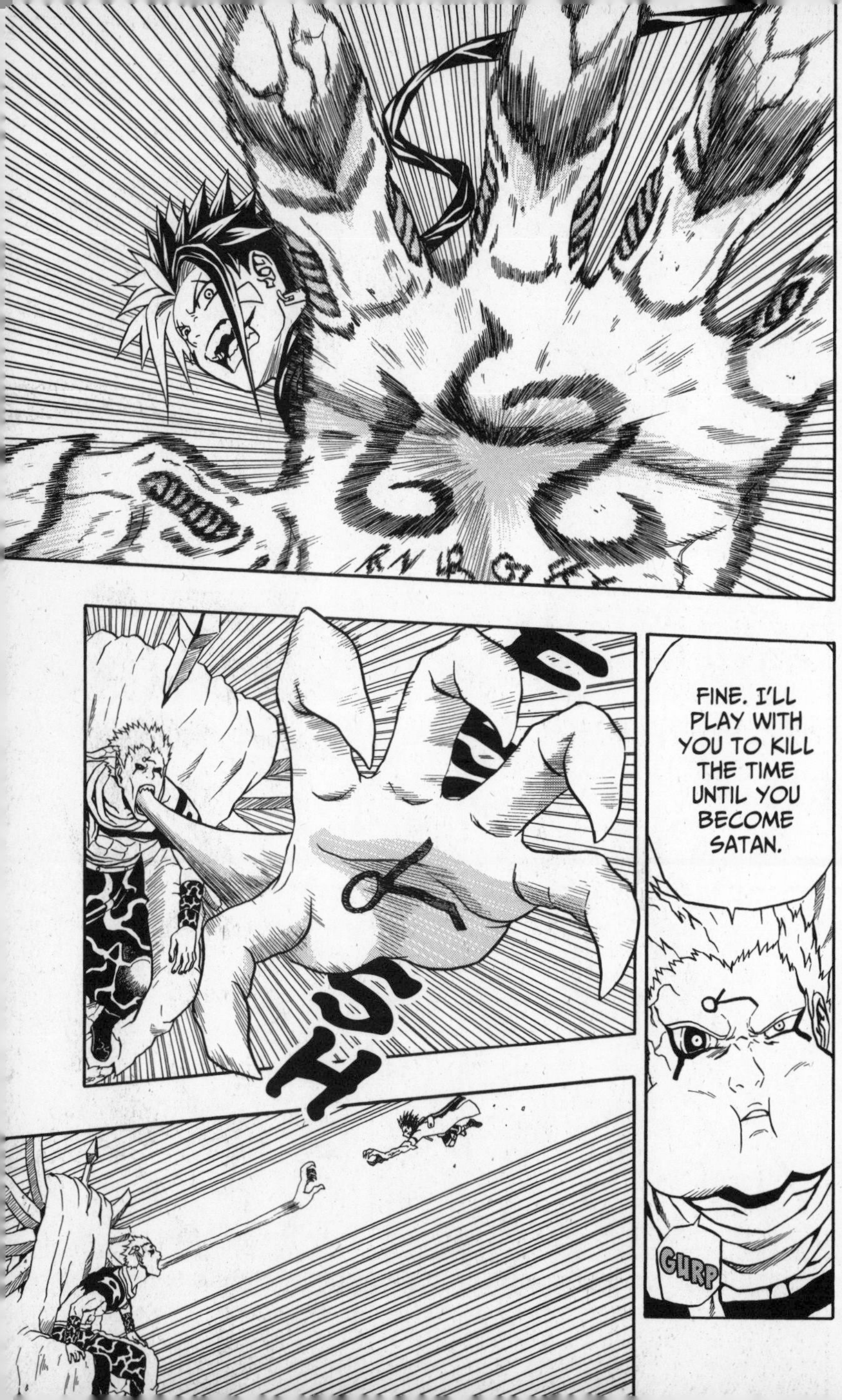
FINE. I'LL PLAY WITH YOU TO KILL THE TIME UNTIL YOU BECOME SATAN.
GURP

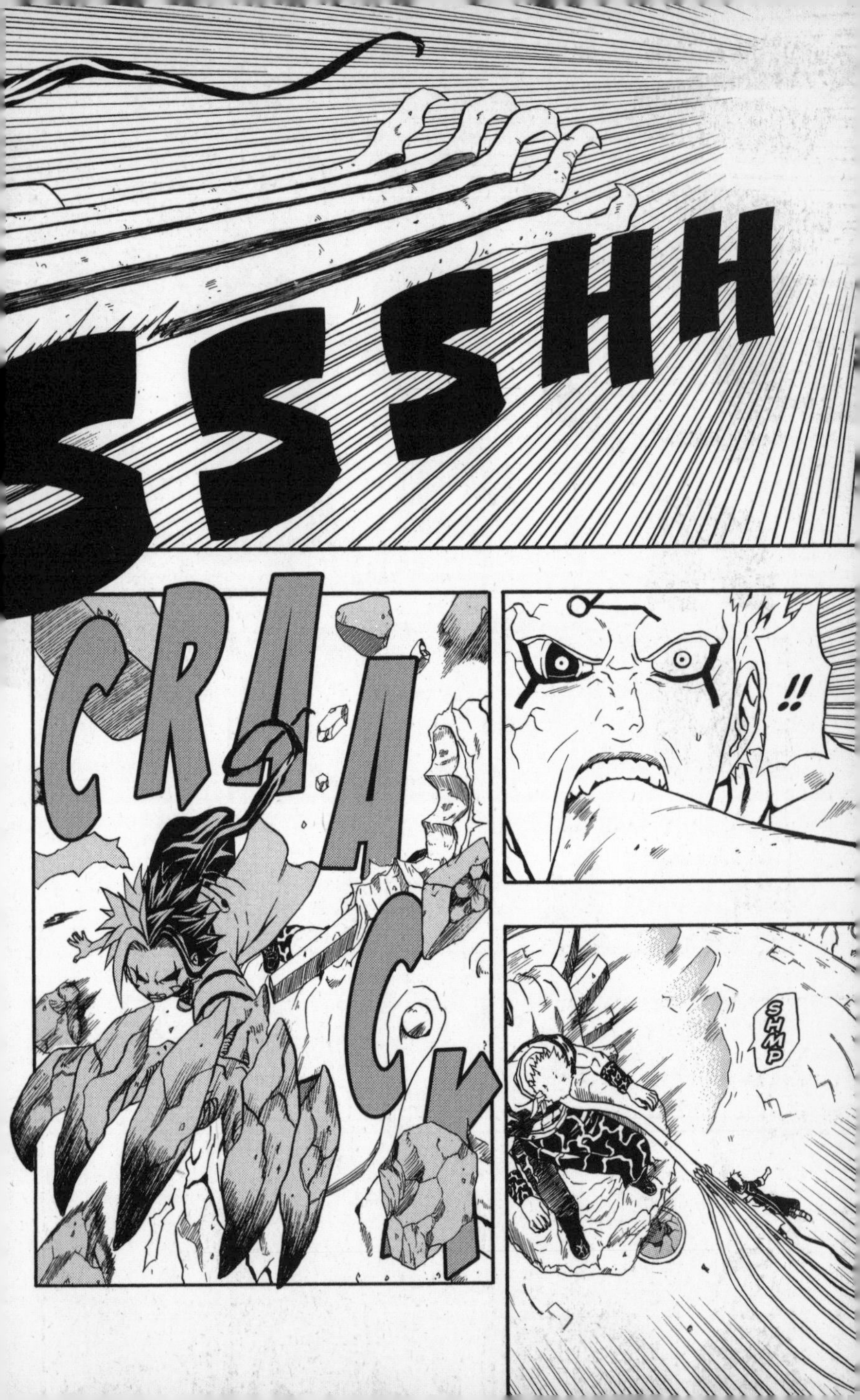
SSSHH
!!
CRAAACK
SHMP

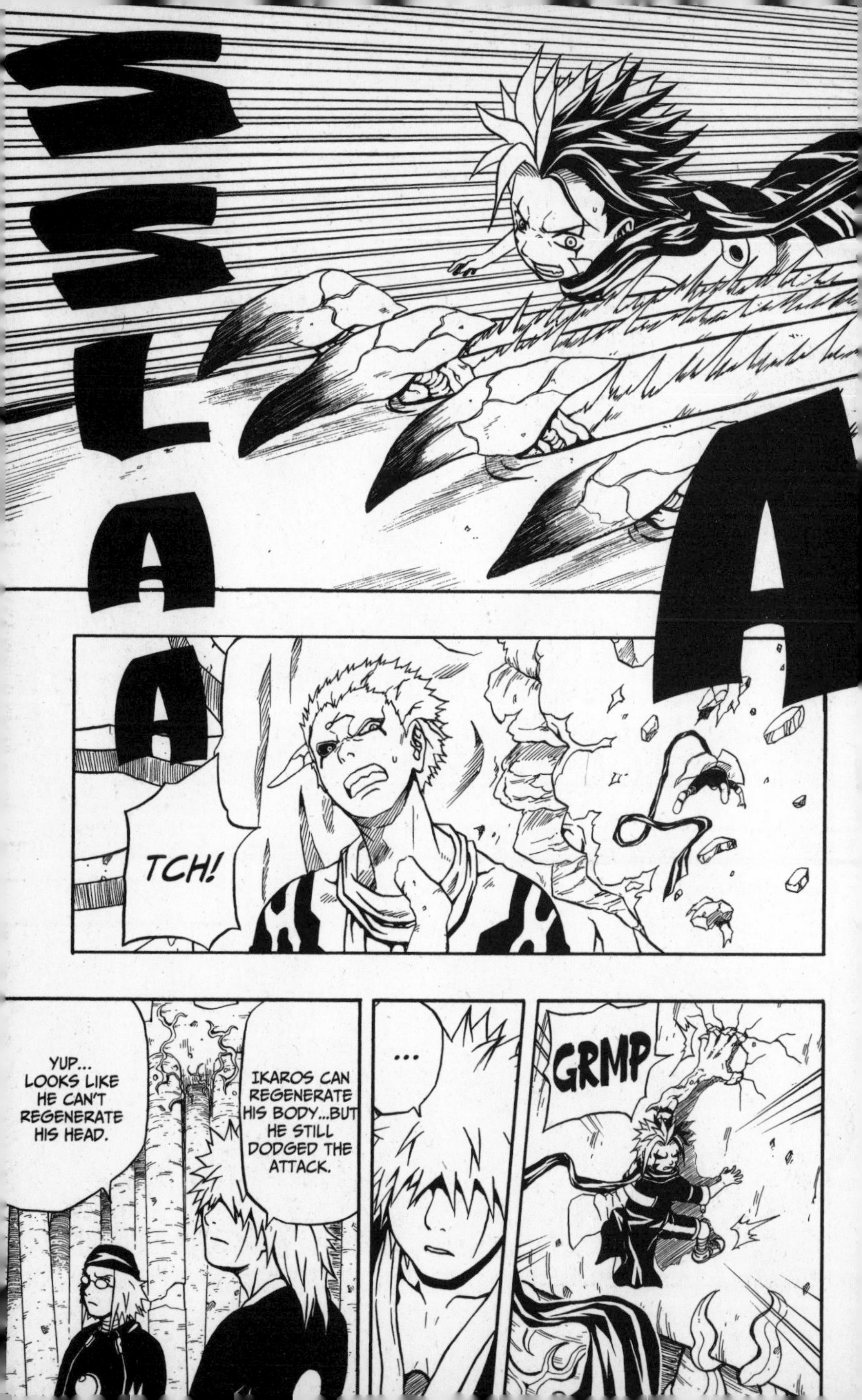
SSLAAA
TCH!
GRMP
...
IKAROS CAN REGENERATE HIS BODY...BUT HE STILL DODGED THE ATTACK.
YUP... LOOKS LIKE HE CAN'T REGENERATE HIS HEAD.

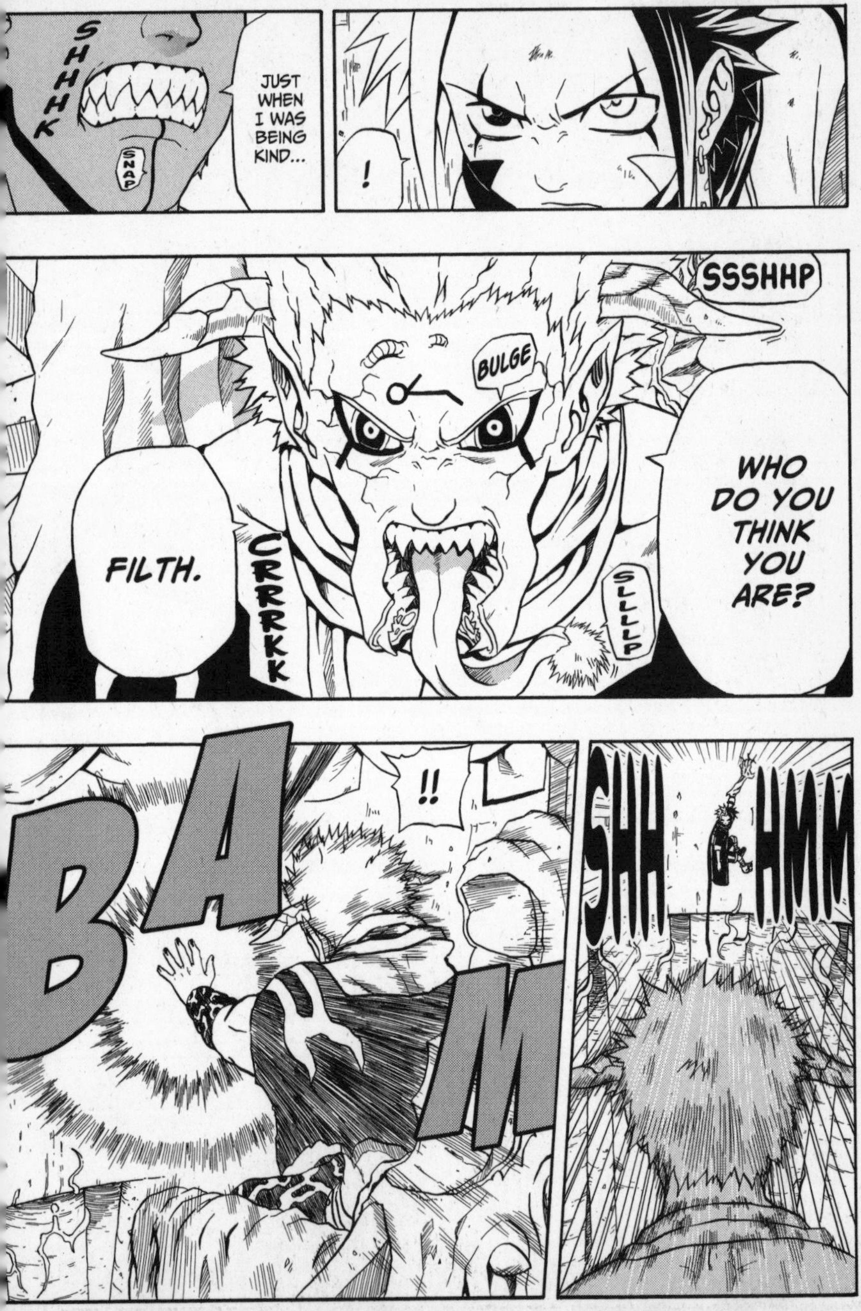
!
JUST WHEN I WAS BEING KIND...
SHHHK
SNAP
SSSHHP
BULGE
WHO DO YOU THINK YOU ARE?
SLLLLP
CRRRKK
FILTH.
SHH HMM
!!
BAM

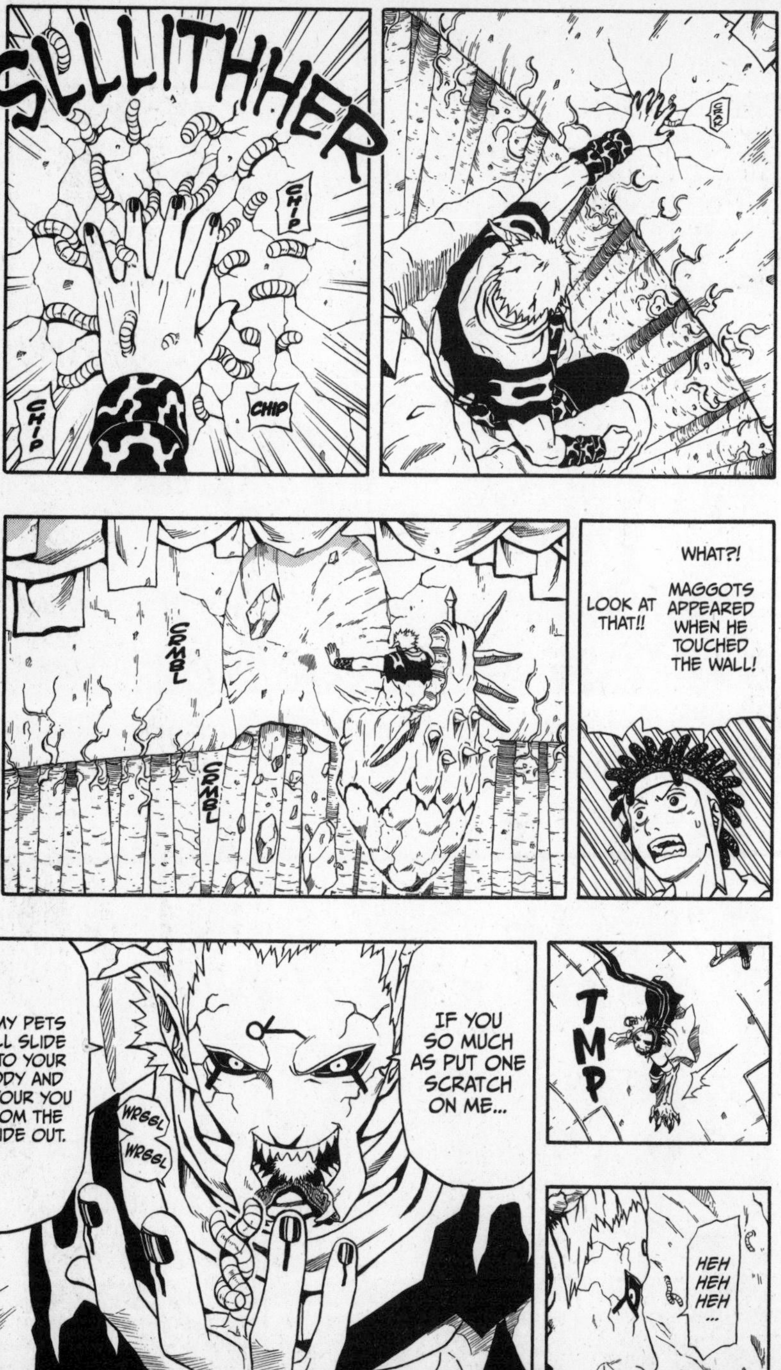
CRAK
SLLLITHHER
CHIP
CHIP
CHIP
WHAT?!
MAGGOTS APPEARED WHEN HE TOUCHED THE WALL!
LOOK AT THAT!!
CRMBL
CRMBL
TMP
HEH HEH HEH ...
IF YOU SO MUCH AS PUT ONE SCRATCH ON ME...
...MY PETS WILL SLIDE INTO YOUR BODY AND DEVOUR YOU FROM THE INSIDE OUT.
WRGGL
WRGGL

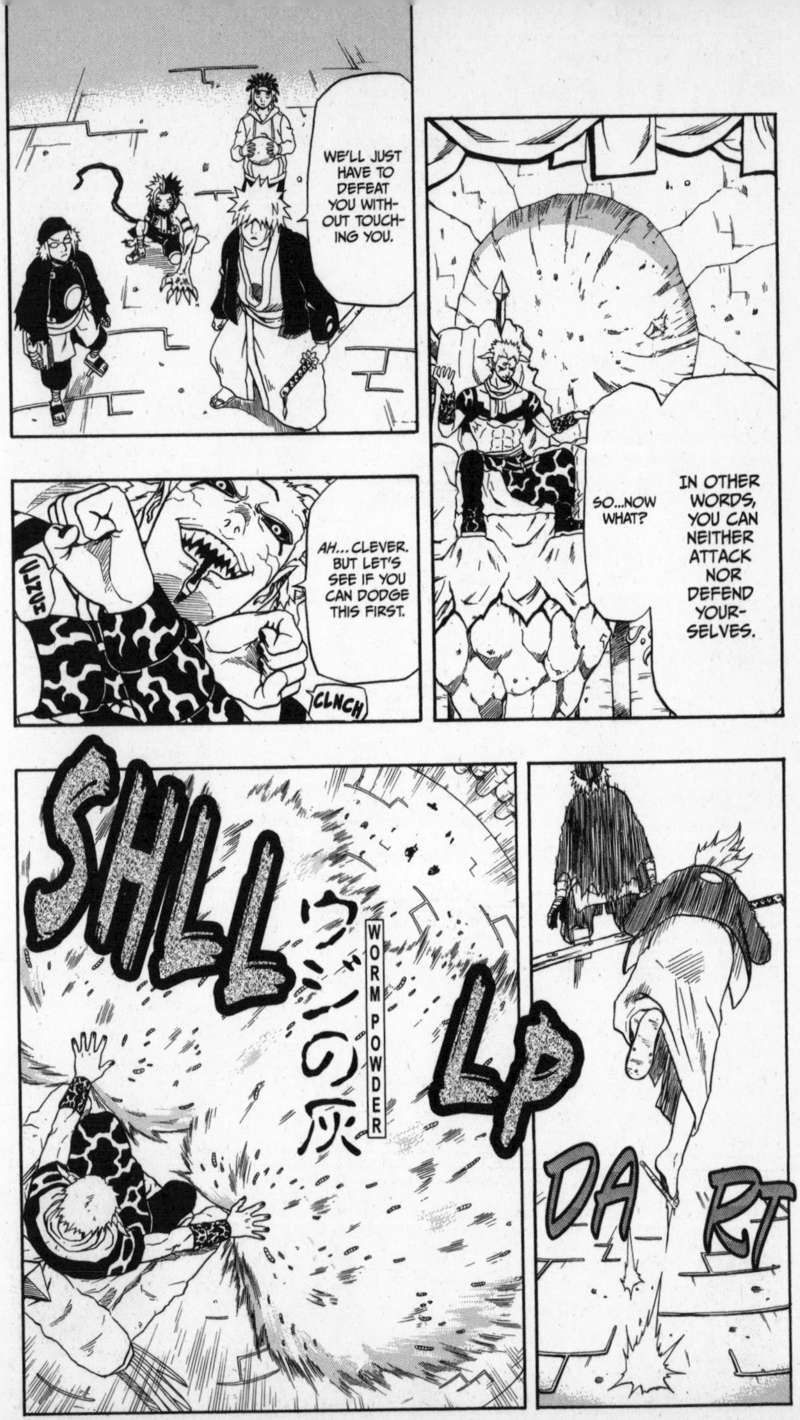
IN OTHER WORDS, YOU CAN NEITHER ATTACK NOR DEFEND YOURSELVES.
SO...NOW WHAT?
WE'LL JUST HAVE TO DEFEAT YOU WITHOUT TOUCHING YOU.
AH... CLEVER. BUT LET'S SEE IF YOU CAN DODGE THIS FIRST.
CLNCH
CLNCH
DART
SHLLLP
ウジの灰
WORM POWDER

THE FLOOR WILL SOON BLOOM WITH THE RED FLOWERS OF YOUR BLOOD.

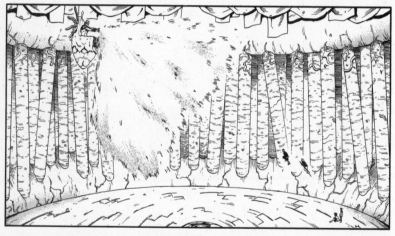

TCH!

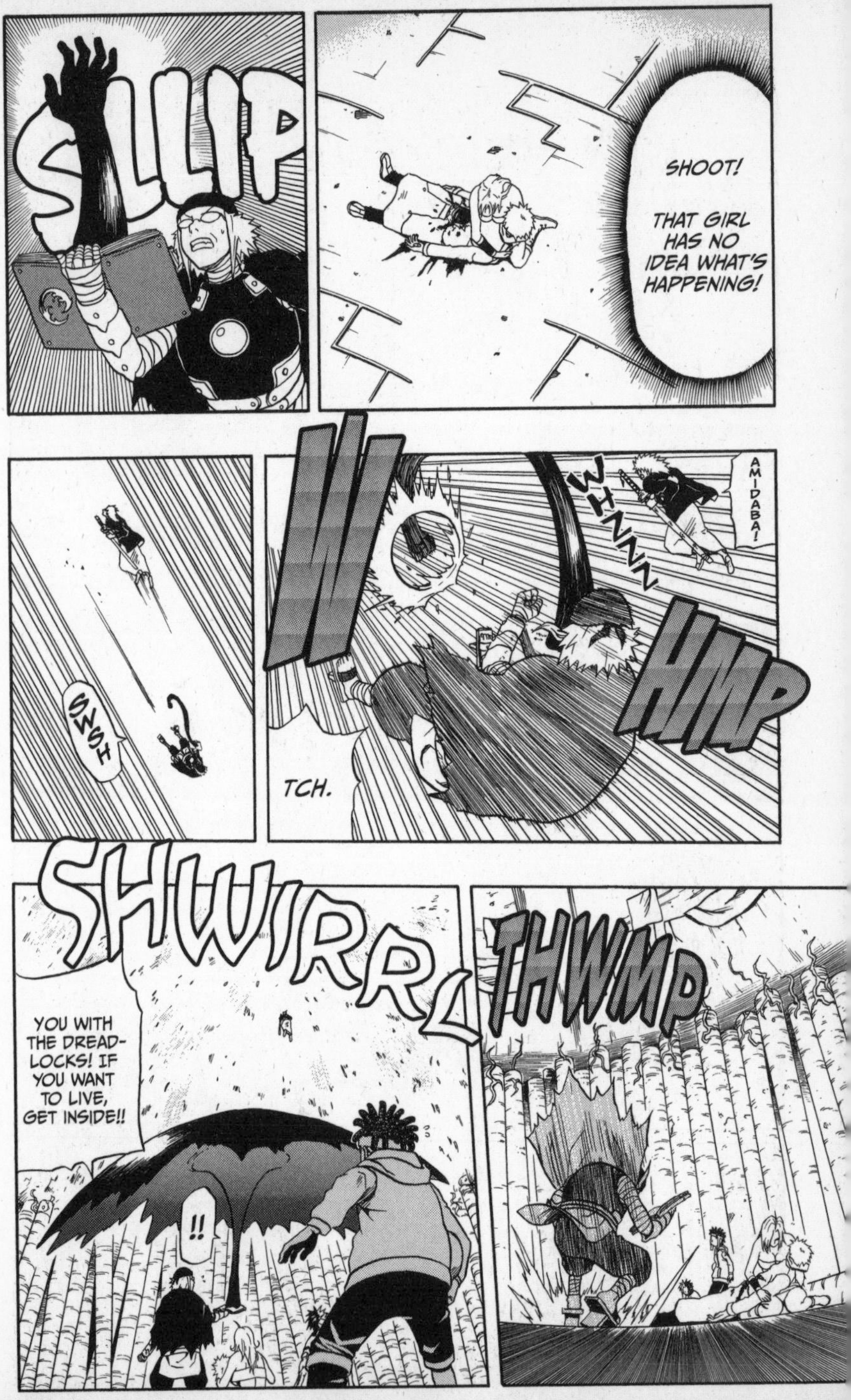
SHOOT!
THAT GIRL HAS NO IDEA WHAT'S HAPPENING!
SLLIP
AMIDABA!
WHNNNN
HMP
TCH.
SWSH
THWMP
SHWIRRL
YOU WITH THE DREAD-LOCKS! IF YOU WANT TO LIVE, GET INSIDE!!
!!

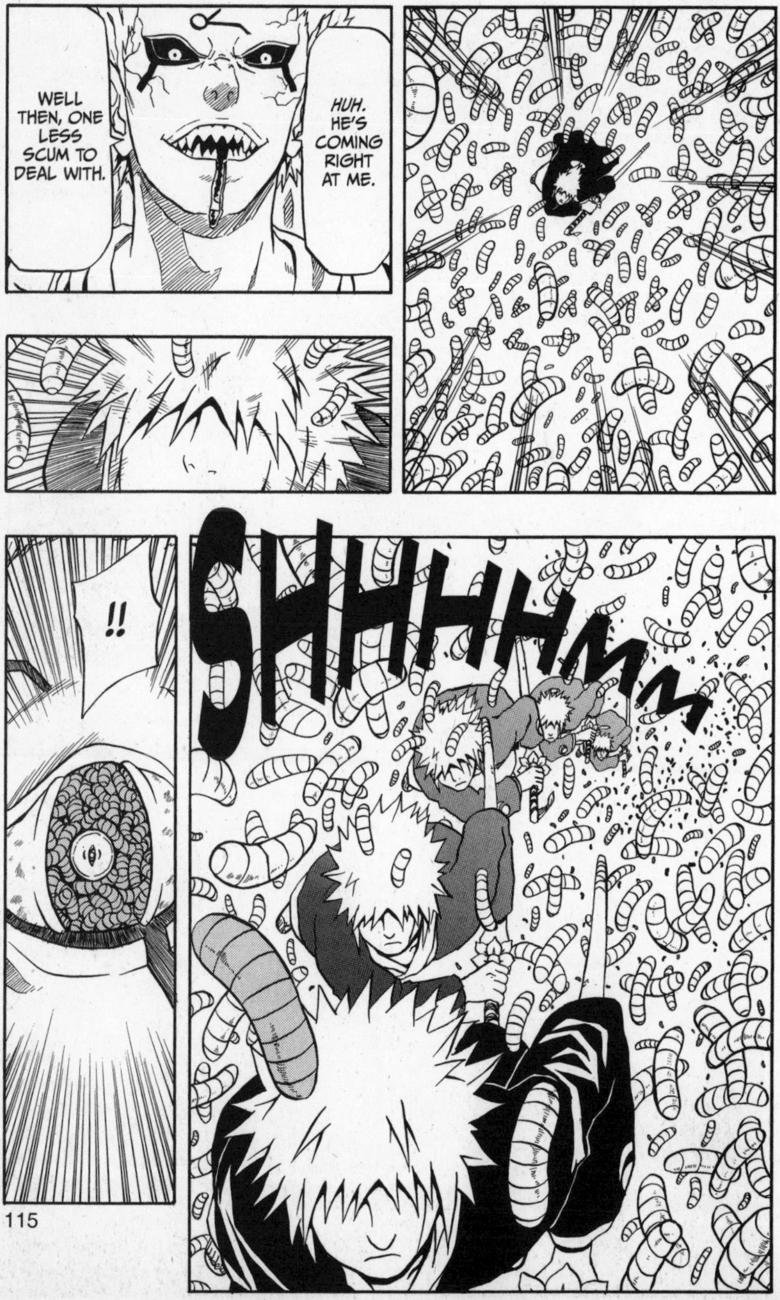
HUH. HE'S COMING RIGHT AT ME.
WELL THEN, ONE LESS SCUM TO DEAL WITH.
SHHHHMM
!!

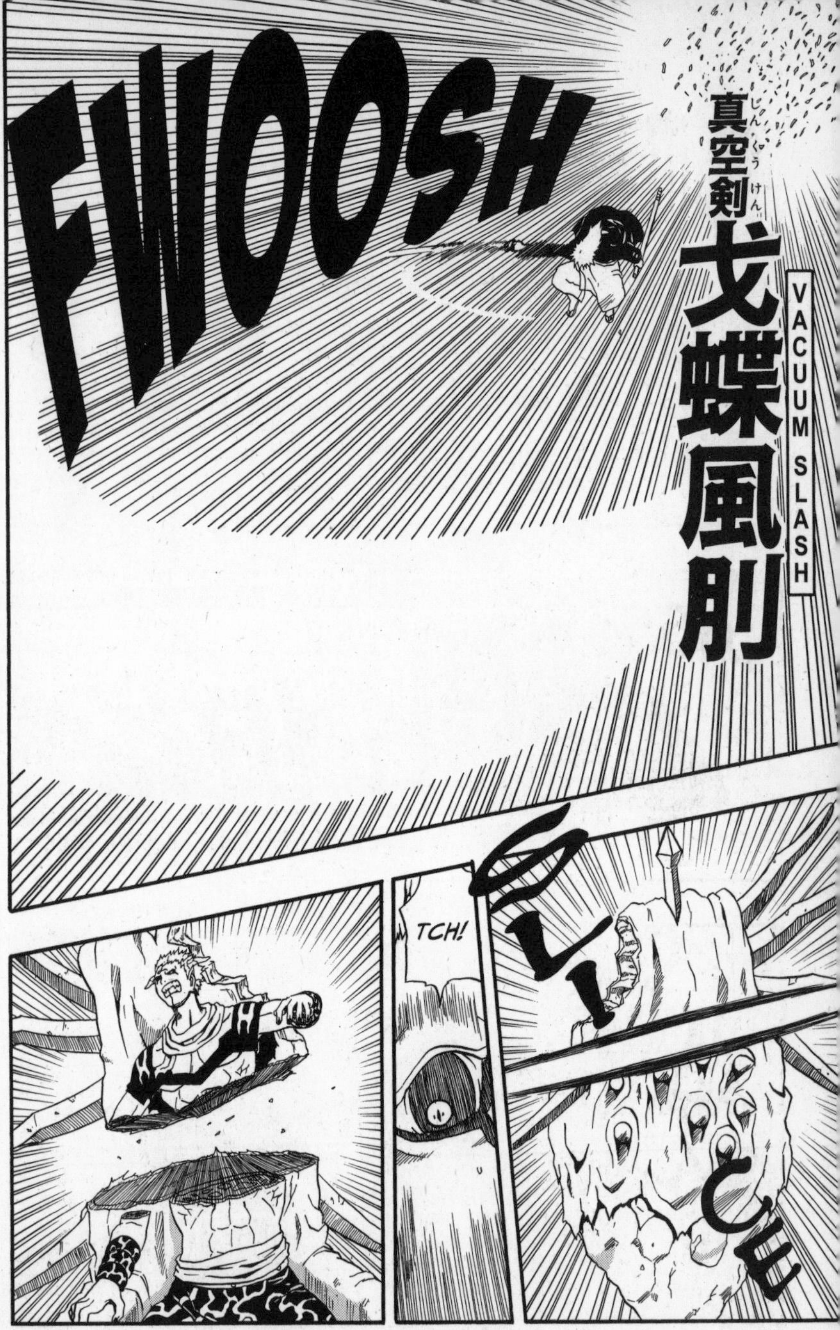
FWOOSH
真空剣(じんくうけん)戈蝶風刖
VACUUM SLASH
SLICE
TCH!

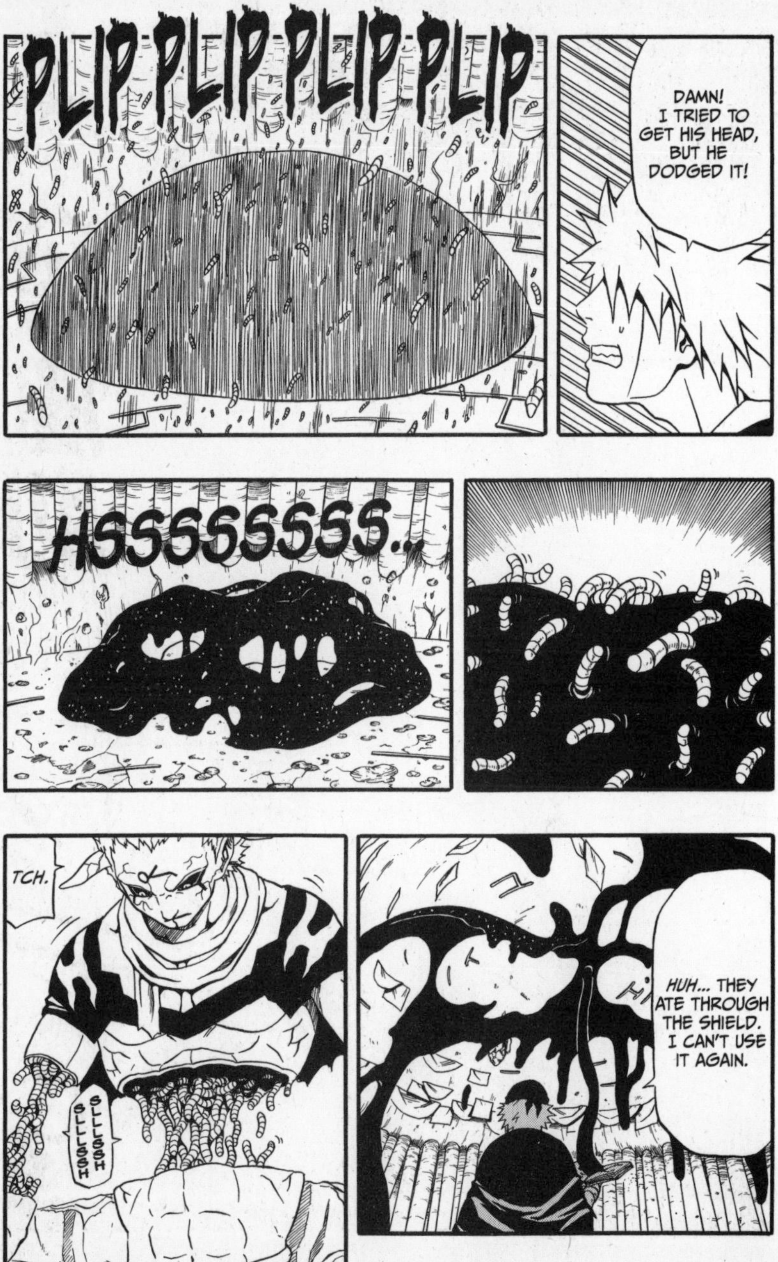
DAMN! I TRIED TO GET HIS HEAD, BUT HE DODGED IT!
PLIP PLIP PLIP PLIP
HSSSSSSSS...
HUH... THEY ATE THROUGH THE SHIELD. I CAN'T USE IT AGAIN.
TCH.
SLLLSSH SLLLSSH

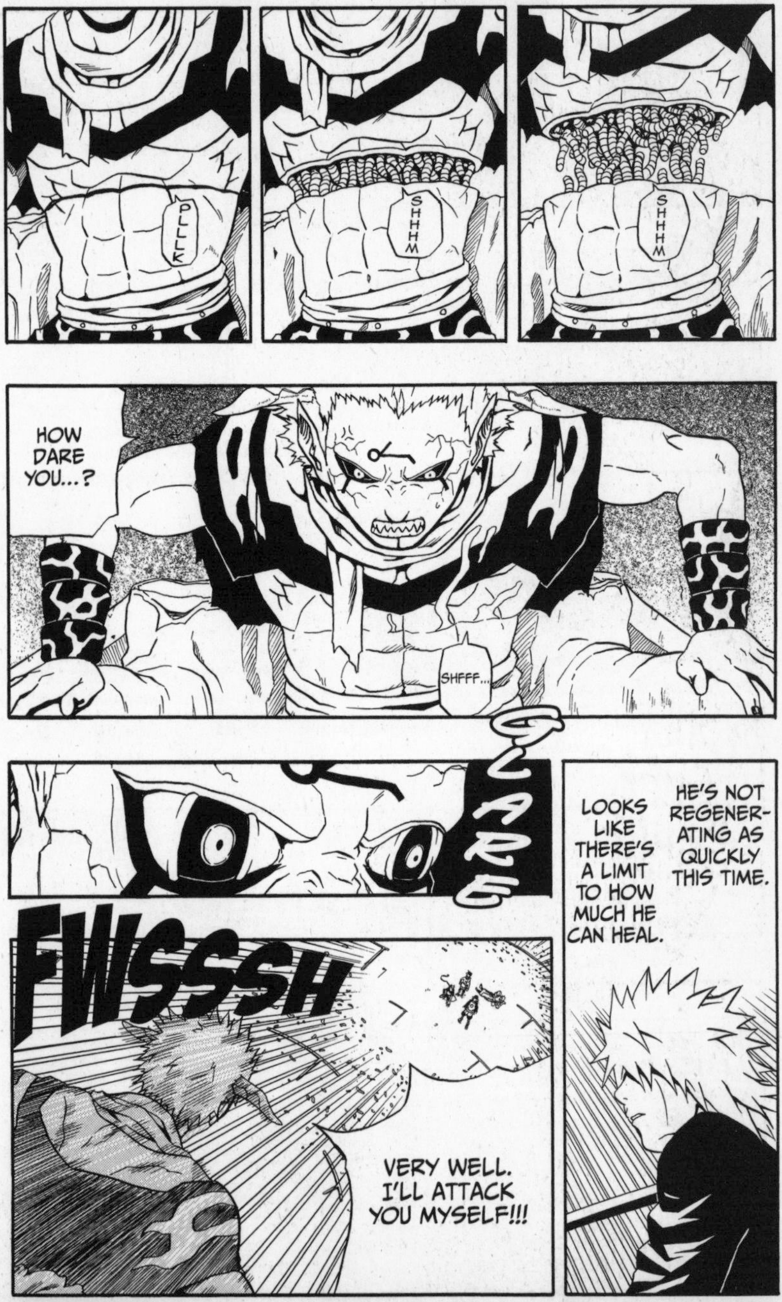
SHHHM
SHHHM
PLLLK
HOW DARE YOU...?
SHFFF...
HE'S NOT REGENERATING AS QUICKLY THIS TIME.
LOOKS LIKE THERE'S A LIMIT TO HOW MUCH HE CAN HEAL.
GLARE
FWSSSH
VERY WELL. I'LL ATTACK YOU MYSELF!!!

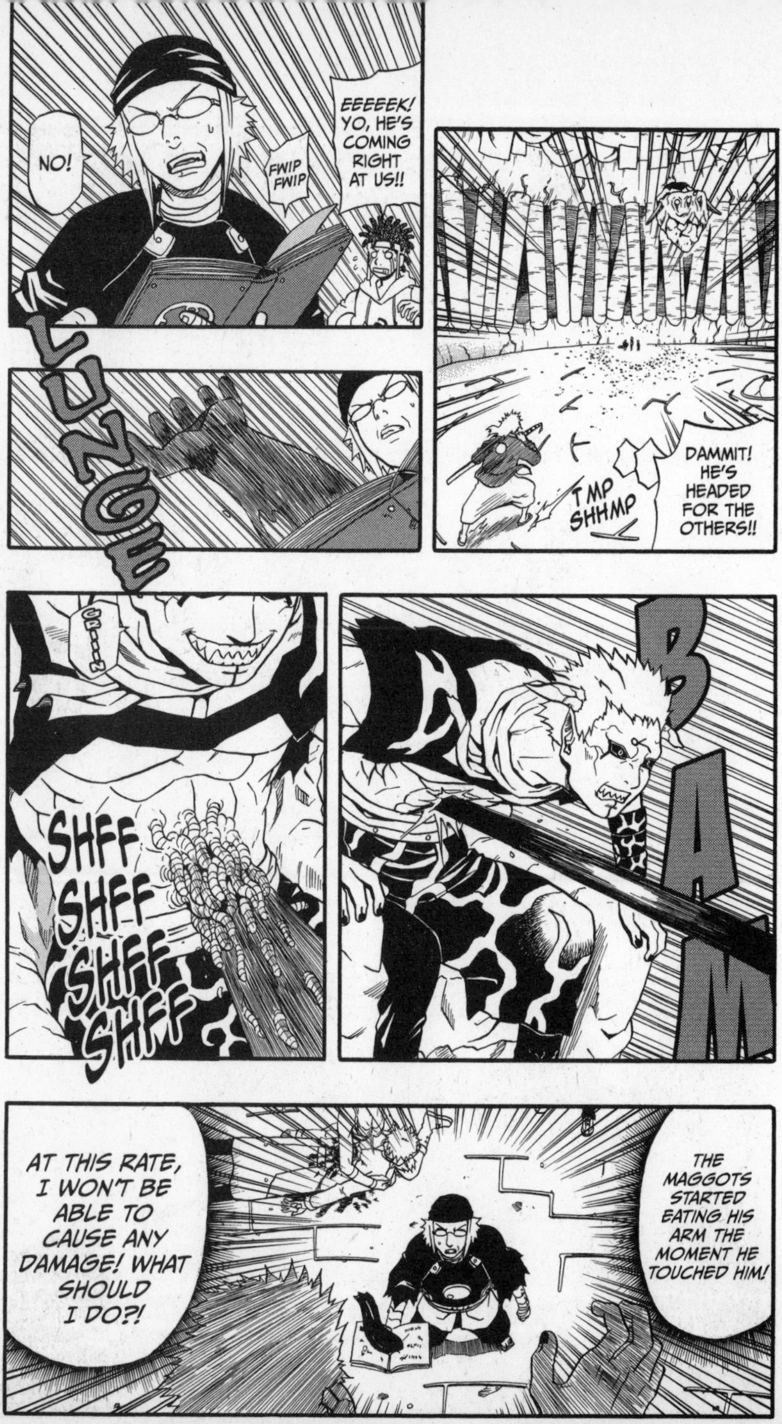
DAMMIT! HE'S HEADED FOR THE OTHERS!!
TMP SHHMP
EEEEEK! YO, HE'S COMING RIGHT AT US!!
FWIP FWIP
NO!
LUNGE
BAM
GRIN
SHFF SHFF SHFF SHFF
THE MAGGOTS STARTED EATING HIS ARM THE MOMENT HE TOUCHED HIM!
AT THIS RATE, I WON'T BE ABLE TO CAUSE ANY DAMAGE! WHAT SHOULD I DO?!

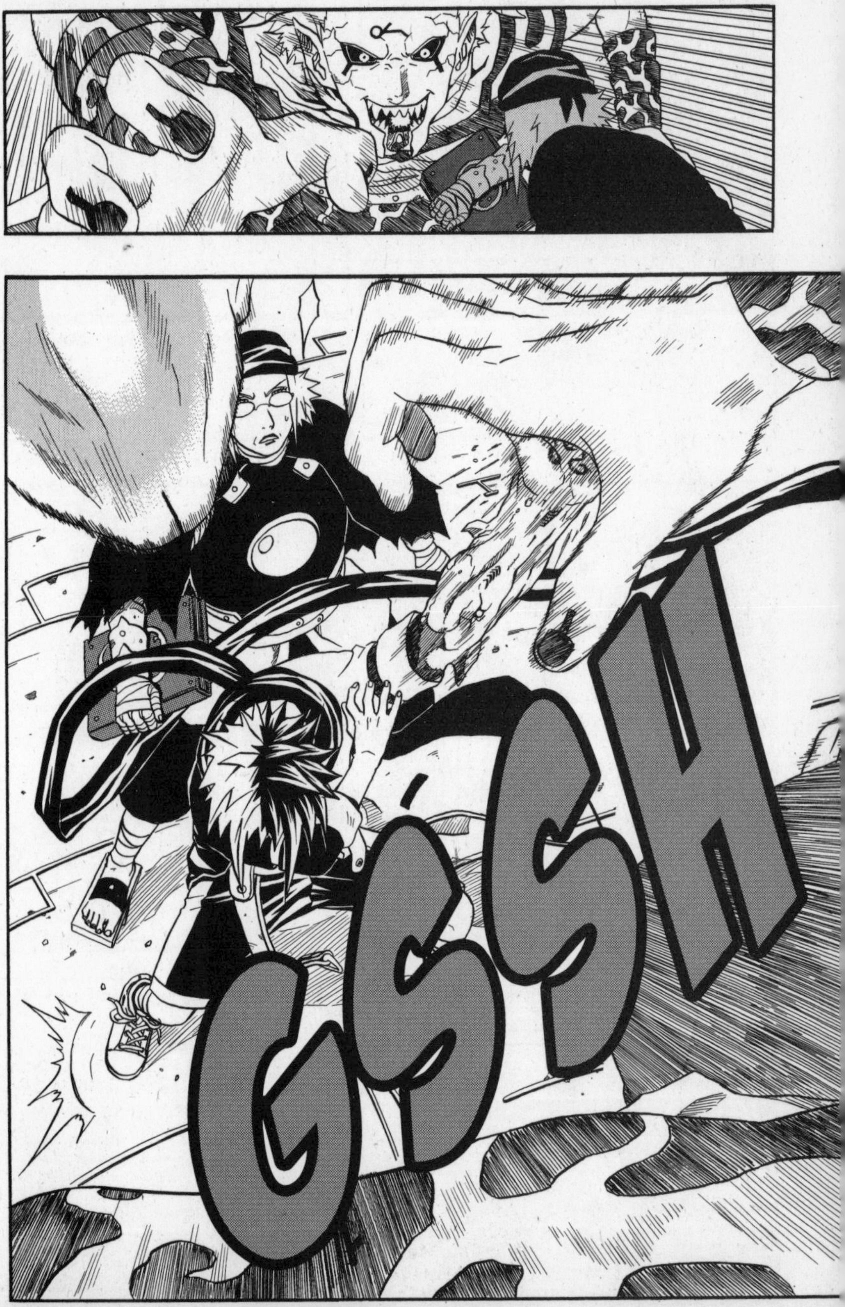
GSSH

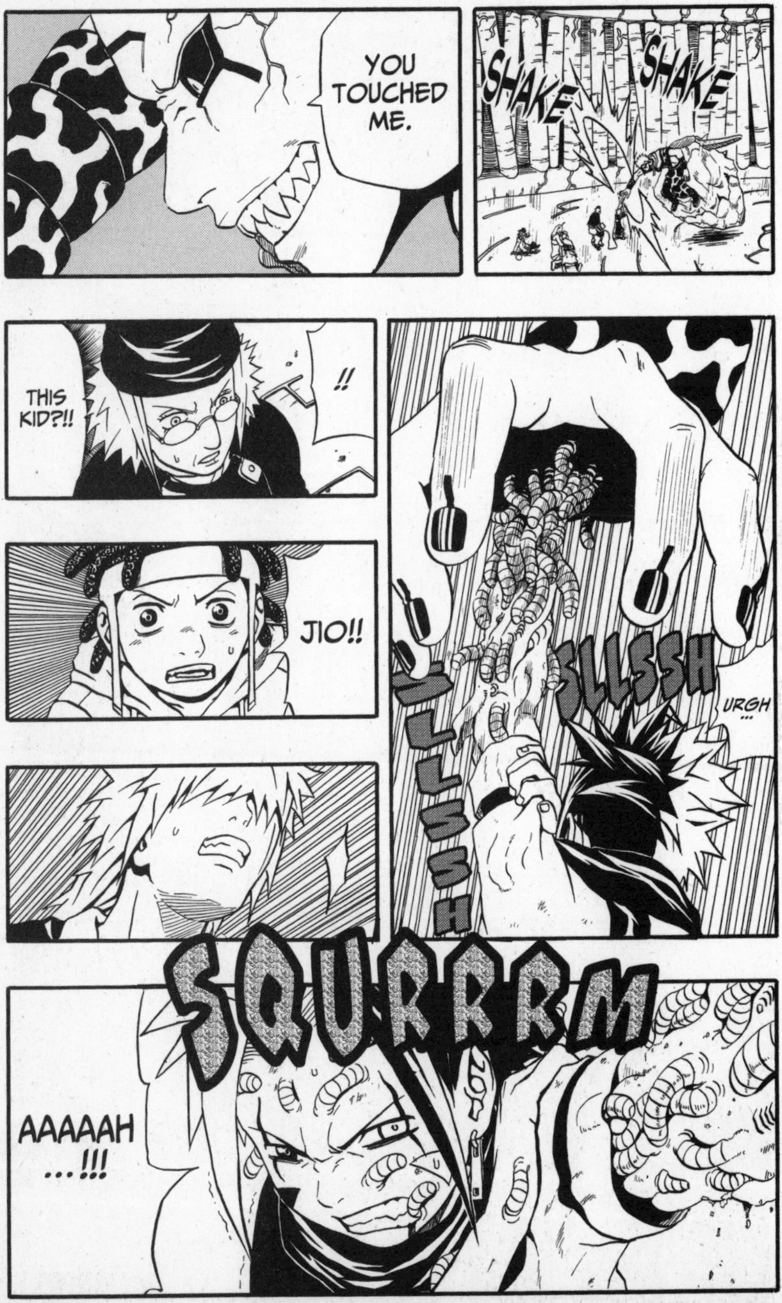
SHAKE
SHAKE
YOU TOUCHED ME.
SLLSSH
URGH ...
SLLSSH
!!
THIS KID?!!
JIO!!
SQURRRM
AAAAAH ...!!!

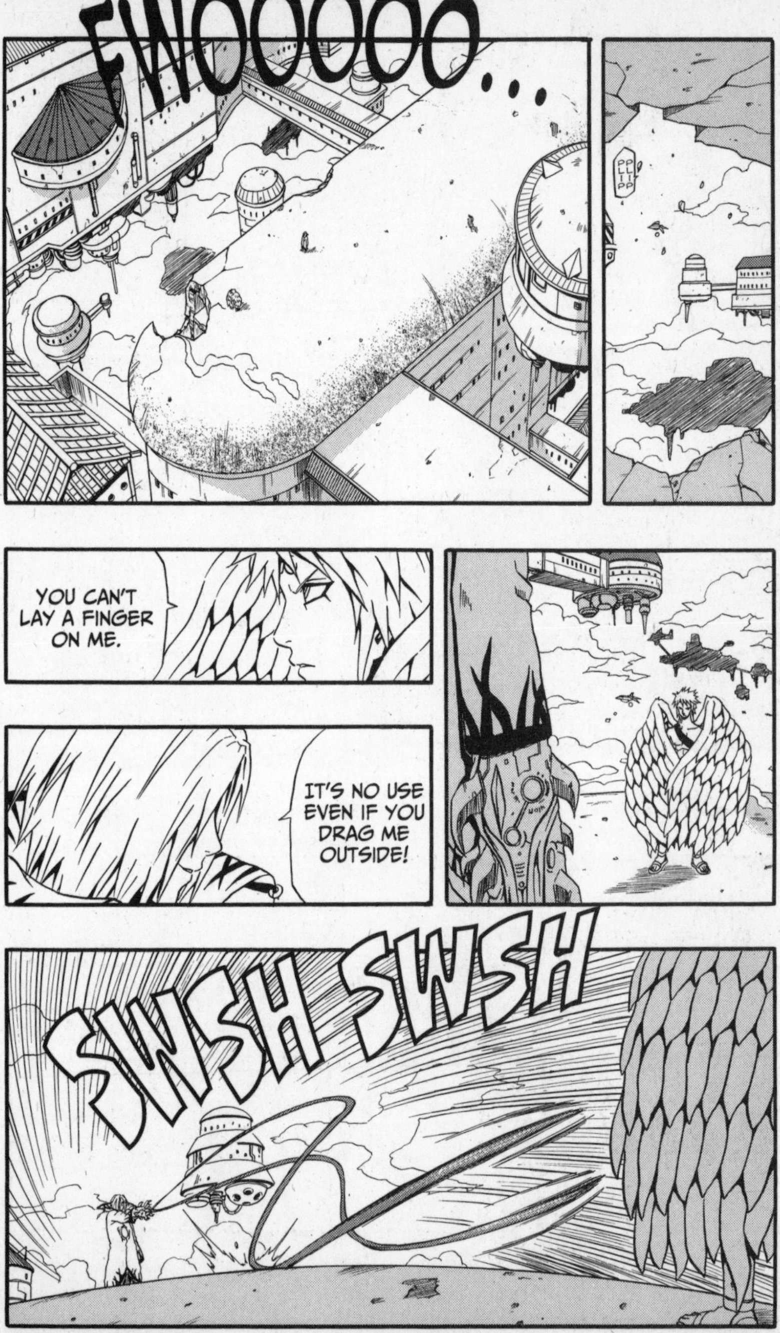
FWOOOOO...
YOU CAN'T LAY A FINGER ON ME.
IT'S NO USE EVEN IF YOU DRAG ME OUTSIDE!
SWSH SWSH

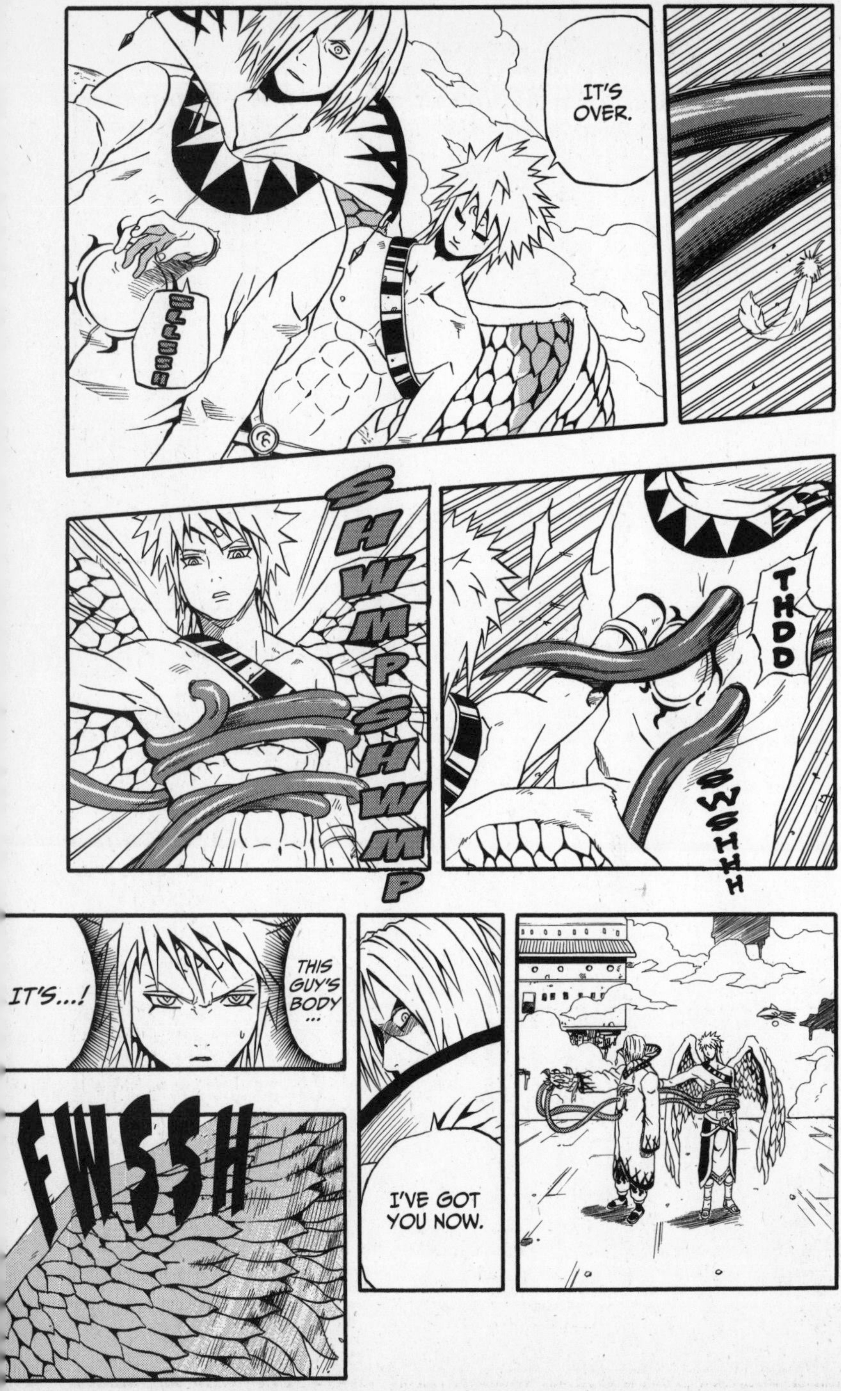
IT'S OVER.
ELLSSH
THDD
SWSHHH
SHWMP SHWMP
I'VE GOT YOU NOW.
IT'S...!
THIS GUY'S BODY ...
FWSSH

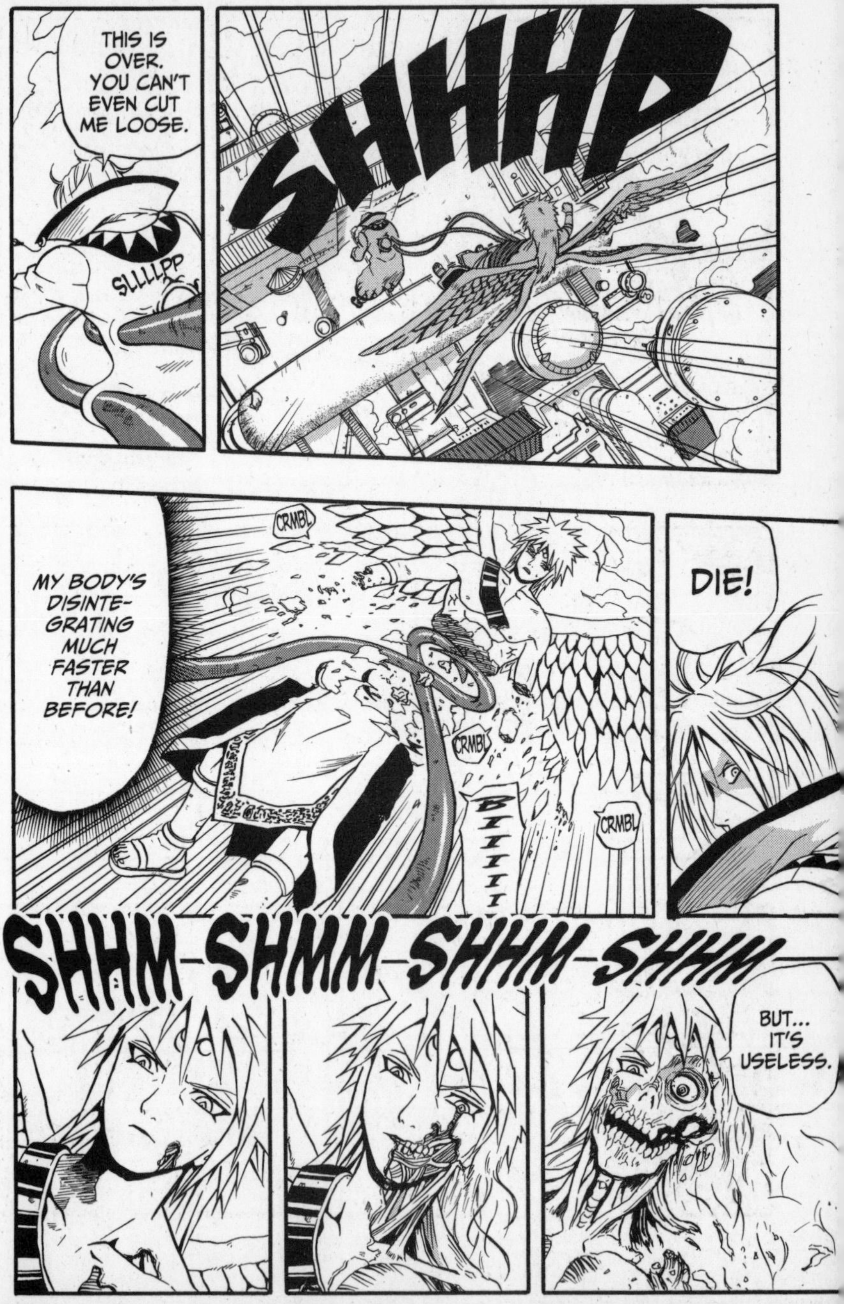
SHHHP
THIS IS OVER. YOU CAN'T EVEN CUT ME LOOSE.
SLLLLPP
DIE!
MY BODY'S DISINTE-GRATING MUCH FASTER THAN BEFORE!
CRMBL
CRMBL
BIIIIII
CRMBL
SHHM-SHMM-SHHM-SHHM
BUT... IT'S USELESS.

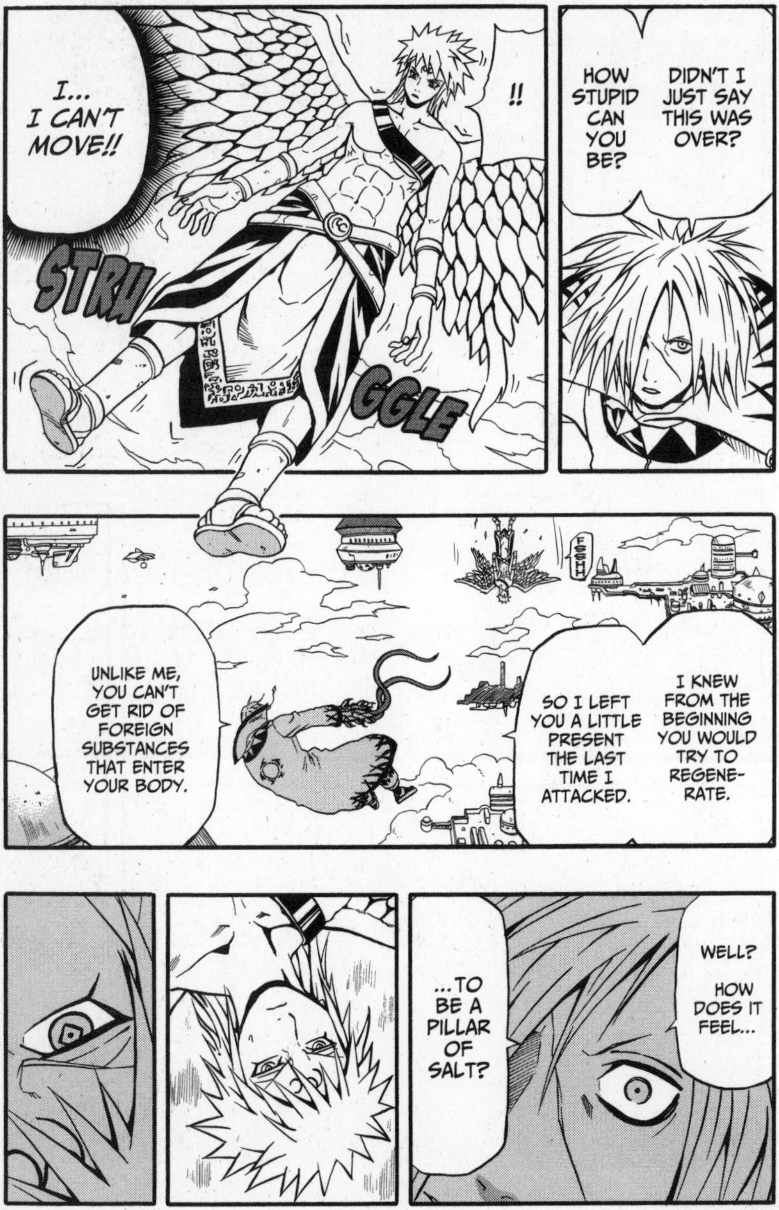
DIDN'T I JUST SAY THIS WAS OVER?
HOW STUPID CAN YOU BE?
!!
I... I CAN'T MOVE!!
STRUGGLE
FSSH
I KNEW FROM THE BEGINNING YOU WOULD TRY TO REGENE-RATE.
SO I LEFT YOU A LITTLE PRESENT THE LAST TIME I ATTACKED.
UNLIKE ME, YOU CAN'T GET RID OF FOREIGN SUBSTANCES THAT ENTER YOUR BODY.
WELL?
HOW DOES IT FEEL...
...TO BE A PILLAR OF SALT?

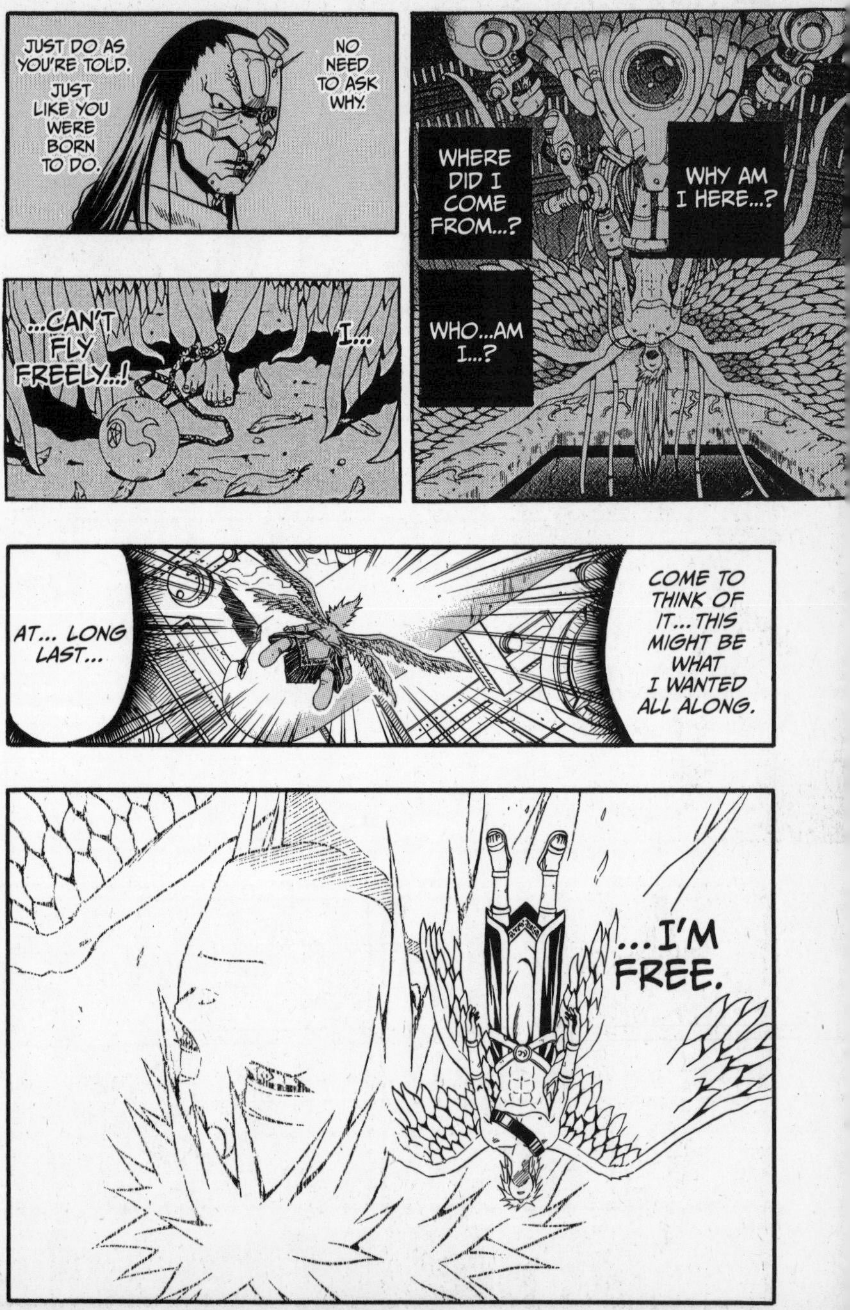
WHY AM I HERE...?
WHERE DID I COME FROM...?
WHO...AM I...?
NO NEED TO ASK WHY.
JUST DO AS YOU'RE TOLD.
JUST LIKE YOU WERE BORN TO DO.
I...
...CAN'T FLY FREELY...!
COME TO THINK OF IT...THIS MIGHT BE WHAT I WANTED ALL ALONG.
AT... LONG LAST...
...I'M FREE.

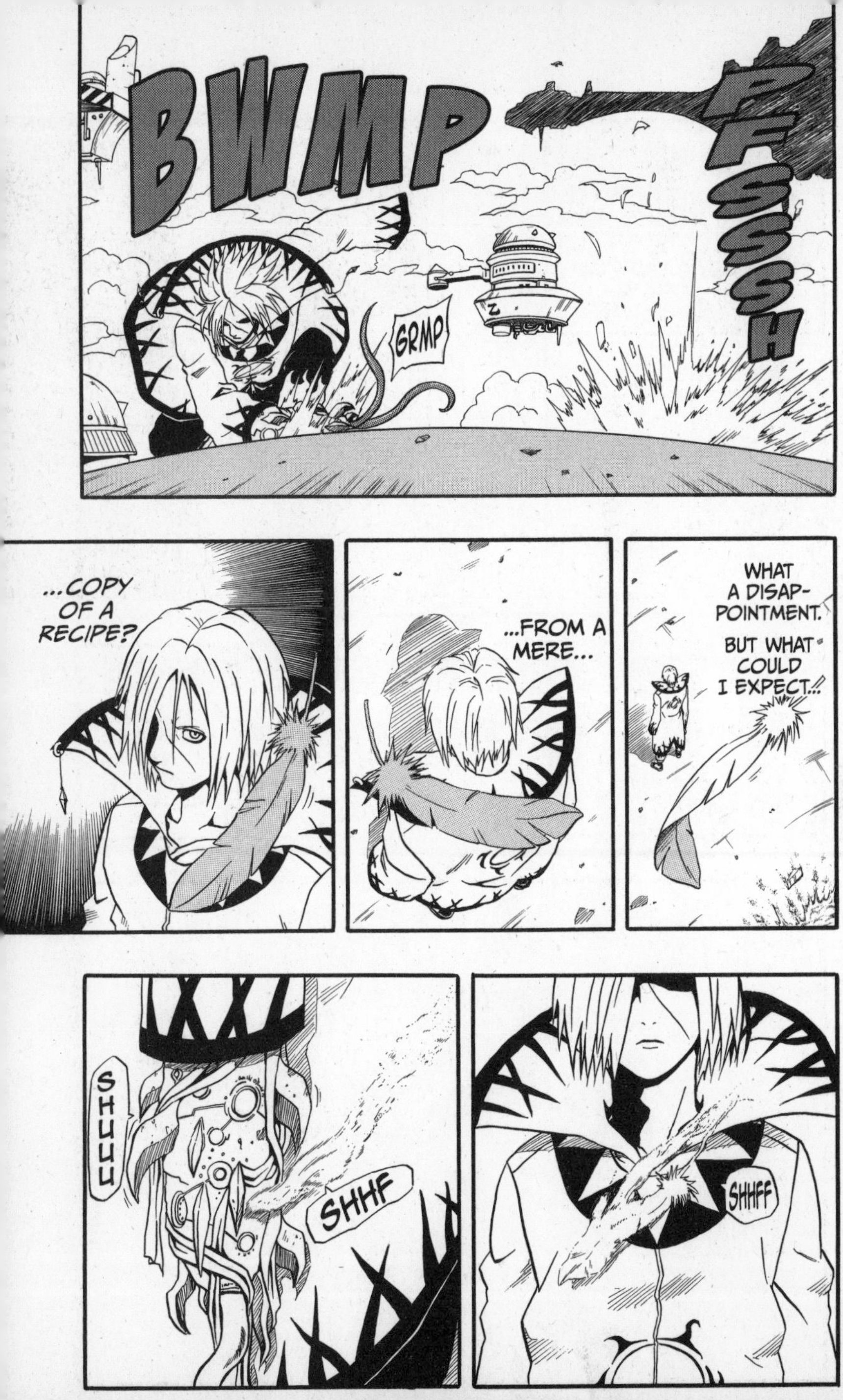
PFSSSH
BWMP
GRMP
WHAT A DISAPPOINTMENT.
BUT WHAT COULD I EXPECT...!!
...FROM A MERE...
...COPY OF A RECIPE?
SHHFF
SHUUU
SHHF

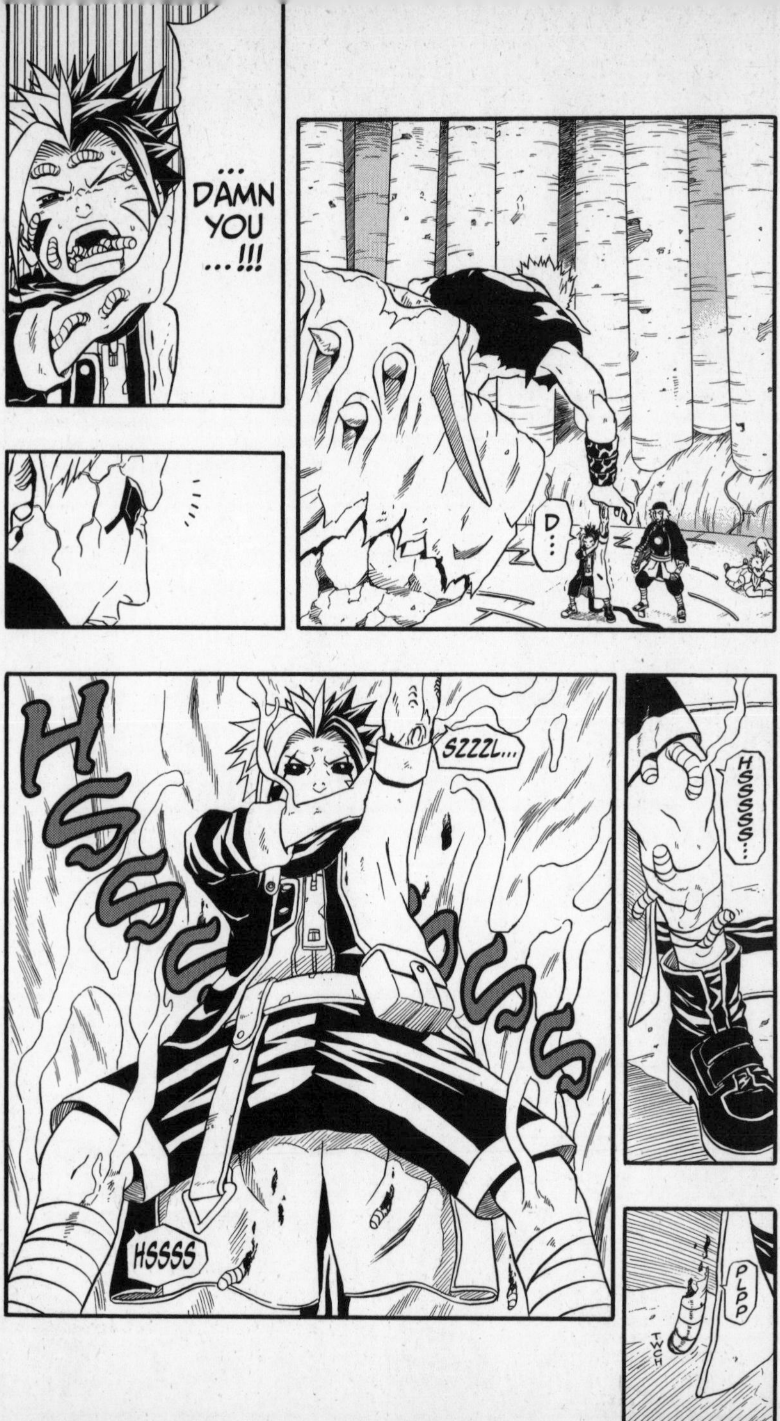
D...
...DAMN YOU ...!!!
HSSSSS...
PLPP
TWCH
SZZZL...
HSSSSSS
HSSSS

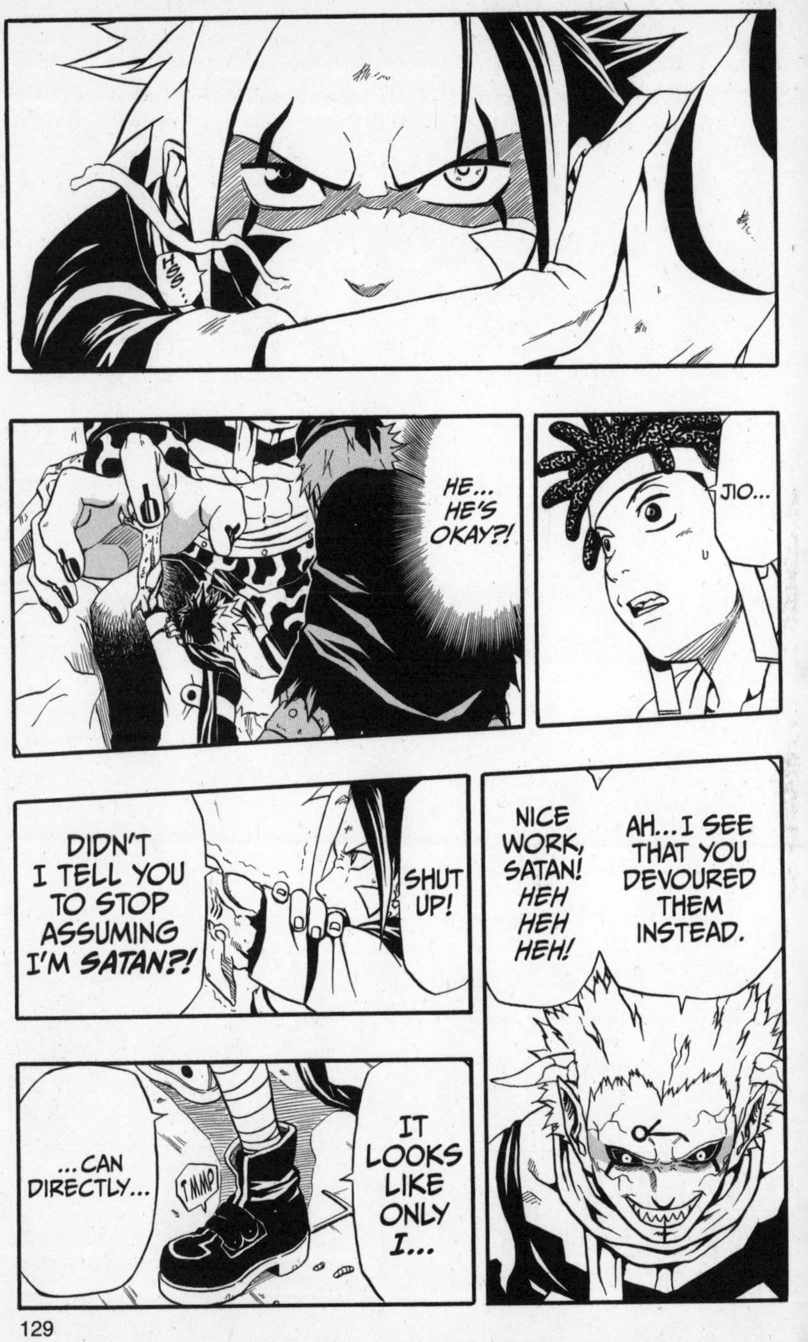
HSS...
JIO...
HE... HE'S OKAY?!
AH...I SEE THAT YOU DEVOURED THEM INSTEAD.
NICE WORK, SATAN! HEH HEH HEH!
SHUT UP!
DIDN'T I TELL YOU TO STOP ASSUMING I'M SATAN?!
IT LOOKS LIKE ONLY I...
TMMP
...CAN DIRECTLY...

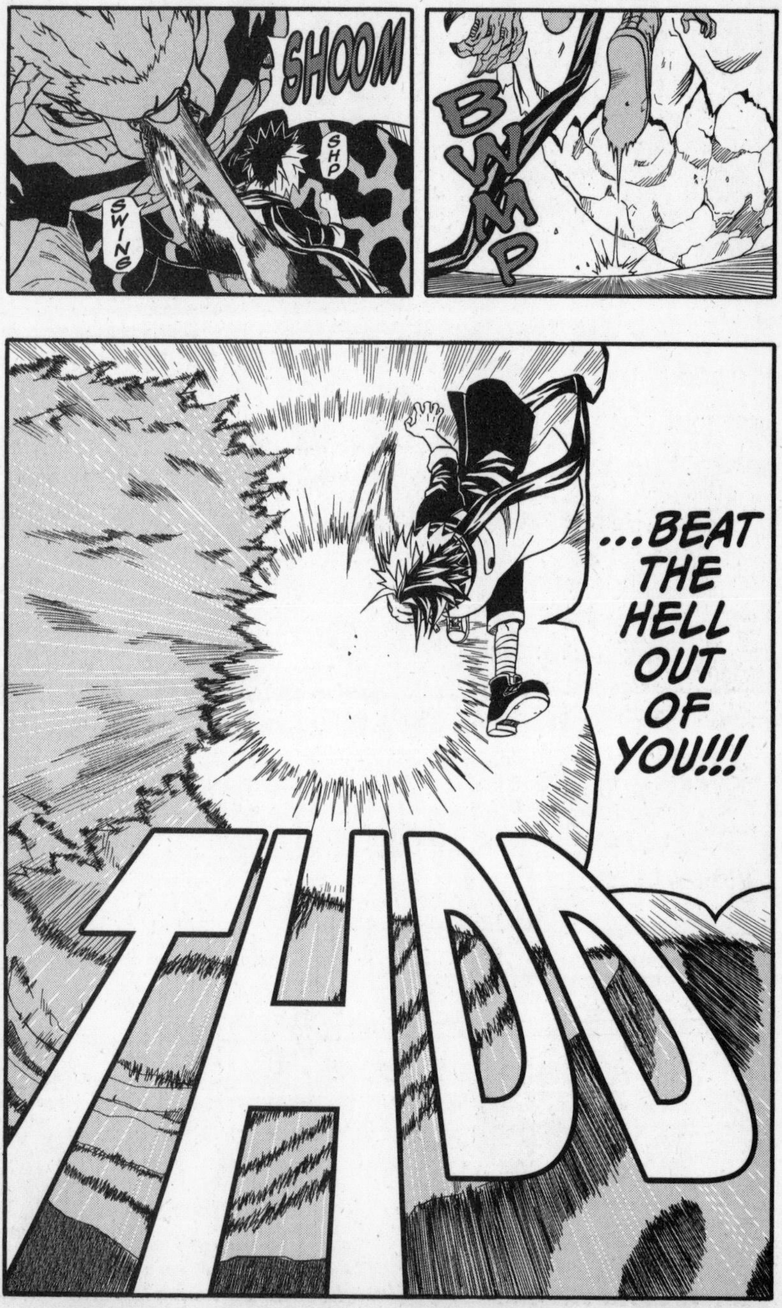
BWMP
SHOOM
SHP
SWING
...BEAT THE HELL OUT OF YOU!!!
THDD

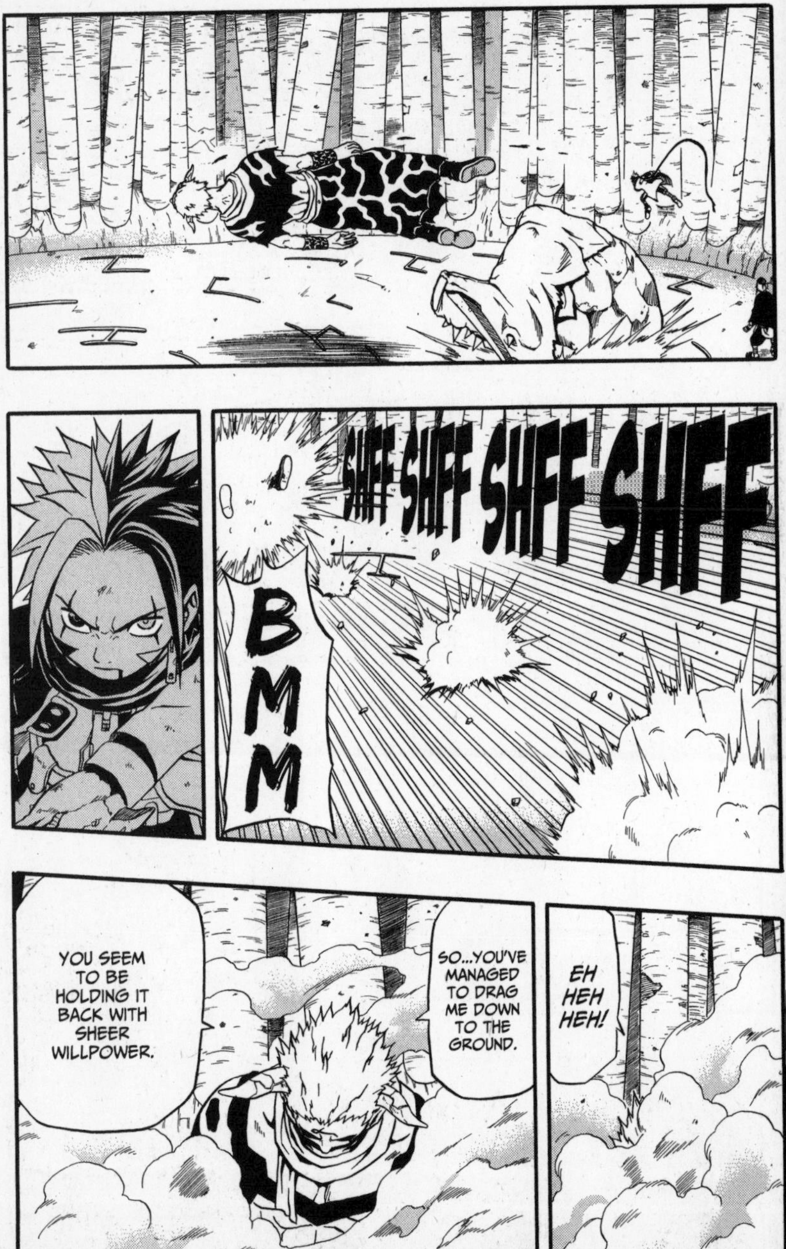
SHFF SHFF SHFF SHFF
BMM
EH HEH HEH!
SO...YOU'VE MANAGED TO DRAG ME DOWN TO THE GROUND.
YOU SEEM TO BE HOLDING IT BACK WITH SHEER WILLPOWER.

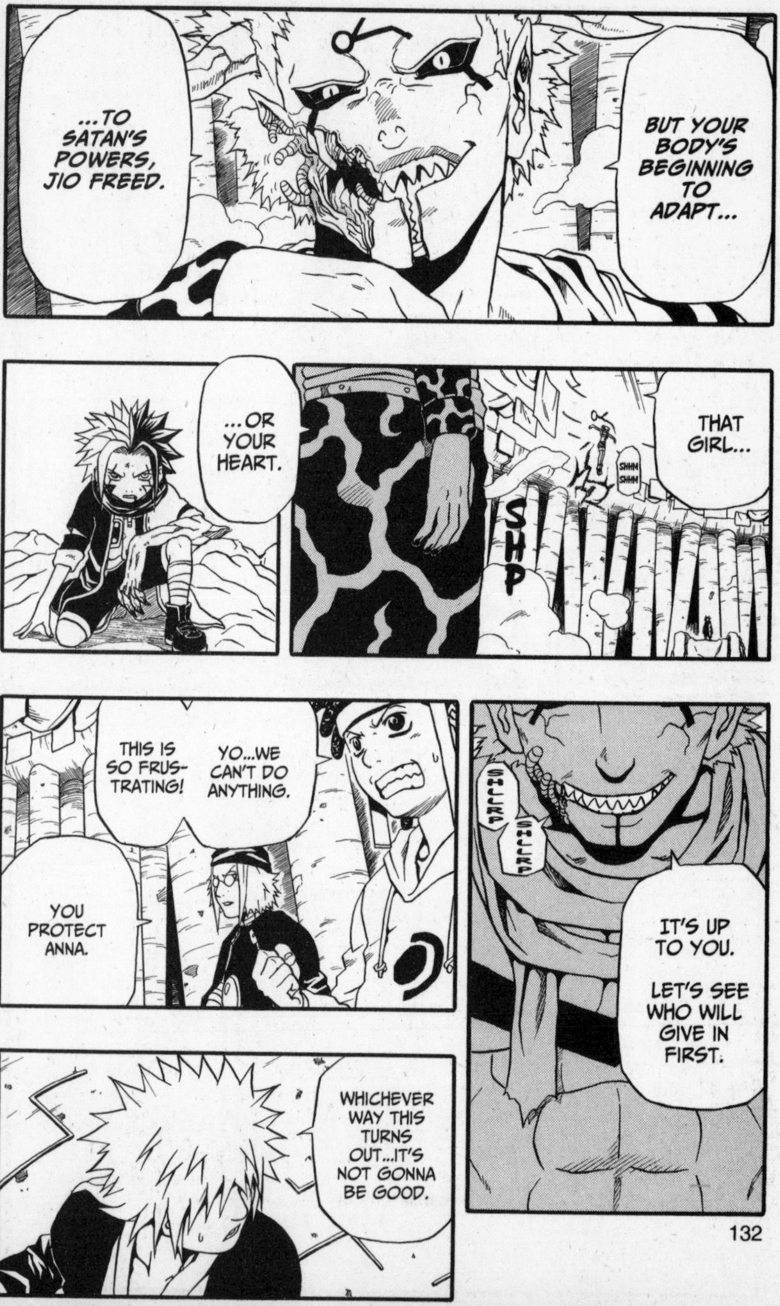
BUT YOUR BODY'S BEGINNING TO ADAPT...
...TO SATAN'S POWERS, JIO FREED.
THAT GIRL...
SHHM SHHM
SHP
...OR YOUR HEART.
SHLLRP
SHLLRP
IT'S UP TO YOU.
LET'S SEE WHO WILL GIVE IN FIRST.
YO...WE CAN'T DO ANYTHING.
THIS IS SO FRUS-TRATING!
YOU PROTECT ANNA.
WHICHEVER WAY THIS TURNS OUT...IT'S NOT GONNA BE GOOD.

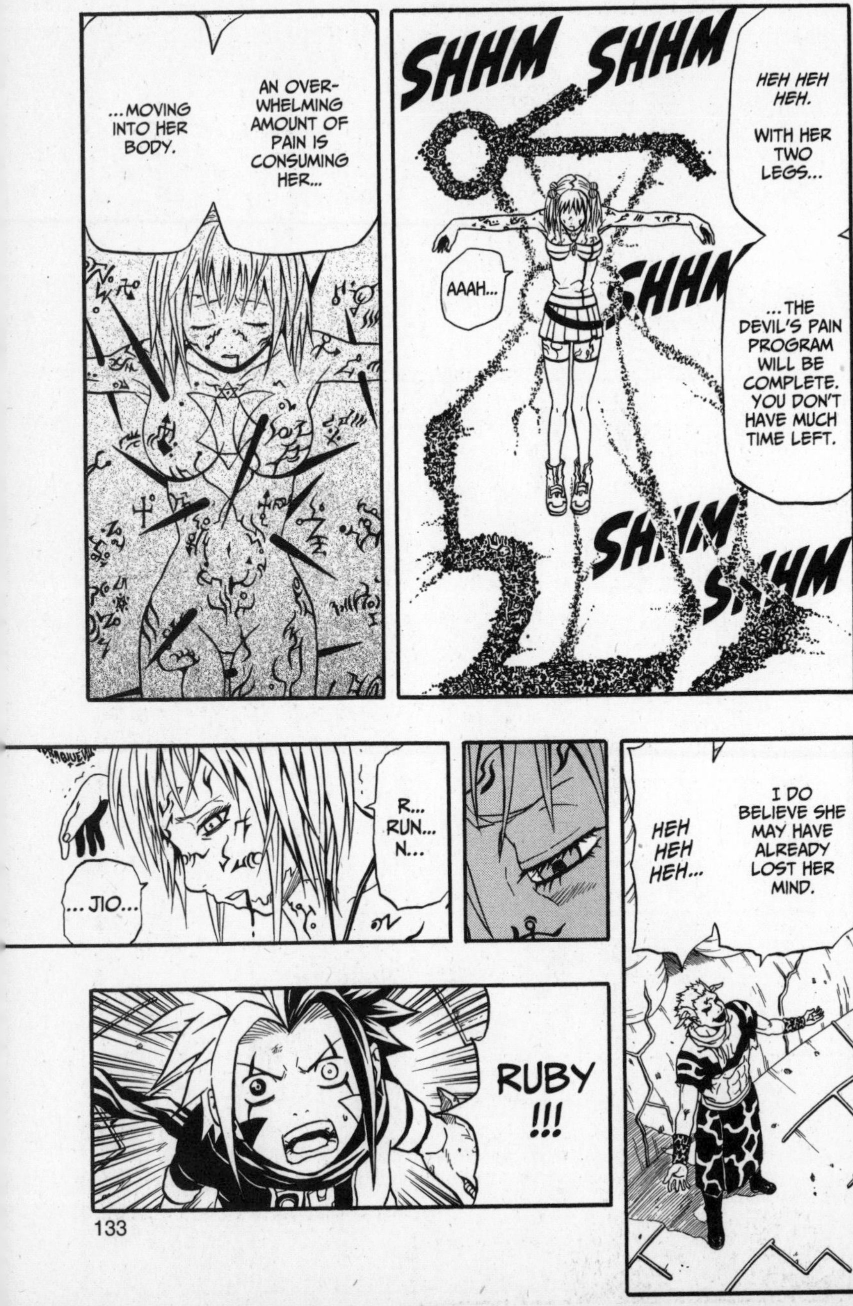
HEH HEH HEH.
WITH HER TWO LEGS...
...THE DEVIL'S PAIN PROGRAM WILL BE COMPLETE. YOU DON'T HAVE MUCH TIME LEFT.
SHHM SHHM
SHHM
SHHM
SHHM
AAAH...
AN OVER-WHELMING AMOUNT OF PAIN IS CONSUMING HER...
...MOVING INTO HER BODY.
I DO BELIEVE SHE MAY HAVE ALREADY LOST HER MIND.
HEH HEH HEH...
R... RUN... N...
...JIO...
RUBY !!!

JIO IS MY FRIEND! I'M NOT GOING TO LET HIM TURN INTO SATAN!

I'LL BE... F... FINE...

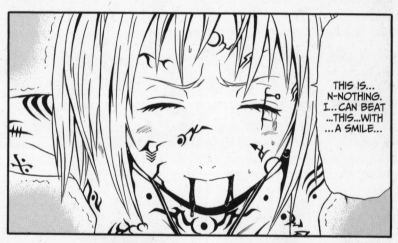

THIS IS... N-NOTHING. I... CAN BEAT ...THIS...WITH ...A SMILE...

HOW CAN WE BE FRIENDS THAT EASILY?!

I HATE PEOPLE LIKE THAT!!!

AND YOU'VE GOT THAT STUPID SMILE ON YOUR FACE ALL THE TIME!!

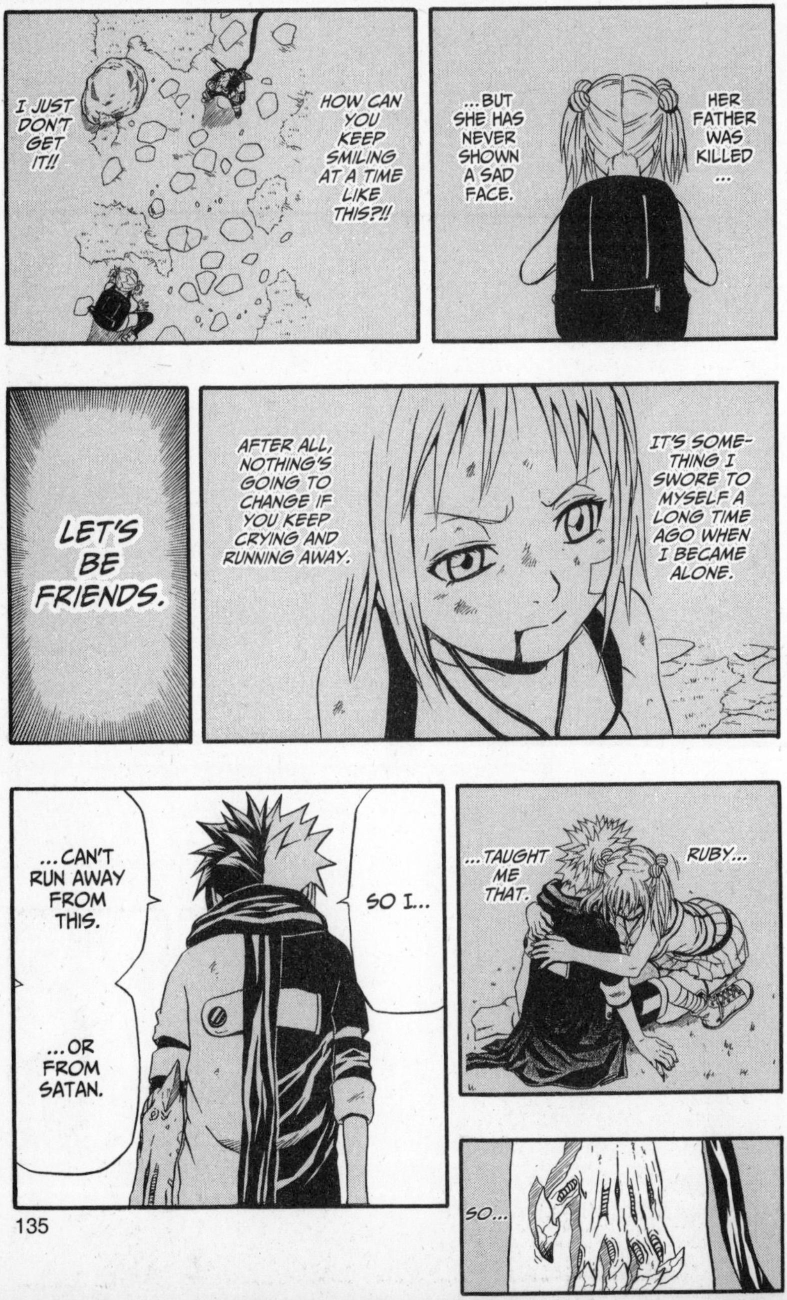
HER FATHER WAS KILLED...
...BUT SHE HAS NEVER SHOWN A SAD FACE.
HOW CAN YOU KEEP SMILING AT A TIME LIKE THIS?!!
I JUST DON'T GET IT!!
IT'S SOME-THING I SWORE TO MYSELF A LONG TIME AGO WHEN I BECAME ALONE.
AFTER ALL, NOTHING'S GOING TO CHANGE IF YOU KEEP CRYING AND RUNNING AWAY.
LET'S BE FRIENDS.
RUBY...
...TAUGHT ME THAT.
SO...
SO I...
...CAN'T RUN AWAY FROM THIS.
...OR FROM SATAN.

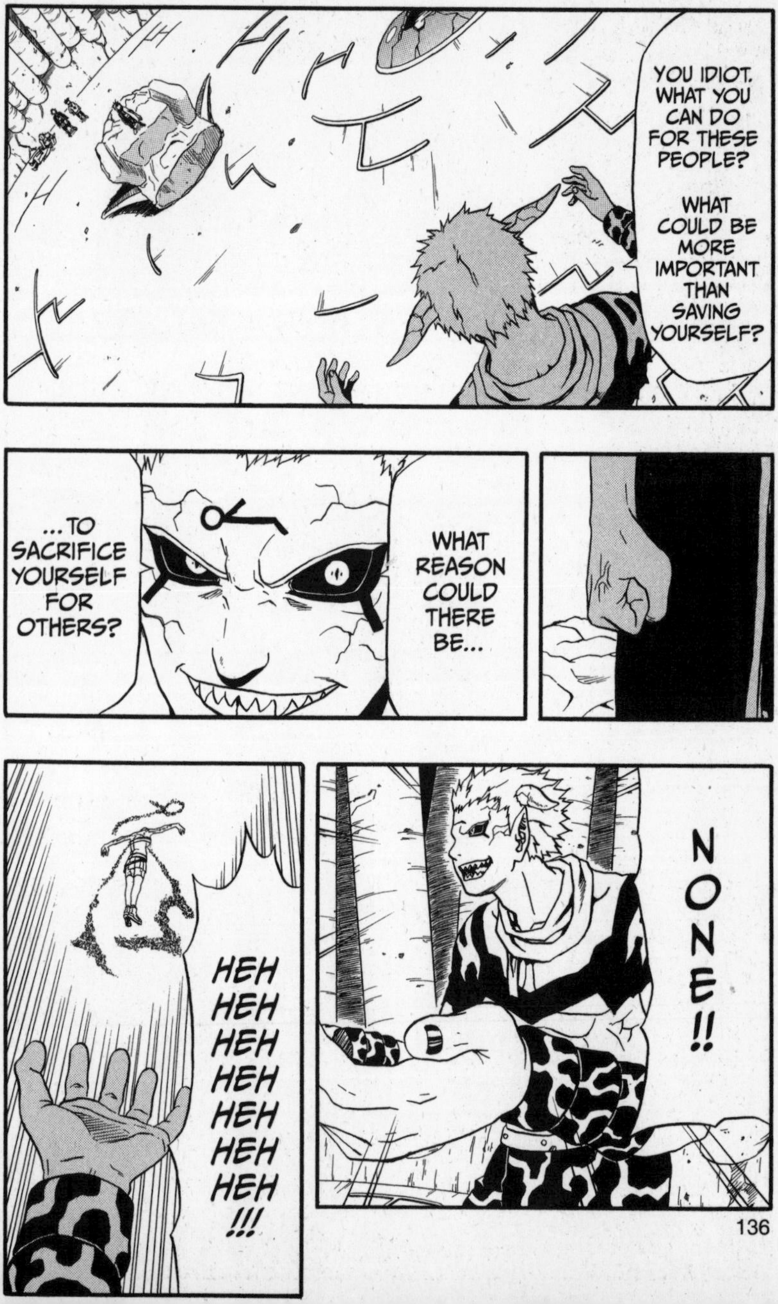
YOU IDIOT. WHAT YOU CAN DO FOR THESE PEOPLE?
WHAT COULD BE MORE IMPORTANT THAN SAVING YOURSELF?
WHAT REASON COULD THERE BE...
...TO SACRIFICE YOURSELF FOR OTHERS?
NONE!!
HEH HEH HEH HEH HEH HEH HEH!!!

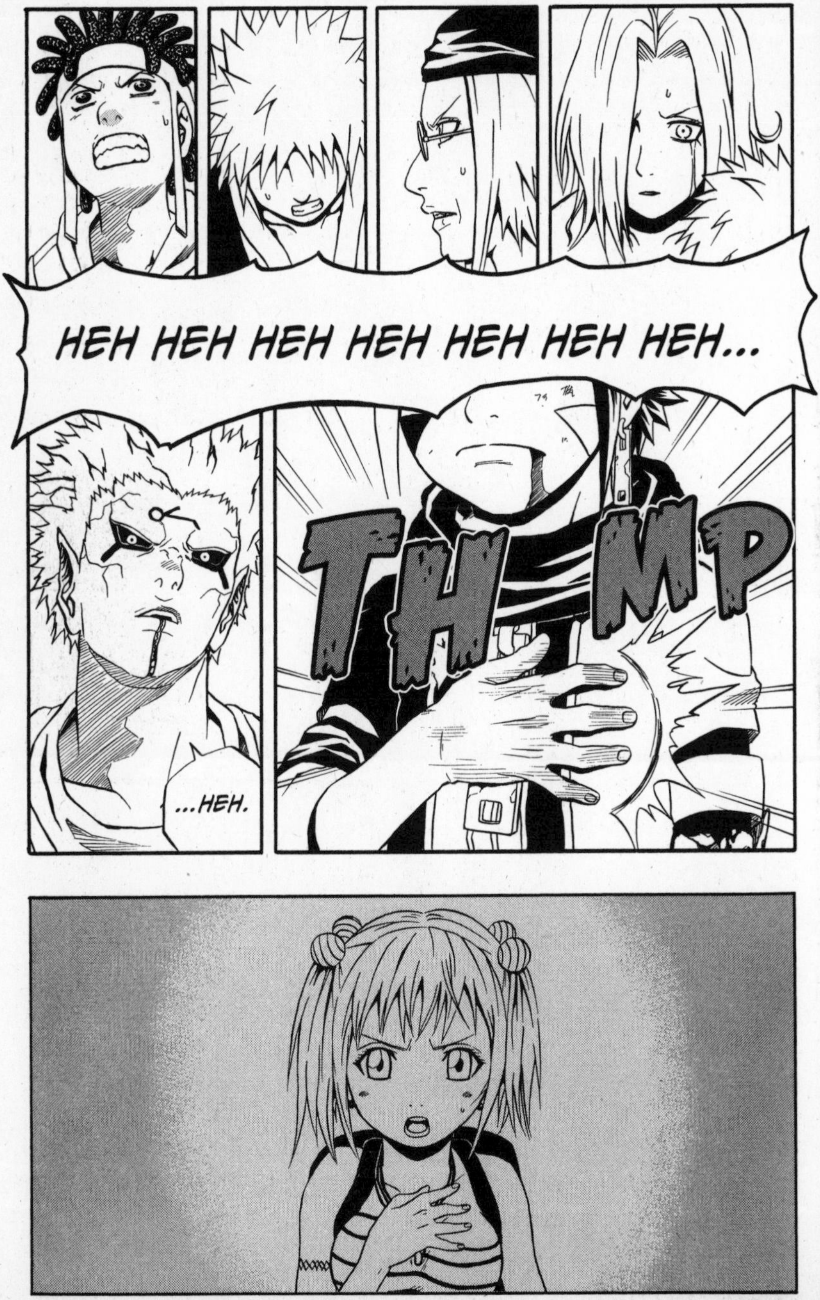
HEH HEH HEH HEH HEH HEH HEH...
THMP
...HEH.

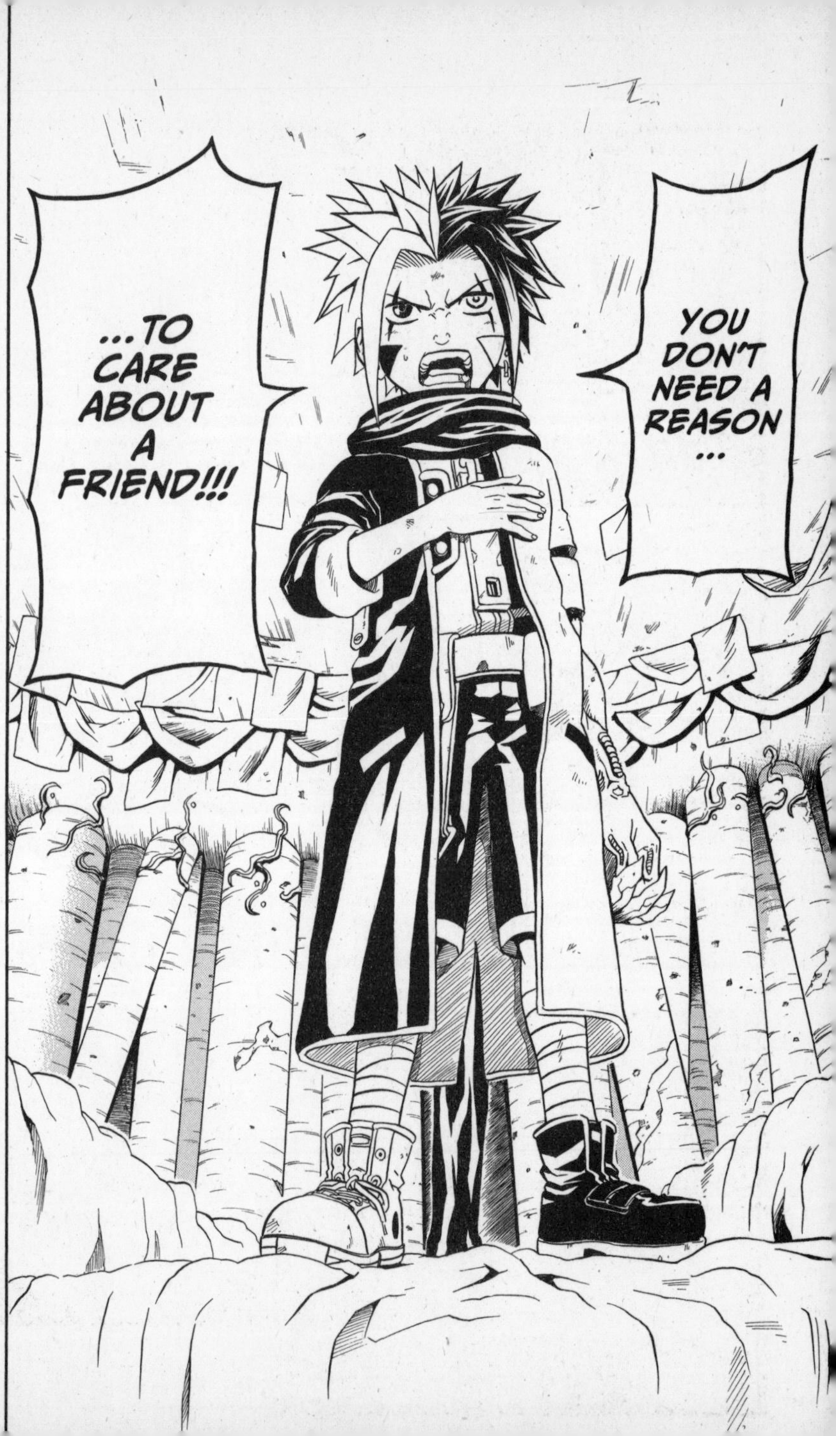
YOU DON'T NEED A REASON ...
...TO CARE ABOUT A FRIEND!!!

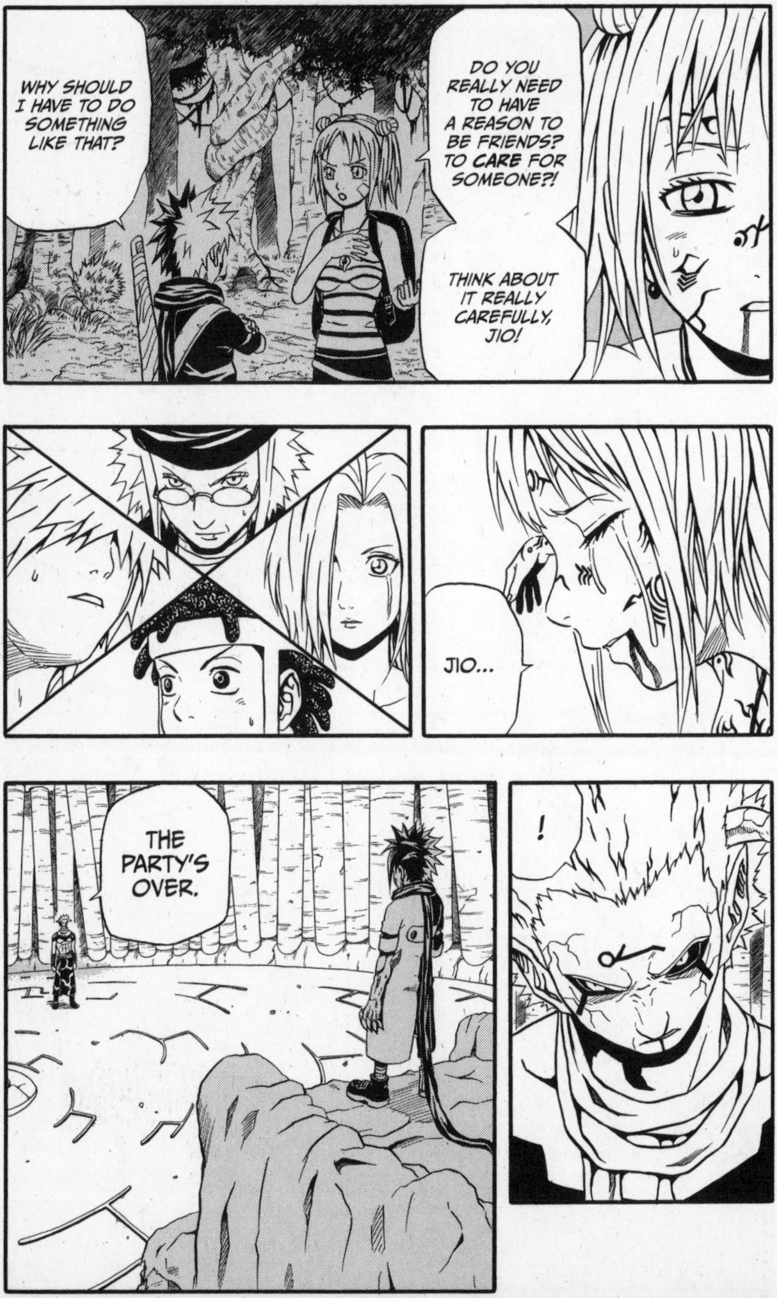
DO YOU REALLY NEED TO HAVE A REASON TO BE FRIENDS? TO **CARE** FOR SOMEONE?!
THINK ABOUT IT REALLY CAREFULLY, JIO!
WHY SHOULD I HAVE TO DO SOMETHING LIKE THAT?
JIO...
!
THE PARTY'S OVER.

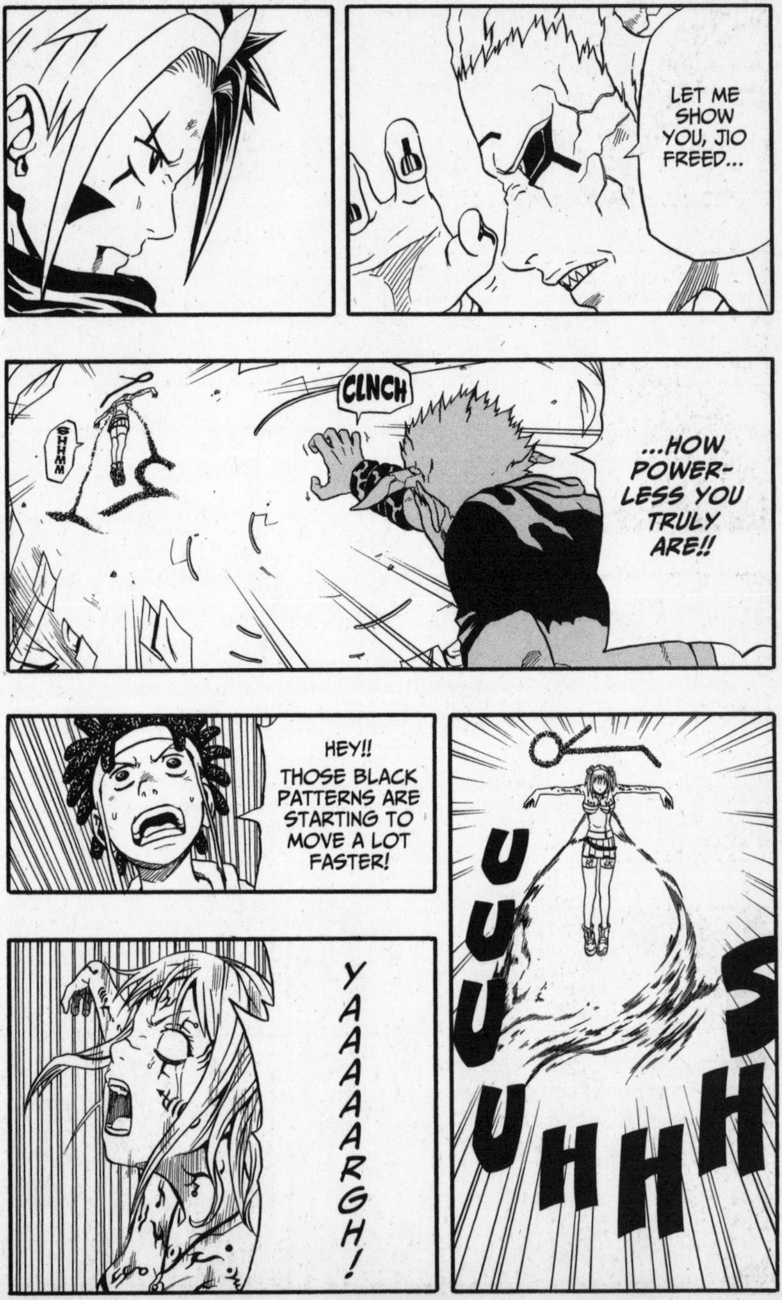
LET ME SHOW YOU, JIO FREED...
...HOW POWER-LESS YOU TRULY ARE!!
CLNCH
SHHMM
SHHHUUUU
HEY!! THOSE BLACK PATTERNS ARE STARTING TO MOVE A LOT FASTER!
YAAAAAARGH!

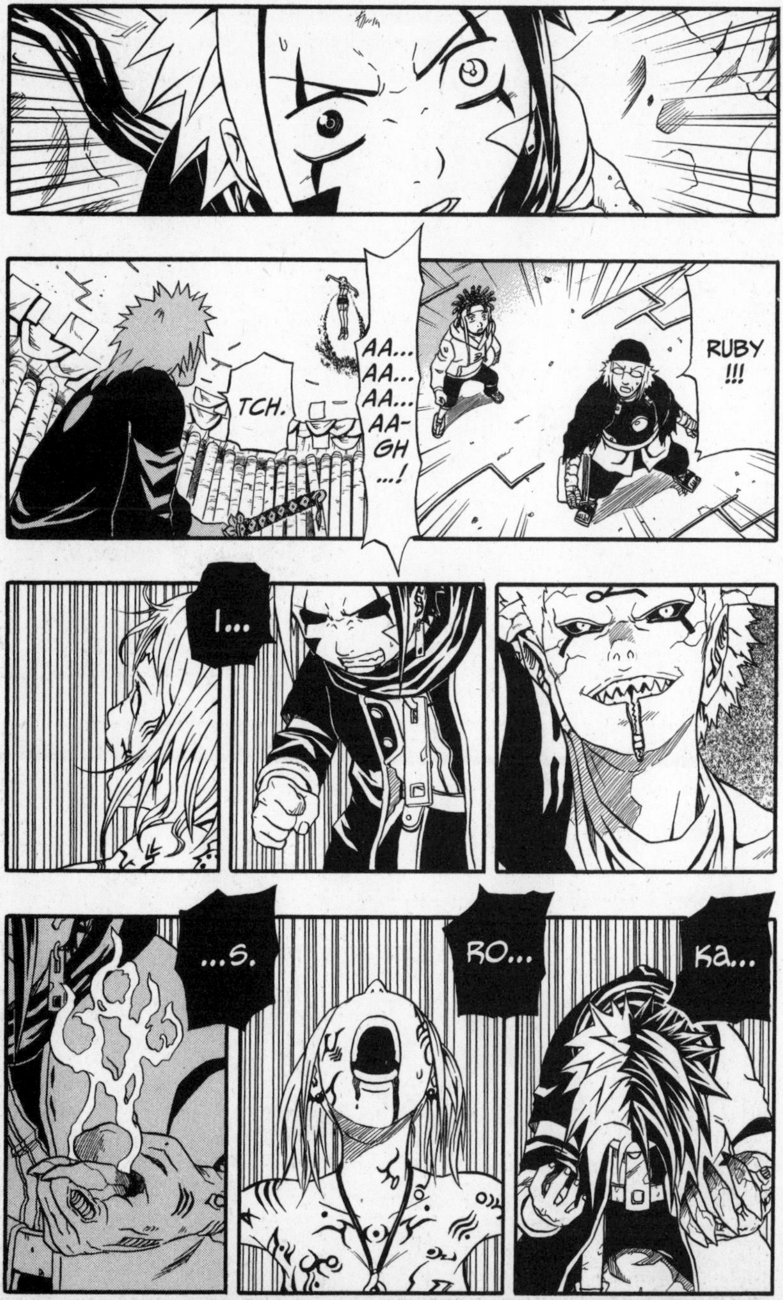
RUBY !!!
AA... AA... AA... AA-GH ...!
TCH.
I...
Ka...
RO...
...S.

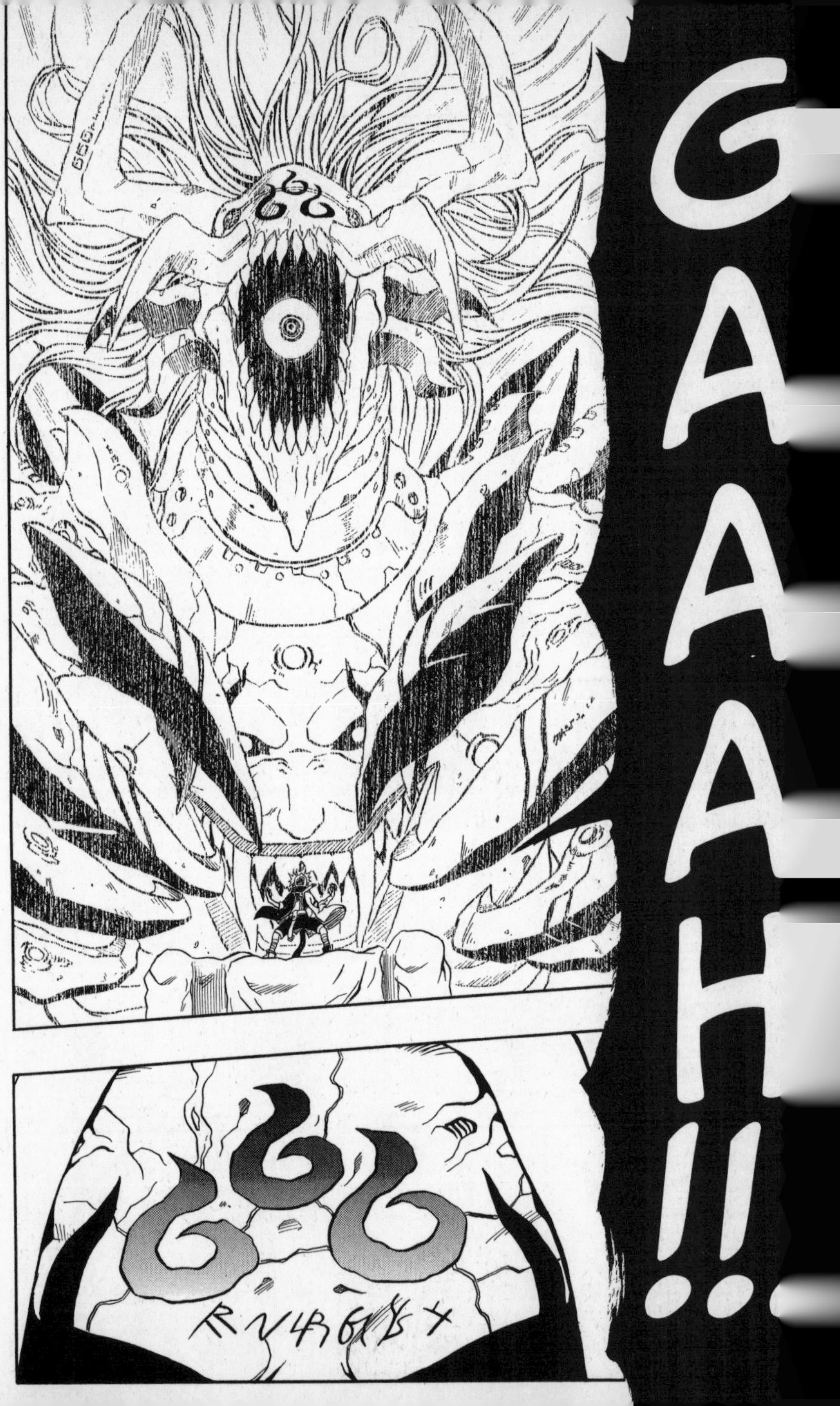
GAAAH!!
666

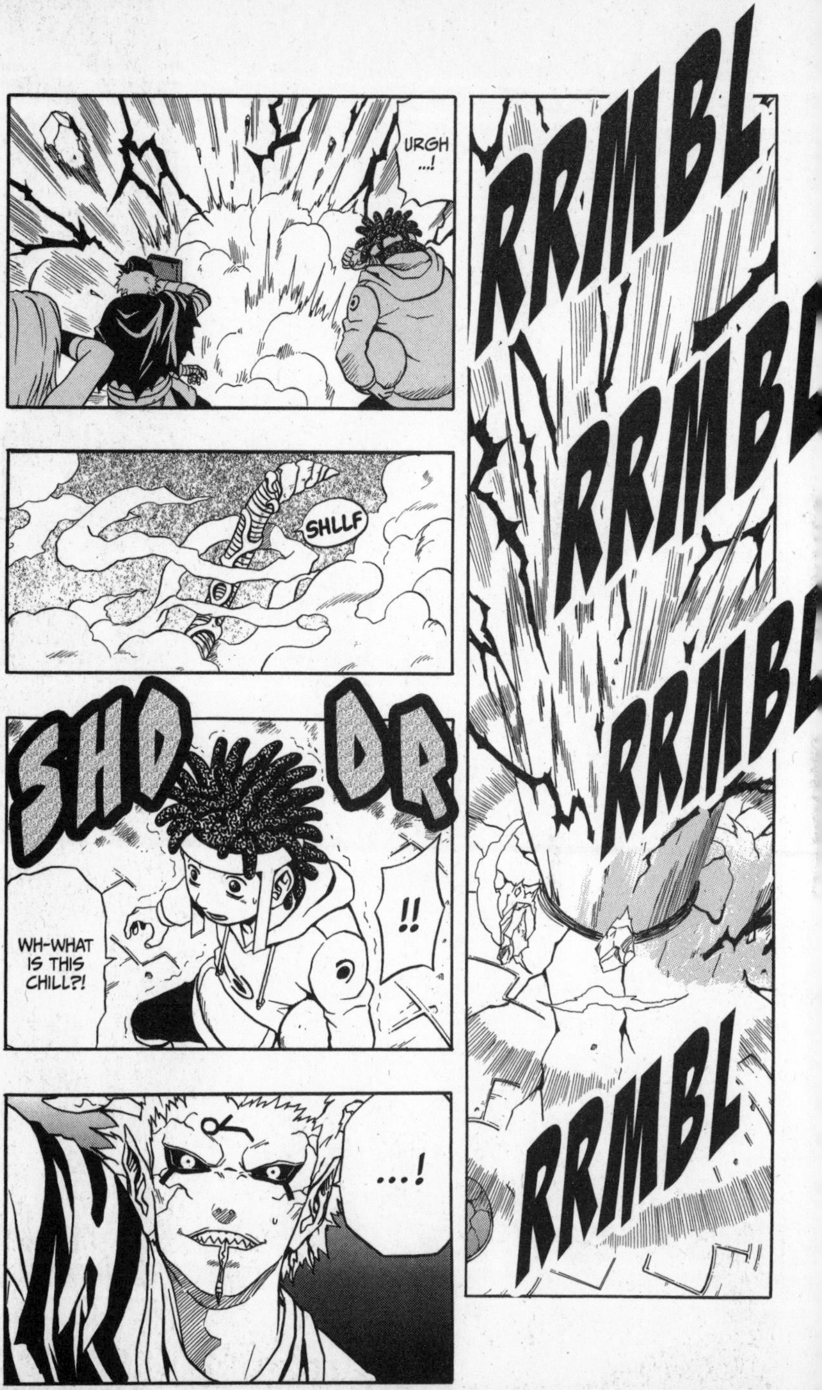
RRMBL
RRMBL
RRMBL
RRMBL
RRMBL
URGH ...!
SHLLF
SHD DR
!!
WH-WHAT IS THIS CHILL?!
...!

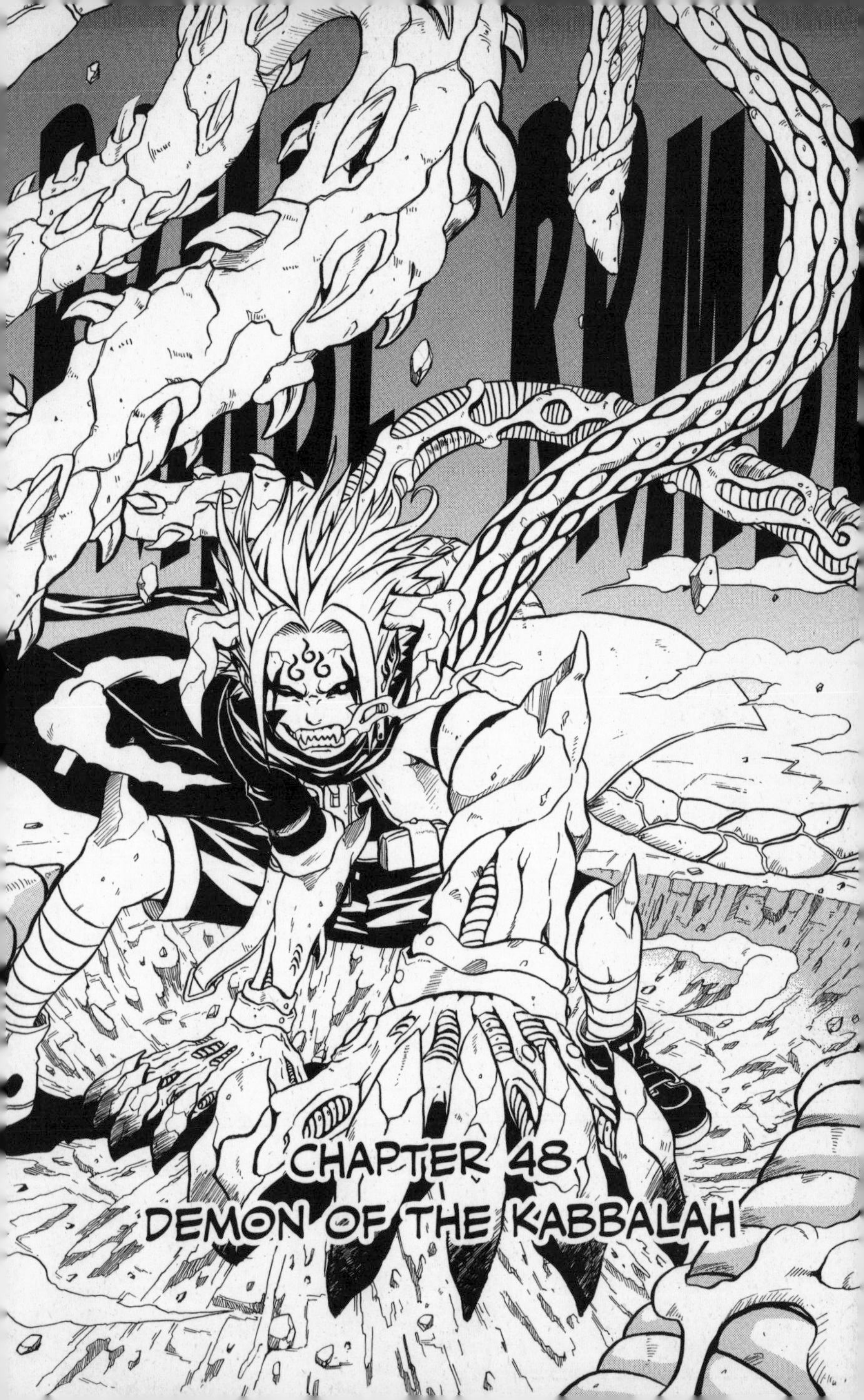
CHAPTER 48
DEMON OF THE KABBALAH

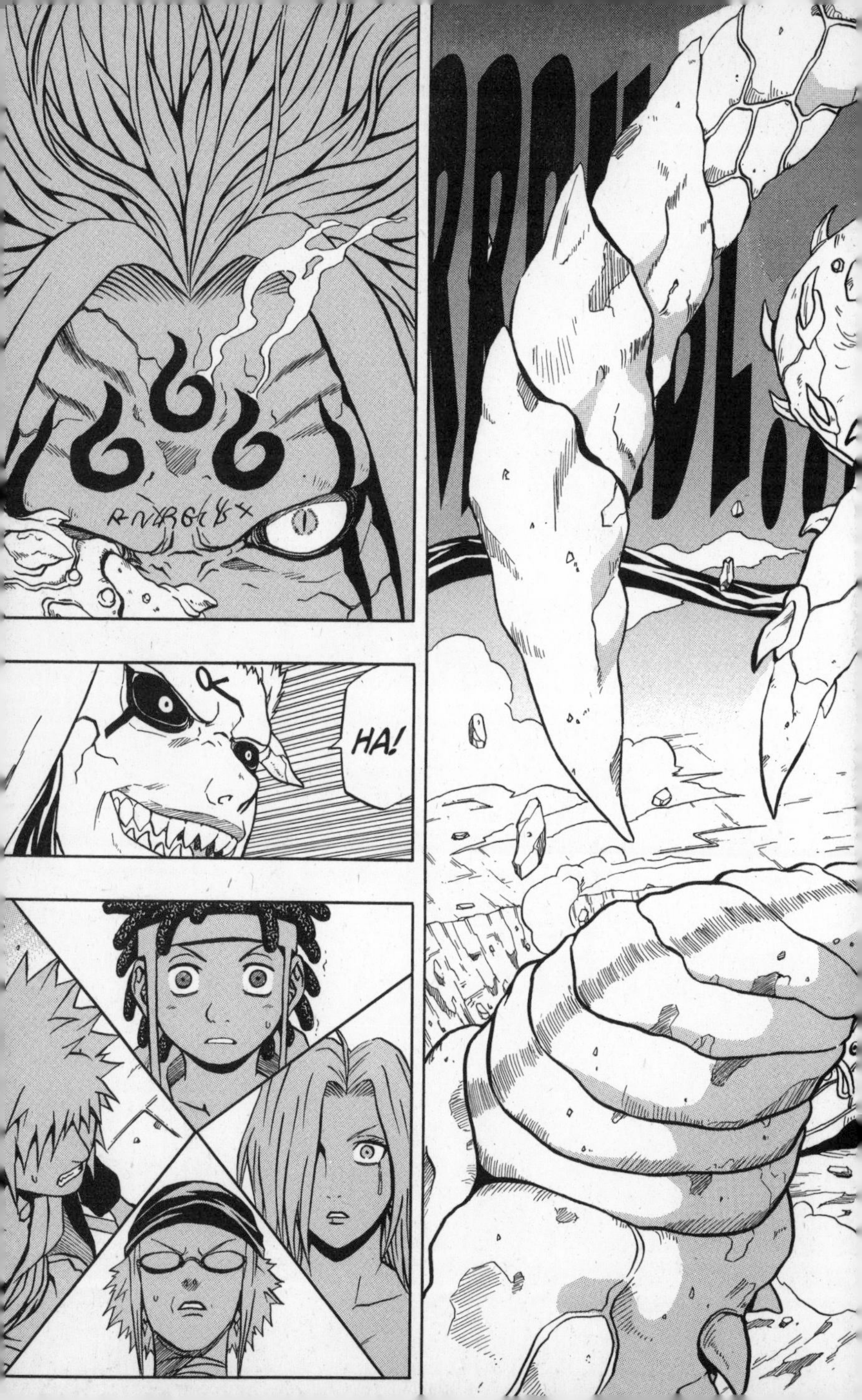
HA!

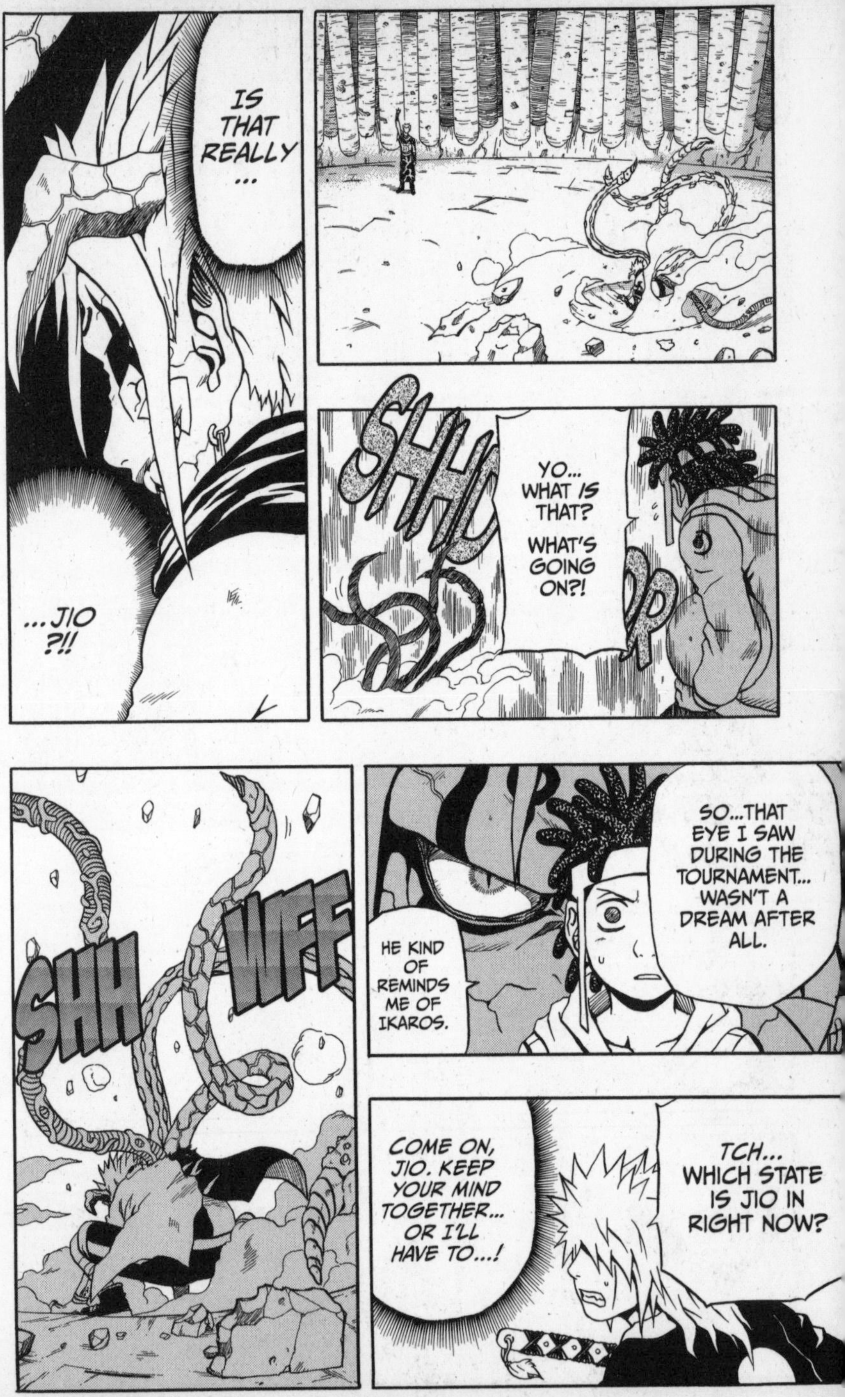
SHHO
OP
YO... WHAT *IS* THAT?
WHAT'S GOING ON?!
IS THAT REALLY ...
...JIO ?!!
SO...THAT EYE I SAW DURING THE TOURNAMENT... WASN'T A DREAM AFTER ALL.
HE KIND OF REMINDS ME OF IKAROS.
TCH... WHICH STATE IS JIO IN RIGHT NOW?
COME ON, JIO. KEEP YOUR MIND TOGETHER... OR I'LL HAVE TO...!
SHH
WFF

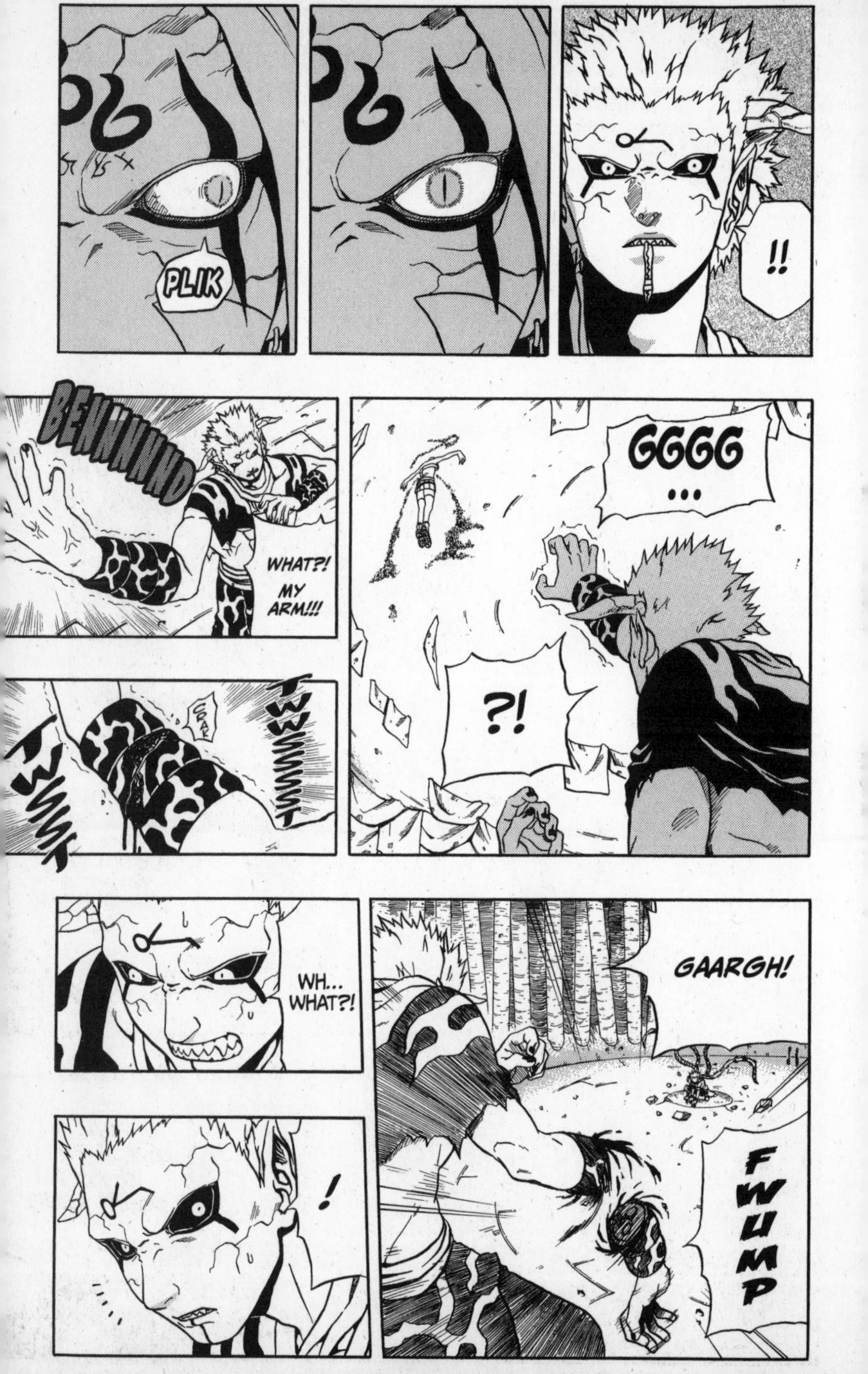
!!
PLIK
GGGG
...
?!
BENNNND
WHAT?!
MY ARM!!!
TWWSSSST
CRAK
FWUNK
GAARGH!
FWUMP
WH...
WHAT?!
!
...

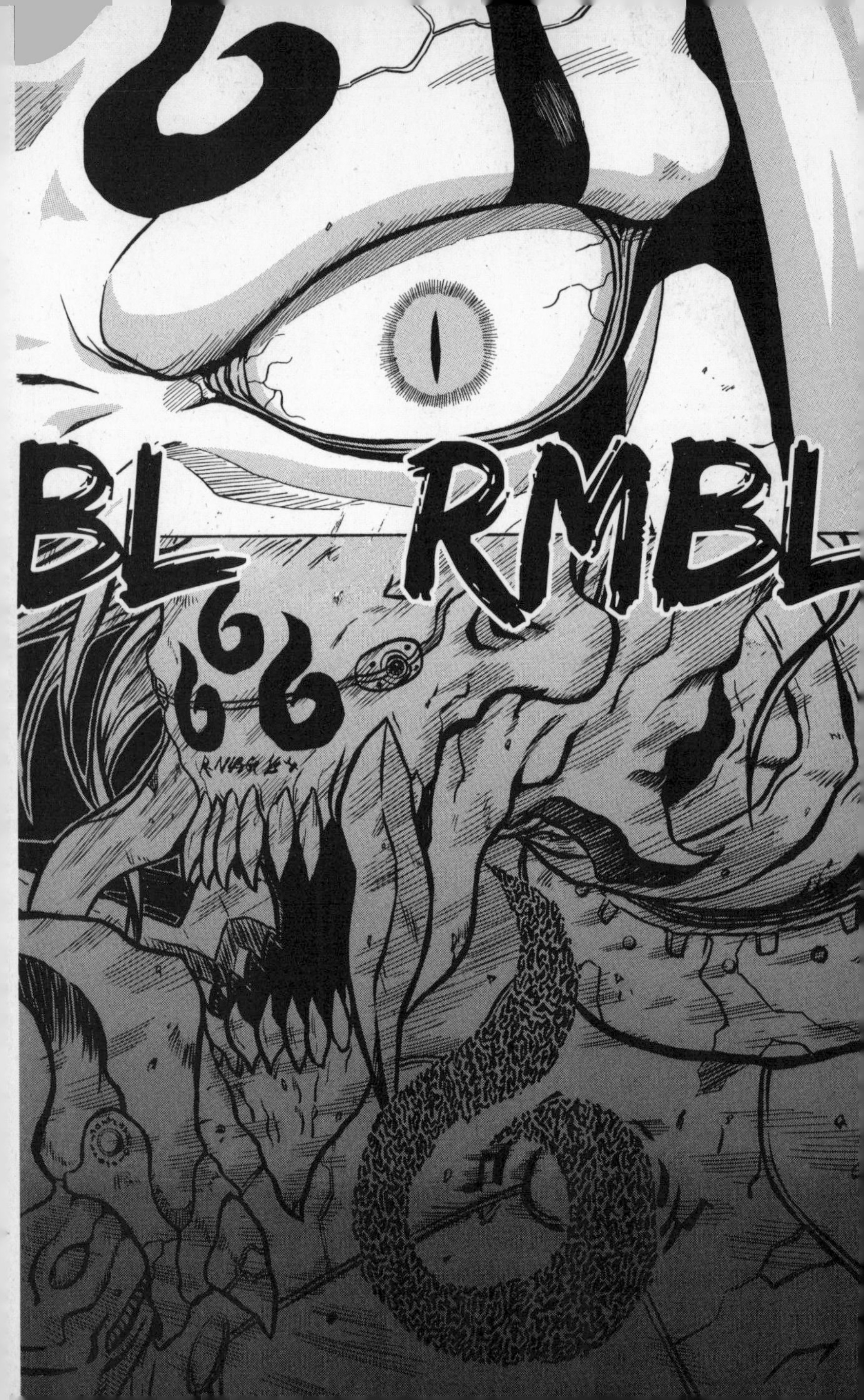
BL
RMBL
666

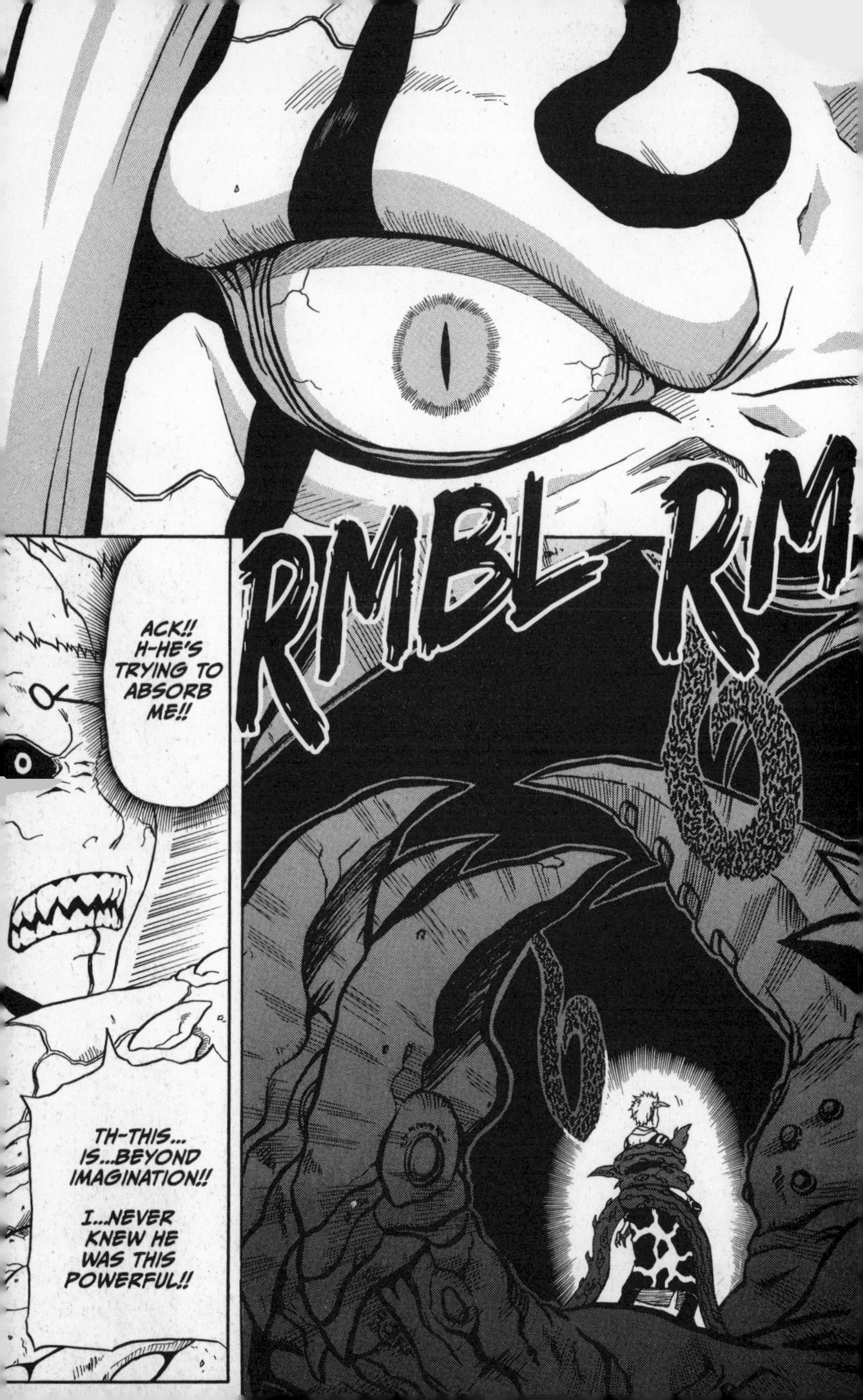

RMBL RM
ACK!! H-HE'S TRYING TO ABSORB ME!!
TH-THIS... IS...BEYOND IMAGINATION!!
I...NEVER KNEW HE WAS THIS POWERFUL!!

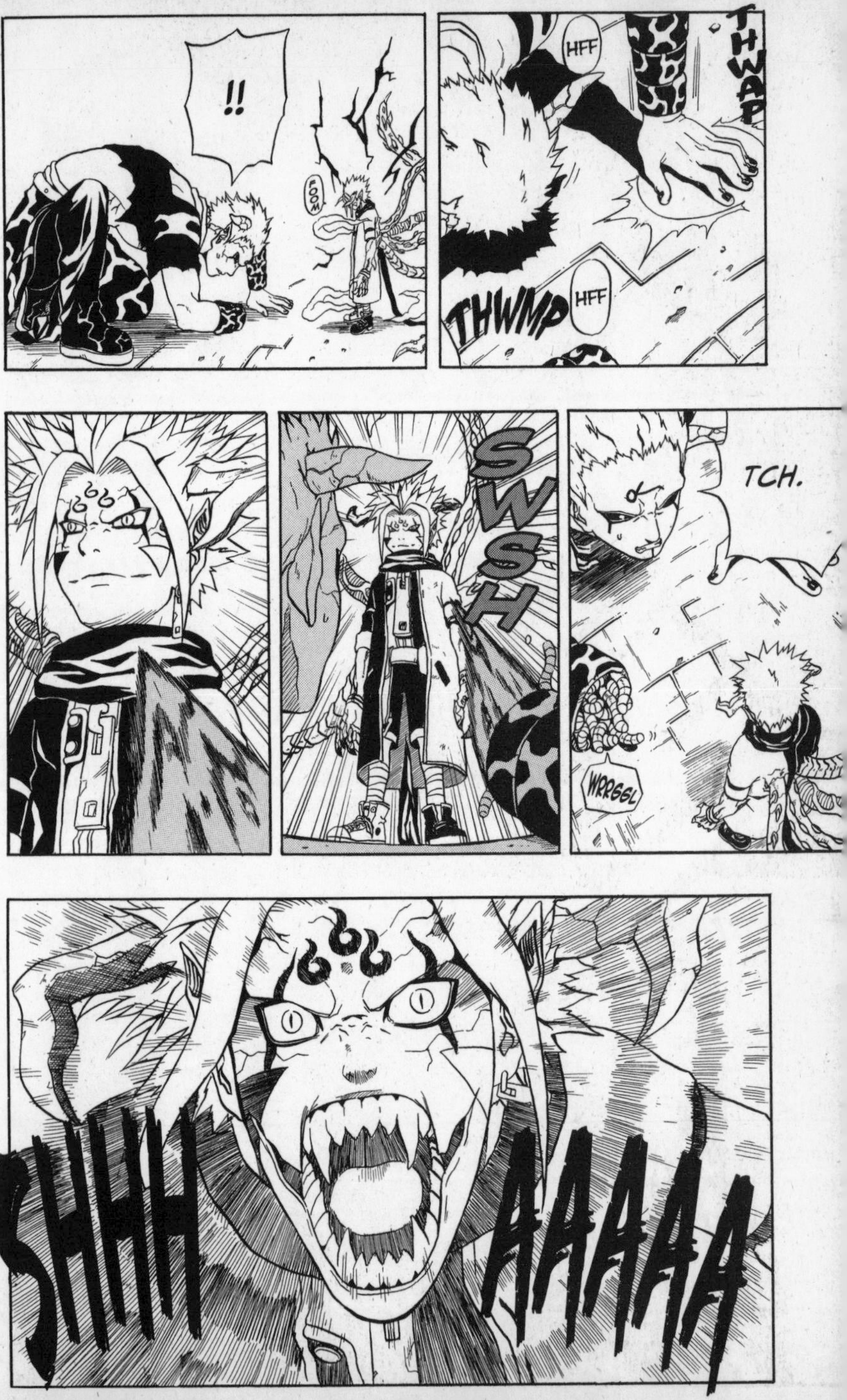
THWAP
HFF
HFF
THWMP
!!
FOOM
TCH.
WRRGGL
SWSH
SHHHAAAA

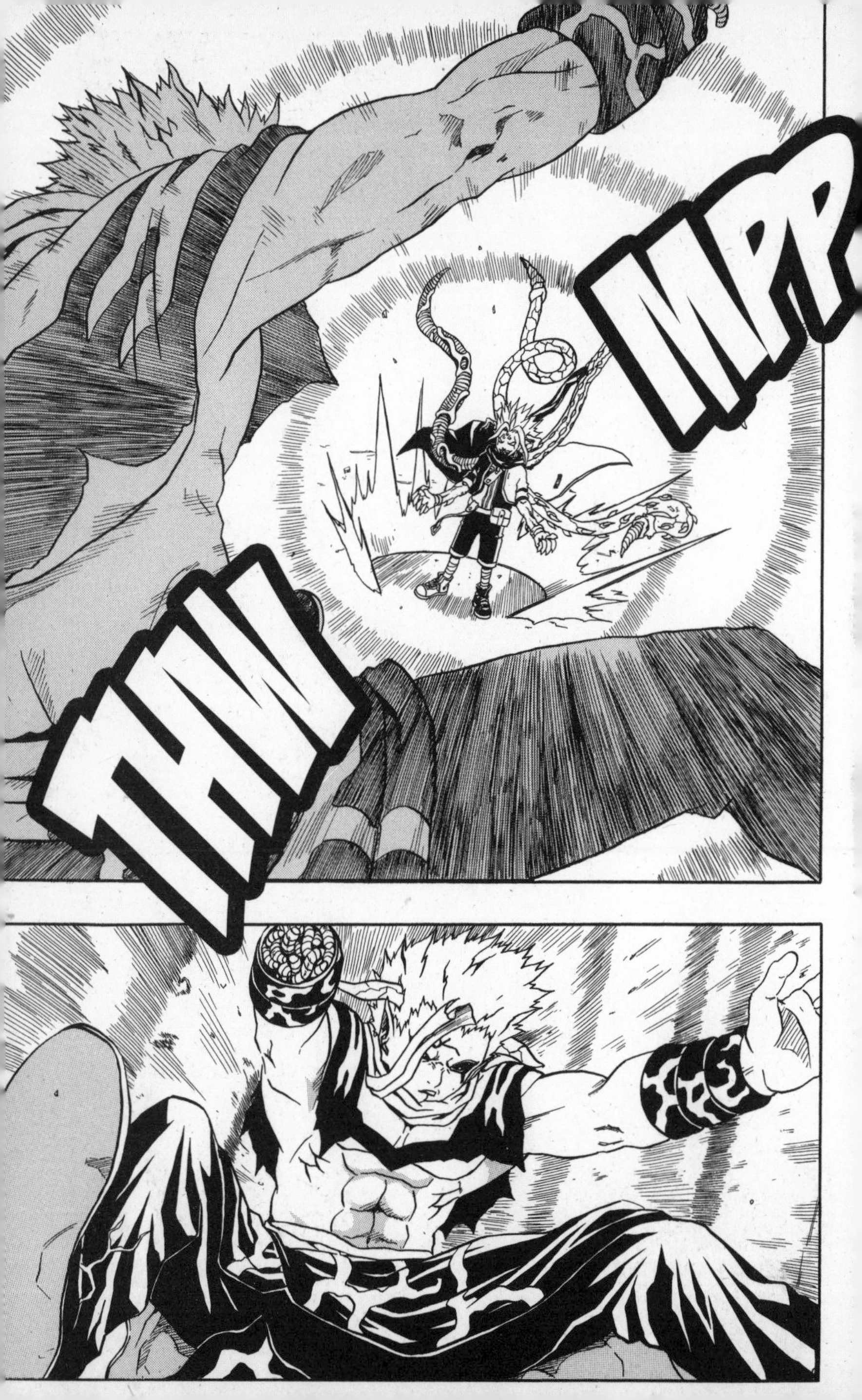
THW
MPP

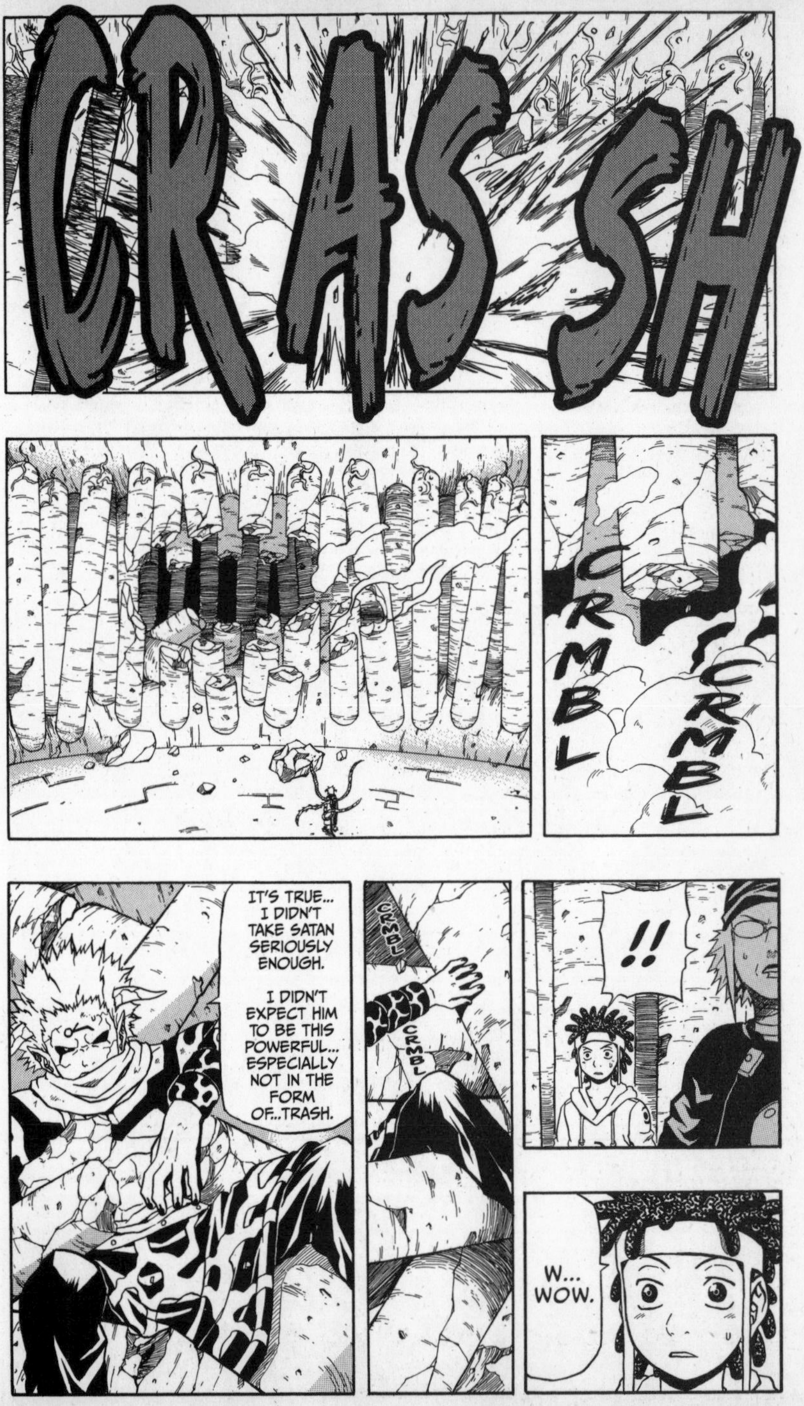
CRASH
CRMBL
CRMBL
!!
W... WOW.
CRMBL
CRMBL
IT'S TRUE... I DIDN'T TAKE SATAN SERIOUSLY ENOUGH.
I DIDN'T EXPECT HIM TO BE THIS POWERFUL... ESPECIALLY NOT IN THE FORM OF...TRASH.

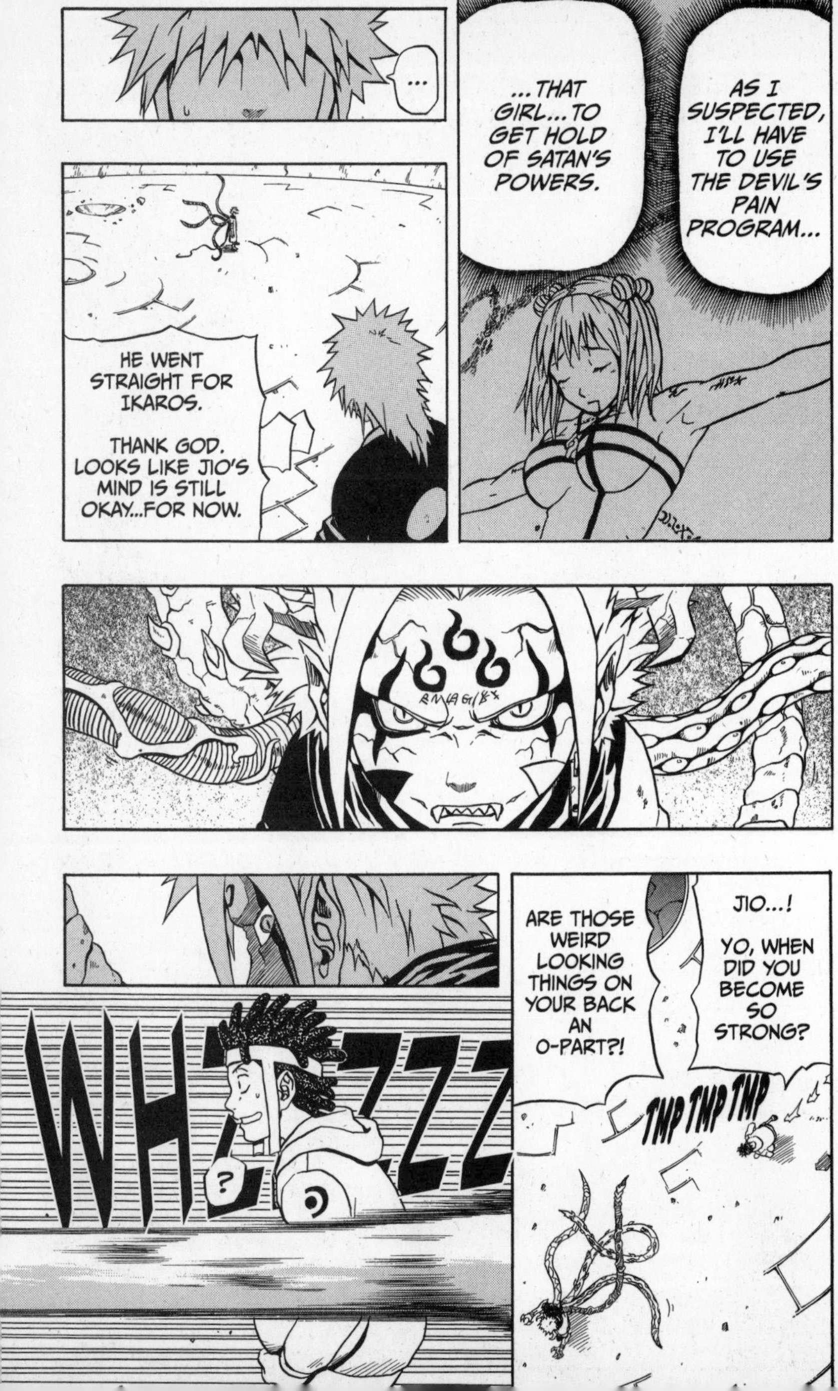
AS I SUSPECTED, I'LL HAVE TO USE THE DEVIL'S PAIN PROGRAM...
...THAT GIRL...TO GET HOLD OF SATAN'S POWERS.
...
HE WENT STRAIGHT FOR IKAROS.
THANK GOD. LOOKS LIKE JIO'S MIND IS STILL OKAY...FOR NOW.
JIO...!
YO, WHEN DID YOU BECOME SO STRONG?
ARE THOSE WEIRD LOOKING THINGS ON YOUR BACK AN O-PART?!
TMP TMP TMP
WHZZZ
?

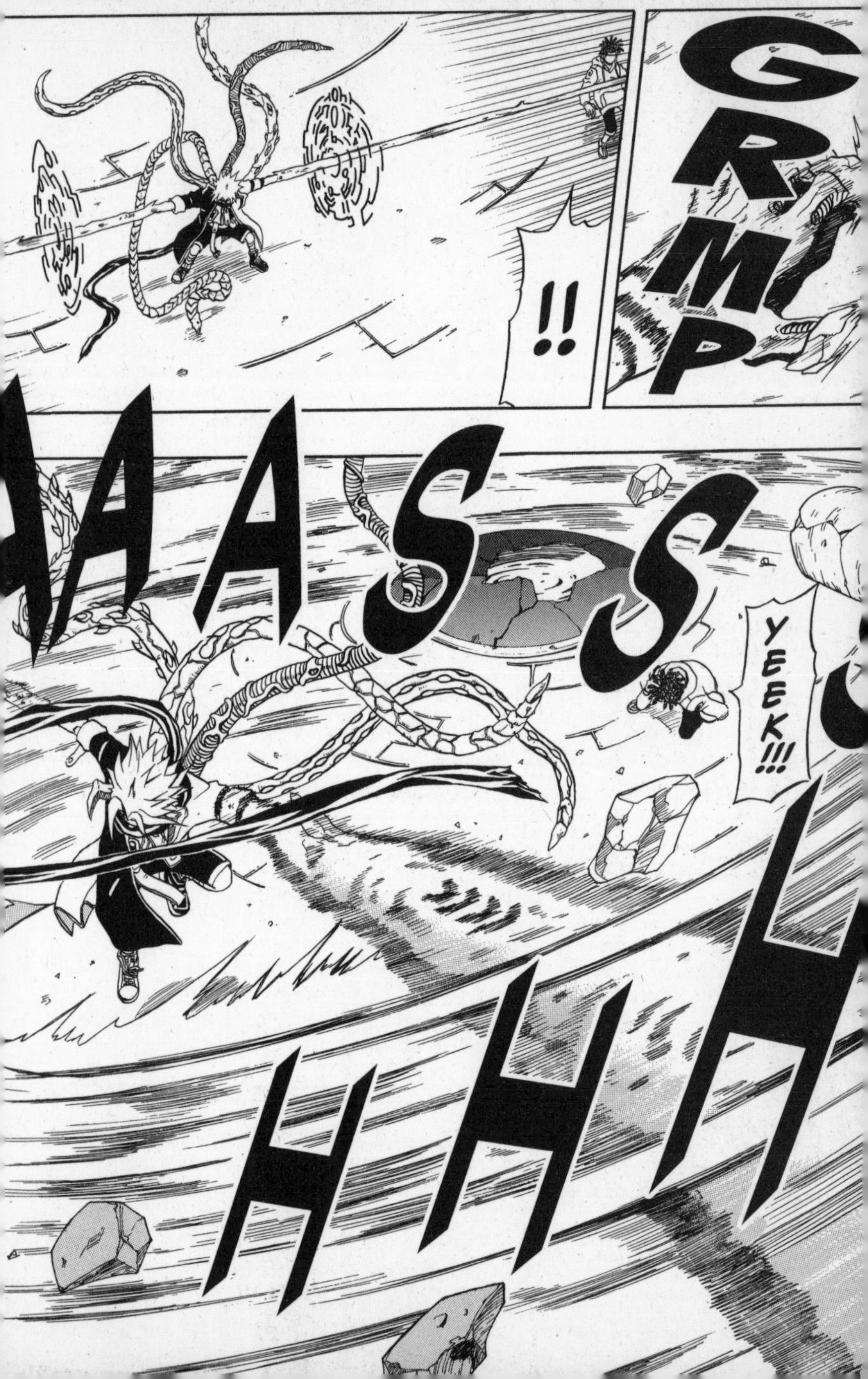
GRMP
!!
AASSHHHHH
YEEK!!!

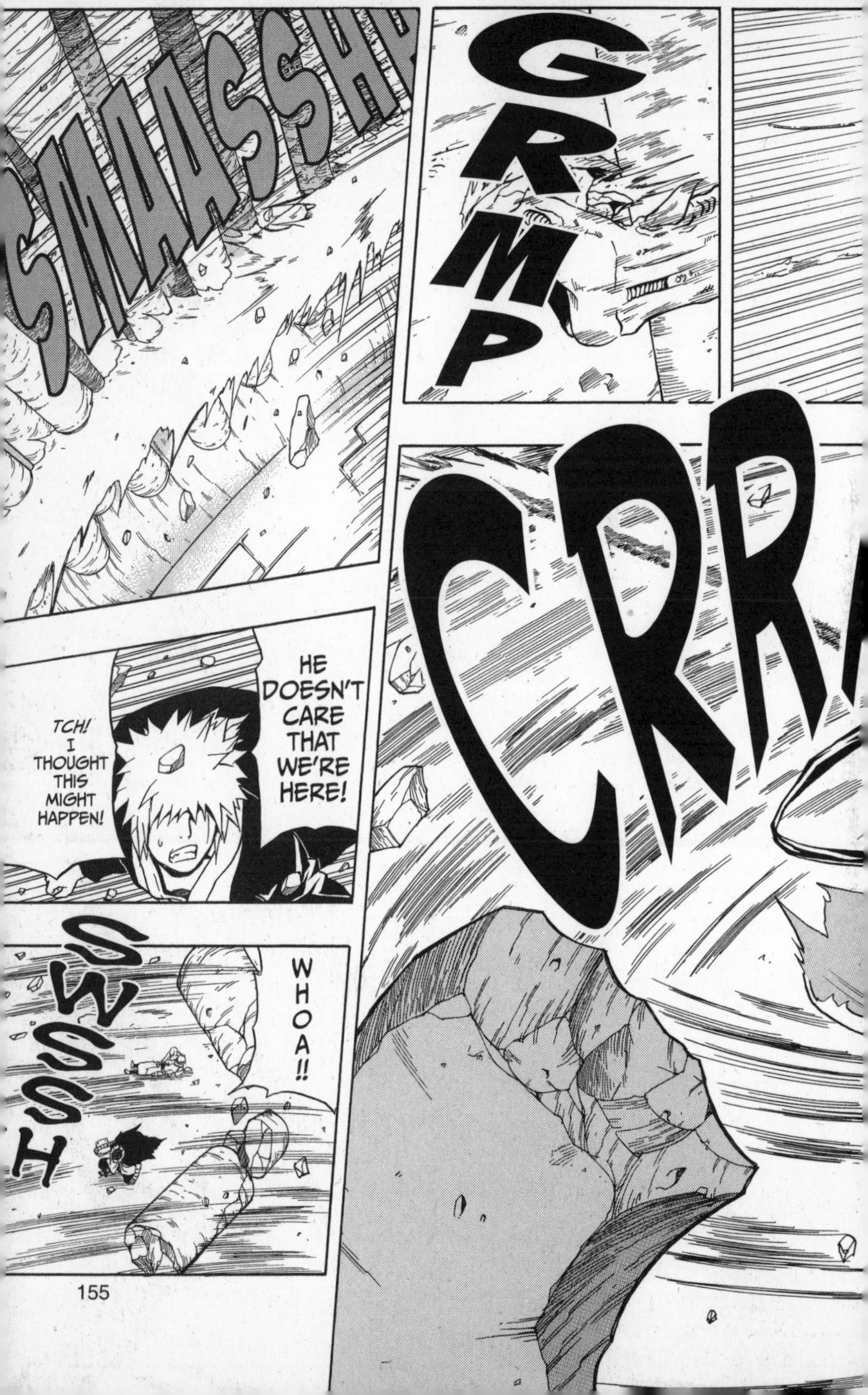
GRMP
SMAASSH
CRR
HE DOESN'T CARE THAT WE'RE HERE!
TCH! I THOUGHT THIS MIGHT HAPPEN!
WHOA!!
SWSSH

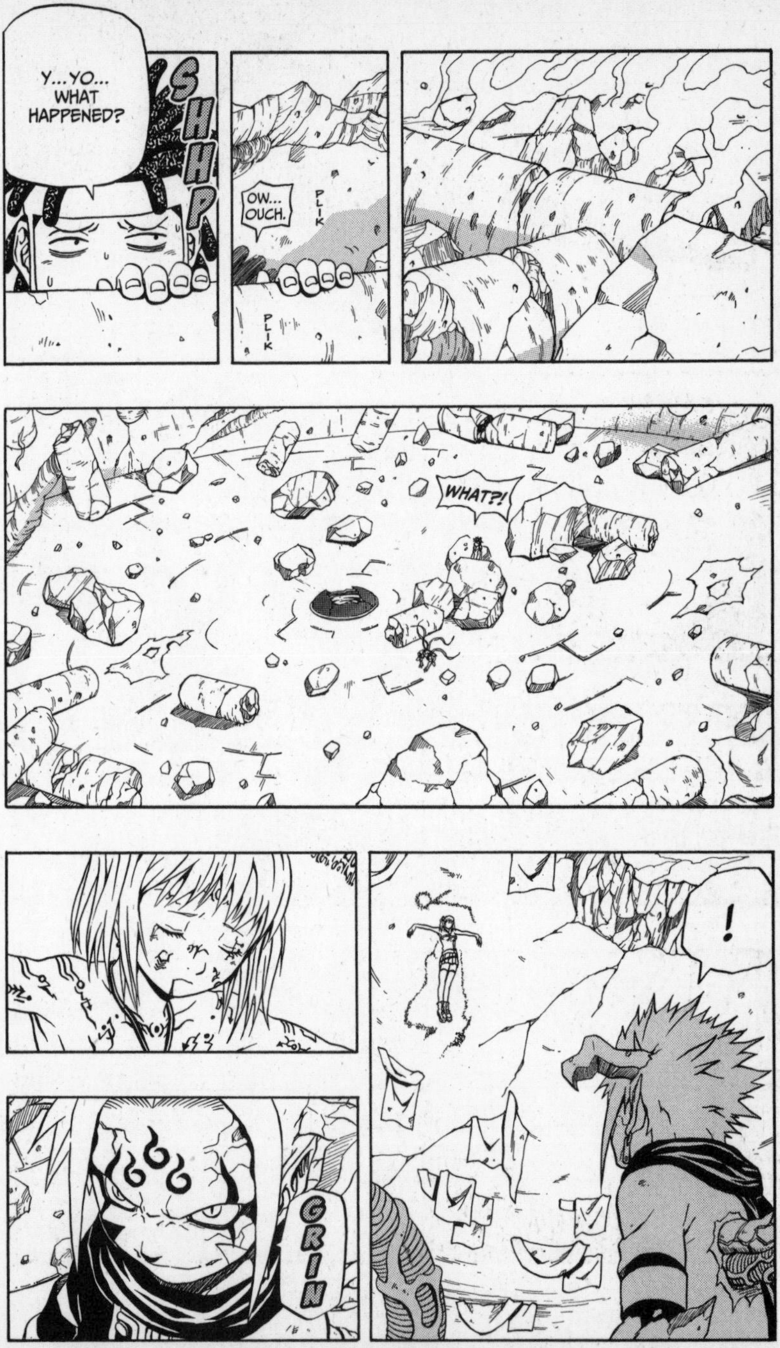
OW... OUCH.
PLIK
PLIK
Y...YO... WHAT HAPPENED?
SHHP
WHAT?!
!
GRIN

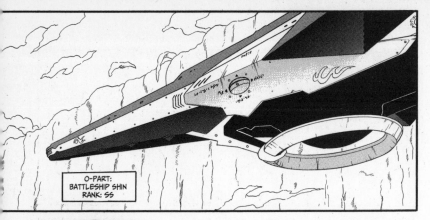

O-PART:
BATTLESHIP SHIN
RANK: SS

SHDDR

!

CHKK

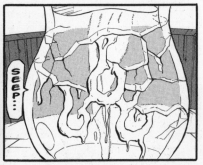

SEEP...

157

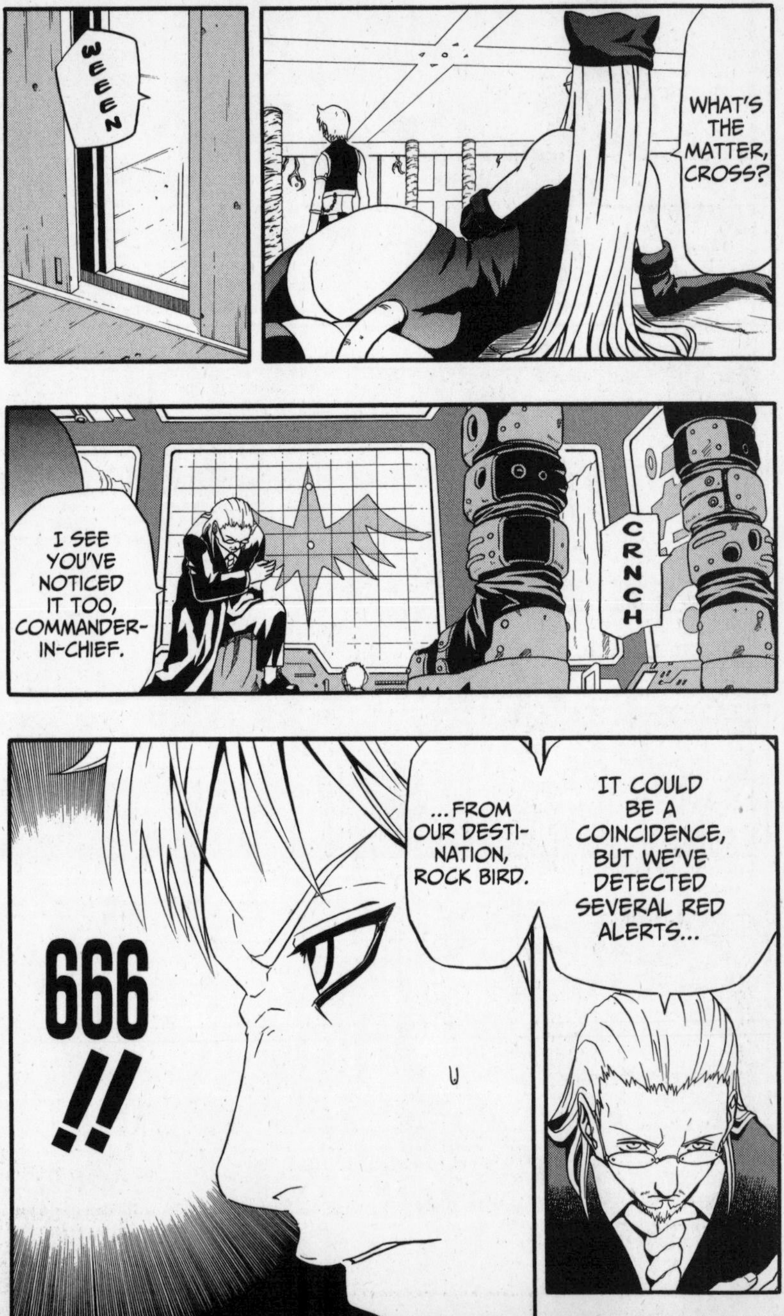
WHAT'S THE MATTER, CROSS?
WEEEN
CRNCH
I SEE YOU'VE NOTICED IT TOO, COMMANDER-IN-CHIEF.
IT COULD BE A COINCIDENCE, BUT WE'VE DETECTED SEVERAL RED ALERTS...
...FROM OUR DESTINATION, ROCK BIRD.
666!!

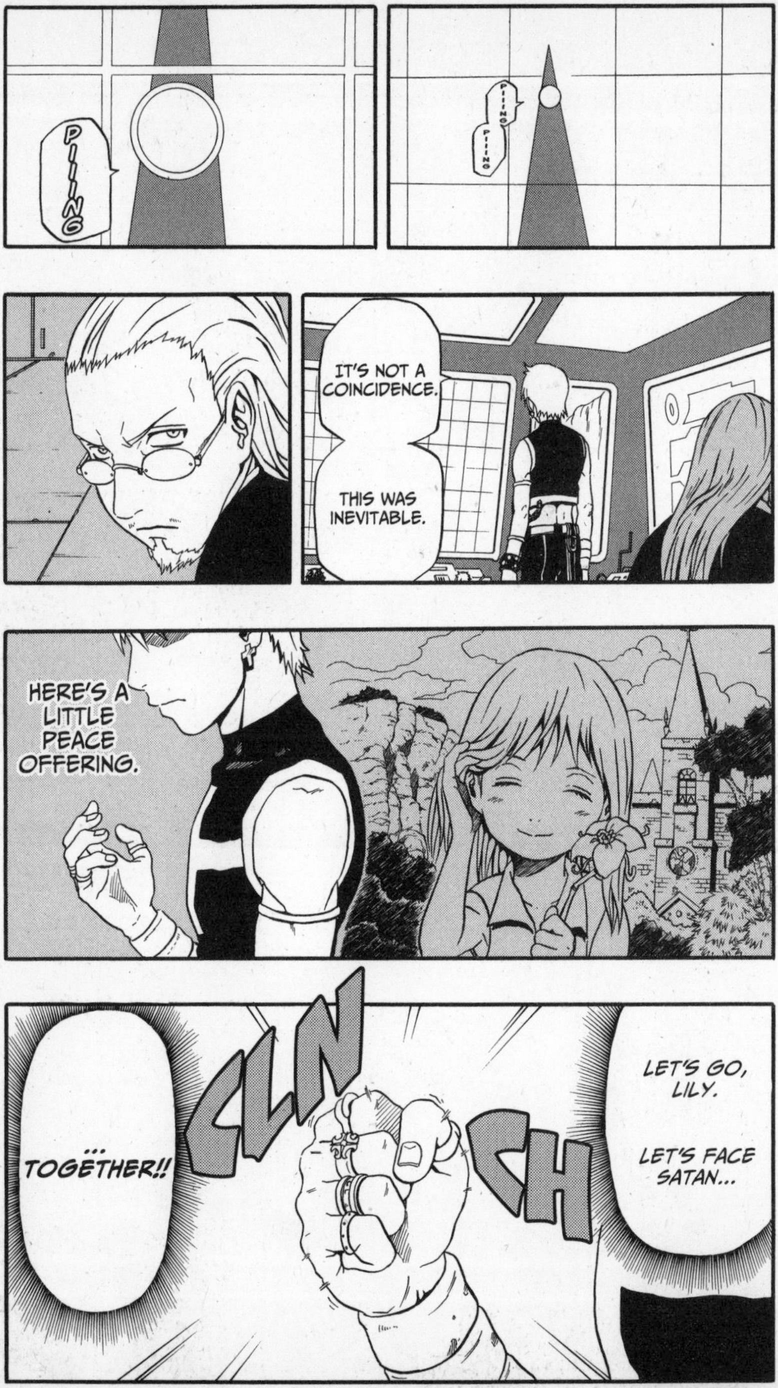
PIIING
PIIING
PIIING
IT'S NOT A COINCIDENCE.
THIS WAS INEVITABLE.
HERE'S A LITTLE PEACE OFFERING.
LET'S GO, LILY.
LET'S FACE SATAN...
CLNCH
...TOGETHER!!

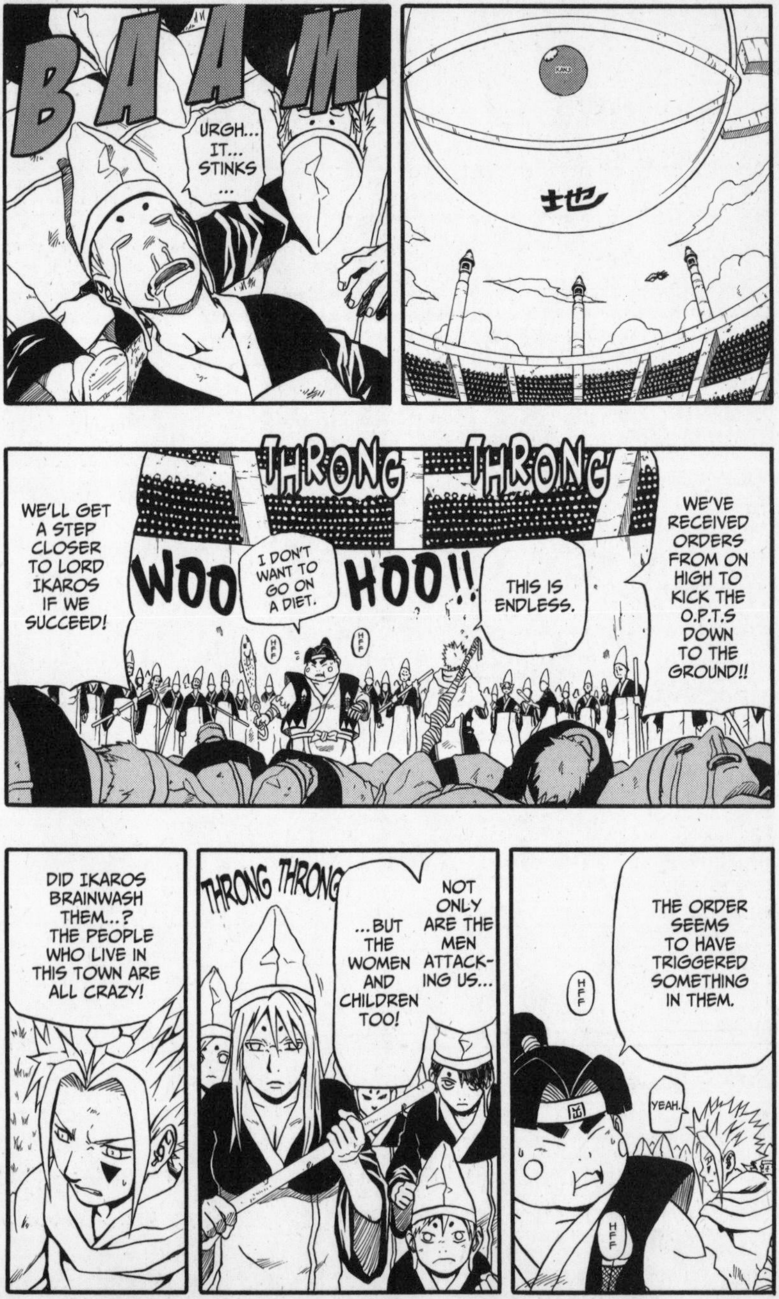
土也
KANJI
BAAM
URGH... IT... STINKS ...
THRONG THRONG
WE'VE RECEIVED ORDERS FROM ON HIGH TO KICK THE O.P.T.S DOWN TO THE GROUND!!
THIS IS ENDLESS.
WOO HOO!!
HFF
I DON'T WANT TO GO ON A DIET.
HFF
WE'LL GET A STEP CLOSER TO LORD IKAROS IF WE SUCCEED!
THE ORDER SEEMS TO HAVE TRIGGERED SOMETHING IN THEM.
HFF
YEAH.
HFF
THRONG THRONG
NOT ONLY ARE THE MEN ATTACKING US...
...BUT THE WOMEN AND CHILDREN TOO!
DID IKAROS BRAINWASH THEM...? THE PEOPLE WHO LIVE IN THIS TOWN ARE ALL CRAZY!

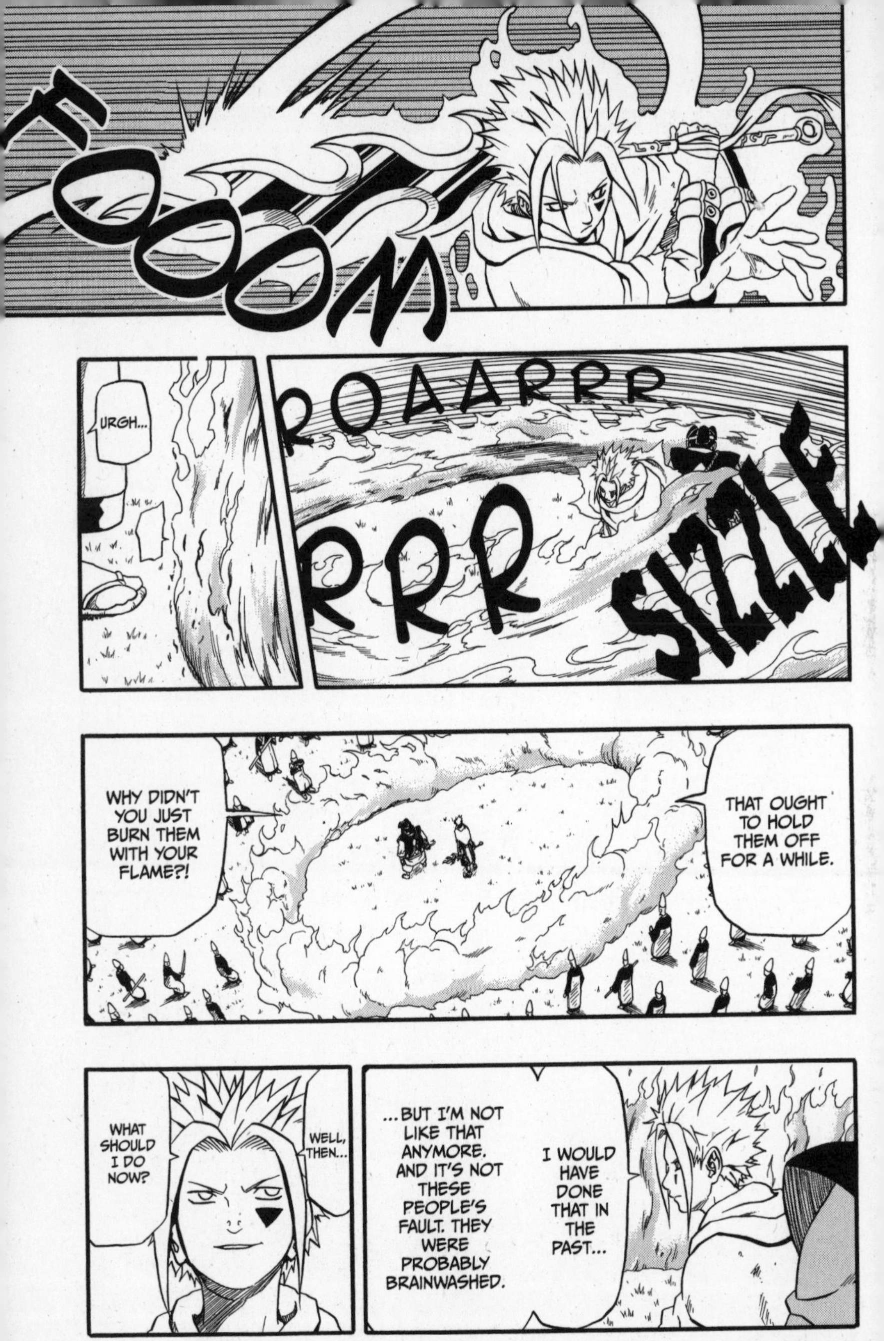
FOOOM
ROAARRRRRR
SIZZLE
URGH...
THAT OUGHT TO HOLD THEM OFF FOR A WHILE.
WHY DIDN'T YOU JUST BURN THEM WITH YOUR FLAME?!
I WOULD HAVE DONE THAT IN THE PAST...
...BUT I'M NOT LIKE THAT ANYMORE. AND IT'S NOT THESE PEOPLE'S FAULT. THEY WERE PROBABLY BRAINWASHED.
WELL, THEN...
WHAT SHOULD I DO NOW?

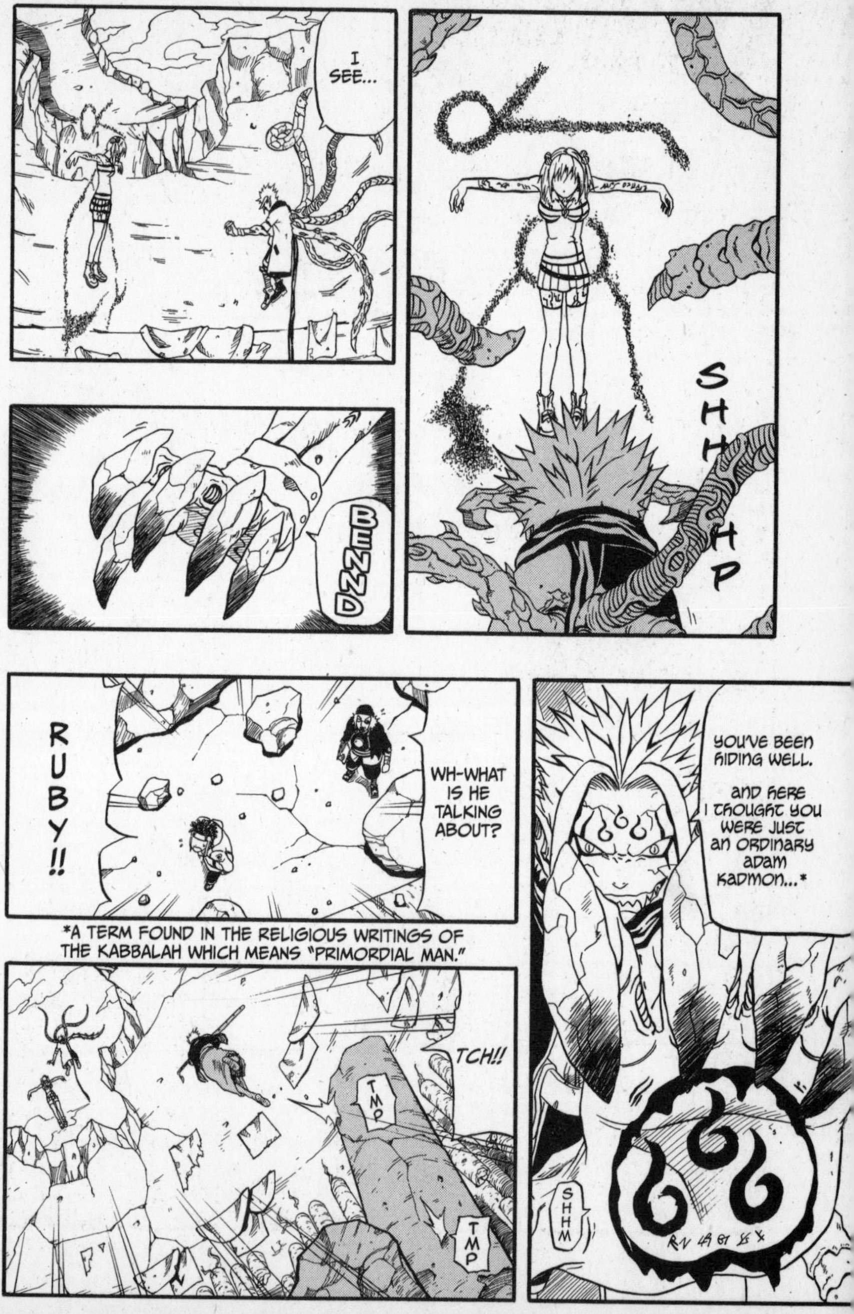
SHHHP
I SEE...
BENNND
YOU'VE BEEN HIDING WELL.
AND HERE I THOUGHT YOU WERE JUST AN ORDINARY ADAM KADMON...*
SHHM
WH-WHAT IS HE TALKING ABOUT?
RUBY!!
*A TERM FOUND IN THE RELIGIOUS WRITINGS OF THE KABBALAH WHICH MEANS "PRIMORDIAL MAN."
TCH!!
TMP
TMP

THWMP

SMAASH

NO WAY!! I CAN'T BELIEVE KIRIN GOT HIT!

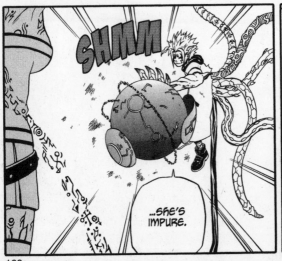

SHMM

...SHE'S IMPURE.

JIO, YOU IDIOT! WHAT ARE YOU DOING?!

GET AHOLD OF YOURSELF!!

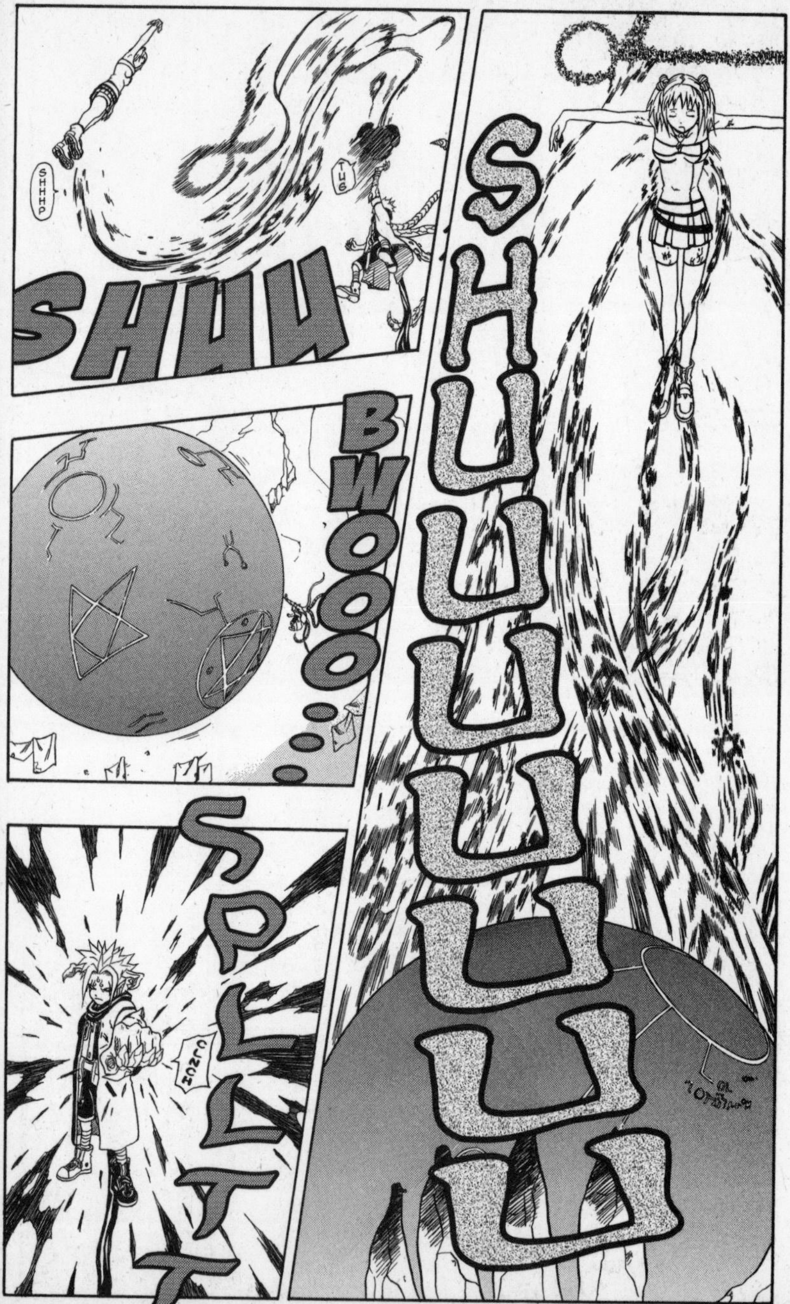
SHUUUUUUU
TUG
SHHHP
SHUU
BWOOO...
SPLLTT
CLNCH

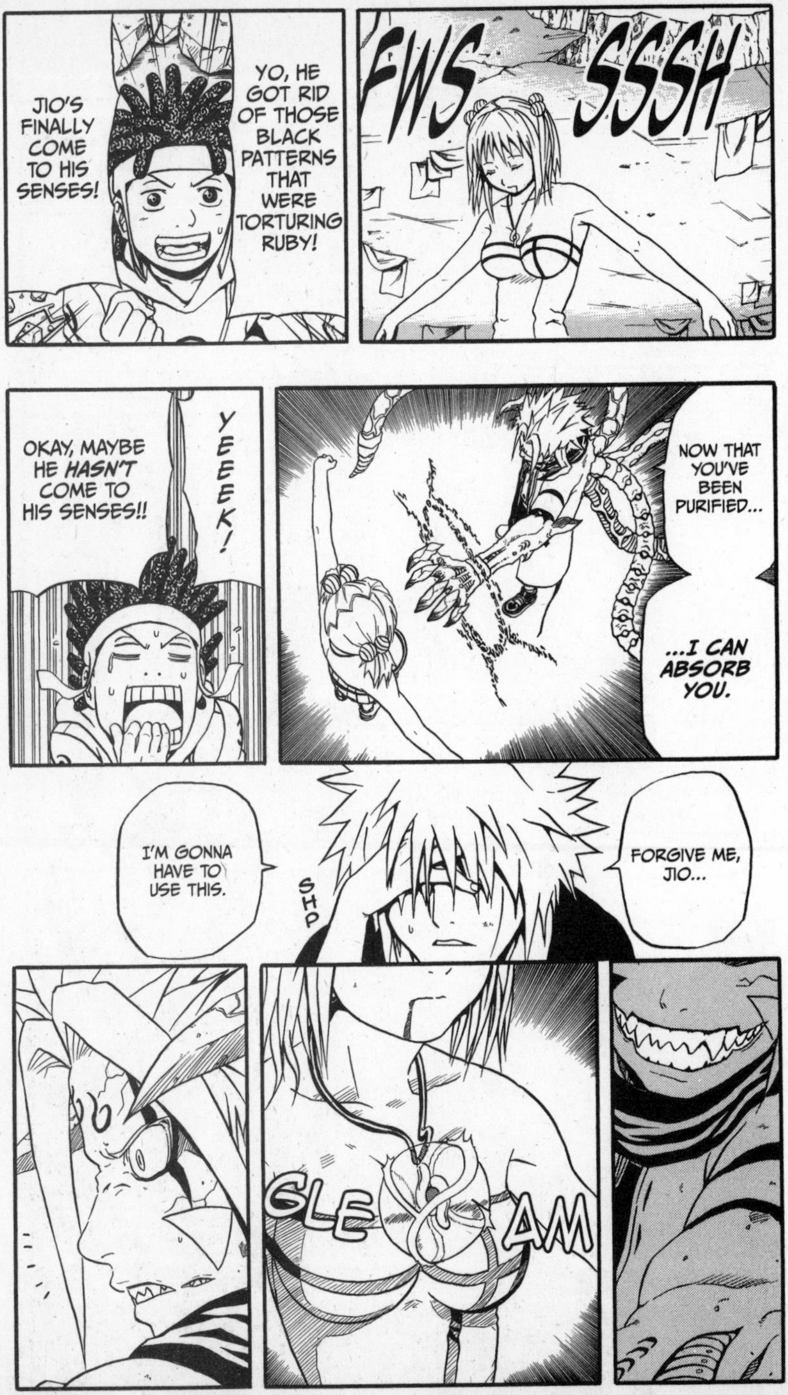
FWS SSSH
YO, HE GOT RID OF THOSE BLACK PATTERNS THAT WERE TORTURING RUBY!
JIO'S FINALLY COME TO HIS SENSES!
NOW THAT YOU'VE BEEN PURIFIED...
...I CAN ABSORB YOU.
YEEEEK!
OKAY, MAYBE HE HASN'T COME TO HIS SENSES!!
FORGIVE ME, JIO...
SHP
I'M GONNA HAVE TO USE THIS.
GLEAM

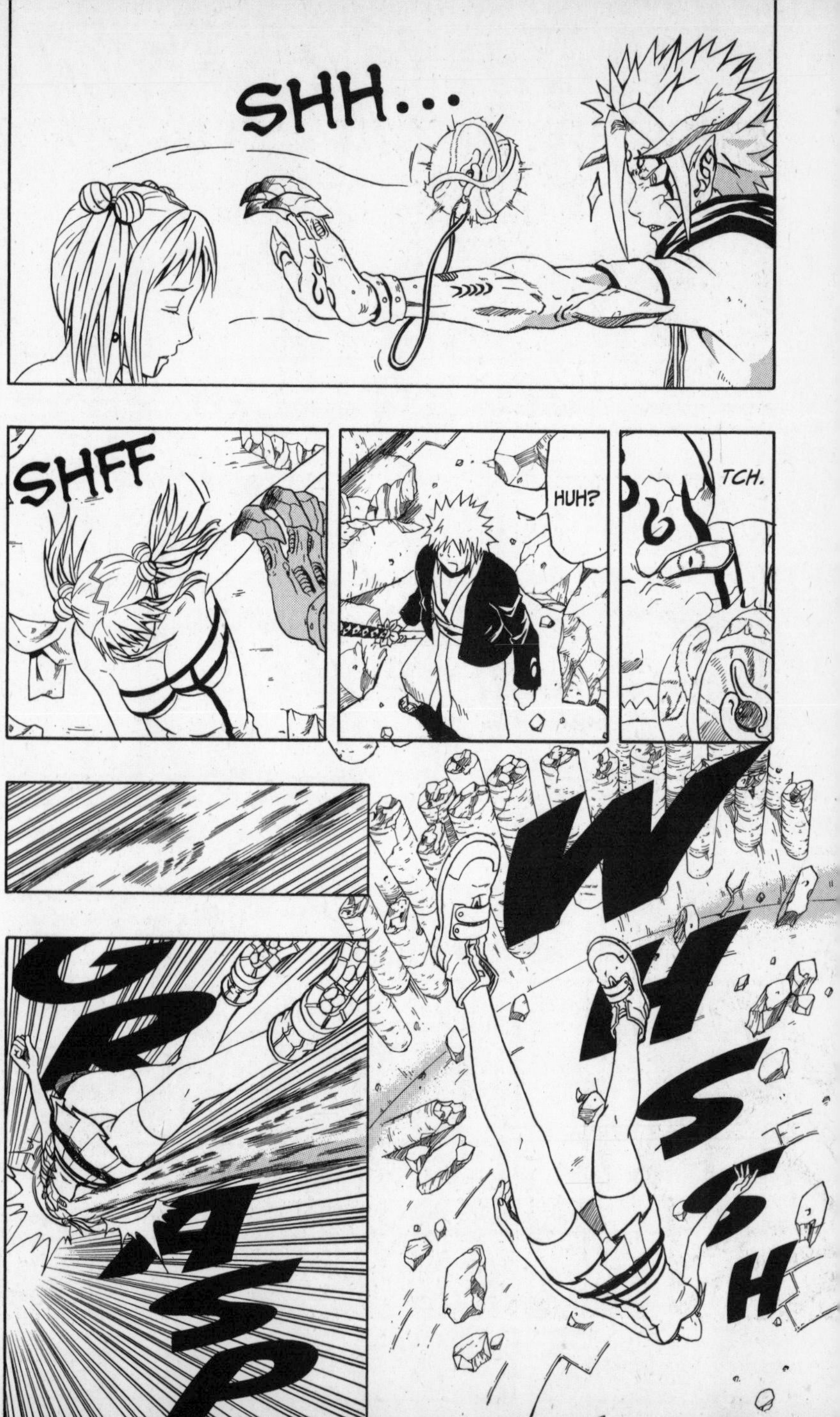
SHH...
TCH.
HUH?
SHFF
WHISH
GRASP

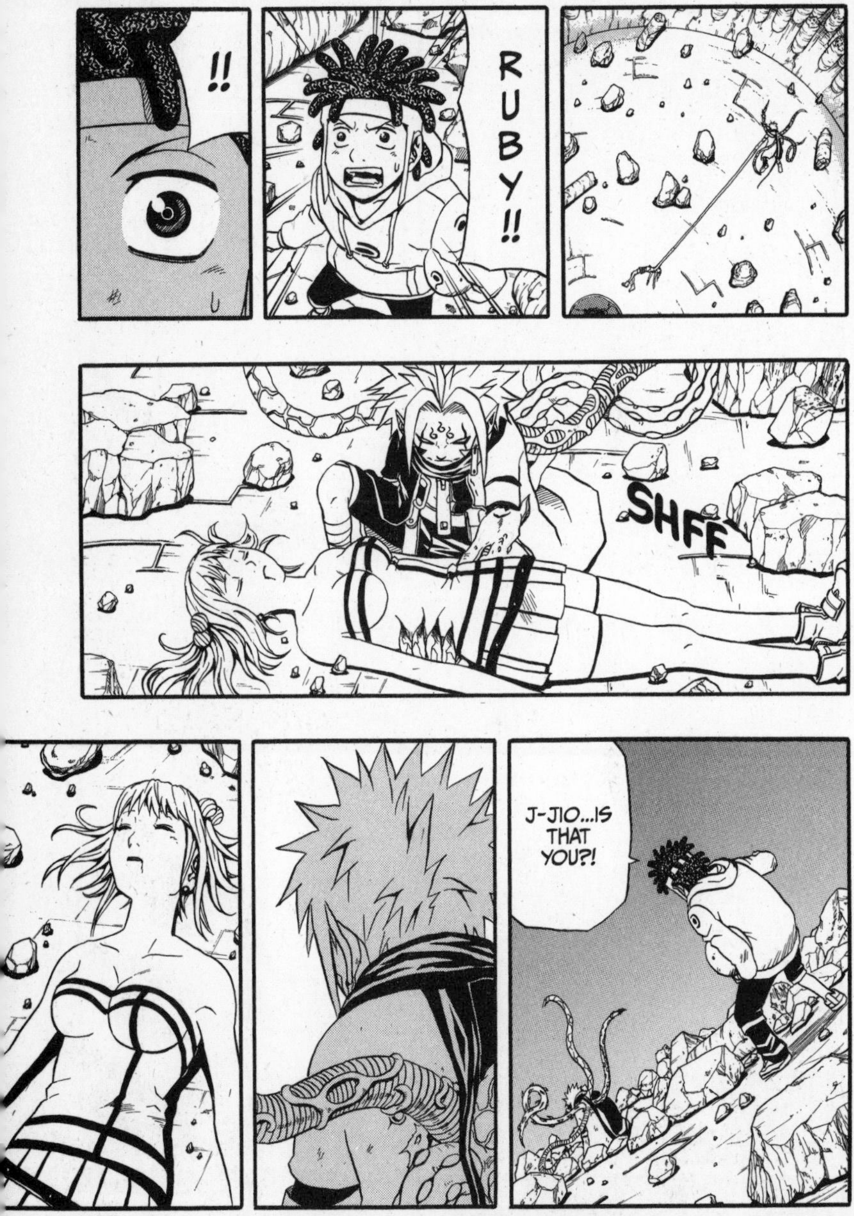
RUBY!!
!!
SHFF
J-JIO...IS THAT YOU?!

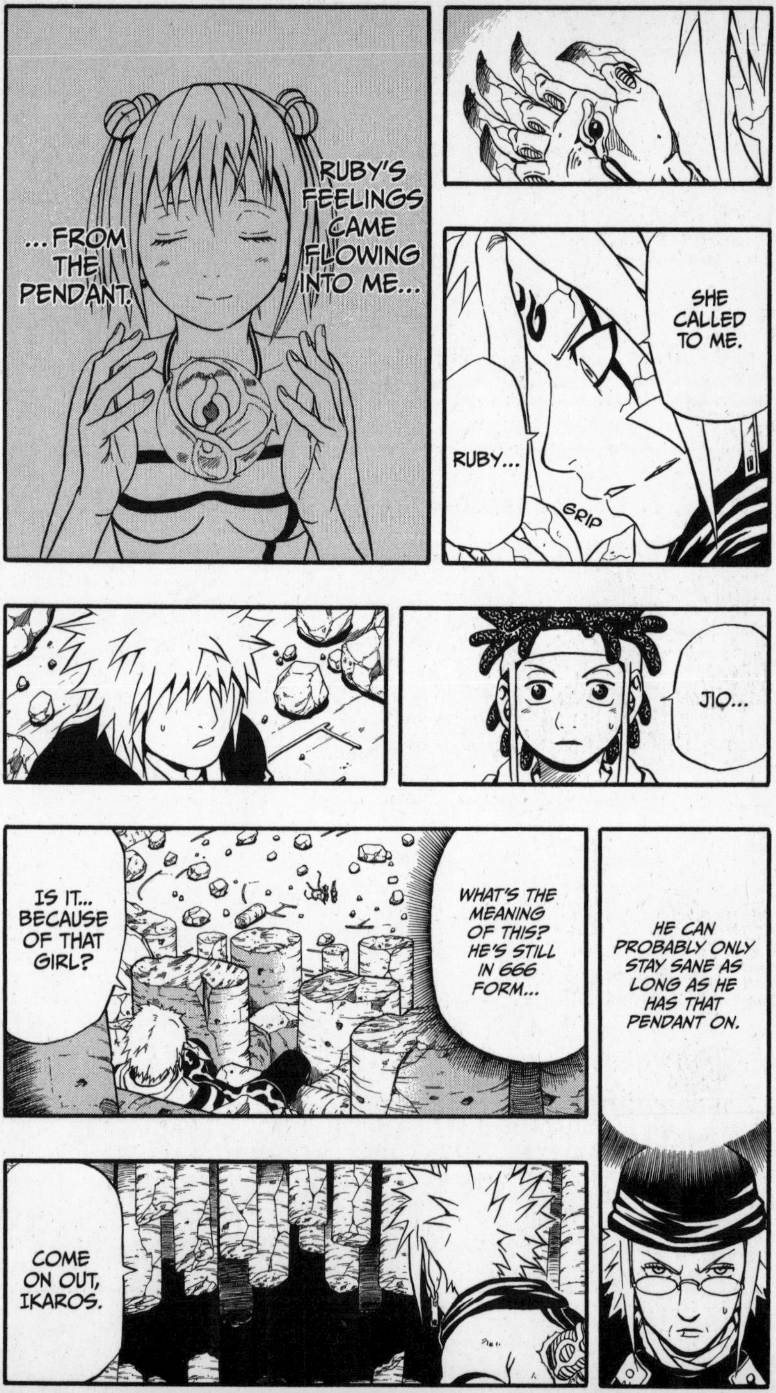
SHE CALLED TO ME.
RUBY...
GRIP
RUBY'S FEELINGS CAME FLOWING INTO ME...
...FROM THE PENDANT.
JIO...
HE CAN PROBABLY ONLY STAY SANE AS LONG AS HE HAS THAT PENDANT ON.
WHAT'S THE MEANING OF THIS? HE'S STILL IN 666 FORM...
IS IT... BECAUSE OF THAT GIRL?
COME ON OUT, IKAROS.

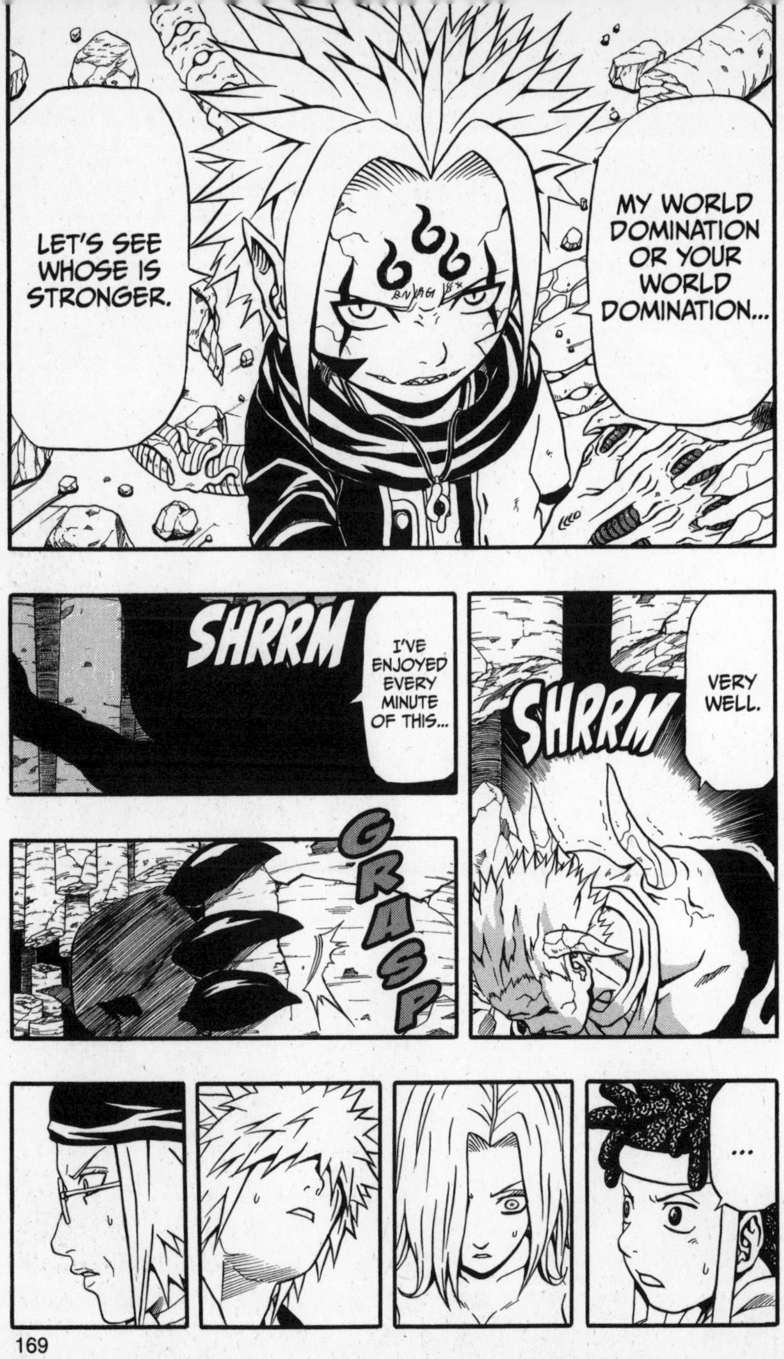
MY WORLD DOMINATION OR YOUR WORLD DOMINATION...
LET'S SEE WHOSE IS STRONGER.
SHRRM
VERY WELL.
SHRRM
I'VE ENJOYED EVERY MINUTE OF THIS...
GRASP
...

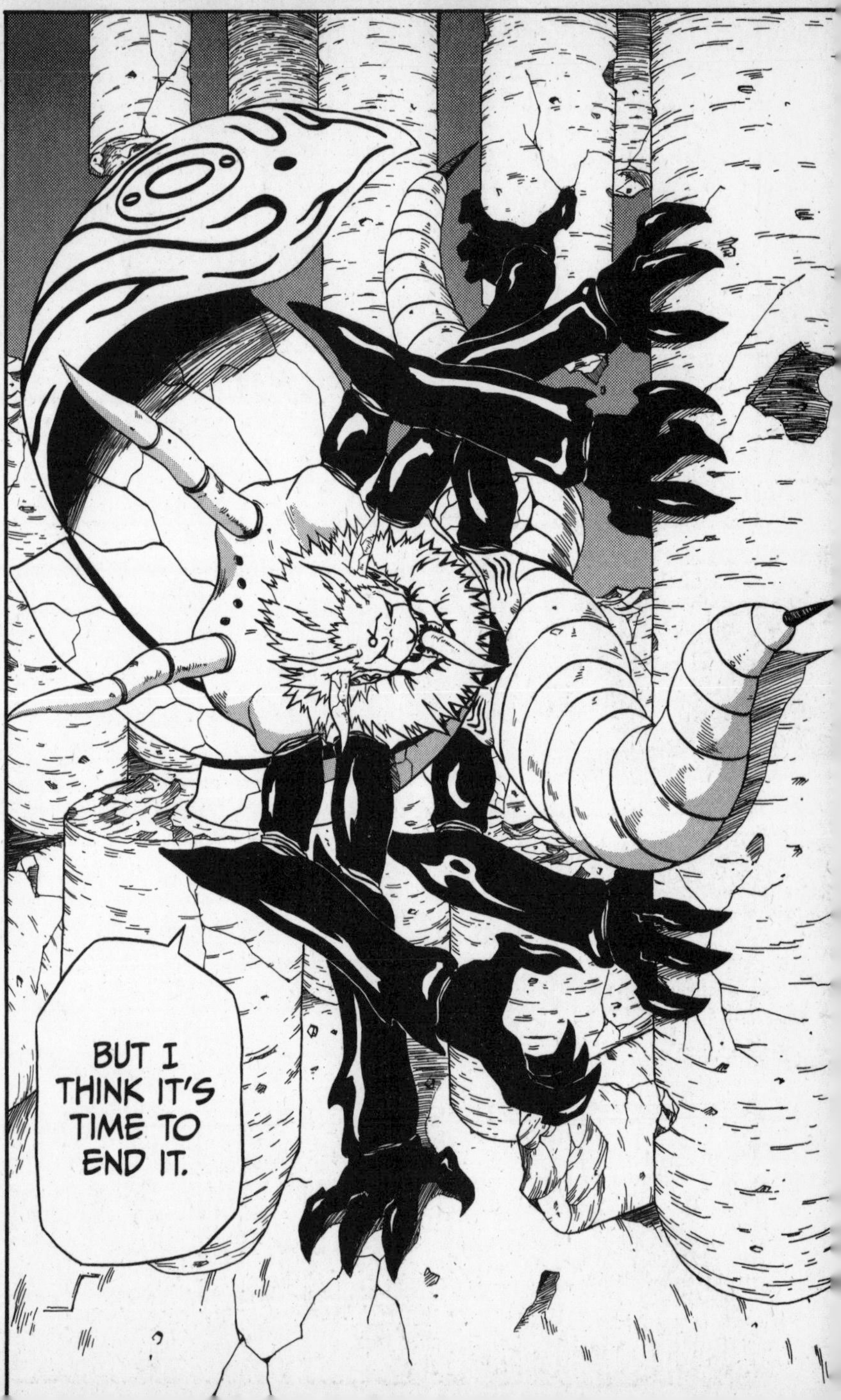
BUT I THINK IT'S TIME TO END IT.

YO...SO THAT'S IKAROS'S TRUE IDENTITY, HUH?

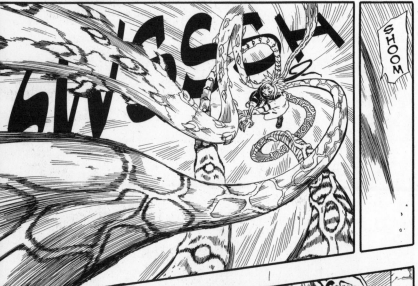

SHOOM

SHHHMM

CLNCH

CLNCH

CLNCH

CLNCH

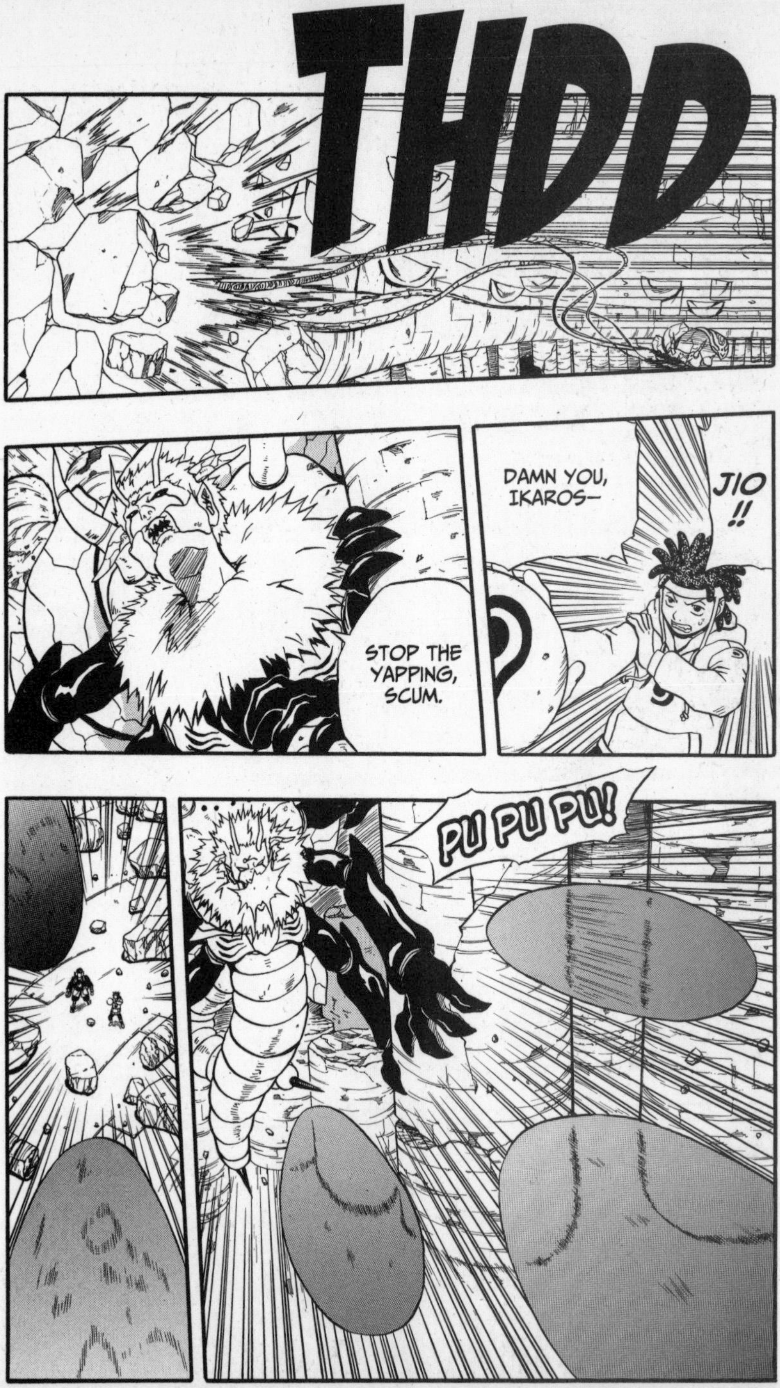
THDD
DAMN YOU, IKAROS—
JIO!!
STOP THE YAPPING, SCUM.
PU PU PU!

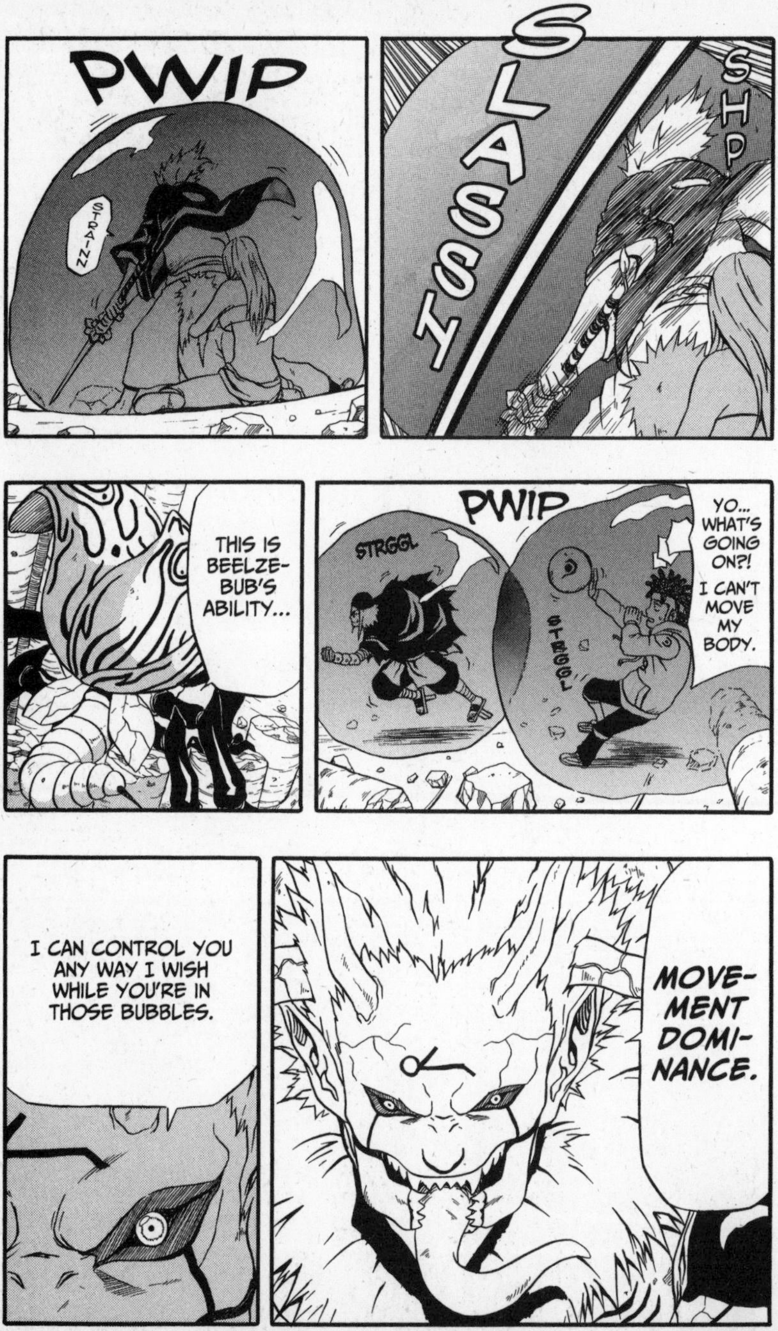
SHP
SLASSH
PWIP
STRAINN
YO... WHAT'S GOING ON?! I CAN'T MOVE MY BODY.
PWIP
STRGGL
STRGGL
THIS IS BEELZE-BUB'S ABILITY...
MOVE-MENT DOMI-NANCE.
I CAN CONTROL YOU ANY WAY I WISH WHILE YOU'RE IN THOSE BUBBLES.

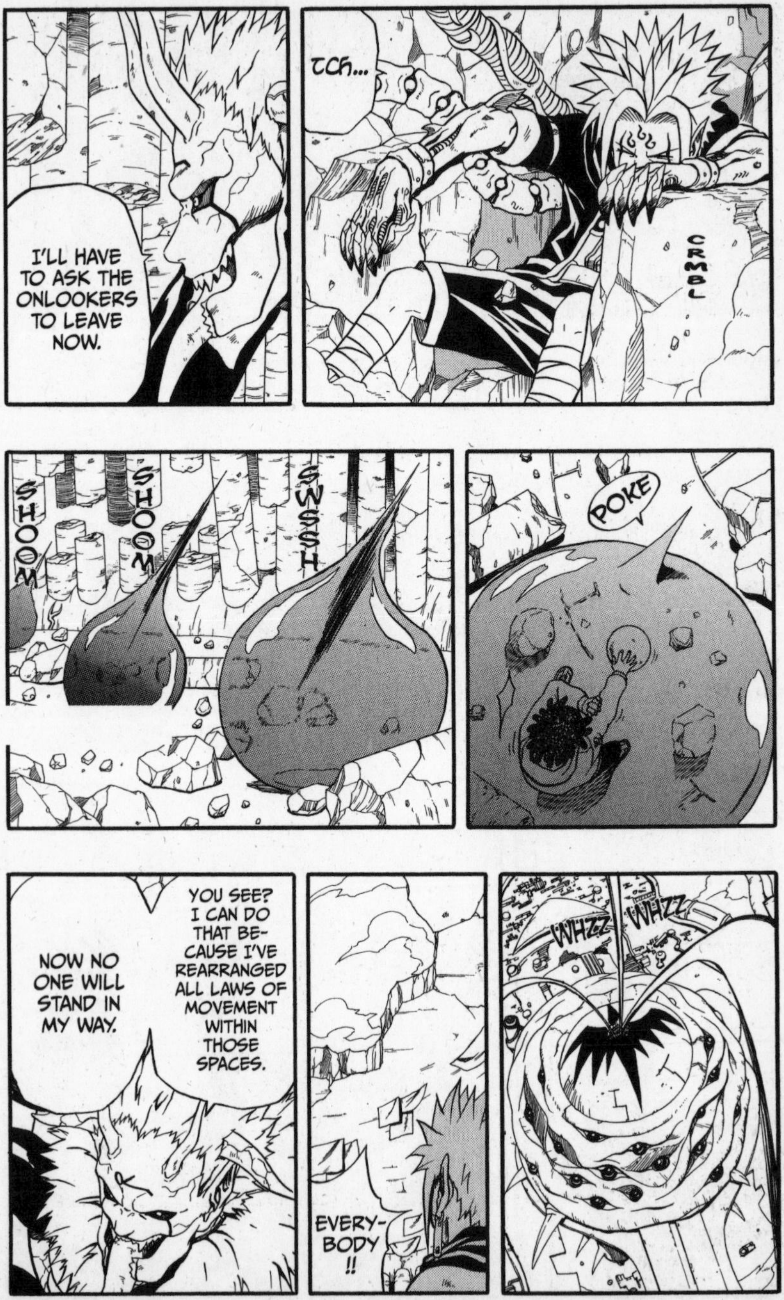
TCH...
CRMBL
I'LL HAVE TO ASK THE ONLOOKERS TO LEAVE NOW.
POKE
SWSSH
SHOOM
SHOOM
WHZZ WHZZ
EVERY-BODY!!
YOU SEE? I CAN DO THAT BE-CAUSE I'VE REARRANGED ALL LAWS OF MOVEMENT WITHIN THOSE SPACES.
NOW NO ONE WILL STAND IN MY WAY.

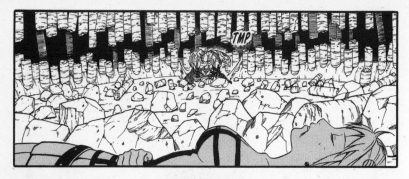

TMP

...

CRNCH

THAT GIRL...

...SEEMS TO BE EVEN MORE IMPORTANT THAN I THOUGHT.

...GO NEAR RUBY!

DON'T YOU DARE...

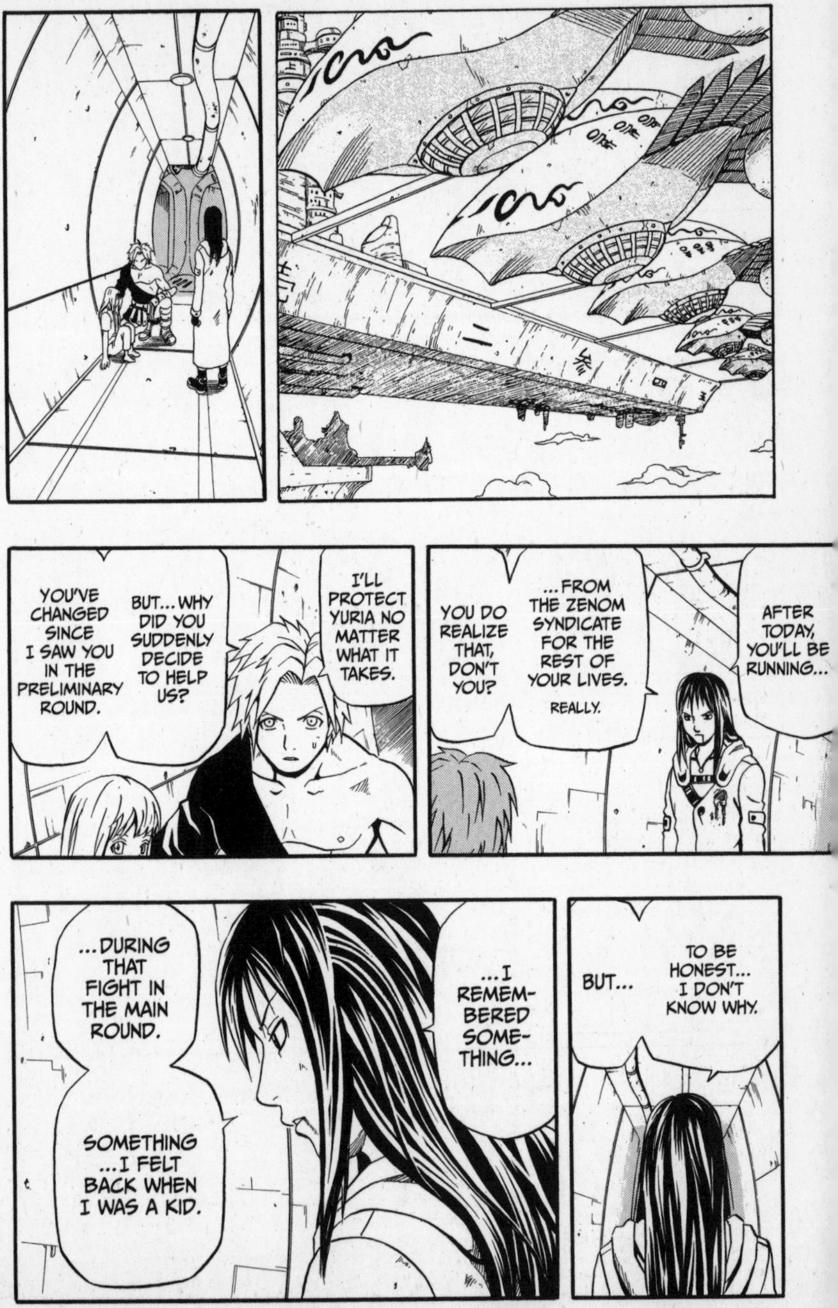
AFTER TODAY, YOU'LL BE RUNNING...
...FROM THE ZENOM SYNDICATE FOR THE REST OF YOUR LIVES.
REALLY.
YOU DO REALIZE THAT, DON'T YOU?
I'LL PROTECT YURIA NO MATTER WHAT IT TAKES.
BUT... WHY DID YOU SUDDENLY DECIDE TO HELP US?
YOU'VE CHANGED SINCE I SAW YOU IN THE PRELIMINARY ROUND.
TO BE HONEST... I DON'T KNOW WHY.
BUT...
...I REMEMBERED SOMETHING...
...DURING THAT FIGHT IN THE MAIN ROUND.
SOMETHING ...I FELT BACK WHEN I WAS A KID.

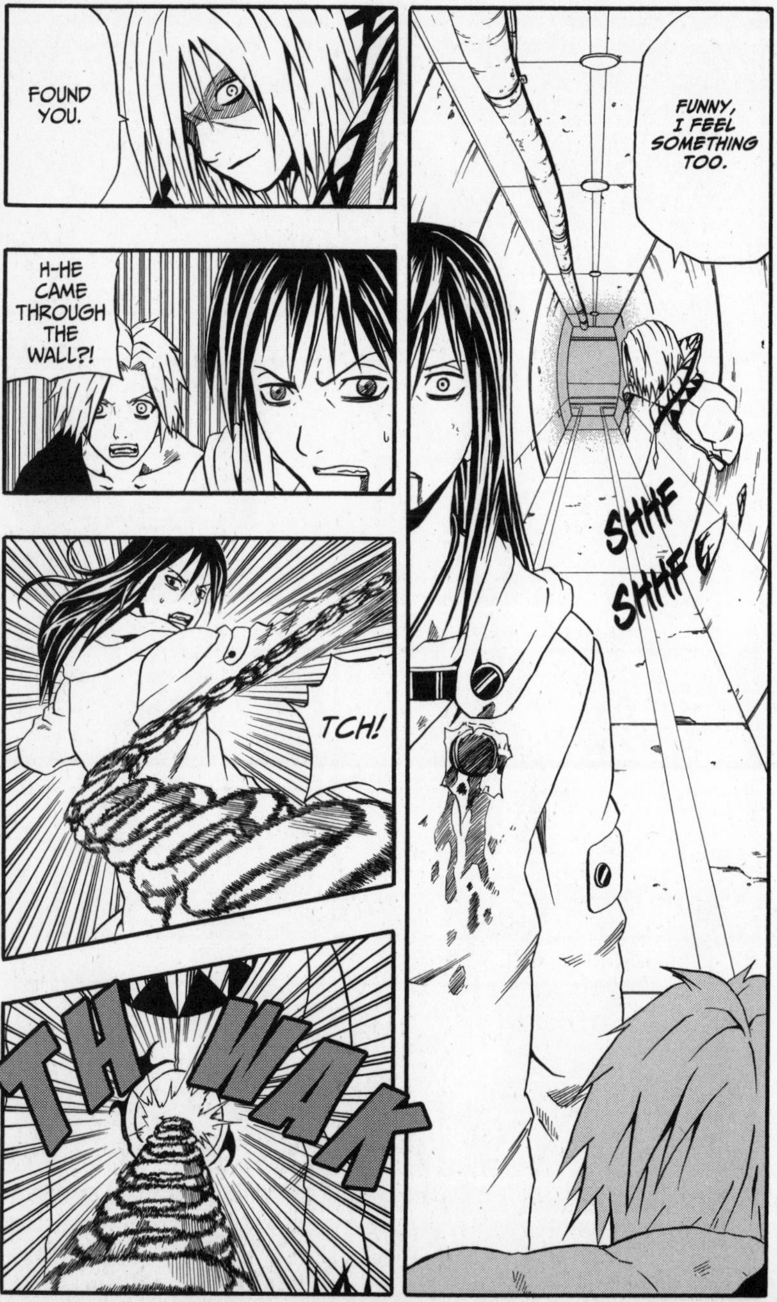
FUNNY, I FEEL SOMETHING TOO.
SHHF
SHHF
FOUND YOU.
H-HE CAME THROUGH THE WALL?!
TCH!
THWAK

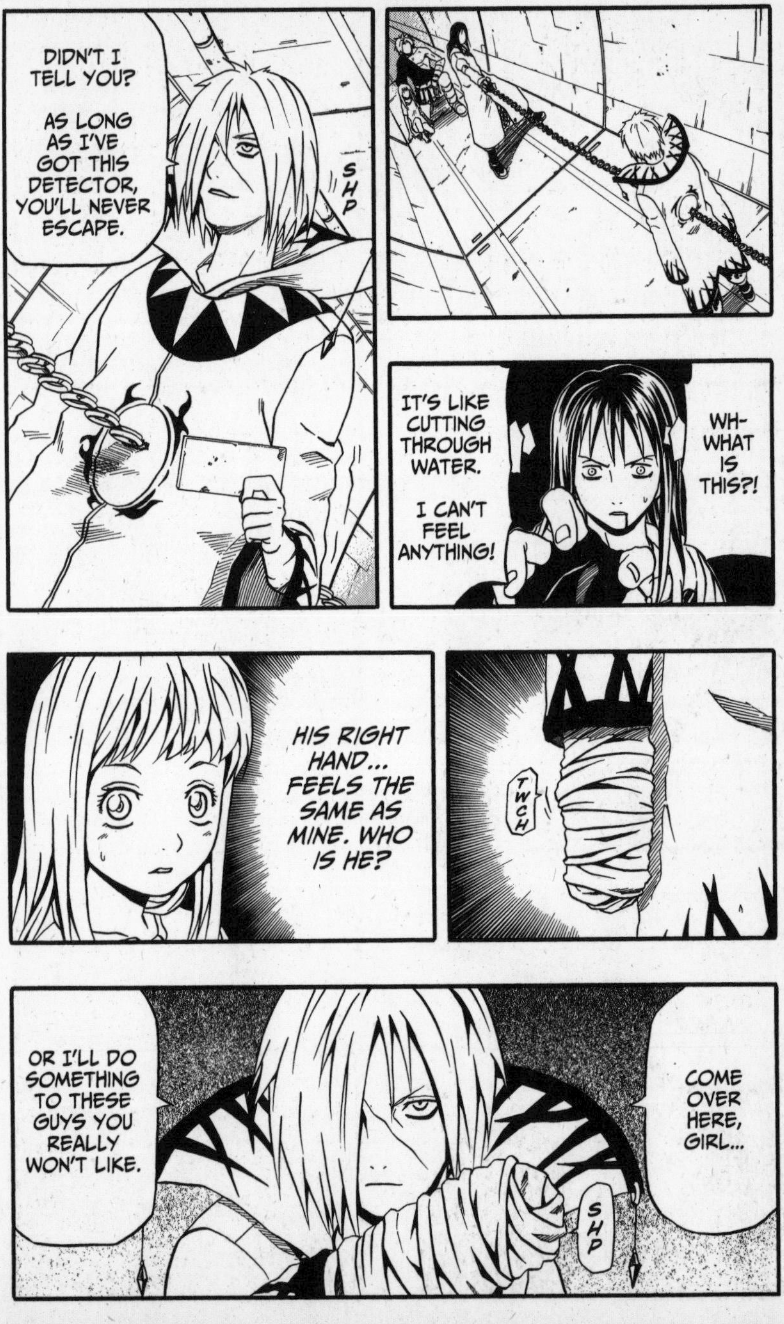
WH- WHAT IS THIS?!
IT'S LIKE CUTTING THROUGH WATER.
I CAN'T FEEL ANYTHING!
SHP
DIDN'T I TELL YOU?
AS LONG AS I'VE GOT THIS DETECTOR, YOU'LL NEVER ESCAPE.
TWCH
HIS RIGHT HAND... FEELS THE SAME AS MINE. WHO IS HE?
COME OVER HERE, GIRL...
SHP
OR I'LL DO SOMETHING TO THESE GUYS YOU REALLY WON'T LIKE.

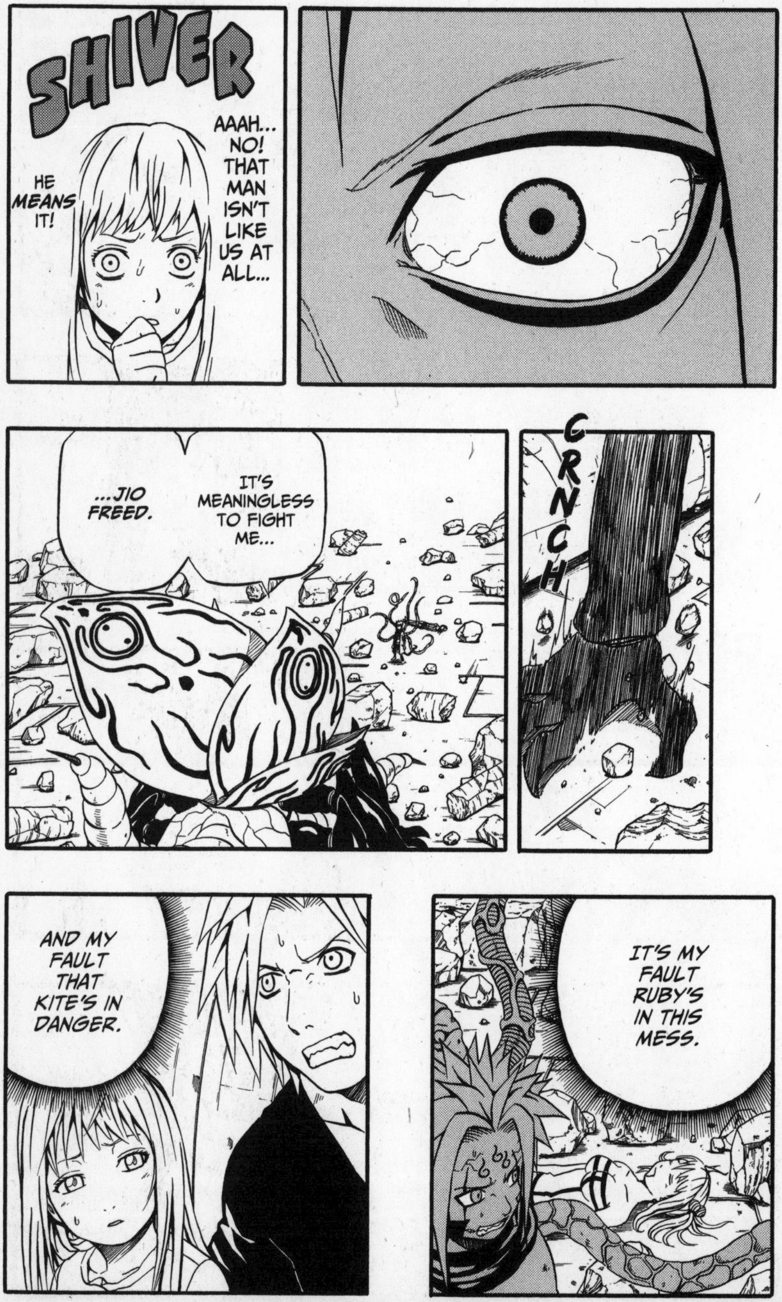
SHIVER
AAAH... NO! THAT MAN ISN'T LIKE US AT ALL...
HE MEANS IT!
CRNCH
IT'S MEANINGLESS TO FIGHT ME...
...JIO FREED.
IT'S MY FAULT RUBY'S IN THIS MESS.
AND MY FAULT THAT KITE'S IN DANGER.

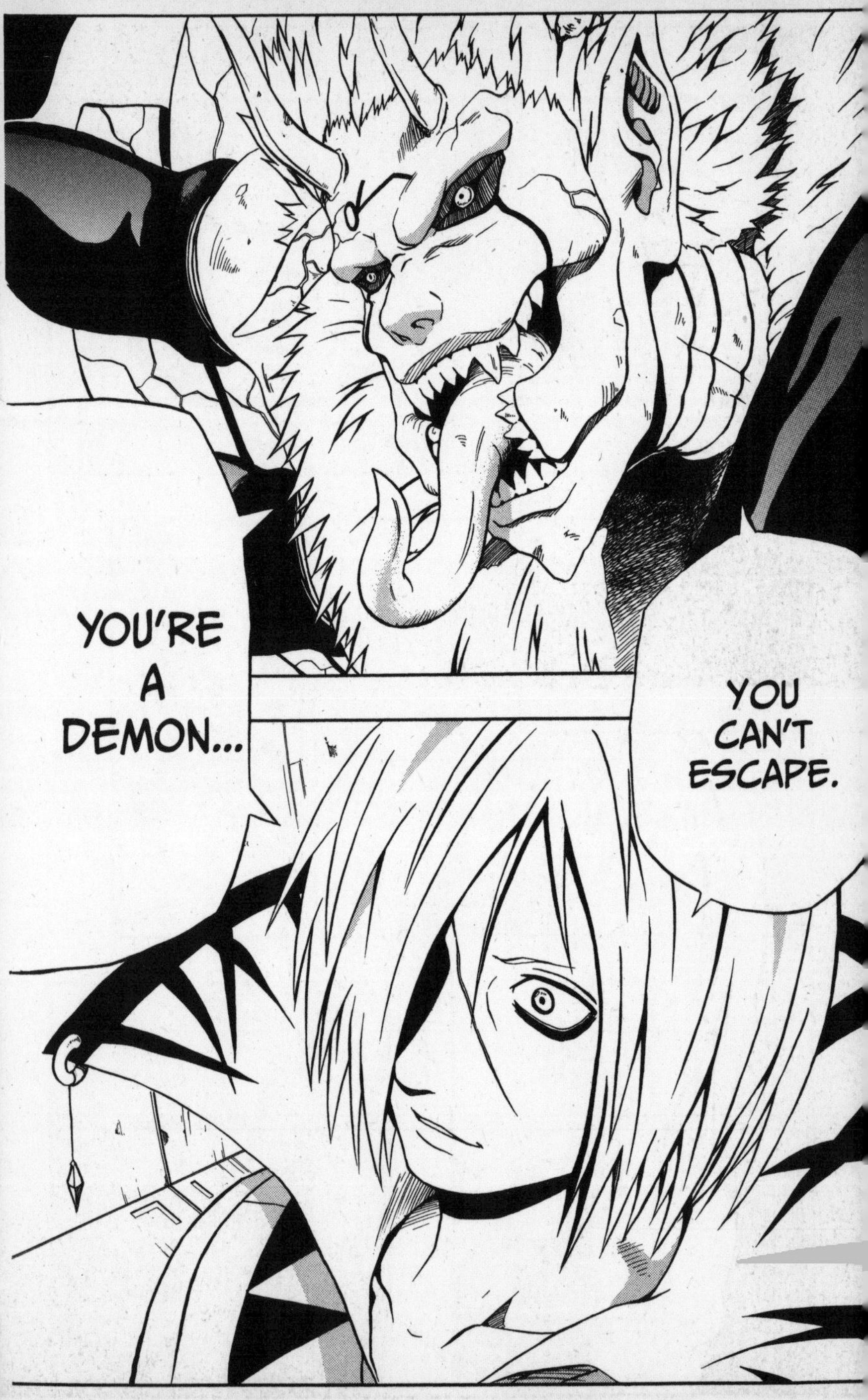
YOU CAN'T ESCAPE.
YOU'RE A DEMON...

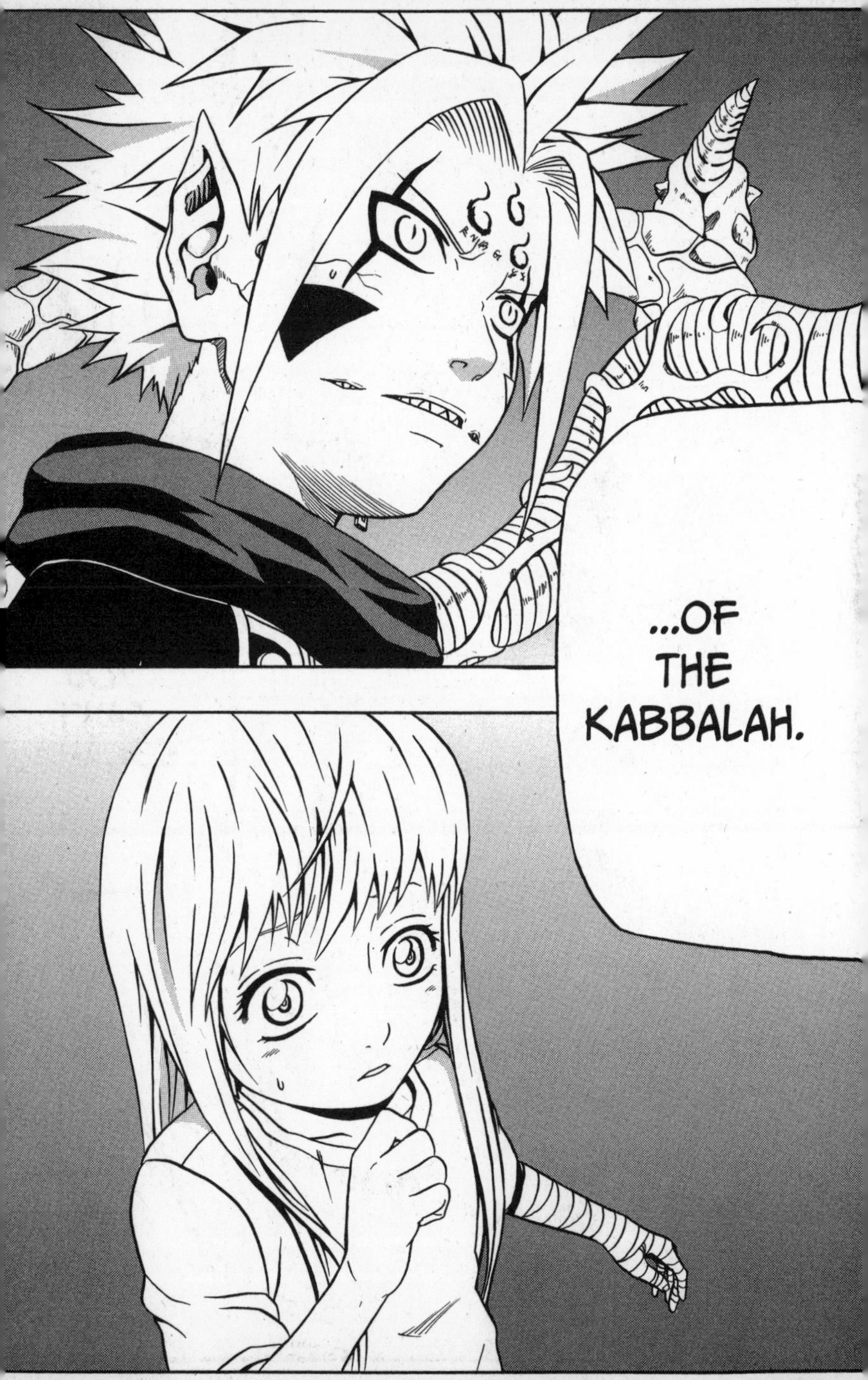
...OF THE KABBALAH.

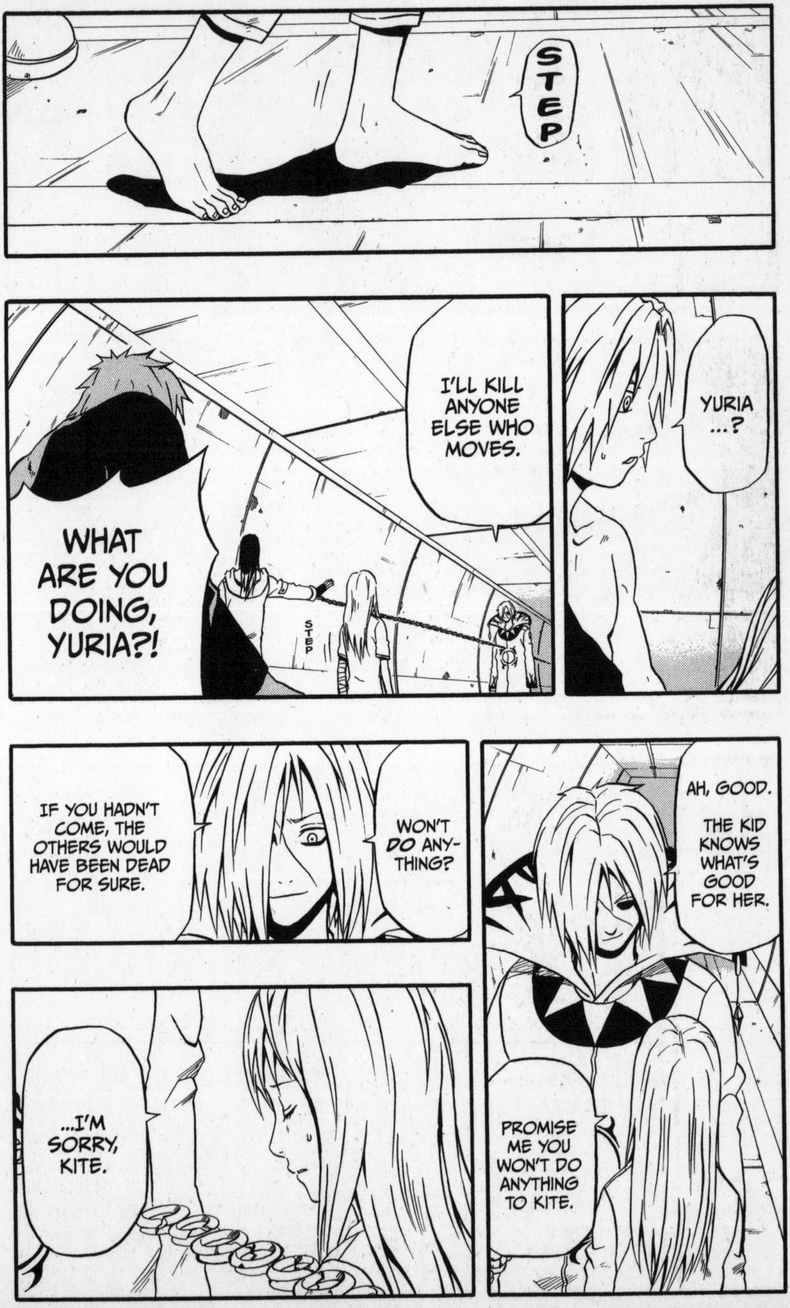
STEP
YURIA ...?
I'LL KILL ANYONE ELSE WHO MOVES.
WHAT ARE YOU DOING, YURIA?!
STEP
AH, GOOD.
THE KID KNOWS WHAT'S GOOD FOR HER.
PROMISE ME YOU WON'T DO ANYTHING TO KITE.
WON'T DO ANYTHING?
IF YOU HADN'T COME, THE OTHERS WOULD HAVE BEEN DEAD FOR SURE.
...I'M SORRY, KITE.

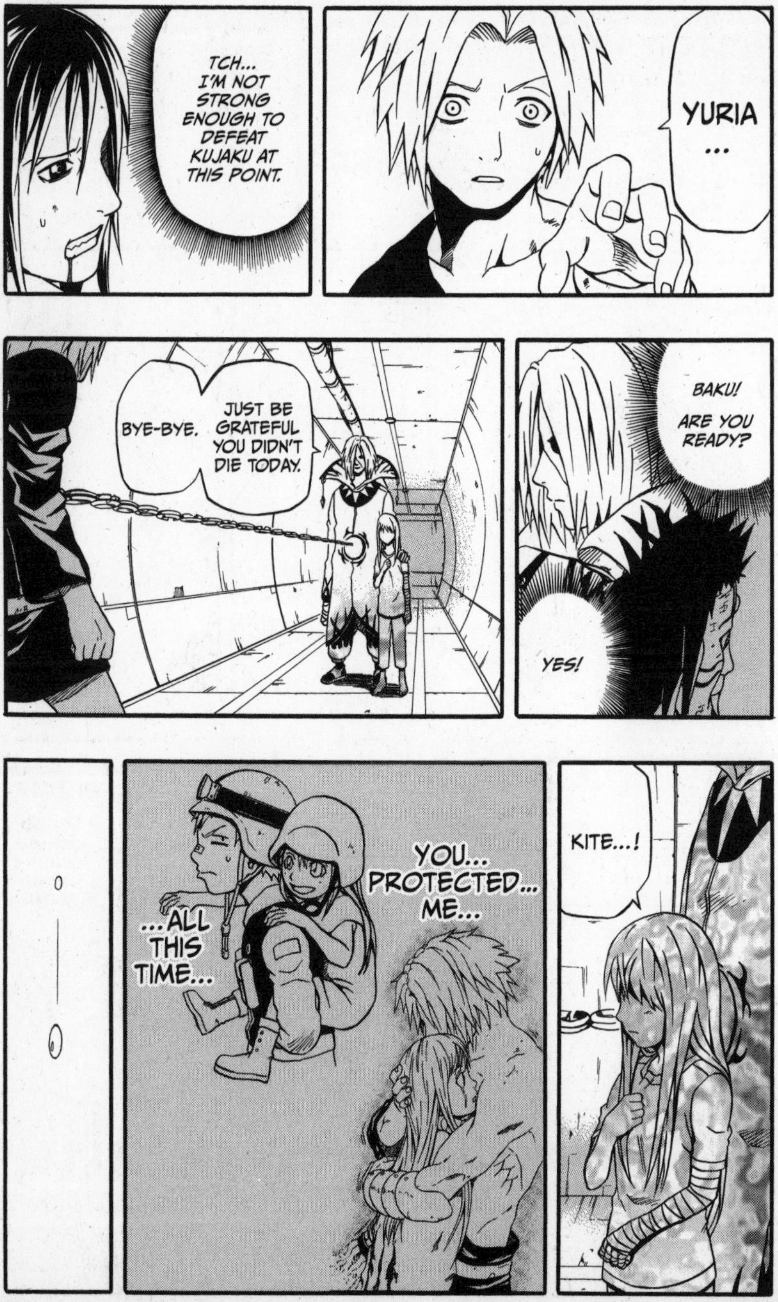
YURIA ...
TCH... I'M NOT STRONG ENOUGH TO DEFEAT KUJAKU AT THIS POINT.
BAKU!
ARE YOU READY?
YES!
JUST BE GRATEFUL YOU DIDN'T DIE TODAY.
BYE-BYE.
KITE...!
YOU... PROTECTED... ME...
...ALL THIS TIME...

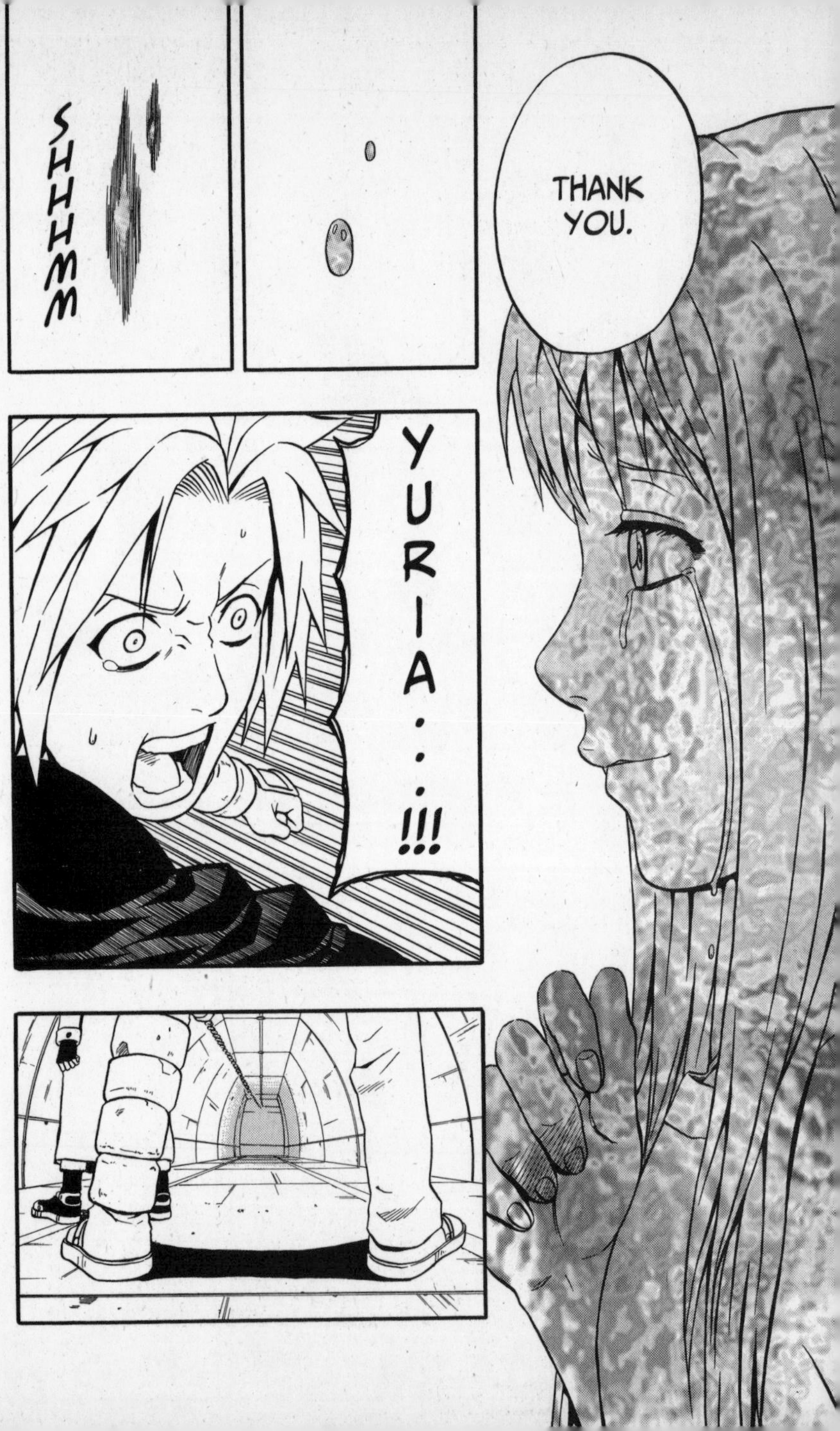
THANK YOU.
SHHHMM
YURIA...!!!

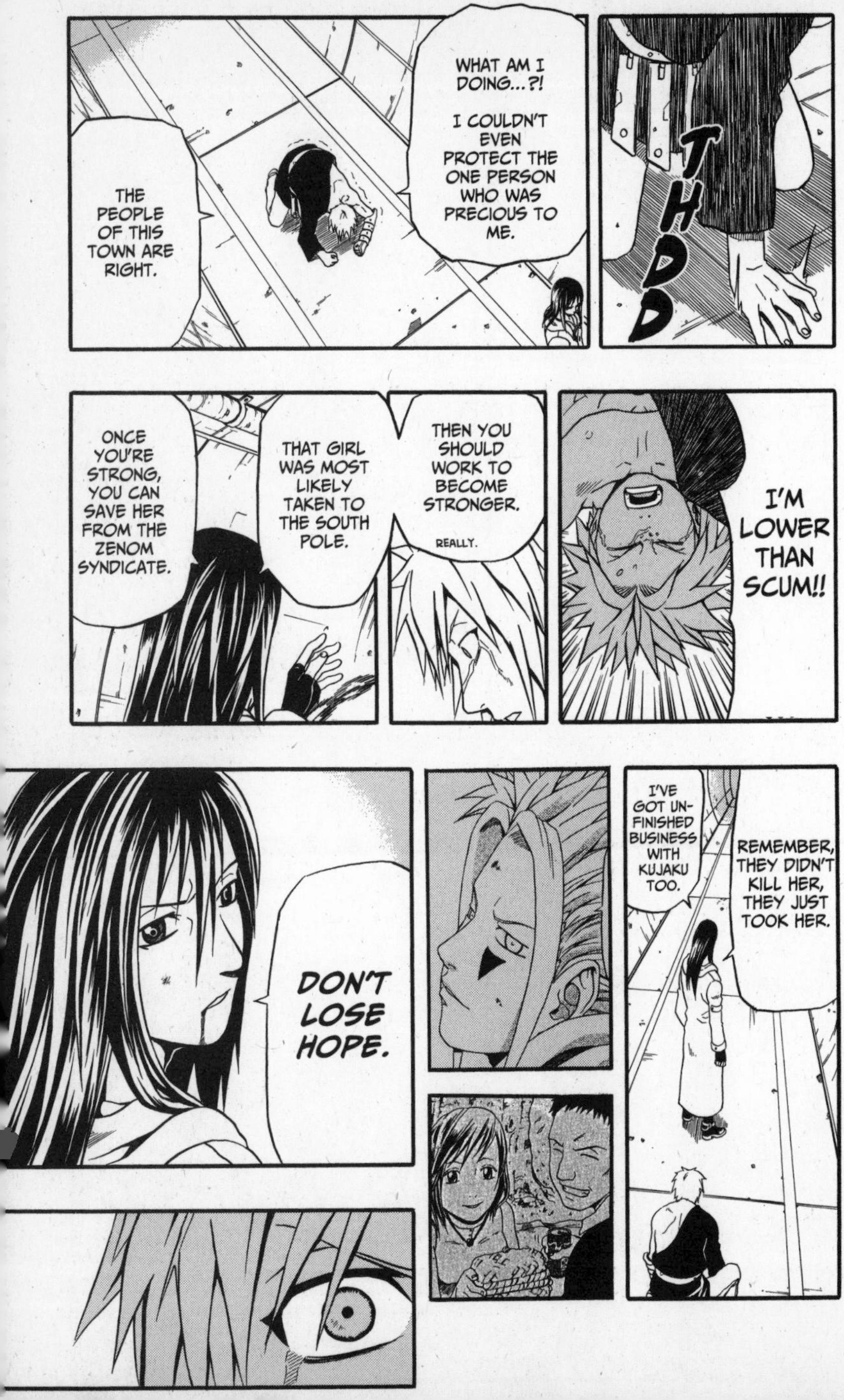
THDD
WHAT AM I DOING...?!
I COULDN'T EVEN PROTECT THE ONE PERSON WHO WAS PRECIOUS TO ME.
THE PEOPLE OF THIS TOWN ARE RIGHT.
I'M LOWER THAN SCUM!!
THEN YOU SHOULD WORK TO BECOME STRONGER.
REALLY.
THAT GIRL WAS MOST LIKELY TAKEN TO THE SOUTH POLE.
ONCE YOU'RE STRONG, YOU CAN SAVE HER FROM THE ZENOM SYNDICATE.
REMEMBER, THEY DIDN'T KILL HER, THEY JUST TOOK HER.
I'VE GOT UNFINISHED BUSINESS WITH KUJAKU TOO.
DON'T LOSE HOPE.

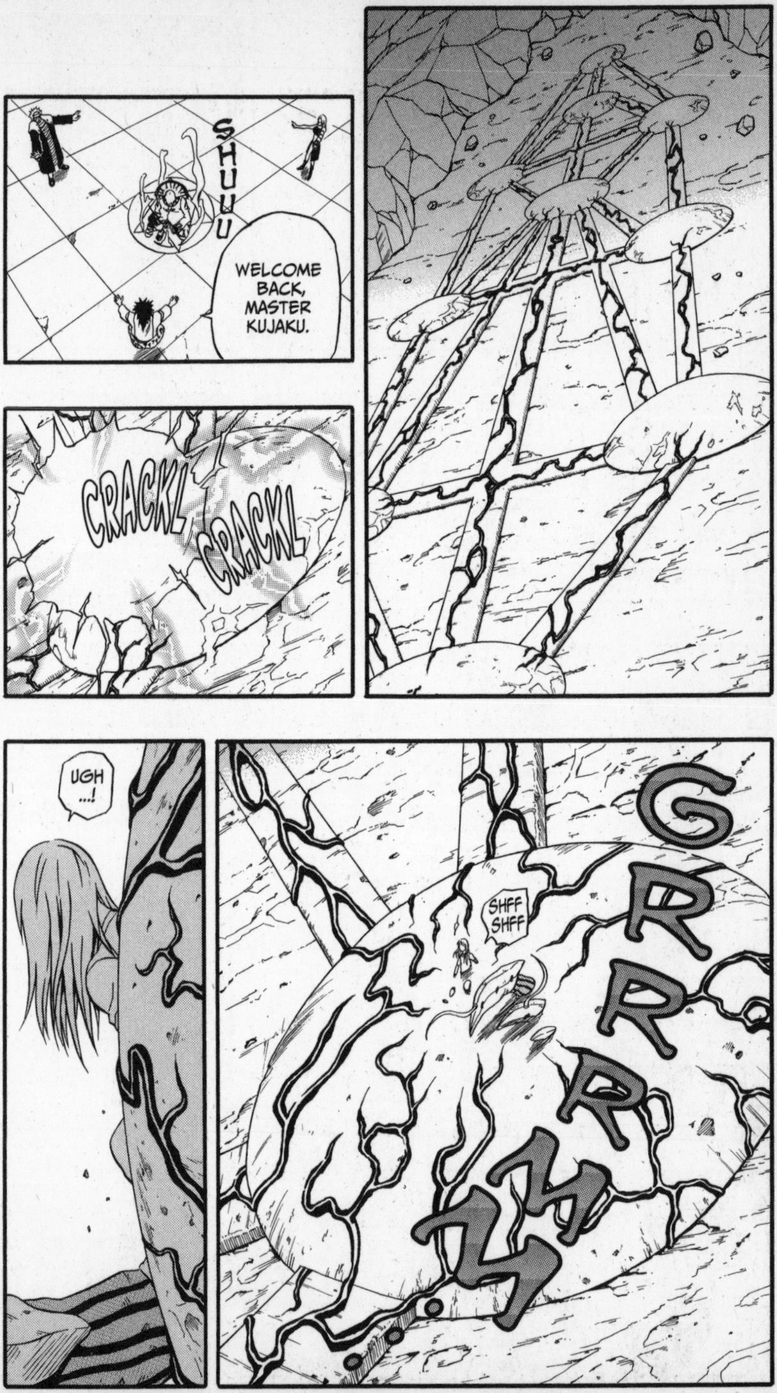
SHUUU
WELCOME BACK, MASTER KUJAKU.
CRACKL CRACKL
GRRRMM...
SHFF SHFF
UGH ...!

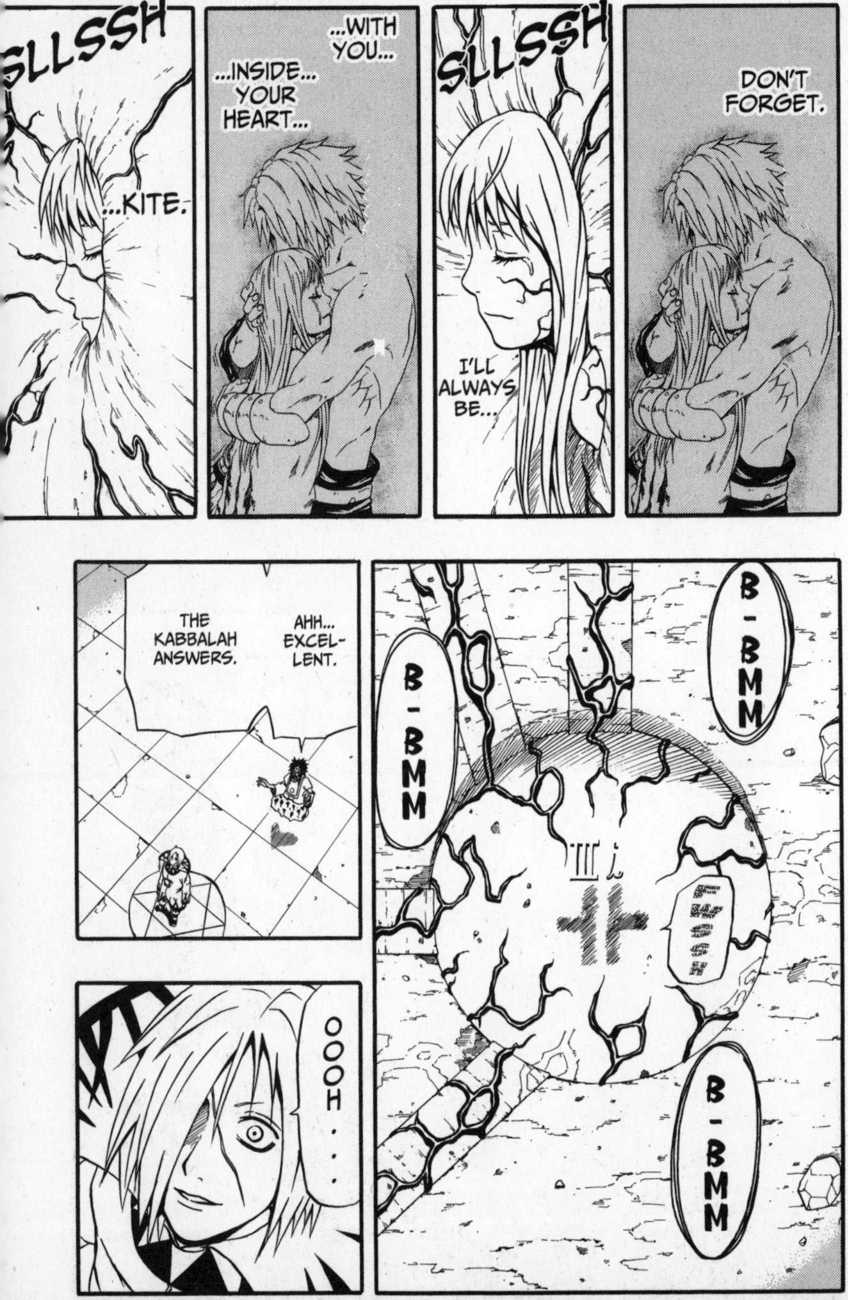
DON'T FORGET.
SLLSSH
I'LL ALWAYS BE...
...WITH YOU...
...INSIDE... YOUR HEART...
SLLSSH
...KITE.
B-BMM
B-BMM
B-BMM
AHH... EXCEL-LENT.
THE KABBALAH ANSWERS.
OOOH...

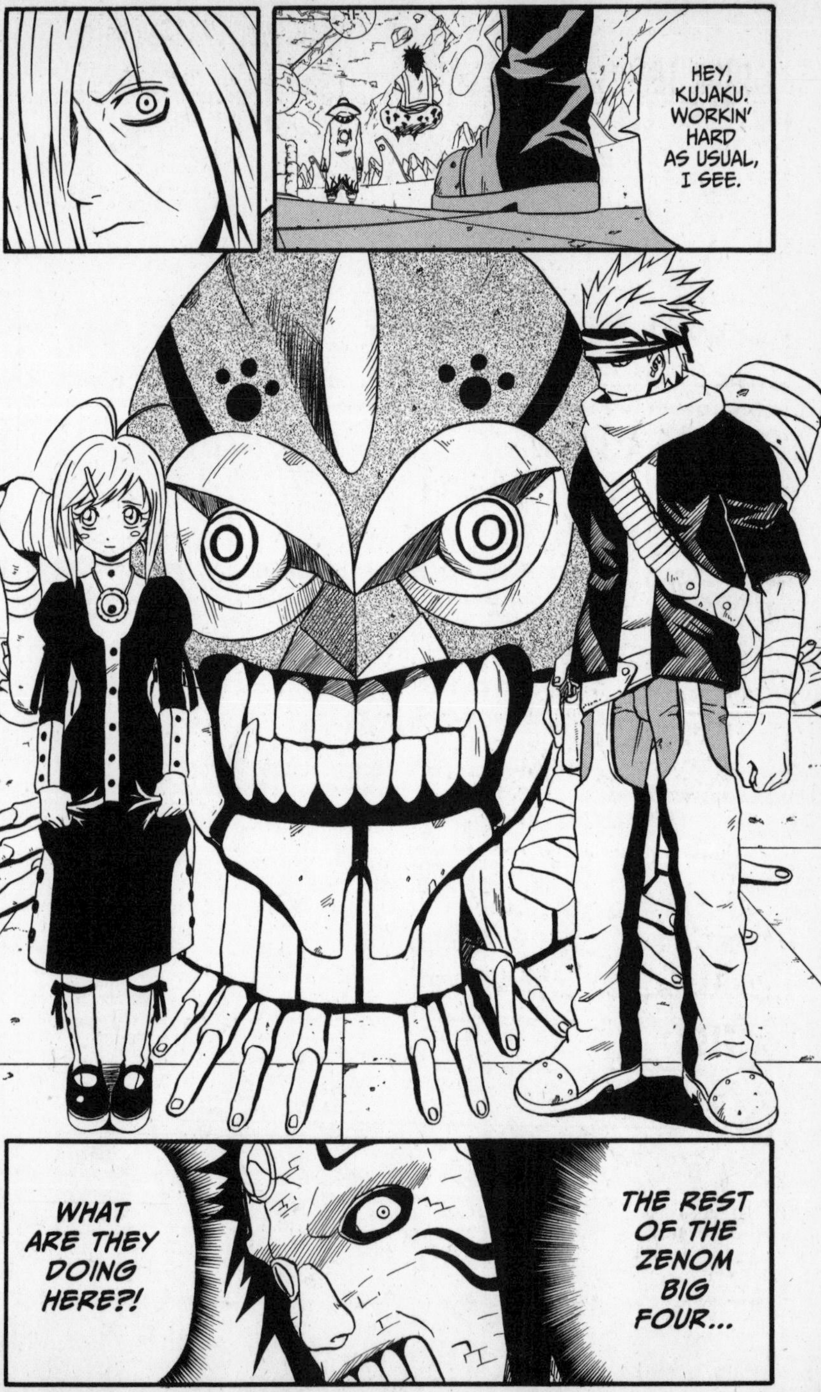
HEY, KUJAKU. WORKIN' HARD AS USUAL, I SEE.
THE REST OF THE ZENOM BIG FOUR...
WHAT ARE THEY DOING HERE?!

SEISHI AND THE CUSTOMER WHO FORGOT HER GLASSES

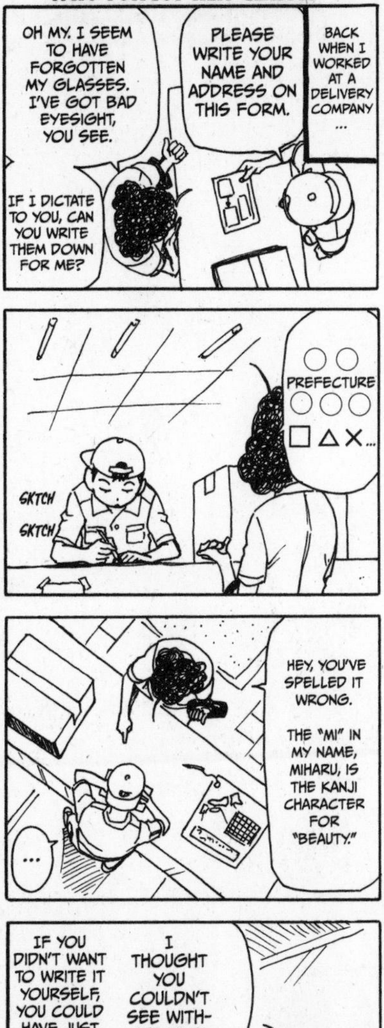
BACK WHEN I WORKED AT A DELIVERY COMPANY ...
PLEASE WRITE YOUR NAME AND ADDRESS ON THIS FORM.
OH MY. I SEEM TO HAVE FORGOTTEN MY GLASSES. I'VE GOT BAD EYESIGHT, YOU SEE.
IF I DICTATE TO YOU, CAN YOU WRITE THEM DOWN FOR ME?
○○ PREFECTURE ○○○ □△×...
SKTCH
SKTCH
HEY, YOU'VE SPELLED IT WRONG.
THE "MI" IN MY NAME, MIHARU, IS THE KANJI CHARACTER FOR "BEAUTY."
...
I THOUGHT YOU COULDN'T SEE WITHOUT YOUR GLASSES.
IF YOU DIDN'T WANT TO WRITE IT YOURSELF, YOU COULD HAVE JUST SAID SO.

SEISHI, THE POOL AND THE DIVE

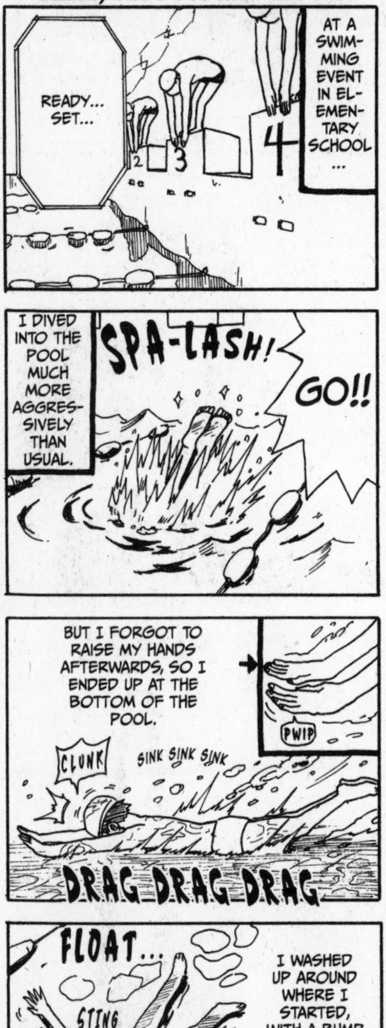
AT A SWIMMING EVENT IN ELEMENTARY SCHOOL ...
READY... SET...
GO!!
SPA-LASH!
I DIVED INTO THE POOL MUCH MORE AGGRESSIVELY THAN USUAL.
PWIP
BUT I FORGOT TO RAISE MY HANDS AFTERWARDS, SO I ENDED UP AT THE BOTTOM OF THE POOL.
SINK SINK SINK
CLUNK
DRAG DRAG DRAG
I WASHED UP AROUND WHERE I STARTED, WITH A BUMP ON MY HEAD AND THE FRONT OF MY BODY COVERED WITH SCRAPE MARKS.
FLOAT...
STING
STING

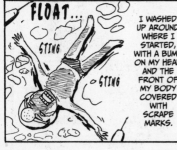

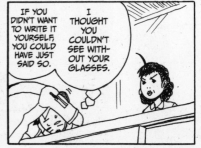

O-Parts CATALOGUE ⑫

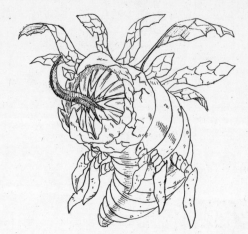

O-PART: FLYZON

O-PART RANK: B

A HUGE FLY CREATED INSIDE IKAROS'S BODY. UNLIKE AGYO AND UNGYO, IT'S VERY FAST. ALSO, ITS MOUTH WILL INSTINCTIVELY SNAP SHUT LIKE A CROCODILE'S THE MOMENT SOMETHING TOUCHES IT.

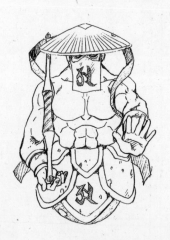

O-PART: AGYO & UNGYO

O-PART RANK: B

TWO GUARDS CREATED INSIDE IKAROS'S BODY. EACH IS 10 METERS (ABOUT 33 FEET) TALL. THEIR MUSCLES ARE ROCK HARD AND EXTREMELY STRONG, BUT THEY'RE PRETTY SLOW. THEY SLEEP MOST OF THE TIME, WAKING ONLY WHEN AN INTRUDER DRAWS NEAR.

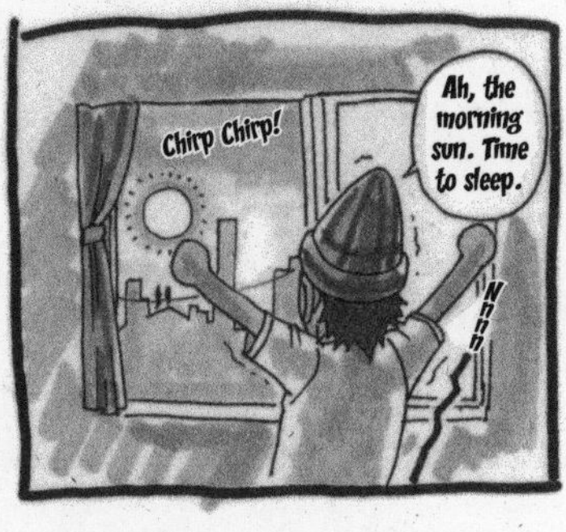
Ah, the morning sun. Time to sleep.
Chirp Chirp!
Nnnn

SEISHI KISHIMOTO

No matter how hard I try, my internal clock always gets reversed and I end up going to sleep when the sun comes up.

O-Parts Hunter 12

VIZ Media Edition
STORY AND ART BY SEISHI KISHIMOTO

English Adaptation/Tetsuichiro Miyaki
Touch-up Art & Lettering/HudsonYards
Design/Andrea Rice
Editor/Carol Fox

Editor in Chief, Books/Alvin Lu
Editor in Chief, Magazines/Marc Weidenbaum
VP, Publishing Licensing/Rika Inouye
VP, Sales and Product Marketing/Gonzalo Ferreyra
VP, Creative/Linda Espinosa
Publisher/Hyoe Narita

Printed in the U.S.A.

Published by VIZ Media, LLC
P.O. Box 77010
San Francisco, CA 94107

10 9 8 7 6 5 4 3 2 1
First printing, October 2008

www.viz.com

store.viz.com

RATED T+ FOR OLDER TEEN

PARENTAL ADVISORY
O-PARTS HUNTER is rated T+ for Older Teen and is recommended for ages 16 and up. This volume contains realistic and fantasy violence and adult situations.

ratings.viz.com